To Mild-

Ch

Where Children Run

Where Children Run

Karen Emilson

NORDHEIM BOOKS
A Division of Nordheim Printing,
Ashern, Manitoba

Published by Nordheim Books, Box 670, Ashern, Manitoba, Canada, R0C 0E0

Editor: Roger Newman, Gimli, Manitoba.

Cover design by: Melanie Matheson, Hignell Printing, Winnipeg, Manitoba.

Cover illustration: David and Dennis Pischke

Photo restoration: Astral Photo, Polo Park Shopping Centre, Winnipeg, Manitoba.

Frontispiece: David and Dennis with their sister Eunice Pischke.

Cataloguing in Publication Data

Emilson, Karen, 1963 -
Where children run

ISBN 0-9681242-0-8

This book was written in cooperation with David and Dennis Pischke, based on recollections from their childhoods. Numerous neighbours, teachers and friends also provided information for this book. Whenever possible, information has been substantiated with government files, records or documentation.

Printed and bound in Canada

This book is dedicated to

the late Gus and Emma Harwart
the late Ruby Ratz
and Jim Deighton
without whom we never would have survived

- David and Dennis

To my husband Mark and son Laurie
for your love, encouragement
and unwavering support

- Karen

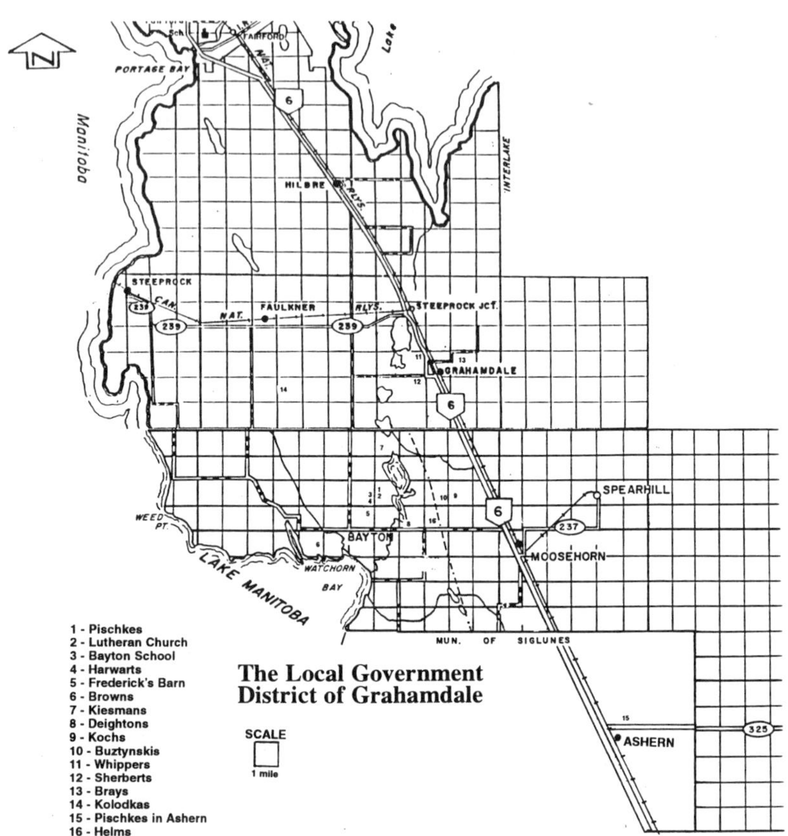

The Local Government District of Grahamdale

Quotes taken from interviews in 1995 and 1996:

"I taught for 30 years, so a lot of kids have passed through my classroom. Sometimes the only ones you remember are the ones who stand out for some reason. I can still picture those poor Pischke children in my mind."

- Leah Gasper

"The Pischke kids weren't bad kids at all. They were never bad in school. They were excellent as far as behaviour was concerned . . . . I knew it wasn't a happy home, but I had no idea of the cruelty. I didn't like the stepfather at all. He made my skin crawl."

- Marion Gering

"I remember those kids coming to my place in the middle of the night. These are awful things to remember - they were all beat up and starving. It was a crying shame that Domko was allowed to get away with it for so long."

- Jim Deighton

"I know exactly who you're talking about when you say the Pischkes. I remember my mother mentioning that family. It was a pretty sad situation."

- Louise Collier

"I was just a little boy, but I remember the night Dave and Dennis came to our house as clear as if it happened yesterday. In my entire life I've never seen sheer terror as what I saw then. It's something I'll never forget."

- Alvin Koch

"The Pischke kids are survivors. So many times I've seen them knocked down but they get right back up again and brush themselves off. And in spite of everything, they've always kept their senses of humour.

- Marjorie Harwart

"After 35 years as a print and electronic journalist, I thought I had heard and seen it all."

- Peter Warren

Thank you

Special thanks to Roger Newman a very talented writer and editor who edited the manuscript.

To Canadian Author Fred Edge and Lorne Reimer for reading the manuscript and offering suggestions.

To Jan Bain, Mary Alards-Tomalin, Darlene West and Bruce Snively for your constant encouragement; Judy Giordano for establishing a web-site, Andrea Dyck, Crystal Park and Villa Leitold for keeping the office running smoothly.

Thank you to Arden and Barb Weigelt - present owners of the former Pischke farm - they allowed us to spend as much time in the area as we needed; Iver and Amanda Bankert and Doug Becker for helping search the area with metal detectors; Marjorie Harwart and her sisters Evelyn, Violet and Linda, Jim Deighton, Leon & Anna Koch, Ken Koch, Alvin Koch, Walter Pischke, Jackie Richter, Leah Gasper, Bernie Gmitzyk, Eunice Bullerwell, Marion Gering, Louise Collier, Margaret Harvey, Mary Burnett, Nina Kiesman, Ida Pollock, Henry Kort, Robert Jeske, Harold Boutilier, Marlene Emilson, Robert Gunnlaugson, Sophie Kolt, Len Kaminsky, Donna Murphy, Vera Johnson, Ken Rutherford and Michael Leitold for agreeing to interviews of varying lengths and supplying photographs and/or other information which contributed to the accuracy of this story.

Thank you to the many reluctant interview subjects and those people who asked not be named.

Thank you to our family, friends, neighbours and readers for their support.

AND FINALLY TO, Peter Warren - Host of the CJOB Action Line Radio, Winnipeg, Manitoba, for believing in the boys and giving us the encouragement to proceed with this book.

Foreword

This incredible story about the Pischke twins needed a writer who as determined not only to lay out the basic who-what-where-when facts of the case, but a person who could be relied upon to probe the mysteries of so many unanswered questions; somebody not scared to ask the infamous 'why'!

Karen Emilson has accomplished this mission, with style, truth, emotion, caring and, because I know the lady, not without much personal foreboding.

As such, she has proved again she is a skilled craftsman both as a writer and as a reporter. There is a vast difference. Combined, those two talents have produced for us - as individuals and as a society - a remarkable end product in the book now in your hands.

Here you will find a story of behaviour which, in places, defies human explanation; a strength of love as once defined only by the Old Poets; serious questions that still have to be answered by churches, social agencies and law enforcement officials.

Here, too, you will find a true story about rural midwestern life that exposes the dark side to those tales about quilting bees, and love-thy-neighbour reports which were paraded out by Hollywood week after week on programs like "Little House on the Prairie."

For this is truth, in all stark nudity.

It is not pretty and heart-warming, but it is factual.

David and Dennis Pischke appeared on my radio program in April, 1995. After 35 years as a print and electronic journalist, I thought I had heard and seen it all.

These two gracious survivors from "Where Children Run," did not need raised, angry voices or challenges of revenge to make us all understand very quickly how 12 years of torment had shredded parts of their very souls.

But, what struck me during that particular broadcast, were the number of on-air calls to the Pischke twins from people in Saskatchewan, Manitoba, northwestern Ontario and from both North and South Dakota - radio listeners who sympathized and ended with simple sentences like: "Thank God you have spoken out," or "It happened to us, too."

Thus, what the Pischke boys suffered and what Karen Emilson has given us in book form, is historical fact, social history and a gut-wrenching story that still begs answers.

Someone, somewhere once said: "Suffer little children to come unto me."

Perhaps only He has an explanation about why it was allowed to happen . . . and why it is still happening.

- Peter Warren, CJOB Radio, Winnipeg, Canada.

"All children are potential victims, dependent upon the world's goodwill."

- Sally Kempton, child welfare activist

The Beginning of the End - February 8, 1966

QUIETLY, CAROLINE SLIPPED OUT of the house. The snow crunched noisily under her boots as she hurried down the driveway. She shivered as she buttoned her dark coat, then pulled a toque over her brown hair. It had been unusually warm for February that day, but the air was cooling quickly as evening approached.

She jumped at the sound of a door slamming behind her.

"I wanna come too!" a young voice whined. Eight year-old Raymond was running to catch up.

"Shhh!" she cautioned glancing nervously around. She hoped her son's wail hadn't been heard in the house. Grabbing him by the hand, she hurried towards the road, glancing over her shoulder once more. She relaxed after a few moments once she was confident they weren't being followed.

Caroline hurried towards a cream coloured pick-up truck parked on the road a short distance away. Her sons were parked in front of the old Lutheran church where the majority of her German-speaking neighbours attended Sunday service. Caroline knew the boys would be waiting by the church since it was one of the few safe places they had ever known. Silently she wondered how many times that old building had saved their lives.

The truck idled quietly, its lights turned off. A frozen cloud of exhaust gently drifting upwards. She recognized the two shadowy figures sitting in the cab as her eighteen year-old twin sons, David and Dennis. Glancing out the back window, Dennis spoke to his brother who opened the driver's side door. Stepping out, David gave his mother a gentle smile.

What a fine young man he'd grown to be, she thought to herself. A tear crept to the corner of her eye at the sight of her ruggedly handsome son. His thick, blonde hair was combed neatly back from his face. His bright, blue eyes smiled gently at her.

"How are you doin' Mom?" he asked in a quiet voice.

"About the same," she said weakly, her words punctuated with a faint Polish accent. "I don't know what I'm gonna to do."

David took her arm, helping her into the truck. He lifted Raymond, his step-brother in behind her. David felt the energy drain from his body as he contemplated his mother's situation. A familiar feeling of desperation gripped him.

How many times had the act of survival consumed his every thought and action? Would they ever be free to enjoy life and live without fear? He tried hard to forget the suffering, hoping the past would become nothing but a bad memory. His only tie to a childhood of torment was his mother who now desperately needed his help.

"He's never been worse," she said. David slid in beside her and pulled the door shut.

"He refuses to take his medication," she said, lowering her voice. "I'm afraid he's gonna kill us."

Caroline looked at Dennis who was studying her carefully. She knew that he had stopped forgiving her years ago, believing she was to blame, along with members of her church, for the horrible suffering they had endured. Dennis could never understand how she let things get so out of hand. His step-father should have been stopped years ago.

"Why don't you come live with us?" David asked breaking the silence. "We've got a good place and lots of money now. Let me an' Denny take care of you."

Caroline smiled but said nothing. Dennis looked deep into his mother's soft blue-grey eyes in an attempt to understand her. She seldom disclosed her feelings and at that moment he realized how little he knew this woman who had given him life.

Suddenly a chill ran down David's spine. His twin sensed the same feeling and they shot each other a quick glance. Swinging around in the crowded cab, both teenagers caught sight of a dark figure running awkwardly towards the truck. The twins immediately recognized the man as their step-father, Bob Domko. He was shaking one fist in the air while clutching a rifle in the other. David's blood ran cold as those familiar childhood feelings returned. Dennis froze in fear, unable to speak or move.

"It's that crazy bastard!" David yelled as he yanked the truck in gear, slamming the gas pedal to the floor. The tires spun in an effort to grip the slick, snow-packed road. Staring intently into the rear-view mirror, David could see Domko stop in the centre of the road and raise his rifle to eye level.

"He's gonna shoot!" David yelled, "everybody down!"

Instinctively Dennis' arms came up over his head as he slid low on the seat. Caroline pulled Raymond down and covered him with her body.

Got to get out of here, David thought to himself, clenching his jaw tight. His heart raced as adrenalin surged into his bloodstream. *We don't deserve to die like this, not after what we've been through. If only I can get out of range -*

Moments seemed like hours as the truck slipped sideways down the centre of the road. They had no way of knowing that this would be the day that would end more than twelve years of abuse and torment at the hands of a madman . . .

Chapter 1

Living in Fear - June 1953

"SSSH!" EUNICE WHISPERED. Pulling her three-year-old sister close, she clasped a hand over little Rosalie's mouth giving her a stern look. 'Rosie' had started crying the moment the yelling began in the kitchen. She was trying to be brave, but tears crept from her tightly squeezed eyes.

Eunice was old enough to understand that the less noise the children made - the better. A cheerful and talkative six year-old, she was mature beyond her years. She felt it was her responsibility to care for Rosie and her five year-old twins brothers since their mother had been so preoccupied with the new baby. Eunice accepted the task willingly, fussing over her younger siblings whether they needed it or not.

Pushing her light brown hair back from her round face she watched silently through soft blue eyes as her nine year old brother Norman, quietly slipped out of the bed. He tip-toed across the floor to the bedroom doorway then pulled the curtain back slightly. Norman could see their mother, Caroline, arguing with her common-law husband, Bob Domko who had come to their farm as a hired hand just over a year ago. A relationship had developed between Caroline and the man, which had resulted in the birth of their step-sister Kathy. That's who they were arguing about this time.

The man who everyone called by his last name, was jealously accusing their mother of infidelities, saying that the baby was not his child. Caroline loudly protested in Polish that the child was indeed his. Norman couldn't understand what his mother was saying, but could tell by her anger and the occasional English word that she was demanding Domko stop accusing her of wrongdoings. They argued furiously, causing Norman to let the curtain go, then walk silently towards the bedroom window. He had decided to slide it open as a precaution. It was important for him to be able to escape if Domko came into the room. Grasping the metal rungs at the base of the frame, he gently lifted upwards. The sound of the window panes rattling from too little caulking rang in his ears. His heart beat quickly as a warm breeze filled the room.

Staring out the window, the boy noticed how surprisingly serene it was outdoors. The sun shone a golden-pink from behind the bush across the road as it set slowly in the western Manitoba sky. Mosquitoes buzzed loudly while the family's cows chewed damp grass in the nearby pasture. A dog barked excitedly somewhere in the distance.

Climbing back into the crowded bed beside his twin brothers, Norman could feel the warm dampness of the mattress on his bare legs. The putrid smell of urine wafted upwards as he lifted the sheet. He shot a disapproving look toward the twins assuming one of them had peed the bed.

"R-r-rosie did it," David whispered.

"Uh-huh," Dennis nodded in agreement.

Norman rolled his eyes. Likely one of them had done it, but it really didn't matter anyway. The bed had been peed in so many times it was likely still wet from the night before. It wouldn't take long and he wouldn't notice the dampness and soon the smell wouldn't bother him either.

"Ssssh!" Eunice reminded her brothers.

Norman looked at the twins who's bright blue eyes were full of fear. Physically they were identical and even family members found it difficult telling them apart. They were big boned, healthy children, but too thin from lack of food. Their blonde hair had been bleached white from the sun, framing their tanned, round faces.

The similarities stopped at their appearance though. David and Dennis had very different personalities. David was the more aggressive of the two boys, with lots of energy and independent streak that often made their mother laugh. He was talkative, good natured and somewhat mischievous.

Dennis was the quieter of the twins. He often went along with what David did, nodding in agreement. He was a thoughtful, sensitive, soft-spoken child who was trusting and naive. Dennis enjoyed sitting on an adult's knee or clinging to an older sibling, a trait that seemed to annoy their mother. Caroline had never been generous with hugs and kisses, which seemed to bother Dennis more than the other children.

The twins were always together, either walking or sitting with Dennis on David's right hand side. They communicated in a strange language only they could understand. They spoke a jumbled combination of low German with many undistinguishable words thrown in for good measure.

Eunice acted as family interpreter when someone wanted to understand what the twins were saying, although Domko was usually the only person concerned with the twins jabbering. Often he would ask Eunice or Caroline what the boys were talking about, then would scowl at them in disbelief. If he was in a good mood, he would chase them out of the house so he wouldn't have to listen to them. If he was in a bad mood, he would beat whichever one he could catch - most often Dennis. Norman wasn't sure what caused Domko's bad moods, but knew that he and his siblings were to blame.

Norman had spent that day in the field picking rocks alongside Domko, watching him grow increasingly irritated as the day wore on. His older brothers Walter, 11, and Steven, 10, had received a beating the day before for not milking the cows thoroughly. When Norman woke up that morning, the window was open and they were gone. This must have been what had annoyed him, since he relied heavily on the children to do most of the farm labour.

The children were beginning to relax as their mother calmed Domko. It was apparent that even she had grown to fear him over the past year.

The bed creaked as the twins shifted their bodies in unison. Norman stiffened as their little sister, Kathy, who was asleep in their mother's room, began to cry. At first the sound was muffled, but soon grew into the loud wailing of a discontented four month old child. Their mother picked up the baby, then began preparing a bath.

The fighting started again, but this time Domko grew angry much faster. He was complaining that the baby was making too much noise and criticized Caroline's inability to silence her. Caroline defended the baby, saying the infant's stomach was cramping because she needed the substance that whole milk provided, not the watery skim milk that Caroline was forced to feed the baby. Unfortunately, Domko insisted that the cream be separated from all the fresh milk daily, so that it could be sold. Domko argued that the children were costing too much money to support, while Caroline shot back that the farm was originally hers and that he was the intruder, not her children.

The screaming intensified, causing the children to get ready to jump from the bed. Their hearts began to race again, in expectation that Domko would come raging into the bedroom. The children could hear their mother trying to give the baby a bath. Kathy's little arms and legs thrashed in the basin, splashing water onto the old linoleum floor. The baby's cries permeated the small house, far beyond her father's tolerance level. Everyone knew it except the crying baby.

The twins sat up, holding each other in fear. Eunice drew a protective arm across Rosie's chest while Norman prepared to flee by sliding one leg out from under the sheet, placing his foot on the floor.

"I's be showink them soneebeech bastards!" Domko roared in his heavy accent. His broken English was difficult for the children to understand and a vocabulary consisting mostly of obscenities set a poor example for the children. It had reached the point where Domko could barely carry on a conversation without screaming insults, although he was careful who he yelled at, never showing this side to Caroline's father, brothers or to his few friends.

The children could hear their mother reasoning with him as she tried to quiet the baby. His voice was shaking violently as he screamed at Caroline to make the baby stop crying. Suddenly, Caroline let out a wild scream as he grabbed the child from the wash basin. He lost control of his senses and muttering something about the child not being his, threw her with all his strength against the kitchen wall. Caroline screamed in agony, as the sickening thud echoed through the house. The baby landed on the cold floor after hitting the wall.

The children could hear their mother's hurried steps across the kitchen.

"Boleslaw!" she screamed frantically. "What have you done to my child? Get out! Get out of here now!"

Domko stormed outside, slamming the kitchen door behind him.

Their mother whispering quietly to the baby who was now deathly silent. Caroline choked back a stream of tears in muffled panic. Her pained voice echoed throughout the house as she prayed that the child was still alive.

Knowing Domko was no longer inside, the children began to cry and moan. No child dared get out of bed to comfort their mother, fearing he might come back inside and lash out in jealousy.

Pulling the sheet up over his head, Dennis tried to hum softly, hoping to block out the sound of his mother's crying. He squeezed his eyes shut tight, hoping to remember his father's face. It was difficult for a five year old though, since it had been almost two years since his father's death. As Dennis searched his memory for his father's smiling face, one memory returned again and again. It was the cold, February day that Bob Domko arrived on the farm. It was one memory Dennis was certain he'd never forget.

He remembered standing in the kitchen, pulling on his mother's dress.

"M-m-momma?" he had asked. "When's daddy comin' home?"

His mother had been busy preparing supper in front of the old wood cook stove. She looked down at him and frowned. His boots had made a wet mess across the clean floor.

"Dennis, why are you crying?" she had asked, walking past him to gather a few potatoes for the soup. Digging through the burlap bag on the floor, she pulled out three large potatoes and snapped off the long white eyes that had grown over the winter.

"When's daddy comin' home?" he had sobbed again, rubbing his wet eyes with a dirty hand.

"I told you before," she'd answered in an exasperated voice. "Daddy died. He won't be comin' home no more."

"I want daddy now," he cried.

"I know you do, but he's not gonna," she said. "Now go outside and play until supper's ready."

Dennis had turned and left the warm kitchen. Stepping into the late afternoon air, he walked towards his twin who was playing in the snow fort just south of the house. He could see the Lutheran Church through the bush just past his brother. Turning, Dennis remembered looking up at the house roof. He'd been disappointed to see that there were no doves perched on the peak. His mother had pointed out a pair of white doves on the roof the day of his father's funeral. She had said that the doves were a sign that their father was at peace. Dennis didn't know where that was, but he wanted to go there. He hoped the doves would return some day to show him the way.

A noise in the barnyard caused him to turn to see what was happening. He could see Bob Domko, the new farm hand, watering the horses and giving the animals fresh hay. His older brothers Walter and Steven stood nearby. They were also watching the man. Irritated by their presence, Domko turned and said something that made the boys quickly disappear into the barn.

Dennis' hands were cold since he'd left his homemade mittens somewhere in the barn. Too frightened to go look for them, he approached David and Eunice, sticking out his small hands to his sister.

"Eunice," he had cried. "My han's are cold."

Looking down at her brother, Eunice could see tears had made clear paths down his dirt stained cheeks. Taking off her mittens she handed them to him. "You can wear 'em 'til my hands get cold then we'll trade back," she said gently. "Where is yours?"

"T-t-they're in the barn," Dennis stammered. "I don't wanna get 'em."

His sister had looked toward the grey shanty-style wooden building. A makeshift fence of old posts and planks that their father had built surrounded the barn yard. Usually Eunice would have offered to find the mitts for Dennis, but not today.

The anger Domko had displayed earlier that morning was still fresh in the children's minds. He had hauled a large load of fresh hay into the barn, then returned to the field to get more. While he was gone, the children had amused themselves by jumping from the loft into the hay. They could never remember being scolded for this before, so they were stunned and fearful when Domko returned and flew into a rage.

Dennis had wanted to tell his mother how frightened he was of this stranger, but feared the new farmhand too much to say a word. Domko had told the children that they were going to have to obey him now that the chores were his responsibility. Fearing his wrath, they decided it would be best not to mention Domko's first day when the stranger had lined them up along the hay rack and strapped each one with his belt. Dennis remembered how the thick leather had stung horribly on his cold legs. The big red welts had made it hard to sit down afterwards.

As he drifted off to sleep, he remembered Domko's warning not to tell anyone about the beating. But now he was beating them all regularly, including their mother.

Chapter 2

Two very different men

CAROLINE STRUGGLED TO KEEP HER EYES OPEN as the rising sun sent soft pink beams through the kitchen window. The night before had been the worst she had endured since Domko had come to the farm. Sitting on a chair with the unconscious baby swaddled on her lap, she replayed the drama that had unfolded the day before.

"You's be seeink your boyfriend again, huh?" he'd accused her after she had returned home late that day. Caroline was careful not to answer Domko immediately, fearing he would misinterpret her reply.

"No, I was looking for Walter and Steven like you asked," she'd said.

"Lazy bastards!" he'd yelled. Then he leaned forward, his eyes blazing and tone sarcastic. "Who's be helpink me with some fence? Dennis? David? Those soneebeech bastards be some goot for nuthink!"

Caroline had discovered much too late that Domko was not particularly fond of work. This was an unfortunate fact given farming was their livelihood. She had wanted to yell at him that the twins were only little boys, but she let it go. Domko was thinking in his odd, one-tracked way about the amount of work that needed doing and about the lack of manpower to get it done.

Domko was irritated that the two older boys had run away, something they had been doing often since he had come to the farm. He had kicked over a full can of milk when she told him she couldn't find either boy. They were likely hiding at a neighbouring farm, but which one?

She knew that when he was having one of his 'spells', it was best not to argue and to stay out of his way. As evening wore on though, he had continued to bait her, pressing for a fight. She had seen the signs many times before as he taunted her children to the breaking point, never satisfied until he lashed out at someone. Last night, it had been his own child.

Caroline had hoped that Kathy's birth would make Domko feel like part of the family. Instead, he had sabotaged his own happiness by believing the child was fathered by someone else. He had berated Caroline for this since the baby was born in February. He reasoned that someone else might be the father since she had spent time picking berries near a neighbouring farm the spring before. Domko had spent enough nights in her bed that she knew who had sired the child. No matter what she said to him though, she couldn't convince him of the truth.

How different he was from her first husband Bill Pischke! Son to Adolph and Pauline Pischke, German immigrants who came to Canada in the early 1900s, Bill was a kind and gentle man. His family had settled near Moosehorn, a small farming community in Manitoba's Interlake Region. Bill lived in the area his whole life, buying his own farm in the Bayton District, seven miles north-east of Moosehorn. He brought his young bride there in 1942.

Caroline remembered how Bill seldom raised his voice and always treated her and the children with kindness. He never hit the children, an odd way to parent during the 1950s, especially in the region where they lived. Her family and most of their neighbours criticized him for his leniency, reasoning that children were meant to be seen and not heard. If children disobeyed, most families of that day believed youngsters deserved a sound licking with either a belt, razor strap or willow switch. But not Bill.

Caroline's brood had the reputation of being naughty, possibly because her husband had been so easygoing. Especially the rambunctious twins who were always getting into things. Bill would ignore comments from members of her church and indulge the boys, who were awfully cute and smarter than most people realized.

The twins called him 'Tatoosh' in their odd language. Bill nicknamed David 'Tush' and Dennis 'Tushie'. Caroline remembered once telling Bill that Dennis was going to have to 'toughen up'. He had scolded her for this suggestion and she wondered if the twin might have been his favourite. He had a special way of looking at Dennis, showing a closeness he didn't have with the other children. Dennis in turn, missed his father horribly.

There were a few neighbours who thought Bill was an exceptional father and they told Caroline so. One such couple were Gus and Emma Harwart who lived a short distance down the road. They were genuinely fond of Bill and his family. The Harwarts would visit Bill in the hospital regularly and watched the children when Caroline had to be at his bedside. They had been quite broken up when Bill died.

Caroline reasoned that since both Bill and the Harwarts were Germans, it was easy for them to be friends. Domko on the other hand was very Polish, harbouring great resentment towards German people since he'd been forced to work in labour camps after Germany and Russia invaded Poland. A veteran of the Polish Army, he had recently immigrated to Canada, and only eight years had passed since the end of the Second World War. Not enough time for Domko to forgive and certainly not enough time to forget.

Caroline's Polish-born father Walter Kolodka wasn't much different. He hadn't liked Bill and didn't hesitate to tell her why. According to Walter, Bill hadn't been a good worker and was financially poor. The fact he was German made matters worse.

After Bill's death, old Walter had been quick to match-make Caroline and Domko.

"What more could a woman want?" old Walter had said, referring to Domko's physical appearance, suitcase full of money and war medallions. He was very pleased when Domko moved into his daughter's house and thrilled once they had a child together.

"Now Caroline has a good man!" he had said happily on many occasions in front of his daughter and her children.

Caroline's first impression of Domko was good. At 38 years old, he was clean and reasonably attractive. She had been raised to believe that she was of little value without a man, and now she was being offered one that had her father's approval. She was finding it impossible to support her family alone and Bob Domko appeared to be as good a catch as any man she'd met so far.

Besides, Domko looked at her with passion and longing, something she'd missed long before Bill had died. This man set her heart racing as his piercing stare cut into her soul. He made her feel like a school girl again, giddy with joy. Domko began working as a farmhand but within a few short weeks, they found themselves locked in a passionate love affair. Suddenly, Domko began dominating her life as it had only been dominated once before - by her father.

As the initial passion began to wear off, the fact Caroline had seven children with another man became less than tolerable to Domko. He refused to accept the children and fooled himself into believing that if he ignored them long enough, they would disappear.

Caroline knew her children were basically good kids, but like all children were noisy and misbehaved occasionally. Domko's response was to beat the poor little things into submission, encouraged by the Kolodkas who thought the children were difficult and needed disciplining.

What they may not have realized was the extreme lengths to which Domko would go. The root of the problem was that the children were not his and that they were only half Polish. Beating them wasn't going to turn them into seven little Pollacks! They were still very German and the more he beat them for it, the more stubborn they became.

Old Walter siding with Domko on most issues involving the children made it even more difficult for Caroline who had learned a disconcerting fact about her common-law husband. The scar on Domko's forehead and the metal plate in his head were not from a war injury as he had claimed. Caroline stumbled upon the truth while talking to friends living in Poland. They told Caroline that Domko had spent his teen years in and out of jail.

Wide lashes across his back showed he had been severely punished at some point in his life, likely while incarcerated. Apparently, he was beaten by a group of people one evening for a crime that in their eyes had gone unpunished. Domko was left at the side of the road to die, but was taken to hospital by a good Samaritan. Doctors had to insert a metal plate in the front of his forehead to repair a caved-in skull.

Domko spent time in a Russian labour camp, then enlisted in the Polish Army in 1942, on the basis of the Sikorski-Maisky (Polish-Soviet) pact of July 30, 1941. During his four years of service he was awarded six medals. These medallions initially impressed Caroline but were offset by his brutal and erratic treatment of her children.

By the time she realized what type of man he was, it was too late - she was pregnant. At first, she had not been happy about her eighth pregnancy even though she enjoyed the attention and controversy it might cause. She worried most about the reaction of members of her church and what they might say about the impending birth. After all, she and Domko weren't married and most people didn't realize the extent of their relationship. She believed news of her pregnancy would send local Jehovah's Witnesses into an uproar. As it was, she had difficulty meeting the standards set by her religion.

Caroline had switched from Catholicism to the Jehovah's Witness faith a few years before Bill's death. She had become disillusioned with the Catholic doctrine when she and Bill had caught the Priest of her congregation in a compromising situation. She liked the ideology of the Jehovah's Witnesses who seemed kind and forgiving. Unfortunately, she had kept one Catholic tradition - the rhythm birth control method. It hadn't worked for the young woman who'd borne seven children by her twenty-seventh birthday.

To avoid confrontation, Caroline had decided not to tell anyone except Domko about the latest pregnancy. The fact she carried the child well made the impending birth easy to hide. She remembered placing her new born daughter in a shopping bag before boarding the bus for the ride from the hospital back to Moosehorn. Of course, Kathy began to cry the moment she stepped off the bus and within a few hours, all the busy-bodies in town knew that she had borne Domko's child.

Kathy was a good baby, but cried too much at night because she had her days and nights turned around. Caroline knew that within a few months she would outgrow this, but until then she had to work extra hard to keep the child quiet at night. Domko couldn't tolerate any noise and many times she had to take the baby outside to lull her to sleep. Had he believed the child was his, Caroline was convinced he would have treated her better.

Now what was she going to do?

Little Kathy had barely moved all night. Her breathing was quiet and her arms and legs were limp to her mother's touch. Domko had gone too far this time. It was one thing to discipline the older children, but a four-month-old baby? Staring at the child's pale face, Caroline wiped a tear from her eye. His headaches and violent outbursts were increasing. He blamed the children for making too much noise, but sometimes he flew into a rage over nothing at all. Since fall, he had stopped bathing and let the hair on his face grow for many weeks before shaving. He blamed her for his odd behaviour, saying she was a terrible wife who purposely tried to make him miserable. She was beginning to fear him more and more.

Quietly, she went to the children's bedroom. Glancing to her right as she passed her room, she could see Domko asleep on the bed. She was relieved to see his back was to the door since she wasn't sure she could face him after the previous night. He had come inside hours after their fight and had fallen asleep without a word. He enjoyed prowling the neighbourhood at night, never explaining where he went or why.

The children's room was furnished with only one bed and a mattress on the floor. The three oldest boys normally shared the double sized-mattress while Eunice, Rosie and the twins shared the big metal bed. There was no need for a bureau since the children had no spare clothing. Everything was bought from the second hand store, then passed down from child to child until it was unwearable. There were no pictures on the wall or rugs to cushion their feet from the cold, wooden floor. While people in cities enjoyed the benefits of hydro and indoor plumbing, they were luxuries that most people in this district of Manitoba could not yet afford. Occasional trips to Winnipeg, the province's capital city, located approximately 125 miles south of Moosehorn, left Caroline with the distinct impression that she was a hillbilly, or 'bushed' as the local folks would say. They were indeed the poorest of the poor, not even well accepted in Moosehorn which was a rather small place in comparison to other parts of the country.

Oh, how she had hoped things would be better than this! Lately she'd spent a lot of time mulling over the state of her life. It wasn't much to be proud of. Sometimes she would sit for hours and daydream about how fine her life could have been if she hadn't married young and had so many children. Now Domko was in her life and she wasn't sure how to get rid of him. She didn't have the energy to decide if leaving would be worth the shame and effort.

* * * * *

The mattress on the floor had been empty since Walter and Steven left. The thin, pale faces of her five sleeping children were dirty and tear stained. Little Dennis stirred. Opening his eyes, he turned to face his mother who was standing in the doorway. She felt a lump rising in her throat as his young eyes pleaded for answers. She moved to the side of the bed, noticing the faint smell of urine as she knelt beside the boy. Feeling absolutely helpless, her words betrayed her heartfelt feelings.

"Everything is going to be all right," she said. "Justice is right around the corner."

Caroline turned and left the room. David awoke at his mother's words, just as Dennis turned and fell back asleep. He listening intently to the peaceful sound of morning. Chickens clucked quietly in the yard, while the rooster began his morning wake-up call. Shifting slightly in the bed, he couldn't move without waking his brothers. It was uncomfortable, but having them close made him feel secure. Since Dennis and Rosie peed the bed when they were nervous, sleeping with them was a smelly ordeal. Forgiving them was easy though, since he had done the same thing a few times.

A mosquito hovered aggressively above then landed somewhere in David's matted hair. Smacking his head in a quick motion, the mosquito dodged the blow and flew for a few seconds before choosing a spot on Norman's arm. David watched silently as the insect's abdomen swelled as it sucked blood effortlessly from his brother.

Blood.

The sight of it caused David's stomach to turn. There had been far too much blood since Domko had come to the farm.

David remembered how in the beginning, the farmhand would come in the morning, do the chores, eat and then go away at night. Some days he wouldn't come at all and David remembered how happy he was. Soon though, Domko started sleeping in the barn and then on the chesterfield. The children learned early to avoid him, but now he was sleeping in their mother's bedroom just a few feet away. His gruff yell and swinging arms often sent David and his siblings in all directions. Unfortunately once Domko moved into their small house, avoiding him became impossible.

The hired man didn't seem to mind Walter and Steven since they were old enough to help with chores. Although he beat and mistreated the older boys, it was the younger children who he sought out when he was angry. The little ones tended to make more noise and were deemed 'useless' by Domko who had a special dislike for Norman, Dennis and Rosie.

David wasn't sure, but he believed that Norman was the most defiant of his siblings. He had a way of smirking that made David laugh. He was a thin boy with a crop of thick brown hair and an irresistible charm that everyone loved. Everyone except Domko. Norman feared the man, but he spoke up anyway and Domko hated him for it. He despised the fact that he couldn't break the boy's spirit.

Dennis was a different story. His twin had a gentle way that made Domko especially dislike him. Dennis preferred drawing and making things with his hands to the rough and tumble activities that David and his other brothers enjoyed. These gentler mannerisms were considered a sign of weakness by Domko, who took advantage of the boy's gallant nature at every opportunity. David wished, for both their sakes, that Dennis could be tough like Norman.

A sickening sensation came over David as he remembered the first beating Rosie ever received. Of all the children she was the most vulnerable. Only two years-old when Domko arrived on the farm, the bright and inquisitive girl suffered horribly from beatings. Too small to jump out the window, Rosie learned to hide under the bed and could lay quietly without moving for many hours.

It wasn't long after Domko started sleeping in the house that the trouble started. After supper one evening, the man went into the bedroom then began yelling something in Polish. Of course the children couldn't understand him, but were startled by the intensity in his voice. Given the numerous whippings they had received during the past few months, they all ran towards the door. David remembered Domko being very close behind him when suddenly, he heard a small scream.

He turned in time to see the man grab tiny Rosie by the arm. For an instant, David was surprised. Domko usually grabbed Dennis, but for some reason his twin had been spared this time. He could see Dennis standing with his back to the wall near the doorway that separated the kitchen from the front room.

Holding Rosie by one arm, Domko slipped his stiff, black belt out of his trousers and began strapping her with it.

"Choklit bar? Choklit bar?" he screamed. "I's be showink you choklit bar!"

As hard as he could, Domko strapped the girl, the force of his blows lifting her off the ground. David remembered how odd it looked, as if Domko were beating a doll. He could see the terror in Rosie's eyes as she screamed for their mother, but she was not there. As each blow struck Rosie's small body, David cringed. Soon, Rosie began to bleed from the fresh gashes the belt made on her young skin. Each time he'd strike her, blood splashed, landing in tiny droplets on the floor. David thought for sure that Domko would stop, but he continued for what seemed like an eternity. Somebody must have eaten one of Domko's hidden chocolate bars. The short, muscular man's eyes flashed in a frightening way.

Suddenly, Dennis stepped forward.

"I d-did it! I did it!" Dennis yelled, waving his arms. "I took the chocolate bar!"

Startled, Domko stared menacingly at the frail boy standing before him. Domko couldn't understand what the youngster had said, but David did. A look of pleasure crossed over Domko's face. Dropping the limp girl on the floor, he lunged at Dennis. Without moving, the boy closed his eyes and grimaced. Domko grabbed him and at that moment David covered his eyes. Each time the strap stung his brother's skin, sharp sympathy pains seared across David's backside and legs. Hearing Dennis screaming in pain felt like a dagger slicing through his heart. With one final blow, he threw the limp boy across the room into the wall, knocking him senseless.

David shuddered as he remembered the look in Domko's eyes that night. From that day forward, he and Dennis called their tormentor Satan, the Devil or anything but his real name.

* * * * *

Caroline spent the morning tending to Kathy. The baby moved very little and didn't respond to voice or touch. The other children sensed the gravity of the situation and did their best not to irritate Domko who barked commands and threatened them as usual.

That afternoon, Caroline's thoughts were interrupted by the opening of the kitchen door as her eldest son Walter walked in. The bruising around his eye was beginning to fade.

"Where have you been?" Caroline asked. Walter looked sheepishly at his mother then shrugged his shoulders.

"Where's Steven?" she asked, holding the quiet baby in her arms. "Is he coming home too?" Walter stood staring at the floor. It was obvious that he wasn't going to reveal where his brother was hiding.

"Well, if you aren't gonna answer you can go help Norman with the milking," Caroline said. "And be sure you stay out of Domko's way."

Walter nodded. He loved his mother more than anybody in the world, but didn't feel he could trust her anymore. If he told her that neighbour Jim Deighton had taken him in, she might tell Domko. Surely he would receive another beating, since Domko despised Jim. As usual, it was best that he say nothing.

Caroline watched her son leave. Almost 12-years-old, Walter was the image of his father. He was a tall, thin boy who had a big nose and teeth that protruded slightly. He was at that horribly awkward age, not a boy and not a man. Walter was immature for his age, preferring to play with children much younger than himself. He could sit for hours and roll a toy car through the mud with the twins. He was likely the kindest of Caroline's children, always sharing with others. He'd inherited Bill's stuttering problem, which seemed to be getting worse lately. The twins appeared to have the same problem and Caroline guessed that was the reason they made up their own words.

Walking towards the barn, Walter dreaded seeing Domko. He suspected the man would be supervising the milking. As he passed the water trough, he remembered the time that he and his father had spent an entire January morning trying to thaw out the square, cement cubicle. It had been a particularly cold night in 1951. His father had been ill and asked Walter to stoke the fire under the box before bed so that the water wouldn't freeze overnight. This chore was a big responsibility for a nine-year-old, but Walter had accepted it willingly. Unfortunately, in the excitement of having his father home from the hospital, Walter had forgotten to make the fire. They awoke the next morning to the sound of bawling cattle standing expectantly in front of the frozen waterer.

Walter remembered his father had been annoyed at first, but within a few moments had patted him on the back and told him it was all right. Together father and son thawed the waterer by dousing it with many kettles of boiling water and building a roaring fire underneath the receptacle.

A lump rose in Walter's throat when he thought about his father. Gently he rubbed his left cheek, still sore from the beating Domko had given him.

He had tried to do a good job milking, but it didn't take much to irritate Domko.

He couldn't understand why his grandfather Kolodka had brought Domko to the farm in the first place. He and Stephen were obviously old enough for the chores, and they were the ones working while Domko just stood and watched. It was he and his brothers who had slept in the pump house to catch thieves after their father had died. But Grandfather Kolodka reiterated many times that Domko was a good man.

"G-good for n-nothing," Walter said outloud as he stepped into the barn.

Domko stood at the far end of the building leaning against a pitchfork. His eyes flashed towards the door as Walter walked in. A surge of anger passed over the man as he looked at the dark haired boy.

Domko didn't stand much taller than Walter, but was as muscular as a gorilla. The sleeves and collar of his soiled long underwear stuck out from under his blackened shirt. His dark green work pants were so dirty with cow manure that they were stiff.

Domko always wore black army issue steel-toed work boots, year round, without socks during summer. His dirty face and hands were almost as black as the clothes he wore. He stunk horribly of body odour, not having bathed in months. On the left side of his forehead was a depression and scar which appeared to change colour when he was angry. His thin dark hair was hidden beneath a dirty beige cotton hat which sat sloppily on his head, its greasy peak rolled tightly towards the ceiling.

As he watched Walter pick up a milking pail, Domko's lips pressed together. His short, thick fingers tightened around the pitchfork handle. The stub of a homemade cigarette hung loosely in one corner of his lips. One sinister looking gold tooth flashed at the right hand side of his mouth when he spoke.

"Vere yous be, Valter?" Domko cooed sarcastically. "At your mommy and daddy's?"

The boy shrugged his shoulders and quickly sat on a milking stool beside the cow farthest from Domko. Reaching under the animal, he squeezed a stream of warm, creamy milk into the metal pail. Norman was busy milking on the opposite side of the barn while flies buzzed persistently overhead. A dozen cows were waiting patiently in their stalls which lined the east and west walls of the barn. Their tails swung from side to side, lazily swishing the pestering flies from their backs.

"Fraa," Domko grunted, dropping the pitchfork. Now that Walter was home, he was satisfied the milking would get done without him having to work. He strode toward the barn door, then paused for a moment. Walter froze as he sensed the man standing very close behind him. He stared silently into the milk pail, trying not to cower. Domko grunted, then disappeared out the door, banging it shut behind him.

Walter relaxed. He knew that Domko wouldn't be back for at least 30 minutes, until he had been to the house for a cup of coffee and another cigarette.

Just then, Norman jumped up.

"Hey, Walter!" he yelled. "Fraaa!"

Norman picked up a small stick and tucked it in the corner of his mouth. Pushing his cap back he puffed up his chest. He stooped slightly, then clenching his fists swung his arms back and forth. Strutting up and down the centre of the barn, he turned his head slowly from side to side.

"Yoooou soneebeeeech!" Norman screeched, imitating Domko's accent. Pointing at Walter, he narrowed his eyes. Grunting, he picked up the pitchfork then strode towards his brother, pretending he was smoking. "You's be at your mommy and daaaaaddy's?"

Walter smiled and then laughed. Norman always make him feel better.

"They's be yittink ant sheetink ant peesink all day long!" Norman mimicked Domko's favourite saying when Caroline would complain that the children weren't being fed enough.

Suddenly, the barn door swung open. Norman turned quickly towards the door and dropped the pitchfork to the ground. He stood in paralyzing fear, as he struggled to adjust to the sudden brightness as beams of sunlight shining on his face. Walter's heart jumped to his throat as he slowly turned towards the door.

Their mother stepped into the barn carrying a milking pail. Walter smiled and let out a sigh of relief. Norman relaxed and began to laugh.

"What are you two doing now?" Caroline asked, her mood brightening.

"Nothin'," Norman said. "Just playin' around."

"The cows won't get milked that way," she scolded in a serious tone. "Hurry up before he gets back."

Caroline was anxious to get back to the house to check Kathy who she'd left in Eunice's care. She wanted to take Kathy to see the doctor, but knew that Domko would refuse to let them go because he might be blamed for the child's injury. She decided that if the baby wasn't better by the next morning, she would sneak out of the house early to see the local doctor.

Caroline wasn't yet 30 years old, but had been to see Doctor Gordon Steenson many times. She cringed at the thought of having to tell him what had happened to the baby. She tried to think of a convincing lie, but Steenson had a way about him that unsettled her. She thought how odd it was that he seemed to know what she was thinking almost before she knew herself. He'd know who was responsible for the baby's injury, and then she would be blamed too.

Caroline preferred to keep her domestic problems to herself. Too embarrassed to confide in others, she made excuses for Domko. If she called the police about his violence, they would expect her to press charges against him. This was something that she was much to frightened to do.

The following morning Caroline awoke in her bedroom to the patter of rain on the roof. The children were all asleep, while Domko snored loudly beside her. Getting out of bed she slipped a cotton print dress over her underwear. It was cool and damp in the poorly insulated house. Glancing out the bedroom window, she could see the beginnings of the day were dull and grey. Water streamed off of the roof, puddling on the ground below. She could tell it had been raining most of the night.

Kathy stirred in her bed along the west wall. Little arms and legs began to move as she started to cry. Caroline lifted the baby and began cradling her. She went quietly to the kitchen and excitedly ladled some milk from a can sitting on the floor into a baby bottle. The child drank hungrily as the nipple was placed in her mouth. Pacing across the kitchen floor, Caroline said a quiet prayer as a wave of relief passed over her. It looked as though Kathy was going to be all right.

Chapter 3

Hiding in the night

SUMMER CAME AND WENT. Good weather meant the children worked long labourious hours outdoors. The cows were milked twice a day by Caroline and the older boys while Eunice was responsible for keeping Kathy out of harm's way. The twins had daily chores that included feeding the chickens, pigs, picking vegetables from the garden and carrying in wood for the stove.

The older children spent most afternoons in the hayfield - cutting, raking and stacking hay. It was necessary for enough hay to be ready by fall, as this is what the cows and horses were fed over the long, cold winter.

Caroline's family stayed mostly on the farm since there was little time for socializing. Few people came by to visit as Domko had alienated most of Caroline's friends and neighbours. Domko only enjoyed visiting his friends in Moosehorn or those who lived north of the farm near the hamlets of Grahamdale and Faulkner.

Caroline looked forward to occasional trips to Moosehorn, the area's largest town. Since the family didn't have a car, they travelled by wagon or sleigh. Often Domko would go by himself, leaving Caroline and the children at home to do chores. He would sell the week's accumulation of cream to the Moosehorn Creamery and buy farm supplies and a few household staples with some of the money. He refused to discuss with Caroline what he did with the remainder, berating her whenever she asked questions.

His spending habits were difficult to question, though, since he had purchased the majority of the cattle on the farm with money he'd earned before his arrival. He goaded Caroline with this fact whenever he had the opportunity. She was made to feel worthless and fortunate that he put up with her and the children.

Occasionally, Caroline went to town and would buy groceries at the local Co-op store. She also picked up the mail, which helped keep her in touch with the world outside the farm. Sometimes they would continue south on the highway for an additional seven miles to the town of Ashern. It was approximately the same size as Moosehorn but in addition to the usual amenities, Ashern had a hospital, lawyer and Royal Canadian Mounted Police (RCMP) detachment.

When autumn arrived, Domko's moods began to worsen. At times, the steel plate in his head caused him excruciating pain and trips to the doctor did little to help. Pounding headaches sent him into a blinding rage, causing him to beat anyone within arm's reach. The children learned to stay out of his way but as winter approached, they began spending more time indoors and underfoot.

There was no doubt that this was a noisy household. Eight children under one tiny roof was hard on Caroline's sanity and it had a devastating effect on the troubled mind of her common-law husband. The fact they were struggling financially, and behind in their municipal tax payments, added to Domko's stress. He was deathly afraid of authority figures and didn't trust the local government district, fearing someone would buy the farm out from under him if he didn't pay the tax bill.

Domko was in an irritable mood late one October evening. The family had just finished a meagre supper when the twins began playing with a small toy truck on the bare floor near the old chesterfield. They chattered to themselves in the strange language they shared, sliding the truck back and forth. Their gibberish particularly annoyed Domko who believed they spoke that way so he couldn't understand them. The boys had lost themselves in their twin world of make-believe when suddenly, Domko flew from the kitchen into the front room. He grabbed both boys and flung them onto the chesterfield. David landed on top, while Dennis slid between the side of the couch and the wall. He began beating each boy with his fist.

"Mommmma!" David wailed, as he pulled his arms up over his head and tried to crawl away. The rest of the children scattered, Rosie and Eunice sliding under the bed in their room while the three older boys ran out the kitchen door. Caroline flew from the kitchen into the living room.

"Boleslaw!" she screamed. "Leave them alone!"

The past few weeks had been unbearable as she watched him many times beat each of her children. Poor little Dennis had received two beatings already that week.

"You're going to kill them!" she screamed, grabbing his arm she tried to pull him away from the cowering boys.

Caroline was a strong woman of above average size, weighing about 150 pounds. She had worked hard her entire life doing manual farm labour but in spite of her 5'10" frame, she was no match for the stocky soldier who'd bragged openly about the brutal acts he'd committed during the war.

Spinning around, Domko slammed his fist into her face, the sound of her shattering nose exploded in her head. Her neck snapped backwards and the force of the blow lifted her feet off the ground. Landing flat on her back, her mind whirled as everything around her turned black. From somewhere above, she felt fists pummeling her head and chest. She tried to raise her arms for protection, but they seemed to no longer belong to her body. She could hear the children screaming and crying somewhere in the distance. Caroline wanted to die. She had endured enough beatings since childhood to last a lifetime. She prayed to God to end her life right then and there.

Kill me now, she said to herself in utter hopelessness. *Kill us all.*

Caroline awoke some time later to the sound of Domko's guttural snickering. It was the sound he made after giving someone a thorough beating. Lately, she and the children had been hearing that sound every day. This time it had been her turn.

She was lying on the front room floor near her bedroom doorway. Slowly she opened her eyes, which wouldn't focus at first. She had no idea how long it had been since Domko had stopped beating her. Once she realized how quiet it was in the house, her heart began to race. Alarmed, she tried to sit up. Where were the kids? Did he kill them?

The change in position caused her head to start throbbing. Blood had dried on her face, hands and shirt. Gingerly touching her nose, Caroline felt sharp pains radiate to her forehead. She could see Domko sitting in his usual spot at the kitchen table but the children were nowhere to be seen.

Slowly standing up, she walked dizzily through the kitchen to the door. The older children's jackets and shoes were gone, while the twins' coats still hung from the hooks on the wall. Domko looked up from what he was reading, then snickered again. Without a word, she lowered her head and slipped outside.

The bitter north wind cut through Caroline's light dress. It was a dark, starless night so it took a few moments for her eyes to adjust to the blackness. The weather had changed after supper, now a light blanket of fresh snow covered the ground. Snowflakes swirled around her as she decided which direction to take. Crossing her arms, she looked around wondering which way the children had gone. Since they had taken the baby with them and the twins were without their jackets, she suspected they couldn't have travelled very far.

Caroline rounded the corner of the house, quickly leaving the yard. She didn't have a jacket or shoes, just thin homemade slippers. Fortunately her feet were calloused and tough, so she barely felt the stones poking her feet. Within a few minutes of walking down the road, she could see a light in the distance. Likely the children were at Gus and Emma Harwart's home, only a quarter mile away. Glancing nervously around, she checked to be sure that Domko wasn't following her.

This wasn't the first time she and the children had fled the house and ended up on the Harwart's doorstep.

He'll be mad if he finds out where we went, she thought to herself. Then defiantly she clenched her jaw. *I don't care if he does get mad. He can't hurt us there.*

* * * * *

"I don't know why she puts up with him," Emma Harwart said, shaking her soft, white head of curls. The heavy set woman was leaning over David, applying a soft warm cloth to the youngster's battered face.

"She should kick him out, that's what she should do," Emma raved in a soft German accent. "The house is hers for goodness sake and it's on her quarter of land!"

Gus stood in the centre of the kitchen floor with his arms crossed. He was a tall thin man with a rather large nose and gentle blue eyes. His brown-grey hair was thinning on top and his skin was weathered and beaten from the sun. The German immigrant had large, farmer's hands with big knuckles and ragged nails. Gus didn't talk much, he left that to Emma. There were some subjects that the 61 year old farmer would discuss though, and Bob Domko was one of them.

Gus had tried right from the beginning to get along with Domko but found him impossible to deal with. Domko was envious and always compared his farm to everyone else's in the community. His healthy herd of cattle, had been built surprisingly fast in the few years since he'd moved to Caroline's quarter section. Neighbours thought he must have stolen the animals, but Gus remembered the children telling him about a suitcase full of money that Domko had brought with him to the farm.

He'd also bought another quarter section of land that year from neighbour Arthur Betker. Unfortunately, these acquisitions did not improve Domko's temperament. He continued to be a jealous, spiteful man who had in a short time alienated most neighbours including Gus.

He looked first at the twins sitting at the kitchen table, then to the boys sitting on the chesterfield in the front room. Eunice was standing in the kitchen holding Kathy, while Rosie hid quietly behind her sister's legs.

"Where did you say your momma was?" Gus asked the older boys.

"H-he was punching her on the floor," Walter stammered. "W-we us guys ran out."

"I think he killed her," Norman added, his chin wavering.

Gus and Emma's nine year-old daughter Marjorie was leaning against the living room wall facing the Pischke children. Her eyes widened at Norman's words. Looking at her father, she opened her mouth to speak.

"Hush now," Emma said, transferring her attention to Dennis. "Your momma will be alright."

Marjorie looked at her playmates. It wasn't the first time they had come to her house for refuge from their step-father. According to her parents, Domko was a monster. She had overheard them talking about him many times, mostly when they thought she wasn't listening. She was frightened of him too, but tried not to let it show.

"Auntie Emma," David asked. "You gots something to eat?"

Emma looked at the youngster. The twins were nearly the cutest little things she'd ever seen, but she couldn't understand a word either of them said.

"What did you say, darlin'?" she asked in a gentle voice.

"They're askin' for somethin' to eat," Eunice interrupted. "Domko don't let us eat nothin', 'cause he eats it all himself."

Emma looked at the boys. Both were watching her expectantly. Their tattered clothes were much too small for their growing frames and their hair was dirty and matted. Neither had on socks, having walked through the snow in bare feet. Their bright blue inquisitive eyes gazed at her lovingly.

"I most certainly do," she said. "As soon as I get these boys cleaned up, you all can have some fresh bread and Saskatoon jam."

Walter and Norman looked at each other. Walter's eyebrows raised high while Norman smiled. Marjorie noticed their reaction and smiled too. They were her friends. Norman was the same age as her and Walter was only two years older. Both boys made the best of every situation and were fun and outgoing in spite of the turmoil at home. Marjorie pretended not to notice when Walter stuttered at school even though some of the other kids made fun of him. She never did though, not ever.

Marjorie was a pretty girl who's blue eyes danced when she spoke. Soft blonde curls framed her round, gentle face. The youngest of Gus and Emma's seven daughters, she was pleasingly bright. She did well in school and enjoyed helping her father with the chores. She loved to socialize and spent most of her free time playing with the Pischke children.

"Marjorie," her mother called. "You come and help me get the lunch ready."

Proudly the nine year old hurried into the kitchen and pulled two fresh loaves of bread from the cupboard. She had helped her mother bake bread that day and was quite pleased with herself. Given the chance, she'd be sure to let Norman know that these were her loaves.

The wind whistled through the trees surrounding the old log house. The inside was warmed by two wood stoves, one for cooking occupying most of the space along a wall in the kitchen. The other, an old wood heater, sat in the middle of the living room floor.

A modest home, it was clean and inviting. Divided into four rooms, the kitchen was spread across the back half of the house. An old wooden kitchen table and six chairs sat in the middle of the floor. The farm kitchen was the life force of the home. Here, people visited, gossiped, cooked and made important decisions. The white paint on Emma's chairs had worn thin from the use they had received over the years. Comfortable and worn was exactly how she liked them.

The front room ran across the front of the house. An old green chesterfield and chair sat along the south wall. The largest window in the house was on the far wall in the front room which faced the road. A small table with knick knacks, plants and pictures sat beneath the window. There were old pictures on the wall and a prized aerial photograph of the family homestead.

Gus and Emma's bedroom sat directly off the front room. Their room contained a double sized wrought iron bed with old fashioned springs and a thick mattress. A bright multi-patterned quilt made from scraps of old clothing covered the bed. There was one dresser and bureau for their Sunday clothes, along with a small cedar chest at the foot of the bed.

Marjorie's bedroom was also off the front room, in the small space between Gus and Emma's room and the kitchen. There was a handmade set of bunk beds along one wall and a small homemade bed which bumped against the opposite wall. Each were covered with thin cotton mattresses and similar homemade quilts. There was a small window on the far wall and a bureau in the corner which held Marjorie's everyday clothes and Sunday dress. Her school books were piled neatly on the bed. The floors throughout the house were made from sanded oak planks which Emma had painted a natural brown colour. Braided throw rugs were in front of each bed and in the centre of the living room floor.

Gus did the best he could with his two quarter sections of land. The district had been settled in the early 1920s primarily by German, Ukrainian and Icelandic immigrants. While the land was full of bush and stones, a man could make a living if he was willing to work hard. On the whole, it wasn't very good farm land, but pockets near Lake Manitoba proved adequate for raising cattle or growing grain.

Gus was respected in the community but not admired. He had too few possessions to be considered well off, but he always put in a full day's work and was careful to pay his bills on time. Raising seven children had left little money for luxuries especially since two of their daughters were stricken with Polio, one of them spending many years in a Winnipeg hospital. Frequent trips to visit the bedridden youngster put a substantial drain on the family's savings, although the Harwarts never blamed their daughter for their lack of wealth. Gus was nearing retirement age and dreamed of building a new house for his wife.

Suddenly, the Harwart's two year old dog, Sandy, began barking outside. Sandy never missed the opportunity to let her masters know that someone was in the yard. She barked quickly three times, then again more cautiously.

Gus could hear the dog moving along the south side of the house and then to the back door. Sandy was a small dog of mixed parentage, with brown hair, floppy ears and a thick tail. Although the dog was short on good looks, she had been Marjorie's favourite pet for years. Sandy slept underneath the girl's bedroom window year round as an act of devotion. In the evening, the girl often slipped the dog table scraps through the window, since food could be scare for a dog in winter. Marjorie saw to it that Sandy always got plenty of food and lots of love.

Gus went to the door and wedged his foot across the bottom. With his right hand on the knob, he braced himself against the frame.

"Who is it?" he asked in his gruffest voice.

"It's Caroline," a woman's voice said. "Are the kids here?"

Gus relaxed. Opening the door he stepped back.

"Come in," he said. "Your kids are all here."

Emma stopped cutting bread and bustled toward the door. She stopped when she saw the young woman.

"My Lord Caroline, what did he do to you?" she gasped.

"I'm alright," she answered, looking toward the floor. "How are David and Dennis?"

"They're fine," she said. "A little banged up but nothing that won't heal."

"And the baby?"

"Eunice has her. Come in and sit down, we were just about to give these kids of yours something to eat."

Caroline flinched as she sat down. Her body was beginning to throb as large, dark bruises formed on her arms and chest. She slowly pulled her cold feet up onto the chair and rubbed them with her hands.

Emma watched Caroline and wondered how such a lovely woman had become tangled up with a man like Domko. Caroline was handsome with dark wavy hair that framed her elegant face. She had high cheek bones and soft blue eyes that danced when she spoke. She carried her weight well on her tall frame and her figure was only just beginning to show the signs of having supported seven pregnancies, including a set of twins. Emma was disappointed to see that the turmoil in Caroline's life was beginning to show on her 31 year-old face.

Caroline's children gradually emerged from the living room.

"We thought you was dead," Walter said his tone serious, while Norman and Stephen stared quietly at her.

"Well, I'm not dead," she said, reaching up to pat her eldest son on the back. The twins pushed their way past the older children to their mother.

"Mamma," Dennis said, his chin wavering. "Did you bring my truck?"

Caroline smiled. Then her shoulders slumped. She brought her hands up to her face and began to sob. "I can't take this anymore Emma, I just can't take it anymore."

Putting the plate of bread on the table, Emma instructed the children to sit down. Obediently, each found a seat with the twins sharing one chair. Gently, Emma took Caroline by the arm and led her into the living room.

"You sit here while I get these children fed," Emma said. "I'll be back in a few minutes."

Hurrying into the kitchen, the older woman gave a few quick instructions to Marjorie. The children had already each taken a piece of bread and were spreading thick globs of wild berry jam on top. They ate hungrily and each drank a full glass of milk. Emma had been accustomed to feeding a big family, so caring for the Pischke children was an easy and satisfying experience.

Caroline sat on the couch and stared at Gus and Emma's wedding picture on the wall. Her children's worn and tattered jackets were strung across the small indoor clothes line over the wood stove. She smiled mockingly and shook her head.

Why has life always been so hard for me? she wondered. *Every decision I've ever made has been wrong.*

Remembering the day she met Bill sent a wave of sadness through her. She had been working at the store in Grahamdale when Bill came in to purchase a few items. It didn't take long before he was spending more and more time dawdling by the counter. Caroline was an attractive eighteen year old who enjoyed chatting and joking with the customers. Bill, who was 15 years her senior, was quite smitten with the slim and vivacious young woman. Caroline remembered being impressed that Bill had a car, enabling him to take her and her friends to dances in town. It didn't take long before a romance developed between them.

They married and moved to the farm, a fertile quarter section of land that Bill had bought on tax sale at a few years before. Neighbours said the farm was cursed but this was something that Bill never believed. As time wore on, Caroline was beginning to wonder if it was true.

Not long after the wedding, Walter was born. She and Bill were poor and the babies came too quickly. Then Bill became sick with tuberculosis. Caroline found herself disenchanted with her new life. While she and Bill got along well enough, it was hard to discard her dreams of having a lovely home and beautiful clothes, things she thought Bill would provide.

Emma handed Caroline a piece of bread with jam then sat down on the couch beside her.

"Am I a good mother?" Caroline asked, taking a bite of the bread.

Emma looked into the young woman's sad and pleading eyes. Caroline's lips were swollen and her eyes were purple from the beating. Almost as purple as the Saskatoon jam she was licking from her lips. Her neck was bruised and no doubt she'd be feeling the effects the next morning. Although Caroline had tried to scratch it off, there was crusted blood on her face and neck.

She is a beautiful woman, Emma thought. *In spite of all she's been through she is still more beautiful than I've ever been. But a good mother? Not really.*

"You do the best you can," Emma said. She wasn't lying to the woman, in fact she spoke the simple truth. Caroline didn't know any better. Rumours were that Caroline's childhood had been rough. She seemed to be rejecting adulthood, preferring to behave like a teenager. Everyone in the community knew that she would put on a nice dress with high heels, then disappear for days and leave the children with Domko. Where she went, nobody knew. Sometimes she would stay away for a week or longer.

During those times, the children would show up on Emma's doorstep looking for something to eat. Emma soon realized the children were neglected and began feeding them - sometimes for many days. She began hearing stories about Domko and at first she thought the children must be lying since the stories made Domko sound like a monster.

Emma remembered how in early March Eunice had brought eggs to the house and had been reluctant to go home. This surprised Emma who knew that Caroline had arrived home the day before with a new baby - a big event for a country family. Later that afternoon, Emma overheard Eunice and Marjorie talking and was horrified to discover that Eunice was frightened to go home because Domko had locked her in the crawl space under the house for most of the previous day. Emma's heart broke as she overheard the tiny, sweet girl describing Domko's brutality when he didn't want to take her to Moosehorn with him to pick up Caroline and the new baby at the bus depot. Instead he'd grabbed Eunice by the hair, then dropped her into the cold, dark place.

After overhearing the girl's fears, Emma began hiding the children when Domko came looking for them. She stood many times in the doorway facing the sinister looking man while the children hid quietly in the bedroom. He was the only person she could look directly in the eye and tell a boldfaced lie. For some reason, lying to Domko about those children didn't feel like lying at all.

Emma couldn't understand how Caroline could live with a man like that. Why she left the children with him when she went to town was a mystery. She certainly wasn't an easy person to understand.

Emma hoped that Caroline would muster the courage to send Domko packing. If he refused to go, then possibly Caroline could move to town and ask for welfare. It was an embarrassing thing to have to do, but it appeared she had little choice. She'd been on welfare while Bill was sick - how bad could it be? Surely no worse than living with Domko.

The most important thing is for somebody to start feeding those children, and that they're kept away from that poor excuse for a stepfather, she thought to herself.

"What are you going to do?" Emma asked, hoping Caroline would seek her advice.

"I don't know," she answered, caressing her fat lip. "I can't go anywhere looking like this."

"What about your father?" Emma asked. "Have you told him what Domko does to you and the children?

Caroline laughed mockingly. Then a sad expression came over her face. She lowered her eyes and began twisting the edge of her dress around her index finger. Emma began to feel uncomfortable as she waited for the woman to speak.

"He wouldn't believe me anyway," Caroline said quietly. "He always sides with Domko. The kids are too noisy and bad and of course he hates the twins. I see how he looks at them. He was so glad when me and Domko got together that I don't want to disappoint him now."

"What about Bill's family? The Pischkes are decent folk, I'm sure they'd help you out if they knew Bill's kids were in danger."

Caroline grimaced, then her eyes stared vacantly past Emma to the wall over the woman's right shoulder. Emma sensed that there was some history between the families that Caroline wasn't willing to discuss.

Too bad, Emma thought. *People let their petty differences get in the way and it's the children who always suffer.*

Suddenly, the dog began barking furiously under the front room window. Sandy howled in a frantic, almost vicious way. Emma looked at Caroline who turned to Gus who was standing at the edge of the kitchen listening to the women's conversation. Moving quickly, he dimmed the oil lantern hanging over the kitchen table. The children were oblivious to the commotion, busily eating the last pieces of bread and jam.

Caroline sat upright. She could feel her heart begin to quicken in her chest. Gus walked cautiously to the front room window. Lifting his finger to his mouth he motioned to the women to be quiet. Pulling back the thin curtain he peered outside. The snow was falling heavily now, whipping furiously against the glass panes by a strong north wind. Gus hoped the dog had overreacted to a rabbit running through the yard or a deer at the edge of the bush. Glancing down, he could see Sandy bristling at something moving near the trees in the front yard. Squinting, he tried to make out the figure. As the shadow moved closer, Gus could see the outline of a man walking in a wide circle around the house. The dog continued to bark furiously, then suddenly lunged forward as the man attempted to move closer. There was only one person who the dog barked at with such utter hatred.

"It's Domko," Gus whispered loudly, as he turned towards the women. "And that crazy bastard has a gun."

Chapter 4

Hiding out

THE WORD 'DOMKO' SENT THE CHILDREN running in all directions. Within moments, the older boys slid under the table while Eunice picked Kathy up and scurried between the cook-stove and cupboard.

The twins jumped off the chair they were sharing and ran one behind the other towards their mother. Ignoring Caroline's outstretched arms, David ran past her, then squirmed into the small space between the back of the couch and wall. His little arm reached out and grabbed Dennis' shirt, pulling his brother into hiding. Rosie closely followed Dennis. Her eyes were wide and her bottom lip began to tremble. She ran straight to her mother and wrapped her young arms around her mother's waist as Caroline struggled to stand up.

What is Domko doing? Caroline asked herself, as she held Rosie and crept toward the window. *Is he going to shoot us?* For a moment, Caroline confused her feelings of fear with pride as she thought of Domko's passion for her. She was ashamed of the excitement she was feeling.

Marjorie stood silently by her bedroom door. "Momma," the young girl asked with pleading eyes, "Domko's not going to shoot Sandy, is he?"

"No, I don't think so," Emma answered firmly. "Now you go and climb onto your bed and don't come out of your room until I say so."

"Yes, momma," she said, turning into her room.

"Where is he now?" Emma asked her husband who was still standing at the window.

"From what I can tell, he's circling the house," Gus said quietly.

"Circling the house?" Emma asked. "What's he doing a fool thing like that for?"

"Maybe the dog is keeping him away," he said. "Or maybe he's trying to see in one of the windows. Either way, I don't like it."

Gus turned on his heel and quickly went into the bedroom. He emerged less than a minute later holding a rifle.

"Gustav!" Emma whispered loudly. "What are you doing?"

Giving his wife a stern look, Gus loaded a bullet in the chamber.

Unsure how she should be feeling, Caroline looked at Gus. "What should I do?" she asked.

Gus motioned for her to be quiet. His look showed he was slightly annoyed at the young woman and Caroline's face reddened as she ashamedly realized she had put the Harwarts, once again, in the position of having to defend her.

"Get Caroline and the children into the cellar and do it quickly before he sees them," he said sternly to his wife. Emma could feel her heart in her throat as she motioned for Caroline to follow her to the cellar door in the middle of the kitchen floor.

"What if he asks if they're here?" she said hurriedly, lifting the heavy hinged door. "What are you going to say?"

Gus didn't answer as he walked past his wife to the back door. He couldn't hear her as he was listening intently to the little dog who was barking sporadically while circling the house. Within a few minutes, the dog was protecting the back stoop from the intruder.

Emma could feel a cold draft on her legs as she stood holding the cellar door open. "Caroline, c'mon, get those children of yours into the cellar while I get the twins," she said.

Emma hurried to the chesterfield where she spent a few moments coaxing the frightened boys out from their rather ingenious hiding place. She returned with a boy in each hand in time to see that Walter, Steven and Norman had lowered themselves into the dark hole. Emma was momentarily surprised at the youngsters' lack of fear of the dark, unfamiliar place. Caroline followed the boys with Rosie, who'd refused to let go of her mother since the commotion started outside. Caroline reached up for Kathy, who was in Eunice's arms. Emma lowered the twins, then stepped back so Eunice could follow.

"Can I go to Marjie's room instead?" Eunice asked nervously.

"No, you come down here with us," Caroline answered. "We've caused the Harwarts enough problems without you bein' in full view."

The girl stood staring at the hole in the floor. Her brothers had already found themselves some potato bags to sit on. Walter saw his sister's reluctance and went to the opening.

"C'mon Beanie, grab my hand an' I'll help you," he said, calling his sister by her pet name. Reluctantly, Eunice reached out and gave a fearful squeal as she put one leg over her brother's shoulder.Walter held her tight then set her down on a bag of onions.

"I'm going to close the door now," Emma said. "Will you all be okay?"

Caroline nodded as she ducked out of the way.

Emma looked at the sad, dirty faces below her. She felt bad having to put them in such an uncomfortable spot, but they had no other choice.

"I'll let you know as soon as he's gone," she said lowering the door.

Emma turned to see her husband pulling on his work boots. Lifting his coat from the the hook by the door, Gus quickly put it on.

"You sit here and pretend like nothing is happening," he said pointing to the kitchen table. "Get your knitting."

Emma gathered her latest project, a new pair of grey wool mittens she was making for Marjorie. Sitting in her usual spot, she reached across the table and turned on their old wooden battery operated radio in the corner. Gus nodded approvingly. She gave him a nervous smile.

Opening the door, he stepped out onto the stoop. "Sandy, come here girl," he called, quieting the dog's frantic barking. "Who's there?!"

The gun hung loosely by his side as he tried to shield his face from the wind with his other hand. Sandy slowly approached the stoop, glancing protectively over her shoulder. Her lip quivered back, showing a row of sharp, white teeth.

Gus strained to see as his eyes adjusted to the darkness. The wind was cold, as hard snow whipped his cheeks. "Who's there?" he called aggressively. A few moments passed and then a figure appeared from around the corner of the house.

"Domko," a familiar voice with a heavy accent answered. "Where's be Carlorka?"

Gus could see his neighbour clearly now. The darkness shadowed Domko's face, making the short, dirty man look sinister, an appearance that was accentuated by his shining gold tooth creating a ray of light. Gus looked cautiously at the gun Domko held in in one hand.

"Caroline isn't here, so you can stop walking around my house," he answered coldly, hoping the little man would leave.

"You's be shootink me?" Domko smirked, examining the gun at Gus' side.

"I didn't know who I'd find out here," Gus said trying not to apologize. He raised the gun slightly to make a point. "The dog doesn't usually bark like that."

Domko moved closer to the door as he tried to peer over Gus' shoulder into the house.

Sandy, who'd calmed somewhat, growled deep in her chest. Her small body, pressed against the front of Gus' leg, was beginning to feel penned in as Domko stepped closer.

"Caroline isn't here," Gus said again, this time more firmly. He was uncomfortable in the lie so avoided Domko's eyes. "Did you check anywhere else?"

The intruder shrugged his shoulders, then his eyes narrowed. "They say it be goot at Harvarts."

"By jimminy, they don't come here because they like my farm!" Gus challenged, knowing that the man was trying to antagonize him. "They come here for something to eat. If you'd feed them more often, the kids might like you better."

"Yit, Yit, that's all they's be do," he laughed, spitting on the ground.

As she pretended to knit, Emma strained to hear what the men were saying. Domko's cold-hearted stare over her husband's shoulder sent a chill down her spine. She dropped a few stitches as her hands shook nervously.

"They're children and you shouldn't treat them like workhorses," Gus said trying to distract Domko from staring at his wife. "Now go home before I charge you with trespassing."

"Trespass?" Domko chuckled, his laughter turning quickly to anger. "Vat? Me? I's be showink you some trespass!"

Knowing better than to turn his back on Domko, Gus took two steps backwards. He stepped back into the house, then slammed the door. Sandy took that as her cue and began barking again.

"Is he gone?" Emma whispered.

"I hope so," he said angrily. Gus stood in front of the kitchen window with his hand blocking his reflection on the glass. "I don't see him, but that doesn't mean he's left the yard. I can see Sandy looking towards the barn, maybe that's where he went."

"When should we bring Caroline and the kids up?" Emma asked as she looked admiringly at her husband. She always trusted his opinion.

"Not yet. We'll wait until Sandy stops barking. He just might come back to the house."

Gus still held the gun firmly in his hand. Tiny droplets of water covered Gus' jacket and hat as the snowflakes melted quickly in the warm kitchen.

It didn't take long for Caroline's eyes to adjust to the cellar's darkness. Looking around, she saw the room was similar to the crawl space under her own house. Jars of preserves were stacked neatly in one corner, while bags of potatoes were in the other. There were two crocks of sauerkraut aging next to the potatoes, and beside them a few bags of carrots. The older children sat on top of the bags, while the twins played together on the dirt floor. Rosie sat pressed against her mother while Kathy gurgled softly.

Glancing around, Caroline could see that Emma had worked hard this fall to prepare for winter. The smell of sauerkraut filled the space, bringing back memories of the fall of 1942, just shortly after Walter was born. She and Bill had spent a full day chopping cabbage and preparing brine in what she had learned was a fall ritual for German people. Bill had loved the pungent food, especially when it was served with boiled sausage. Now, those days seemed so very far away.

The only thing she and Bill had ever fought about was her religion. They had bickered about the same things that irritate all married couples, but were always able to make up later in bed. Religion was the only exception. Caroline had tried to persuade him to join her as a Jehovah's Witness but while he was polite to her friends, he refused to study. When his illness progressed, doctors recommended an operation that required a blood transfusion. She had tried to persuade him not to have the procedure, but he had ignored her. Shortly afterwards he had died, reinforcing her belief that taking blood from another person is evil and wrong. She concluded that by undergoing the transfusion, he had written his own death certificate. Caroline vowed to never forgive him for that.

"I'm c-c-cold," Walter said, interrupting her thoughts.

"Me too," Eunice added. "We shoulda brought our coats down here."

A feeling of dread swept over Caroline. The children's coats were still hanging in full view above the wood stove in the living room. If Domko looked in any window or door, he'd be able to see them.

Listening carefully, she could hear the dog still barking outside. The noise had subsided earlier, but had started again so Caroline was reluctant to push open the cellar door, fearing that Domko would be standing in the kitchen. The floor creaked every time Gus and Emma moved across it.

The children were becoming restless in the tiny crawl space. The twins examined the stone crocks, discussing what might be inside. Dennis stood and watched while David reached into the crock pot and lifted up the glass plate that was pressing the thinly sliced cabbage into the brine. Smiling, he reached in and pulled up a fistful of cabbage, showing it to Dennis. Taking that as his cue, Dennis stepped forward and placed his hands in the pot. Both boys put some of the cold, fermenting cabbage into their mouths.

"Get out of there," Caroline scolded. "Eunice, put the lid back on and make the boys sit with you."

The boys turned to their mother and grimaced. David dropped the cabbage back into the crock, while Dennis rubbed his hands across the front of his shirt.

"What? You don't like raw cabbage and vinegar?" Caroline laughed as she rocked Kathy in her arms. *Those two sure love to eat,* she thought and a smile crossed her face. The twins were hearty children who could take the cold and lack of food better than the others.

Sandy stopped barking and a few minutes later, heavy footsteps moved across the floor above. Caroline's heart skipped a beat as the door to the cellar was slowly lifted. It was Emma who peered in.

"Is he gone?" Caroline asked, squinting as light from the oil lamps streamed in and hurt her eyes.

"I think so," Emma replied, reaching down to grasp Caroline's hand. "C'mon out of that cold cellar."

With Kathy in one arm, Caroline hoisted herself out of the hole. Gus stood behind his wife, watching as the children emerged from the darkness. Eunice had pushed her way past the boys to be first in line. The chatter that ensued once the entire family was in the kitchen prompted Marjorie to emerge from her bedroom.

"Can I come out now?" she asked in a fearful voice.

"Yes, you can come out, but only for a short while," her mother said. "It's getting late and already past your bedtime."

Walter herded the children into the living room while Caroline turned to Gus and Emma.

"What happened?" she asked.

Gus sat down at the table. He knew Emma would want to tell the story.

"Well, Domko was here alright," Emma began. "He came looking for you and the kids. Gus told him that you weren't here."

Caroline sat down beside the man who had been a father figure to her the past few years. "Did he believe you?" she asked.

"Gus isn't a very good liar," Emma said, pushing her knitting aside. She poured Caroline a cup of hot tea from the pot that sat on a warming pad in the center of the table. "And you know how strange Domko is. He's doesn't trust us at all."

Gus could never remember meeting a more suspicious man. There was a word to describe his odd behaviour, but Gus couldn't think of it at that moment.

"Those devil eyes of his darted around so much I couldn't tell if he believed me or not," Gus said. "I tried, but he may have seen the children's coats. We should have taken them down, but I didn't think of it." He didn't appreciate being caught in the middle of a lie, even if it was just by Domko.

"Now it's not your fault," Emma cooed. "You scared the fool off, didn't you?"

Caroline flinched at the woman's comment. She suddenly felt the need to defend her common-law husband. After all, he did have some good qualities in spite of his erratic behaviour. For instance, when he wasn't in a bad mood, Domko could be quite charming and good company. He had told her many times how lovely she was and was quite an ardent lover. It was as if he had two personalities - one loving and cooperative, the other suspicious and violent. She and the children seemed to inspire his violent side and lately Caroline was beginning to wonder if it wasn't there fault.

After all, who else would want a woman with seven, rather eight children? The whole incident would probably not have happened if she could just teach the children to be quiet.

A feeling of guilt washed over her. This was all her fault. She was involving the Harwarts in troubles of her own making. Her father and brothers had told her many times that the children were bad and needed more discipline. This would never have happened if she had taught them to be well-mannered and respectful. The twins were too noisy, always causing disruptions in the house. And that crazy chatter of theirs! No wonder Domko lost his temper with them. Caroline decided she would try to make them behave, then Domko wouldn't be so hard on them.

"I think it will be best if I go home and talk to him," Caroline said. "Can I leave the kids here tonight?"

"Are you sure you want to go over there? He still looked pretty mad to me," Emma said, not hiding her surprise very well. "Of course you're welcome to leave the kids here, but I'd rather you stayed too."

"I'll be alright. He's probably cooled off by now."

Gus and Emma stared at the young woman as she got up from the table.

Her reflection in the mirror near the door caused Caroline to look twice.

The sight of me will make him feel bad, she thought. *I'll try to be a better wife and this won't happen no more.* Turning, she gave the Harwarts a faint smile.

"Take my coat and boots," Emma offered. "It's too cold to go out dressed like that. And make sure you come back here to stay if he's acting crazy."

Without a word to the children, Caroline slipped out the door.

Finding enough quilts to cover eight youngsters was not an easy task. There was a time when the house was full of beds and blankets. Now that six of the seven Harwart daughters were grown, all that was left were worn blankets that had survived numerous trips to town on the old sleigh. When Gus bought a car a few years earlier, the old linen had been stored under Emma and Gus's bed. She pulled out a box and shook out the musty blankets.

"These will just have to do, but I don't have enough pillows for you all," she said as she fussed over the sleeping arrangements.

"That's o.k. Mrs. Harwart," Norman said cheerfully. "We don't got no pillows at home anyways."

It was decided that Eunice and Kathy would share the extra bed in Marjorie's room, while the twins shared the bottom bunk. The boys were happy about this as they chattered to themselves and climbed into the bed, pulling a thick blanket behind them.

Walter was given a quilt and told to sleep on the chesterfield, while Norman and Steven shared the thick rug in front of the wood stove. Marjorie invited Rosie to share her bed.

Eunice took Rosie aside as the children were stripping off their dirty clothing.

"Now don't you go peein' in Marjie's bed," Eunice warned.

"I won't," Rosie said indignantly, giving Marjorie a quick glance.

Marjorie's eyes widened.

"Don't worry, she only does it if she's scared," Eunice said, trying to reassure her friend.

"You're not scared now are you?" Marjorie asked.

The youngster smiled. "No Marjie, I like your high bed."

Steven and Norman began squabbling about who was to sleep closest to the wood stove. Gus acted as referee, grabbing the rug and turning it so the feet of both boys were close to the heat. Then he covered them with a thick, wool blanket which seemed to satisfy the youngsters.

As everyone settled in for the night, Emma dug an old baby bottle out of the cupboard. Caroline had left it there on an earlier occasion, so Emma put it to good use and fed Kathy warm milk. The woman stared thoughtfully at the baby who seemed unusually quiet and passive. She wasn't able to make eye contact with the child who stared aimlessly into space.

This worried Emma who wondered what might be wrong with the child. More than anything she was relieved that Kathy wasn't crying for her mother.

After tucking the baby in beside Eunice, Emma put on her night dress and climbed into bed. Gus added a little extra wood to the stove since the night promised to be cold. She could hear the wind blowing outside, whistling through spaces in the thick sheets of plastic that were nailed around the outer edges of the windows. Emma dreamed of owning a new home some day, but looking around that night, admitted to herself that she would miss this place. After all, she and Gus had shared a lot of memories in this old log home. She wished that Caroline could also find happiness.

"Life doesn't have to be easy to be good," Emma said, as Gus slid his long legs in beside her. "I wonder if Caroline knows that."

Gus thought for a moment. "I don't think Caroline knows much of anything."

Emma nodded as she stared at the ceiling. She often discussed the day's events with her husband at night, lulling him to sleep with her soft chatter. Emma had a lot to say since this had been a particularly interesting day.

"Did you see how the children didn't even notice when their mother left?" she asked. "Did you see how satisfied they are to stay here? I wonder what goes on in that house. It must be pretty awful when kids don't want to go home."

Gus turned on his side to face her and draped a long arm across his wife's waist.

Emma wondered to herself how Caroline could go back to Domko. She wondered what the woman would have to do tonight to make up to him. Emma couldn't understand how she could let a man like that into her bed. Shuddering, she pushed the thought from her mind.

"Gus," she whispered.

"Hmm," he murmured with closed eyes.

"Did you notice anything peculiar about that baby? You know I think there is something wrong with that child. Caroline seemed pretty careful with it, much more so than she's ever been with the others. Did you notice? I think it might be retarded or something like that. Her eyes roll around and she can't control her head yet. Yes, I'm quite sure that I've seen a retarded baby before and that's what they are like, you know, kinda' dull and slow. What do you think?"

"Hmm," he answered.

"I just wish there was more we could do for those kids. Honestly, Bill would turn in his grave if he knew how Domko treats them! And that crazy religion of Caroline's doesn't help. I know that if Bill had been healthy, he wouldn't have allowed her to convert. She should be a Lutheran, like Bill and the rest of us around here."

"Now Emma, you know full well that he couldn't make Caroline do anything, just like the rest of us," he said quietly. "Bill was too soft for his own good. She took advantage of that all the time."

"I know," she said. "But I just can't stand this! Caroline is going down the wrong road and I can see it plain as day but I can't stop her."

"Well, we're her neighbours not her family," he said. "It isn't up to us to tell her what to do."

Emma sat in silence for a few moments. Gus was right. It was not her place to interfere in Caroline's personal life. If anyone was going to say something to Caroline, it should be her family.

Emma said a quick prayer, thanking God for her husband and her life. She drifted off to sleep only to be was awakened a few hours later by Sandy's bark. A sound came from the living room and her first thought was that Domko had come back for the children. The sound of Caroline's whispering voice reassured her. It sounded as if she would be staying too.

A few moments later, the older children began protesting that they didn't want to go home. Caroline's tone was firm as she roused the children from their makeshift beds. The twins and Rosie began to cry as their mother hushed them all.

Emma sat up. Gus reached over to stop his wife from getting out of bed. It was clear to him that Caroline did not want them to interfere. It was best they pretend to be asleep.

"But Gus," Emma whispered. "She's taking them back! I can't believe she's taking them back in the middle of the night!"

"There's nothing we can do," he said. "They're not our children."

"Maybe so, but I love them like they are!"

Gus swallowed hard. He cared for the children too, but was careful not to show it. "We can check on them tomorrow," he offered. "Nothing more will happen tonight."

Emma laid back down and listened intently to the children pulling on their jackets and shoes. Caroline continued to whisper as she instructed Walter to help her take the other children home. Within a few minutes they were gone.

Emma turned to face the wall. The flurries had stopped and the moon shone brightly through the window. A tear welled in her eye as she stared at the light and shadows the moon cast throughout the bedroom. She fell into a fitful sleep, marred by dreams of running from Domko with the twins crying in her arms.

Chapter 5

Trying to get help

I'M GONNA FIND US A PLACE TO LIVE," Caroline said as she pulled on her best dress. It had been two weeks since the family had sought refuge at Harwarts and she needed to get away from the farm. Aside from sporadic visits from Emma, Caroline hadn't seen another adult except Domko for months.

He was berating her and the children constantly now and she was not looking forward to another long, cold winter in virtual isolation with him. She should have kicked him off her farm a long time ago, but was too frightened of him to do so.

"No, Momma," Eunice begged. "Don't leave me. I wanna come too."

"I can't take all you kids," she said, walking past the girl to the kitchen. Eunice followed quickly behind.

"He'll put me in the hole," the frightened girl said, her eyes welling with tears. "I'm too scared to go in there again."

Reaching into the cupboard, Caroline found a small piece of red crepe paper. Moistening it with her tongue, she dabbed it against her pale mouth. Then pursing her lips, she rubbed the ruby paper gently across both cheeks. The paper added just enough colour to brighten her face.

"Eunice, I need to you take care of the twins," she said. "Domko is in a better mood today, so just stay out of his way and I'll be back before dark. I'm taking Kathy and Rosie with me, but you and the boys have to stay here."

Tears streamed down the girl's cheeks. "But Momma," she whined, "I should come with the girls too."

Her objections were cut short as the twins came bursting into the kitchen from outside. Chattering to themselves, they stopped suddenly when they saw their mother. They knew that Caroline's best dress and shiny black shoes meant she would be going away for a while.

Caroline pulled a small piece of charred wood from the stove. Gently she rubbed it across her brows accentuating her large eyes. Standing back she looked at herself in the mirror. The swelling on her face was gone now, although her nose was still sensitive to touch.

Dennis started to cry. David stood with his hands at his sides, his little shoulders drooping.

"Where are your brothers?" Caroline asked the twins.

David told her the boys had gone to school.

"I wanna go too," Eunice cried.

"You hafta stay home and watch your brothers," Caroline said kneeling in front of the twins, putting a hand on each of their shoulders. They stared at her solemnly, big blue eyes shining with tears. "You be good for Eunice. Things will be better when I find us a place to live."

Caroline knew that the twins would not tell Domko where she had gone. They never spoke to him and even if they did, he couldn't understand them anyway.

"If Domko asks where I went, you tell him I've gone to town for groceries and that I'll be back this afternoon," she told Eunice firmly.

"What if he gets mad at me?"

"He won't. There's soup on the stove. Have it warm when he gets in."

Caroline disappeared into the bedroom, emerging with Kathy in her arms and Rosie tagging close behind. She wrapped the baby in a blanket and put a worn coat and boots on Rosie . She hoped to get away without having to explain to Domko where she was going. She estimated he would be outside for at least thirty minutes, almost enough time for her to get to the neighbour's house.

Stepping into the cool autumn morning, she felt a chill run through her body. Her heart began pounding hard in her chest as she glanced towards the barn.

"C'mon Rosie ," she whispered to her daughter who would be turning three in just a few days. "You've gotta hurry so Domko won't get us."

The child let out a squeal, and began running ahead of her mother down the driveway. The baby grunted softly from somewhere beneath the blankets as Caroline's feet pounded along the dirt road. Once they were out of view of the farm, she and Rosie slowed their pace. Caroline hoped that Emma and Gus wouldn't see her as she passed their farm. She didn't like the way Gus had furrowed his brow when they discussed Domko the other night. Since Gus wasn't her father, she didn't appreciate his disapproving tone. Caroline decided to ask a different neighbour to help her this time.

Rosie 's rubber boots, at least one size too big, made a clucking noise on the frozen road as they walked towards Jim Deighton's house. The bright, cheerful child asked a steady stream of questions as her mother answered absentmindedly. For now, Caroline's main objective was to get out of that house, and she wondered what she should do next. She considered for a moment stopping at a neighbours to ask for a ride to Moosehorn, but decided against it. There were only a few families she felt comfortable asking for help and they were the Harwarts, Deightons and the Gall families. Everyone else either avoided her and Domko, sided with her common-law husband or lived too far away.

Caroline and Rosie turned east on the Township Line road. The three mile walk to Ruby and Jim Deighton's house would be worth it. She knew Ruby would welcome her with a smile and invite her into a warm kitchen.

It was late in the fall. The leaves had fallen and the landscape was stark and quiet. They passed hayfields filled with large stacks as well as open fields of grain that had been cut and threshed two months ago. The sun shone brightly in spite of a cool wind that whipped leaves across the road in swirling gusts. A small flock of Canada geese flew overhead, honking as they migrated south towards their winter home. Earlier flocks had eaten all the grain left in the fields, so the late travellers passed through the area without stopping in favour of abundance further south.

Caroline tried hard to appreciate the autumn beauty of the area but the grim reality of her situation clouded any happiness she could muster. Winter would soon be upon them, a time that Caroline once loved but no longer anticipated. The thought of being cooped up in that tiny house with the children and Domko was more than she could stand. Domko hated the winter and the previous year he had been relentless in beating the children. Caroline was certain she wouldn't be able to stand another month on the farm. She knew that the beating she had received two weeks before was a prelude of what was to come.

As she approached the Deighton farm, Caroline wondered about Ruby and Jim's relationship. Ruby had two sons from a previous marriage and Jim seemed to like the boys just fine.

The Deighton's house stood amid a clump of trees on the north side of the road. As Caroline drew closer, she could see Jim splitting wood in the yard and piling it high along the fence. Some of it would be hauled into the house now, while the remainder would have to wait outdoors and be hauled in as needed. When Jim noticed Caroline approaching, he stopped to wave. He watched as the young woman with her children turned into the yard.

Jim Deighton was born a Canadian to British immigrants. He had grown up in the Moosehorn area and had served in the Canadian army during the Second World War, returning home to farm afterwards.

Jim was a tall, slim, wiry man with high cheek bones and a chin that jutted straight out. He was a man who liked to work and had a reasonably successful farm because of it. Jim always spoke his mind and was quick to anger when irritated. He could be stubborn and sometimes that trait got the best of him.

"Hello Carrie," he said cheerfully, calling her by a pet name. Beads of sweat had formed on his forehead and chest as he quartered fallen willows and oak with an axe. Lifting one leg onto the block, he removed his cap and pulled a handkerchief from his pocket. Smiling, he wiped the sweat from his forehead. Jim was lightly dressed in jeans, a checked shirt and a pair of coveralls. "What are you out doin' out walkin' with those children?"

"It's Domko again, he's been . . ." she began, letting her sentence trail off. Looking towards the ground, she kicked a small chunk of wood with her shoe. "Is Ruby home?"

"She's in making lunch, or at least I hope she is. I'm getting hungry. Come on and have something to eat." Jim reached down and grabbed Rosie under the arms. He swung the youngster overhead. "How are you doin', pipsqueek?" he asked, shaking her in fun. Rosie giggled, her brown eyes sparkling.

The Deighton home was a large two-storey log-chinked house covered in white plaster. A red brick chimney protruded from the centre of the wood-shingled roof. There were two windows at the front of the house, which Ruby had covered with thick dark curtains. A small lean-to made of tin shielded the door from cold winds.

The house was reasonably well furnished, decorated and clean. The kitchen took up at least a quarter of the house. It had a large table, a cook stove, a wooden two-piece cupboard and a pantry. The staircase leading to the upstairs bedroom was in a corner of the kitchen. A front room with a chesterfield and two chairs, a thick braided rug and the master bedroom ran along one side of the house. A guest room was beside the back door.

Ruby had just taken four fresh loaves of bread out of the oven when the door opened.

"I brought company home with me," Jim said cheerily to his wife. "And word has it they're mighty big eaters."

"Caroline! What are you doing here?" Ruby said greeting her good friend with outstretched arms. Caroline stood sheepishly in the doorway, knowing she'd soon have to explain her plans to the exuberant woman.

Ruby took the baby from Caroline, then encouraged her to remove her coat and have a seat. Ruby was a curvaceous woman with curly brown hair, dramatic eyes and round, red lips. She was rumoured to be a passionate woman whose French-Canadian heritage gave her an air of mystique. She had an accent and an appealing way of referring to the person she was speaking to as 'dear'. Ruby was a divorcee from Winnipeg who never quite fit into farm life, preferring to be well-dressed and socializing in town. She was a good cook who loved to entertain. The Deighton's marriage was turbulent, but the couple were regarded as kind, honest and sociable people.

"So what's this about Domko?" Jim asked, hanging his coat on a hook by the door. He slipped off his boots and put on a pair of thick moccasins. "Is he after the kids again?"

Ruby's eyes narrowed. She could tell by the look on her friend's face that something was wrong. She also knew that Caroline didn't like to be prodded for information. She invited her friend to join them for lunch. Caroline smiled as she avoided Jim's question.

"So, what's Domko up to now?" Jim asked again. Ruby sent him a disapproving look and he gave her one back. He was beginning to tire of the game he was expected to play with the women.

Ruby served a lunch of warm bread and hot soup. Caroline looked into her bowl and stirred with her spoon. Ruby knew she was getting ready to tell them why she was there, they just had to be patient.

"Domko's having one of his spells again," she said. "He's gettin' worse every day."

"Spells my ass!" Jim retorted. "The only thing wrong with that buggar is that he's a miserable cuss, that's all. He shouldn't be pickin' on little kids and a fine wife like you."

Ruby gave Jim a firm kick under the table.

"I need to go see the welfare," Caroline continued. "I want to move to Moosehorn."

"Well that's about the smartest thing I've heard anybody say about Domko in a long time. You should've done this . . ."

"Does Domko know?" Ruby interrupted, giving her husband a stern look.

"Not yet," she answered. "And I don't want anyone to tell him."

Ruby never could understand the relationship between Domko and Caroline. She was such an attractive, vibrant woman while he was foul tempered and unsociable. She and Jim had tried visiting them on more than one occasion, but it seemed the more Jim and Domko got to know one another, the more they hated each other.

"The health nurse is the woman you need to see," Jim said. "I'll drive you to see Margaret Burnett in Grahamdale if you like. She'll be able to give you all the help you need to get on welfare. And don't you be ashamed about that. I mean what's a woman like you with all them kids gonna do anyhow? It ain't your fault Domko's a crazy ass."

Ruby interrupted, offering to keep Rosie and Kathy while she was gone. Caroline smiled with gratitude at the suggestion. "And you take as much time as you need," Ruby said.

"You are good friends," she said, looking first at Ruby and then Jim. His ravings about Domko never seemed to bother her.

"I don't know what I'd do without the both of you," she said.

* * * * *

The house was so small that there were few places to hide. The obvious spots, under the bed and chesterfield or between the cupboard and stove, were the first places Domko looked when searching for the children. The twins hid in the bedroom after their mother left. They knew that Domko soon would be in for lunch and might be angry that she was gone.

Eunice added a block of wood to the stove, then put the soup pot on top. As it warmed, she spooned a small amount for herself into an old ceramic bowl. She ate the soup hungrily before it was fully warmed, knowing that there would be nothing left after Domko ate. Within a few minutes, she had finished and wiped the bowl clean. The kitchen door opened and in walked Domko. Eunice's heart jumped.

"Vere be Carlorka?" he asked suspiciously, hanging his old buffalo coat on a hook by the door. The sight of it reminded Eunice of a stinky old buffalo, like the ones she'd seen in history books at school.

She froze, suddenly feeling trapped with her back to the stove and Domko in the doorway.

"She went to Moosehorn to get groceries," she said quietly. Her hands shook as she lifted the hot soup from the stove and placed the pot on the table.

"But a some town?" he asked. "Ven?"

"About an hour ago."

"Huh!" he grunted as he sat down at the table. He pulled the soup pot forward, filling his bowl. He kept his eyes on Eunice while he greedily ate the hot mixture of potatoes, chicken and carrots.

Eunice stood awkwardly in the middle of the floor. To get outside or into the living room, she would have had to walk past him so she slowly backed up and began putting dishes away and tidied her small area of the kitchen. When Domko finished eating, he pulled a fat homemade cigarette from the plastic container in his shirt pocket, then reached for the firebox on the stove. Opening it, he gingerly pushed the cigarette inside, lighting it on the burning wood. Eunice jumped nervously when he stood and poured himself a cup tea from the pot on the stove. She relaxed slightly as he sat down, then shoveled two heaping teaspoons of sugar into his cup. He took an old piece of sliced lemon and squeezed it hard so that the juice squirted into his cup. He studied her carefully while the metal spoon clanged methodically on the sides of the cup as he stirred.

Reaching down, he took a farm paper from the stack sitting on the floor behind his chair, then sat back and began reading while he stirred his tea. He lit another cigarette from the stub in his mouth while he continued reading. When he was finished, he stood, folded the paper and stuffed it in the stove.

"Veres be some David ant Dennis?" he asked.

Eunice cleared the dishes from the table then filled the wash basin with warm water. She didn't want to tell Domko where the twins were hiding but also didn't want to face his wrath.

"They're in the bedroom," she whispered, wincing at the sound of her voice revealing her brothers' hiding place.

Turning on his heel, Domko stomped into the other room. Dropping her dish rag on the floor, Eunice ran as fast as she could out the kitchen door, letting it slam behind her. Stones and twigs poked the bottom of her dirty feet as she ran into the bush at the edge of the driveway and down the well-worn path. Tears of both fear and relief streamed down her cheeks as she sped toward the schoolhouse.

The twins sat huddled under a blanket between the bed and the wall. The smell of warm soup wafted through the tiny house, making each boy's stomach ache with hunger. They had felt the pangs of hunger many times, especially since Domko had arrived on the farm. He often ate most of what was prepared, leaving just a little for Caroline and the children.

The twins, being only five years old, often lost out to their older siblings when the food was shared. Walter frequently felt sorry for the twins and would give them part of his ration. They had listened quietly as Domko came in and ate his lunch.

A small mouse scurried across the floor under the bed. It stopped for a moment to sniff Dennis' leg then raised it's small head to listen. The pounding of Domko's feet toward the bedroom sent the rodent scurrying back to its hole.

Suddenly, the hiding place became bright as the blanket covering their heads was whipped back. Too afraid to look up, the twins buried their heads under their arms. Domko reached down and grabbed each boy by the hair. They screeched in pain as he lifted them over the bed, dropping them on the floor at his feet. He kicked them each once, hitting David in the legs and Dennis in the back. The boys scrambled to their feet in an effort to escape.

"Fraa!" Domko roared, pointing towards the front room. The boys ran to stand beside the heavy table which sat in the middle of the floor. Large wet stains appeared on their pants as Domko went to the porch then returned with a long piece of twine.

The boys flinched as he told them to take off their pants then grabbed their arms and shoved them onto the floor by the table.

"You's be peesink ant sheetink ant do nuthink all day" he said sarcastically, kicking their pants aside as they scrambled under the table.

The boys sat with their backs to the base of the large oak table, arms pressed tightly against their sides. Both started to cry as Domko took the twine and wrapped it around them. After tying a knot in the rope Domko faced David. His gold tooth shone and his eyes were a flashing white.

"She's be beechin' around," he said, lips curling back.

David wanted to bring his hands up to cover his face but couldn't. Instinctively he lowered his eyes, hoping Domko would go away.

Satisfied that the twins wouldn't escape, Domko turned on his heel and swung open the heavy cast iron wood stove door. The boys flinched as he tossed three large logs into the fire. Crumpling paper in one hand and lighting a match with the other, he watched as the paper caught fire before tossing it in the stove. Domko disappeared from sight, but the boys could hear him preparing to leave the house. Within a few moments the man had taken his heavy coat and left. All was quiet except for the crackling in the stove as the paper ignited the well-seasoned logs.

"Is Satan gone?" Dennis asked, relieved that Domko was out of sight.

"Yep, he's gone," David said, rocking back and forth to see if the twine would loosen. Dennis squirmed but couldn't pull an arm free.

"I'm stuck," David said. "How 'bout you?"

"Me too," Dennis said.

Each boy gave up struggling, hoping their mother would be home soon. The twins jabbered back and forth, until they noticed it had become hot in the small house. Domko had put too much wood in the stove so it was burning far too hot for an early November day.

"Daddy said not to puts no more than two logs in," Dennis said to his brother.

"'Cause the house might catch fire," David added, finishing Dennis' sentence. "An' Domko put in three."

They watched solemnly as the stove pipe that ran from the stove across the ceiling into the kitchen grew hotter. Soon it was a blazing red over their heads .

"The h-house is gonna b-burn," Dennis stammered. David could hear the panic in his brother's voice. "Where's momma?"

"Momma's gonna find us some place to live," David said. He remembered months before when their mother had left, she had promised to move the family to town but nothing had happened when she came back from Moosehorn. David was skeptical, but wanted badly to believe that she would not let them down this time. "There was no places b-before, but they gots more houses in Moosehorn now."

"Do you think Momma gots us a house?" Dennis asked hopefully.

"Yep, she's gonna 'cause she promised," David answered, his voice confident. "Then Domko can't h-hit us no more."

Dennis squirmed. His wet underwear were making his skin itch.

Chapter 6

She's not quite right

"WELL WE'D BETTER GET GOIN' THEN," Jim said, glancing at his watch. "The public health nurse won't be there much longer. Margaret's got a family at home too."

Ruby waved from the front door as Caroline and Jim drove away in his 1949 Chevrolet. The pair rode quietly towards the gravel highway for a few moments before curiosity got the best of Jim.

"So what's made you finally decide to leave Domko?" he asked softly.

Caroline hesitated, then suddenly she began pouring out the events of the past six months.

"He was good to me and the kids at first but then he started gettin' these moods. You know, he worked the kids like slaves in the summer which wasn't too bad since kids gotta learn to work, but then in the fall he'd start beating them for little things like not closing the door on the grainary or puttin' the pitchfork down in the wrong spot. And not just a little whippin' but a big one. He started hittin' me too and then just awhile ago, well, he even hit the baby."

"The baby?" Jim asked. "He hit the baby?"

"Yeah, and you know she hasn't been the same since," she said lowering her voice. Caroline fought back tears as she continued. "He really hurt her bad Jim. I thought at first she was gonna die and I didn't know what to do. She came around but you know, I'm pretty sure she's not right no more."

Jim listened in silence as Caroline poured out her heart. He turned onto Highway No. 6, one of the province's main highways and began driving north to the Grahamdale Nursing Station.

"What do you mean she's not right?" he asked cautiously.

"You know, I don't think she's the same," she explained. "I don't think she can see no more."

"She's blind?"

"I think so."

"Are you sure she could see before?"

"Yeah, she used to laugh at the kids and look at me when I came in the room. Now she looks the wrong way. You can put your hand by her face but she won't move to get outta the way."

"That's terrible!" Jim said as his face began to redden with anger. "How could he do that to one of the kids? His own kid, to boot!"

It was like a giant weight had been lifted from Caroline's shoulders as she confided in Jim, describing the terror her family had lived with during the past 18 months.

"It's been bad Jim," she said. "I think he really wants to kill the kids." Caroline related how just two days before, Domko had become so enraged with Steven that he hit the youngster over the head with his rifle, knocking him unconscious. He then dumped the boy somewhere in the bush, returning home to tell Caroline that he 'hoped the wolves would eat him'. He wouldn't allow her to leave the house to go looking for the boy and forced the rest of the children to continue working so they couldn't go either. The following afternoon the ten-year-old staggered home. He was still in a daze and badly dehydrated.

"It's a miracle the boy didn't freeze to death!" Jim said incredulously.

"That's what Domko wants," she said unhappily. "If it hadn't been for the dog stayin' in the bush with him, he probably would be dead right now."

Jim and Caroline drove the rest of the way in silence. They arrived at the nursing station to find that the health nurse, Mrs. Burnett, was not available. She had gone to a nearby farm for a post-natal visit and wouldn't be back until later. Caroline decided she would wait for the nurse to return, rather than ask Jim to bring her back the following day. Besides, she didn't want to go home to Domko that night. Especially not after confessing to Jim.

"I can stay here by myself," she said as they stood in front of the brick building. "I'll be able to find a ride home later."

Jim hesitated. He didn't want to leave her alone, but had to get back to finish chores. The days were getting shorter so he'd be finishing in the dark as it was.

"Only if you'll be alright," he said. "Ruby'd have my hide if anything happened to you."

"I'm okay now," she laughed, motioning for him to get in the car and go home. "And by the way, thanks for listenin' to all my problems. I feel a lot better now that I've told someone."

Jim smiled and waved as he backed onto the road. He drove back through the small village, acknowledging people he knew with a quick wave. As he pulled back onto the highway, he wondered if Carrie would tell Mrs. Burnett all that she had told him. With Carrie you never knew what to expect. Sometimes she'd tell you the most intimate details of her life while at other times she would clam up and say nothing.

Domko was the opposite. With him, you always knew what to expect.

Ever since Domko had come to the district, things had changed for the worse.

He's no good. A curse, that's for sure, Jim thought to himself. He wondered why Carrie's family didn't help her, but remembered how he'd heard rumours that her family wasn't much better. Some said that old man

Kolodka ruled with an iron fist.

There's a fine line between discipline and a beating, Jim thought. *Some of those old european bastards can't tell the difference.*

Jim wondered how Caroline could have chosen such different men as partners. Bill Pischke had been kind and generous but Domko was the opposite. At first, Domko seemed like a decent fellow but soon he began taking advantage of his neighbours. Then people began noticing that his behaviour was queer.

Once he'd moved to the farm, support from Bill's family became almost non-existent. By that time Caroline was already pregnant with Domko's child. If she wouldn't kick him out, how could Bill's family help her or the children? What made matters worse was that Domko bristled at the mention of the name Pischke.

Jim remembered an incident just a few months ago that sent shock waves through the community. Bill's brother, David went to Caroline's farm to claim the seeder that he had shared with his brother. David had gone to make a few minor repairs to the equipment, and to ensure that it was in good shape and that it hadn't been disposed of by his sister-in-law. This had also given him an excellent excuse to check on Caroline and the children. He'd heard about Domko's odd behaviour and wanted to see for himself what Domko was like.

David and Domko had a disagreement when Domko refused to let him take the seeder. Both men became angry and when David turned to leave, Domko lunged at him, kicking him in the back. Domko was convicted of assault and ordered to pay a $12 fine.

Since then, all the Pischkes had stayed away from the farm. Most of Bill's ten brothers and sisters, all who had families of their own to worry about, were likely unaware of what was going on.

Thinking of this made Jim angry. He made up his mind that Domko wouldn't push him out of Caroline's life. "He'd better not try to kick my ass," Jim said out loud. "Or I'll give that sonofabitch exactly what's coming to him."

* * * * *

The school day always seemed much too short for Eunice. She had missed morning class, but had arrived in time for a whole afternoon of learning.

She loved Bayton School which sat on the opposite side of the road, just south of their farm. Attending class gave Eunice the opportunity to socialize with children her age and escape Domko's watchful eye. One of the youngest students at the school, Eunice loved the smell of chalk and the squeaky sound the hardwood floor made as her teacher, Mrs. Kiesman, walked slowly up and down the centre isle.

This was a typical one-room school in the area. The desks were arranged in rows and the teacher's desk was positioned at the front of the room. Slate blackboards hung on the wall behind the teacher and along the side wall. A row of large windows along the south wall let in ample sunshine most of the day.

The entrance was located at the back of the room through a small vestibule where children left their boots and hung their jackets. The building was heated by a large, round wood stove that stood along the back wall. Eunice's favourite place, the library was near the front of the room.

The interior walls were painted a light green while the outer walls were covered with grey insulated brick material.The school was administered by a board of local directors who were responsible for the upkeep of the building and the teacher's salary.

The youngest students sat in one row, the middle students in the centre and the older students in a row to the left of the teacher. Eunice had a seat beside her best friend, Larry Meisner. Larry was a quiet boy from one of the largest families in the district. People would say that 'you couldn't swing a dead cat without hitting a Meisner in the Bayton area'. To this people would laugh because most people were either born a Meisner or related to one by marriage.

Larry was a farm boy with a round face and timid disposition. He and Eunice shared jokes and helped each other complete assignments. He treated everyone with kindness and to Eunice, this was the most important quality a friend could have.

Norman was in grade three, sitting in the middle row across from Eunice and a few seats back. Walter and Steven were both in grade five and sat together near the back of the room behind Norman. The Pischke children were not considered very bright in school and each child had failed at least once. Their marks would have been much better had they had been encouraged to attend regularly and if obtaining an education had been valued at home. As it was, the children were nothing but farmhands to Domko.

It was difficult to explain to him that the children needed an education. He was proud of the fact that he had a grade four education and had managed just fine. Caroline wasn't much better, having only completed grade six.

The classroom broke into loud chatter as the teacher, Mrs. Nina Kiesman dismissed the students for the day. Eunice dawdled, hoping the teacher would ask her to clean the blackboards.

"Eunice, it's time to go home," Mrs. Kiesman said as she slipped on her coat. "Where is your jacket and shoes?

"I was in such a hurry to get here that I forgot 'em," Eunice said bashfully.

"Well, you'd better hurry home then," her teacher said. "Otherwise you'll catch a chill."

Nina Kiesman was a young, married woman who had been teaching at the school for a few years. She and her husband George lived just north of the Pischke farm. They were nice people who were helpful to Caroline after Bill died. Initially, George was friendly to Domko but one day after witnessing Domko's brutality gave him a lecture.

"Those boys are going to grow up someday," George said. "And if you keep this up then one time those boys are going to kick your ass all the way to Moosehorn."

To that, Domko promptly threw George off the farm.

* * * * *

Stepping out into the cool afternoon, Eunice could see her older brothers playfully teasing Marjorie and the other girls nearby.

"Marjie!" Eunice called, running up to her friend. "Can I come home with you?"

"Sure," Marjorie said. "I've got some chores to do but you can help me."

The two girls walked across the field, while the Pischke brothers went in the opposite direction. As they neared home, they could see that Domko was not waiting for them in his usual spot at the edge of the driveway. The house looked very quiet and there was no smoke coming from the chimney.

"He's gone!" Walter cheered. "Let's go."

The boys' spirits lifted immediately. Turning, they gave a few hoots as they began running south down the road.

"Eunice said Mom is gone again too," Norman said as he ran beside Walter. Steven, still a little dazed from his head smashing a few days earlier, struggled to keep up. "Let's go to Ruby's. She'll give us something to eat."

They ran through the ditch into the church yard. Soon they were on their well-worn trail that took them through the thick bush to the Deighton farm.

"Maybe we can stay there for a few days," Walter added. "I like them guys."

The twins weren't accustomed to sitting in one spot for hours. Being tied forced each into a fitful and uncomfortable slumber. The afternoon wore into evening and soon the heat from the fire had all but disappeared. Now the cool evening wind began whistling through cracks in the floor as it swirled in the crawl space underneath the house. The house chilled quickly and sitting on the cold floor was becoming harder to bear.

"Where's momma?" Dennis asked. "You said she was comin' home."

"She will," David said. "She'll come home an' untie us."

The twins could hear cattle bawling outside. They wondered where their older brothers were. Usually the boys came home right after school and went straight to the barn to do chores. Still tied to the table, the twins had lost all track of time. It appeared that their brothers hadn't fed, watered or milked the cows.

As if David could read Dennis' mind he answered the question before his brother spoke.

"They're at Deightons," he said, the thought cut short by the sound of a tractor outside. "Sshh," he whispered. "What's that?"

"Domko?" Dennis asked fearfully.

"Or maybe it's momma," his twin said hopefully.

Suddenly the door swung open and Domko came storming into the house, spitting and cursing.

"Valter! Steven! Norman! you bastards!" he screamed, his heavy feet moved swiftly across the kitchen floor into the front room. A shaking Dennis looked up to see the short, stocky figure standing before him in the dark. The gold tooth flashed and he could see his eyes darting from side to side in anger. The scar across his forehead was beginning to turn white. His arms were shaking uncontrollably. The twins had seen the signs before. Domko was mad at the older boys for not doing the chores and now was looking for some excuse to beat them.

David and Dennis began to cry. Both boys had soiled their underwear. Domko sneered as he pulled a pocket knife out of the breast pocket in his coat and lunged at the boys. Both David and Dennis screamed in fear, their eyes squeezed tight as Domko sliced through the twine that bound them. Slamming the knife down on the table top, he slipped his black leather belt off in one motion. Before the boys could stand, he began whipping them mercilessly.

"Sheetink again!" he screamed. "Steenkink soneebeech bastards sheetink in but a some pant."

The room whirled around David as he scrambled between the table base and the wall. Dennis tried to crawl into the kitchen, but searing blows kept knocking him to the floor. Each boy screamed in agony, until finally their senses became blunted from the beating. Soon, neither felt pain as they floated far away.

"Where are the twins?" Ruby asked when the three eldest Pischke boys showed up at her door.

"With our Mom," Norman said innocently. The boys explained that Domko was not home and that Eunice had went home with Marjorie after school.

Ruby was puzzled. Keeping track of eight children all going in different directions was not an easy task. Everyone seemed accounted for except the twins. Ruby guessed they must be at home alone. She decided to tell Jim once he came in from chores. She fed the boys and then filled the wash tub with warm water so that they could take a bath. They were so filthy that she didn't dare put them to bed until they were scrubbed clean.

Jim came in about 9 p.m., just as the boys were settling in for the night.

"I think the Pischke twins are home alone," Ruby said. "Should we check on them?"

Jim thought for a moment. "I saw a tractor go by about 15 minutes ago and I think it was Domko. Carrie hasn't come back yet?"

"Not yet," Ruby said. "I'm worried those boys might be outside by themselves or worse yet in the house with Domko. Who knows when Carrie is coming home?"

Jim nodded. For the second time that day, he was coming to the aid of Caroline and her family. He gave his wife a tired smile then went out to the garage. The car sputtered and coughed as he turned the ignition. Flipping on the lights, he backed slowly out of the bumpy driveway. It was just less than a three mile drive to Caroline's house.

Domko always felt his best after administering a beating to one of the children. Slipping his belt back on, he pulled a cigarette from his breast pocket. It looked as if he would have to do the evening chores since the older boys were not around. He sat for awhile at the kitchen table while he finished his cigarette. His low guttural chuckle was interrupted by a knocking sound. He grunted as he went to the door. Opening it, he found Jim Deighton standing in the doorway. Jim stepped back a little surprised.

"I'm just checking on the twins," Jim said, shocked by the almost pleasant look on Domko's face. "I thought they were at home alone."

"Vere's Valter?" Domko asked, his mood quickly shifting. His eyes narrowed as he tried to stare down the man who stood a healthy four inches taller than he.

"The boys are at my place," Jim said. "They came because nobody was home and there was nothing to eat."

Domko thought for a second. "Yit, yit," he said, spitting on the floor. "That's all they's be doink."

Jim stiffened. It was no wonder the house was a mess and the children stank so bad. How in heaven's name did Carrie tolerate this? "Where are the twins?" he asked gruffly.

"How's I be know?" Domko said, lifting his shoulders innocently. "They's not be here when I gets home."

Jim listened carefully but could hear only the rumble of his car's engine in the driveway. Domko pushed his way past Jim then pulled the door shut behind him.

"I's be doink the chores," he said sarcastically as he strode across the yard. "Tell them lazy bastards that I's be doink it."

Jim stood and watched as Domko opened the fence and a stream of bawling cattle followed him into the barn. Jim waited for a moment then cautiously opened the kitchen door.

"Dennis? David?" he called quietly, poking his head inside. "Are you boys here?" Stepping into the kitchen he called out again. The house was unusually quiet.

They're probably hiding outside somewhere, he thought. Backing out the door he pulled it shut. Jim felt bad that he hadn't found the boys but was anxious to get home since it had been a long day. *I hope they've found a safe place to sleep,* he thought. He too was looking forward to a good night's rest.

Caroline found a ride from Grahamdale to the Deighton farm two days later. She arrived to pick up the girls and discovered that her older sons had spent the entire time there too. Ruby and Jim waved off her apology, saying that the boys had been good and were in school at the moment. Caroline avoided discussing where she had been, but assured the Deightons that things were going to be alright. She gathered up Kathy and Rosie who started to cry the moment she saw her mother. Caroline waved a tired hand and in an instant, Ruby's kitchen was quiet again.

"What do you think?" she said to Jim, suspicious about the length of Caroline's absence, her hands placed solidly on her hips.

"It takes a few days to make those kind of arrangements," Jim said. "I just hope she gets out of there soon."

Ruby nodded in agreement to that. It was time that she finished her mending, a job that she had set aside while Carrie's children were there. She made a mental note to pass on a box of used clothing to the Pischke boys the next time she saw them. Her boys had outgrown the clothes and wouldn't need them anymore.

Eunice's heart sank when she saw her mother standing with her two little sisters at the end of the school laneway. She and her brothers walked slowly down the steps and towards her.

"D-d-did you find us s-someplace to live?" Walter asked. He hoped that their mother would take them immediately since he wasn't looking forward to facing Domko. "Eunice said you went to Moosehorn to get us a house."

"No, but I talked to some people who are gonna help us," she said. "Us leavin' isn't the right thing to do."

The children groaned as their mother led them down the road to the farm. Their minds shifted to thoughts of the punishments Domko would have waiting for them. Caroline walked assertively, as the children lagged behind.

"Hurry up," she said impatiently. "We've been gone long enough."

Caroline was confident that Domko would greet her in a pleasant mood. He reminded her of a needy child who took advantage of her mercilessly, but craved her at the same time. His need for affection was insatiable, although he never gave anything in return.

She had been right. Domko was happy to see her and the children. He was beginning to wonder if she had left for good this time. He dreaded the thought of having only the twins to help him do chores. They had been some help over the past few days, but were limited by their size.

"Carlorka!" he said, meeting them in the yard. "Vere yous be goink for but a some time?" He tried to hide the suspicion in his voice.

"I went to Moosehorn to get groceries," she said, reciting her carefully orchestrated answer. "But I couldn't get no credit at the co-op or the supply, so I went to talk to some people about getting welfare."

Domko's eyes narrowed as he studied her closely. Standing about three feet apart, they both looked ready to fight and neither was prepared to back down. Turning to the children, Caroline told them to go inside. Thankful that Domko wasn't going to hit them, the children dashed into the house.

"I also made plans to meet with some people about the kids." she said. "There might be some city people who will take Rosie and the twins," she said. "They can go live there until we get back on our feet." Caroline was confident Domko would like the suggestion since he regarded the younger children as nothing but pests.

"I don't know for sure when they'd go," she explained. "It's being done quietly so that there won't be no social worker comin' around."

"Vere did you sleep?" he asked, satisfied with her explanation but still suspicious that she may have been unfaithful.

"I stayed with friends from the church," she said. "They're comin' to visit soon, so you can ask for yourself if you don't believe me."

Caroline turned and walked confidently into the house. Domko was hesitant to pick a fight with her when she was on the offensive, usually preferring to catch her off guard. Besides, he was too tired to start anything because of all the work he had done in the past two days.

In mid-November a man came to the farm to discuss foster care with Caroline. It was early afternoon so the older children were in school. Domko sat in his usual spot in the chair beside the cupboard with his back to the wall. He stirred his coffee continually while he sucked on the stub of a cigarette, a blue haze rising above him.

They exchanged small talk for a few moments, then Caroline called Rosie and the twins in the house. The children had hid in the bush when the stranger arrived.

"This is Rosie ," Caroline said, "and this is David and Dennis."

The dishevelled children looked solemnly at the man.

"I know of a place for the twins," he said. "Some people I know from Winnipeg want to take them. They can't have children themselves. It might take a little longer to find a place for Rosie ."

Caroline nodded. She invited the man to stay for coffee but he declined. "I'll phone them when I get back to town and you can expect to see them here next Friday."

Caroline smiled nervously as she waved goodbye to the man. She knew in her heart it was the best thing she could do for her sons.

* * * * *

The week went by quickly. The evening before the twins were to leave, friends from Caroline's church stopped by the house for a visit. They sat around the kitchen table chatting and discussing bible passages. Caroline and her friends had been trying to coax Domko into switching faiths, but so far had had no luck. Caroline worked on him when he was in a good mood, hoping that Domko's mean-spirited ways would be tempered if he embraced her religion. She was hushed by church members who discouraged her from moving to town and leaving her domestic troubles.

Domko was especially quiet and obliging this evening as he sat in his usual chair. The children were told to sit and behave themselves and listen to what the visitors were saying.

"David and Dennis are goin' to live with city people tomorrow," Norman said, breaking what had turned into an uncomfortable silence. The Witnesses turned to Caroline in disbelief.

"What's this Norman is saying?" a man asked. "Are you sending the twins away?"

Caroline swallowed hard. She could sense by his tone that this was not considered appropriate by the church's standards. She had suspected this, but had hoped to feign ignorance when confronted after the boys were gone.

"Yes," she answered. "We're struggling and it'll be best for the whole family."

The man thought for a moment. "No, Caroline I don't think you understand," he began. "This is frowned upon. The family is the foundation and by sending those children away, you will be removing bricks of your family's foundation."

Caroline looked at the twins playing on the floor, oblivious to the conversation that was happening on their behalf.

"Are the family Witnesses?" he asked.

"I didn't think to ask," she said.

"Witness children cannot be sent to a non-believing family," he scolded. "Otherwise they will be raised without an understanding of the truth.

Caroline was confused by what she was being told. When Jim had taken her to see the health nurse, she was convinced that she was going to take the children and leave Domko. After staying with her friends from the church and confiding in them, they persuaded her to stay with Domko while she tried to change what was causing him to become angry.

Disciplining the children was their solution - Caroline had tried but the effort had failed miserably. The following day she met with the health nurse who suggested a foster home for the boys - a solution that sometimes worked in situations where stepfathers and children didn't get along. This had seemed like a reasonable idea to Caroline, but now she was being told it was the wrong solution.

Caroline was careful not to show the anger that she was beginning to feel. She didn't like it when people challenged her decisions, since she was having a hard time making up her mind about whether to send the boys or not. When she was undecided she was easily swayed, but once she made up her mind about something, she never changed it.

"Well there is still time to decide," she said, quickly changing the subject. The Witnesses stayed for another hour, focusing their discussion on the importance of the family unit. Caroline was exhausted by the time they left.

"I will never understand," she whispered, as she fell into the bed beside Domko. "I will never be the saint I must be to be accepted into Jehovah's Kingdom." Domko agreed, saying she was a poor wife, mother and Witness. She tried to ignore him as he continued to chastise her. She had thought that sending the twins away had been the least selfish decision she had made in a long, long time.

The following morning Caroline awoke to the realization that her beautiful twin boys would be leaving. The older boys were outside doing chores while she prepared breakfast. She filled the wash basin with warm water then called the twins. Conversations from the night before had cast doubts into her mind, doubts she was having a hard time shaking. She put the twins in the wash tub on the kitchen floor, then went to prepare a small bag they would take with them. It was then that she realized how little she had to offer her children. There were only a few items of clothing. Their only toy, the truck they had been playing with on the floor a few weeks ago, had been confiscated by Domko.

"David, Dennis, come dry off," she said, pulling an old towel from the cupboard. Within a few minutes, they were dressed in the cleanest hand-me-downs Caroline had in their size.

"The nice people from Winnipeg are comin' today," Caroline began. "You can go live with them for a while and then I'll come get you."

The twins stared at their mother in disbelief. Their older brothers had mentioned something about going to live in Winnipeg, but they thought that everyone was going to come along. Everyone except Domko.

"But momma," David said. "you gots to come too!"

"No, David, I can't," she said. "They don't want me, they want you."

David looked at Dennis who was starting to cry.

"Momma, you gots to come," he begged. "We's gonna live in Winnipeg."

"Now stop your crying," she scolded, wiping the tears that had crept into the corners of her own eyes."The people are gonna be here soon and we don't want them to think you're crybabies."

While their mother packed a few clothes in a paper bag, the twins sat quietly in the kitchen. David thought about the situation, deciding that moving to Winnipeg was a good idea even without his mother. He didn't want to go without Dennis, though, and it looked as if his twin wasn't planning to go along.

"Satan's not comin'," David said trying to persuade his twin. "He won't get us there an' the nice people will get us toys an' candy."

Dennis didn't want to leave his mother and his home, even though it was not a happy place. But he liked candy and missed all the toys that Domko had gradually thrown out during the past year. He was beginning to warm up to the idea since David was making it sound like a very interesting adventure. Bored, the twins decided to go outside to play for a while.

Opening the door, they stepped into the cool November air. They didn't bother putting on their jackets as they kicked a can back and forth to each other. Instinctively, David glanced over his shoulder to see if Domko was standing nearby.

A rumble in the south caused him to look down the road. He could see a car approaching, a cloud of dust behind it. Both boys stopped to watch as the large, white vehicle slowed, then turned quietly in the driveway. It was about the biggest, most beautiful car David had ever seen. He liked cars and hoped that these were the people who were going to take him and Dennis to Winnipeg. The people got out and smiled at the boys. They stood for a moment, waving at the twins, trying to coax them to come closer. David took the first step, with Dennis a few feet behind. Both knew it would be best to be quiet and just smile at the people.

David liked the looks of them. They had crisp, bright clothes and nice smiles. The man was tall like Gus, but the woman looked different than anyone he'd ever seen before. David imagined she looked like the fairy princesses from the stories that Eunice told them at night.

The boys waited outside while the people went into the house. Glancing toward the barnyard, David could see Domko standing by the fence watching him and Dennis. The sight of the cruel man scared David so badly that he suddenly became anxious to get away.

"I'm goin'" David said quickly. He told Dennis to go wait by the car while he ran into the house to get the bag. Dennis cried softly but obeyed his brother. David hurried past the people as they came out of the house. He ignored the sight of his sisters standing in the kitchen as he grabbed the bag from the table. This was his chance to escape a living hell and although less than six years old, he knew it was an opportunity that he might not get again.

David ran out the door towards the big car. He could see the beautiful woman getting in the passenger side and she was crying. The man looked back at him, then said a few angry words to Caroline who stood between Dennis and the car. David wanted to say goodbye to his mother, but the people seemed to be in a hurry. He ran up and grabbed Dennis' hand, pulling him towards the shiny vehicle which suddenly began backing down the driveway. David stopped and stared in disbelief as the people from Winnipeg gave him a half-hearted wave then disappeared down the road. The boys weren't leaving after all because their mother had changed her mind.

Now it was David's turn to cry.

Chapter 7

The brave escape

THE MONTHS WORE ON. Soon the most dreaded month of the year was upon them. January days were short and the temperatures frigid.

A storm early in the month dumped more than a foot of snow in the district. Poor weather combined with Domko's unsociable behaviour gave neighbours good reason to stay away from the farm. Caroline was longing for contact with other adults and feeling downtrodden under Domko's tyranny.

By the end of the month, at least one of the children was receiving a beating each day. Caroline was at her wits end trying to keep peace in the house. There was nothing for the children to look forward to each day except for school and work. Many days the older boys didn't make it to school because they had to do chores until late at night. Most often they were hungry and poorly dressed for the weather.

Kathy was growing and it was apparent that something was seriously wrong with the child. Her development seemed slow and her eyes did not focus. It appeared that she could hear and understand, but lacked the confidence to crawl forward or stand up. Everyone knew the child was blind and within the confines of the house, Caroline berated Domko about this. He began accepting Kathy as his own child and was remorseful that he had injured the girl. He vowed never to hit her again and soon a close relationship developed between the father and daughter. Unfortunately for Caroline's other children, no amount of cajoling made him feel badly about how he treated them. He tolerated the older children but hated the twins and wasn't afraid to make his feelings known.

Caroline hoped again to move herself and the children to town, but had to wait patiently for the weather to clear. A tremendous amount of snow had fallen, making it difficult to manoeuvre outdoors. Norman and Walter scrambled out of the house one night after being badly beaten. This left a shortage of manpower for the chores, enraging Domko even further.

David and Dennis went to their bedroom one evening and found a sick Rosie who had spent the day alone in their room. She lay quietly in the bed underneath one of the few warm blankets in the house.

"Hey, Rosie move over," David said as he tried to crawl in the bed beside his sister. The house was cold and he was anxious to warm up.

The girl didn't move.

"Rosie?" he said, lifting the heavy blanket. Steam rose from below as the cool air with the warm dampness underneath. The blanket was oozing with Rosie's blood, sticking to her body as David tried to lift the blanket to see his sister who lay motionless underneath.

David cringed at the sight of the blood. Rosie was lying on her side facing him, raw bleeding gashes covered her arms and legs. Her eyes were closed and she wheezed softly as she slept.

"What's wrong with Rosie?" Dennis asked.

"He got her," David said. "I'm gonna tell momma."

Quietly, David crept into his mother's bedroom. He wasn't sure where Domko was, so he whispered softly. "Momma, come an' see Rosie, she don't look good."

Caroline was lying on the bed with Kathy beside her. Reaching up, she motioned for him to come close. He moved quietly to the edge of the bed as she pulled his face close to hers.

"Ssshh," she whispered through swollen, bleeding lips. "If I go there, Domko might notice and get mad again. Just pretend everythin's alright and sleep beside Rosie. She'll be o.k. 'til morning."

David nodded then crept back to his room. He motioned for Dennis to climb into bed, then slid in beside him. The boys were careful not to touch the fetid blanket which was beginning to stink badly. David fell asleep a short time later to the sound of Eunice crying softly as she slept nearby on the floor.

Caroline awoke the next morning with a start as Domko roused everyone out of bed.

"They's be lazy ant goot for nuthink," he said, referring to the older boys. He blamed Caroline for the boys' absence, saying that if she disciplined them more often, he wouldn't be forced to do it and the boys would not dislike him. He called Walter and Norman 'lazy like their father', a comment he had heard from Caroline's father and brother. As she spooned porridge from a big pot on the stove into small bowls, she tried to pacify him by saying she would milk the cows. Domko ate his breakfast and watched suspiciously as she and Steven left the house.

Once outside in the fresh, cold air, Caroline began planning their escape. She'd had enough of Domko and his ravings. His beating of Rosie the day before had been unprovoked and sadistic. She had tried to step in, but had been unsuccessful in stopping him from whipping the youngster. This time she didn't care what members of the church thought or how community members would gossip. She made up her mind she was taking the children to town and nobody was going to stop her this time.

"Get the horses and sleigh ready, while I go into the house" she said to Steven when they finished milking. "But be sure Domko doesn't see you. We're goin' to town but I don't want him to know."

Inside, Domko drank a cup of coffee while the twins and Eunice sat at the table. Neither child dared look into Domko's eyes for fear he would interpret it as a challenge and start taunting them. He surveyed each child, looking carefully for a missing button or tear in their clothing. Satisfied that the children had done nothing to deliberately antagonize him, he suddenly got up and took off his belt. The children froze and their hearts raced as they wondered which one of them was going to get a beating. Domko strode into their bedroom and each child began to weep tears of relief and remorse.

"Lazy soneebeech bastard," he grunted as he threw the blanket back and began beating Rosie again. Unable to move, the little girl made no sound as the belt whipped against her blood-caked skin.

Caroline came in and began putting milk through the cream separator. Eunice cleared the dishes while the twins were sent outside to bring in wood for the stoves. Satisfied that everyone was busy, Domko went back to the bedroom for a nap.

Caroline motioned for Eunice to follow her outside. They met the twins at the doorway. Each boy was carrying an armful of wood.

"We're goin' to Moosehorn today but everyone be quiet," she whispered raising her finger to her lips. "Go wait in the sleigh."

The children's eyes widened, then they turned and ran towards the sleigh sitting along the fence by the barn. The children piled on top and began kicking off the snow which had accumulated on top. They could hear Steven getting the horses ready in the barn.

Caroline quickly gathered a few belongings while Kathy and Rosie slept. She stacked the few things she wanted to take outside, then slipped off her work clothes and put on her best dress, coat and boots. She did this quietly to avoid waking the baby, while wondering how to bundle Rosie so that nobody would notice she'd been beaten. Taking a warm cloth she cleaned the girl's face as best as she could. Rosie moaned softly as the cloth scraped across her battered skin.

"Shhh, Rosie," Caroline said. "It's gonna be o.k. I'm gonna take us away from here."

Wrapping a fresh blanket around the little girl, she carried her to the kitchen door. She left Rosie lying on the floor while she went outside to get the sleigh. She decided to load everything, then come back for Rosie and the baby.

The horses, Queenie and Jack, were standing nervously along the fence as Steven laboured to attach the traces to the double tree that fastened the team to the sleigh. These were uncooperative horses that often behaved wildly and were difficult to control. Their ears pricked as they watched Caroline approach She climbed into the driver's seat just as Steven finished fastening the team. The twins were so excited they began jabbering loudly.

"Be quiet now, we're not gone yet," she said. "Hold on, because it's gonna pull a little rough at first." She clucked gently as the horses jerked the sleigh toward the house. Pulling back on the reins she stopped in front of the door.

"Hold the horses while Steven and I load the sleigh," she said to Eunice. Jumping down the mother and son quickly placed the small stack of dishes, blankets and spare clothing in the back.

"Be careful with that," she said to Steven as he lifted a can full of cream into the sleigh. "Whatever you do, don't spill it."

Steven packed the can solidly then climbed back on the sleigh and took the reins from Eunice. Caroline went quickly into the house. The children waited in silence until their mother emerged with Rosie wrapped in a big blanket. She laid the girl across the twins' laps and told them to hold her tight. They sat obediently clutching their sister.

"I'm gonna get Kathy," Caroline said as she walked back towards the house. She opened the door then jumped back, letting out a tiny scream. Domko was standing on the other side of the door.

"Veres yous be goink?" he commanded.

Caroline tried to steady her nerves as she took a deep breath. The horses raised their heads, then snorted while Steven pulled back gently on the reins hoping to quiet the animals.

"We're going to town," she said.

Domko stared at Caroline with piercing eyes until she finally had to look away. She could hear the baby crying inside.

"I'm going to get Kathy," she said, trying to push her way past him as he blocked the doorway.

"I's be keepink her," he sneered.

"I want to take her too," she said in a calm voice. "She needs to see the doctor."

"She's be seek?" he asked sarcastically. "Maybe yous not be comink back?"

"Of course I'll be back, we'll all be back tonight" she lied. "I'll see if I can find Walter and Norman too."

Caroline could tell that Domko didn't believe her story. He was beginning to shake, an indication that he was becoming angry and frustrated. She argued lamely that the baby needed to see the doctor as she slowly backed towards the front of the sleigh. Convinced that Caroline wouldn't leave without the baby, he stood in the doorway with his arms crossed confidently across his chest.

Sensing this would be her only opportunity to escape, Caroline jumped aboard the sleigh and grabbed the reins from Steven. Flicking the reins, the horses jumped forward and the sleigh took off with a jolt. Everyone but Caroline flew backwards as the animals broke into a quick trot. Caroline pulled in the left rein and the horses quickly turned, then straightened as they found themselves on the familiar trail which led east behind the house towards the dense bush that led to the Deighton farm.

Surprised by Caroline's courage, Domko stood dumfounded in the doorway. He began shaking his fist in the air and swearing at her in Polish, commanding them to come back.

"Ee-Yah!" Caroline yelled loudly as she prodded the horses to go faster.

"I's be drownink her!" he yelled, and continued yelling until they were out of range.

Once the children realized Domko wouldn't be following them, they let out a wild cheer. Caroline said a silent prayer of thanks. She tried to push away frightening thoughts about what Domko might do to the baby. She didn't think he'd hurt Kathy, but he'd been so unpredictable lately that she couldn't be sure. Leaving the child was unfortunate but she believed she had made the right decision to get the rest of the children safely away. It took more than 30 minutes to reach the Deighton farm where Caroline thought they could warm up before continuing into town.

Ruby and Jim were sitting at the kitchen table listening to Walter and Norman pleading that they should stay home from school for fear of seeing Domko on the road. They were interrupted by a knock on the door.

"Come in," Ruby said, not at all surprised to see Caroline. "The boys told us what happened. Are you alright?"

"We're fine," she said. "I've got some things that I'm taking to town in the sleigh. I was wondering if me and the kids could warm up here first."

Jim raised his eyebrows. "You're going to town? What does Domko think about that?"

"He doesn't really know what we're doing'" she said. "I'll tell him later when I go back with the Police."

"The police?"

"He made me leave Kathy there, he wouldn't let me take her so I gotta take the police there to get her."

"You left the baby there?" Ruby asked, not able to hide the shock in her voice. "With him? He nearly killed her once, didn't he?"

"I had no choice. He blocked the door and if I had got past him, he never never would have let me out. I don't think he'll hurt his own child."

Ruby looked at her husband who was putting on his coat and boots.

"I'll go get the car started," he said. "Then I'll take you and the kids the rest of the way to town. The sooner you get to the police station and come back for that baby the better."

Caroline smiled. She had hoped Jim would offer to help.

Ruby poured Caroline and herself a cup of coffee. "Would you kids like some hot cocoa?" she asked as she began warming a pot of milk on the stove.

"Yes, aunt Ruby," they said. The twins were quite happy about going to Moosehorn and ran around the kitchen in excitement. Ruby stirred a cocoa and sugar mixture into the milk then poured it into mugs for the children.

"Here you go," she said handing a cup to each child. "Now be careful it's hot."

Eunice put the cup to her lips. She took a sip of cocoa that scorched her tongue. The warm milk tasted incredibly good, especially since she loved chocolate and so seldom had a taste of it.

"What about Rosie? Is she sleeping?" Ruby asked.

Caroline held the girl protectively in her lap.

"She's not up to it, I'll just keep her covered like this until she's feeling better," Caroline said, implying the girl was ill.

Ruby nodded but said nothing more.

The family's belongings were transferred from the sleigh to Jim's car. The children piled in the back, the younger ones sitting on top of the older ones. Within a few minutes, they were on their way. The children waved to Ruby as the car backed out of the driveway. The snow was piled high in banks along the road it was ploughed just enough to let one car through at a time.

"Where do you want to go?" Jim asked. "Moosehorn or Ashern?"

"I was thinking I could go to Moosehorn, but I need some welfare and I don't think the council will give any money without passing it at a meeting first," she said. "I heard that in Ashern, the administrator can give some out right away. Besides, Ashern will be good 'cause I don't want Domko comin' to find us right away. I want to be as far away from him as I can get."

Jim nodded in agreement. "I'll take you to the municipal office and see if we can find you a place to live, then we'll go to the police."

Caroline nodded. The ride to town was making her feel better. The further away from the farm she got, the stronger she felt. There was still the matter of going back to get Kathy, but she felt the police would help her do that.

Caroline asked Jim to stop at the creamery so she could sell the cream and then at the Co-op store in Moosehorn. While she met with the manager to discuss her account, the children looked around the store. It was one of the few times the twins had ever been in town. They were amazed at the many wonderful things to eat in the store. Shoppers stopped to watch the children who begged their mother to buy them candy. Caroline tried to hush them, since all she had was the $8 cream cheque which was needed to buy groceries. Jim walked up to the whimpering children carrying seven boxes of Lucky Elephant popcorn. The children were so surprised and delighted that it was hard for them to also be grateful. They grabbed the popcorn and began to greedily eat the shiny pink candy coated treat. Caroline smiled at Jim's generosity, wishing that someone as wonderful as him had come into her life, only much sooner and under better circumstances.

It was starting to snow lightly as they pulled onto the gravel road. As they travelled south, they met a north bound train travelling along the tracks paralleling the highway. The children watched in amazement as the train chugged along, effortlessly ploughing snow from the tracks. David and Dennis had never seen a train before. They were amazed as Jim explained the train was on its way north where the cars would be loaded with lime from the stone quarries, then hauled back south. He told them that if they continued to follow this highway past Ashern, it would eventually take them to Winnipeg.

Caroline only knew a few people in Ashern, having grown up on a farm northwest of Moosehorn near the hamlet of Faulkner. The only people she knew in this unfamiliar community were members of her church. She was anxious to see a familiar face after being cooped-up on the farm with no visitors for the past four months. A little worried about the reaction of church members to her leaving Domko, Caroline peeked under the blanket at Rosie who sat silently bundled on her lap.

I'm doing the right thing, she thought to herself.

It was Friday afternoon and Ashern's Main Street was busy. Cars lined the street, parked diagonally in front of the stores, cafes and hotel. The business section of town was primarily at the east end of Main street and along Railway Avenue which crossed it. Jim stopped in front of the municipal office.

"I'll check to see if they know of a place for rent," he said. "You might have to come in to apply for welfare, but I'll see if I can get it for you."

She was thankful for Jim who always knew what to do.

The municipal office was a wooden, remodeled, two-storey house and the hub of activity around town. People wanting information always stopped to inquire there. The building smelled of old paper and documents. Some people avoided the building, especially if they were behind in their tax payments.

Olive Porteous, the secretary-treasurer was sitting behind a big wooden desk. The hardwood floor creaked softly as she stood with a pleasant smile and greeted Jim at the counter. He was pleased to see a woman in charge, since she might be more sympathetic to Caroline's plight.

"I'm looking for a house to rent for a friend of mine," he said. "Would you know of a place?"

Olive thought for a moment. "How big a place are you looking for?"

"She's got eight kids," he said. "I think she'd like to live somewhere in town, maybe close to the school."

"I do know of a place near the school, but it won't be available until the end of the month," she said.

Thinking for a moment, she wrote a few names on a slip of paper. "There is one place right in the middle of town but it's pretty small. Call this man here," she said pointing a well-manicured finger to the top name on the list. "He can give you all the information you need."

Jim thanked the kindly woman then stood for a moment, not sure how to ask his next question. He'd never asked for money before and felt awkward almost as if he was asking for himself.

"Do you know if she could get some money here?" he blurted.

Olive thought for a moment then glanced at her watch.

"You get her settled in and tell her to come back and see me in the morning," she said. "We won't be able to give her much, but we don't want any starving kids in town either."

Jim smiled. He was glad he had brought her here since her past wouldn't be thrown up in her face.

"I'll tell her that. Thank you ma'am," he said as he closed the heavy door behind him.

An operator at the public telephone office placed Jim's call about the house. Caroline met with the landlord in front of a small white house in the middle of the town's residential area. The man agreed to let Caroline and the children stay there for a few weeks until they could find a larger place.

The landlord unlocked the door and immediately lit a lamp in the kitchen. The children brought in their belongings while Jim lit the oil heater in the middle of the floor in the front room. The house was clean and furnished with necessities.

"Carrie, you've got oil heat in this place," Jim said as he emerged from the front room. "That's good because it's a bad time of year to try and find wood."

Caroline smiled at her friend as she made arrangements with the landlord to pay her weekly rent.

"I'll see the social worker as soon as I can. It doesn't take long for the money to come," she said bashfully. "I . . I've done this before."

He smiled at her genuinely as he handed her the house keys.

"Not that you have much need for these around here," he said. "But it's good to lock up if you're going to be away for a while."

Shortly after the man left, Jim offered to take Caroline to the police station.

"You'd better get over there before they close for the afternoon," he said. "It's getting late and I don't think you want to leave Kathy with Domko overnight."

Caroline agreed, buttoning her coat and pulling her boots back on. Turning to the children she asked them to stay behind and behave themselves for Walter.

"Lock the door, Momma," Eunice begged. As much as she was glad to be away from the farm, she was frightened by the unfamiliar environment. "What if Domko comes when you're gone?"

"D-don't worry Beanie, h-he can't find us here," Walter said confidently. "We's all the way in Ashern."

Jim and Caroline drove to the RCMP office in the residential section of town. It was a large, white, two-storey house with many windows and a hip-style roof. The front part of the house was divided into an administration office and jail cells. The Sargeant and his family lived in the back and on the second floor.

Jim stood with his arms folded as Caroline explained what had happened to the officers on duty. She left out many details, but did say that Domko had been 'too hard' on herself and the children. The two officers stood and listened, but didn't seem too concerned about her plight. They'd heard of Domko all right and the report was that he was backward, of below-average intelligence and could barely speak english. He was about the last person they felt like visiting that night.

"Why did you leave her there in the first place?" the older officer asked in an exasperated tone.

Caroline looked at the floor. "He wouldn't let me take her."

"Wouldn't let you? You managed to get all the other children out of the house, why not her?"

"I was gonna go back but he blocked the door."

"Why didn't you take her out first? If he's that bad, why did you take a chance?"

"It was cold and I had to get the sleigh ready and I didn't want her to start crying. She was sleeping, but she must have woke up."

"But you left her alone with him, weren't you afraid he'd hurt her?"

"No, he won't hurt her because she's his daughter. It's my kids he hates."

"Then what's the big hurry to go get her then?"

"Well, he said he'd drown her if I left."

"But I thought you said he wouldn't hurt her?"

Caroline didn't know what else to say. Fed up with the interrogation, Jim interjected.

"Listen," he began. "That Domko's off his rocker and about as predictable as a bull elk in rut. I've seen it for myself, he's nuts I tell you, and it is about time somebody did something about it. Now, if one of you don't take her back to the farm to get that baby, then I'll do it - but I'll take a loaded gun with me."

The officers studied him carefully. They didn't appreciate being lectured about how to do their job properly.

"Now Jim, it's not that we don't want to go," the younger officer began. "We just want a full understanding of what we're walking into, that's all. We don't want to go barreling in there and run the risk of somebody getting hurt. You're right, the baby should be with its mother and we can make him give her up on those grounds."

"Then what are we standing around gabbing for?"Jim asked. "It's getting late and I have chores to do when I get home."

The young officer pulled on his heavy RCMP issue coat and fur hat. "I'll go," he said to his partner. "This shouldn't take too long."

Jim said good-bye to Caroline. Within a few minutes, he was turning north on the highway, heading for home. It took a few moments for the officer to get ready and as he opened the cruiser door, Caroline noticed he was carrying a gun. Although it's something she'd never admit to, she was excited by the prospect of a shoot-out taking place on her behalf.

They soon caught up to Jim's car and passed him in a burst of speed. Caroline gave a small wave as the police car whizzed by.

Now he's in a hurry! Jim thought.

The he realized his anger was misdirected towards the officer when it should have been aimed at Domko. *He seems like a decent enough fellow, he'll see. Once he meets Domko then he'll know what I'm talking about.*

The police hated intervening in domestic turmoil. Too often they were expected to side with one person over the other without full understanding of the circumstances. It was difficult to prove that a crime had been committed when a husband and wife were battling. Children under twelve years of age were not considered credible witnesses so what they said didn't matter to the courts.

It wasn't the RCMP's job to take action against the husband - it was up to the wife. Police needed a woman to press charges, follow it through the court system then stay away from her husband so that the judge would take her seriously.

Unfortunately, few women did that, though. Often they went back to their husbands within a few days. Charges, if laid, would be dropped and then the pattern would start all over again within the year. It was frustrating for police as they tried to get foolhardy women to listen to reason. How bad could it be, if they kept going back?

Sure, an officer could arrest the husband, but he'd have to witness the crime taking place or believe that the woman and her children were in immediate danger. It was a judgement call, each and every time. And it was a tough call to make. Some officers did arrest husbands, but more often than not the wife would show up at the station begging for his release. For some officers it was just easier to not get involved - especially if the man was a well-respected member of the community.

All a police visit did was create hard feelings between the officer and the husband. The ensuing ripple of gossip through the community hardly seemed worth the waves.

"Tell me about your common-law husband," the officer said.

Caroline hesitated. She wasn't sure if she wanted this handsome young man to know the details of her sordid love affair with Domko and the birth of his illegitimate child. It seemed rather stupid to have a child with a man and then show up at the doorstep to take it away from him.

"He's like the devil," she said. "This is all his fault. He starves the kids and works them in the fields and has spells which make him act crazy. He never bathes or cleans up after himself. You should see what he did to little Rosie. That was it, after that I said 'no more' and took the horses and sleigh and left."

Caroline described Domko as best as she could, without revealing the shame of the constant beatings she and the children had been receiving. The officer listened intently as she spoke. Domko did sound like a monster and the officer was more than a bit curious to see the man face to face.

Caroline gave him directions and soon they pulled off the highway and had passed Jim's farm. They turned north again and were in front of her house within a few minutes. The officer pulled quietly into the driveway.

Caroline strode bravely into the house with the officer close behind, his holstered gun tucked neatly inside his heavy coat. Domko was sitting at the kitchen table with Kathy on his lap. He had made a supper of boiled potatoes and freshly killed chicken. He was wearing clean clothes and was freshly shaved. The baby cooed softly as he carefully guided the spoon into her mouth. Feigning surprise, he looked up at Caroline and the officer.

No one spoke for a moment and the ensuing silence became awkward. Caroline finally told Domko why she had come back.

"I came to get Kathy," she said. "Me and the kids are going to live in town and that means Kathy too."

A look of sadness passed over Domko's face. His shoulders slumped as he stood and handed Caroline the baby. Kathy, who was still hungry, began to cry. Sensing where he stood, she reached back for her father. Domko took another step back, causing the baby reach even further.

"Ta Ta!" she cooed in baby language.

"C'mon, it's time to go" Caroline said, trying to console the baby.

"Go!" he said, his voice wracked with pain. "I's not be vantink lazy voman ant keets no more. I's be tryink to make farm goot ant vat you's be doink? Leavink me with Kathy ant goink to town vith all de mooney ant cream."

Caroline was shocked by Domko's attitude. She'd never seen him so solicitous. She looked towards the officer who appeared confused. Domko took advantage of the young man's bewildered expression.

"Look!" he said, waving his arm across the room. "She's not be cleanink or cookink, just sleepink all day."

"I do!" she said defending herself, knowing he had outwitted her. The filth in the house was going to be hard to explain. "You're the dirty one who makes a mess."

"I's be vorkink all day! Vat? I should vork in barn then smell like but a some flower? Ant the kid, vat they's not be doink it, I's be?"

The bickering continued until finally the officer spoke up.

"Well, Mrs. Pischke we have the child, I think it is time to leave," he said.

"I shouldn't have to go, this is my house," she said, angry that Domko refused to let his guard down in front of the officer. "He is the one who should have to leave. He shouldn't even be in Canada. Ask to see his passport and papers!" Caroline knew that Domko feared the threat of deportation more than anything else.

"Maybe I's go," he said controlling his temper. "But vere the farm be then? Who's be payink but a some tax? Jim?"

Seeing that they were getting nowhere, the officer began to tire of the bickering. Taking Caroline by the arm, he escorted her out of the house. During the ride back to Ashern she found it difficult to speak to him as Kathy sat quietly on her lap. She could sense that he was sympathetic to Domko. For a moment began she began to question if leaving her common-law husband had been the right thing to do.

The officer wasn't sure what to think of the scene he had just witnessed. His training in domestic violence had taught him that it was never a clear-cut issue. No one was to blame and everyone was to blame.

Who knows? he thought. *Maybe there is more between Mrs. Pischke and Jim than meets the eye. Everyone has a motive - what could hers be for trying to railroad Mr. Domko?*

He'd met worse characters than Domko and Mrs. Pischke didn't seem perfect either.

Chapter 8

Life in Ashern

SHE'S BE STEALINK BUT A SOME HORSES ant the cream!" Domko said as he stood in Jim's doorway the following afternoon.

"If I remember correctly she lives at the farm too, and you can't steal your own horses," Jim shot back. "You're just lucky she didn't sell them. And as for the cream, who milked the cows anyway? I know it wasn't you!"

Domko turned and stormed towards Jim's barn and emerged a short time later with the horses Caroline had driven there the day before. Domko hitched the animals to her sleigh that sat at the edge of the barnyard. Climbing on the sleigh, he took the reins and whipped the horses' back ends to get them moving. The animals reared slightly, then took off around the edge of bush, pulling the sleigh out of sight.

Jim stood watching in full view from the doorway knowing how much it would irritate Domko.

"Is he gone?" Ruby asked when Jim came inside and shut the door. She was sitting at the table visiting with Emma Harwart.

"He's gone but not forgotten," Jim laughed.

"Honestly, leaving that was the best thing Caroline ever did," Emma said.

Ruby nodded in agreement.

* * * * *

For the first time since Caroline had met Domko, she felt free. She and the children had moved to a larger house just out of town on Highway #325 east of Ashern. Although the house was small, it had three bedrooms, a kitchen and a front room for entertaining guests. The chemical toilet in the basement fascinated the children since they'd never used anything but the bush at home and outhouse at school. The house was sparsely furnished with items scraped together from neighbours and the second hand store in town.

The social worker, a middle aged woman named Martha Jeske paid periodic visits to Caroline and the children.

Martha was a tall, heavy-set woman with a rigid smile and no-nonsense attitude. She had curly graying hair and a booming voice. She seemed genuinely concerned about how they were getting on. She sat with Caroline and worked out a monthly budget based on a family of eight children. Martha explained that because Caroline owned land, there would be a lien against the land payable to the provincial government for the amount of her Mother's Allowance payments if the land sold.

Caroline agreed. Although she and the children were still quite poor, the monthly mother's allowance meant they were well-fed and secure in their new home. Soon the children began filtering home from school.

"Well, who do we have here?" Martha said at the twins.

David and Dennis looked at the big woman and smiled, recognizing a faint German accent.

"This is Dennis and this is David," Caroline said pointing to each twin in turn.

"My aren't they just the cutest little things?" Martha said her voice softening. "And look at those eyes, so blue!"

Caroline beamed. It wasn't often that people were kind towards her boys.

* * * * *

The children walked to school a short distance away. Steven, Norman and Eunice seemed to enjoy their new teachers and classmates. Walter was having a difficult time mixing with town children. Instead of a one room school, the Ashern building was divided into seven rooms, split according to grade level with a teacher in each room.

Walter was an adolescent whose problems stemmed from feelings of inferiority that he and his siblings were 'bushed'. He complained to his mother that the students at Bayton were much kinder to him and that he wished he still went to school there. Caroline brushed off his complaints hoping that he would make a few friends and find the adjustment easier.

Caroline became friends with Anna and Leon Koch, neighbours who lived a short distance away. The Kochs had a daughter and two young sons. The Deightons and Harwarts each stopped by shortly after Caroline settled in. She also received periodic visits from members of her church. Friendships outside the religion were frowned upon, so Caroline found she had few people to confide in.

Unfortunately, some members of the church did not support her decision to leave Domko. They tried to convince her to return to the farm, but she was prepared for the onslaught and refused outright. Widowed at a young age from her first husband she reasoned that her vulnerable situation had led her to the ghastly mistake of co-habitating with Domko.

She asked church members if she deserved to be punished for one mistake for the rest of her life. She pointed out that since she hadn't married him, she was breaking no religious laws by leaving him. This put her in a precarious position with the church and for a while she found herself drifting away from her religion.

* * * * *

Late one spring afternoon, the children were playing a game of tag outside when Walter suddenly came bursting into the house. Caroline was reading in the front room and was startled by the urgency in his voice.

"Mom, D-domko's coming!" he yelled.

Caroline jumped up and peered out the front window. Domko was walking slowly up the driveway carrying a brown bag in each hand. She could see him greeting the children cheerfully.

The older children had retreated to the back yard while the twins and Rosie stood motionless in the front yard. Caroline hurried to the door to meet him before he came inside. Slipping on her shoes, she stepped out onto the porch .

"Carlorka, it be goot to seeink you" he smiled.

Caroline crossed her arms in front of her chest awkwardly.

"How are you?" she asked defensively.

"Goot," he said. "I's be brinkink for you ant keets." Thrusting his arms forward, he motioned for Caroline to take the bags.

She hesitated not wanting to look at him.

"Vat?" he said, smiling wider. "You's be gettink too much food?"

Taking one bag from his outstretched hand, she looked inside. It contained a newly killed, plucked chicken. Setting it down on the porch, she took the other bag and opened it. Inside there were eight bottles of soda pop.

Caroline's resolve softened as she looked at the man standing before her. This was the Domko she remembered when he had first come to the farm. Where had he been these past two years of beatings and horror? More importantly, was he back for good?

"I's be comink inside?" he asked innocently. She hadn't had enough time to decide what she should do. Calling each of the children by name, she reached into the bag and handed them a bottle of pop. They let out a collective gasp.

"Domko brought it," she said. The children hadn't had pop since before their father's death. The twins and Rosie couldn't remember ever having tasted the sweet, bubbly liquid, but knew they would like it by the way their older siblings described it.

Norman put the bottle in his mouth, hoping to pry off the metal lid with his teeth.

Caroline laughed. "That won't work," she said. Looking around for a moment, she pointed to a flat piece of metal on the shed door.

"Walter, you show them how to pry it off over there."

Walter smiled widely as he led the children away. He'd opened pop before and was confident he could do it again without breaking the bottle.

Domko kept his eyes transfixed on Caroline. "I's be comink in?" he asked again, this time gentler.

Caroline could see no reason to be rude to him, especially after his generosity to the children. She picked up the chicken and motioned for him to come in. He sat at the kitchen table while she prepared supper. As they chatted, a wave of normalcy flooded over her.

This is what it is supposed to be like, she thought to herself.

Handing him an ash tray, she smiled. The clean and well-groomed man removed a cigarette from his pocket. He looked like an average fellow and nobody would have been able to convince her about his rages if she hadn't witnessed his brutality first hand.

They chatted and gossiped for a while and she was amazed by the change in him. He seemed entirely different from the person she had fled from a few months before. Almost as if he could read her mind, Domko began to speak.

"I's be better now," he said. "My head be but a some goot."

Domko apologized for his past treatment of her and the kids and asked if they would return to the farm. He told her that he needed her there and loved her very much.

Letting her defenses down, she smiled and invited him to stay for supper. The children were called in and told to sit at the table. Domko was friendly to them which made the older children wary, but the twins were eager to accept his kindness. Domko carefully hid his suspicion as they spoke in their strange language.

Shortly after supper he left, waving kindly as he walked down the road towards the tractor he'd parked in the school yard. Caroline felt a little sad that he was leaving, but relieved that she didn't have to make any decision about returning to the farm, at least not right away.

Domko continued to make occasional visits to the family, but he wasn't the only suitor trying to win Caroline's heart. Several men visited the widow and she enjoyed the attention immensely, openly flirting with them. In May, Domko began pressuring Caroline to return to the farm and she knew it was because he'd need help in the hayfield soon.

"I's be keepink some farm," he said one afternoon in his kindest, most persuasive tone. "I's can't be doink it long."

Caroline thought for a few moments, then offered to take Walter and Steven out of school early and send them to the farm for the summer. This seemed to satisfy Domko who arrived the following week in Caroline's brother's truck to get the boys.

Neither boy seemed to mind going since Domko did seem much better. Steven got along well with Domko, much better than any of Caroline's other children. He was a quiet boy who demanded little attention and was proud of his Polish heritage.

Walter was beginning to forgive Domko, optimistic that he had truly changed his ways. As well, the boy's persistent stuttering caused him embarrassment with the kids at school, so he was happy to go back to the farm.

Norman stayed in school until the end of June, then began raking hay for one of the local farmers. This brought a little extra money into Caroline's household, money she decided she wouldn't tell the social worker about.

The summer came to an end and Steven tired of the heavy workload at the farm. He snuck back to Ashern in time for the Labour Day long weekend. School started soon after that, giving him the perfect excuse not go back to work. Walter decided to stay at the farm and attend school there. This suited Caroline fine because it kept Domko from pressuring her to return.

* * * * *

There were nearly 30 children enrolled in grades one and two that year at Ashern School. On the first day of school, the Pischke twins found themselves in the middle of a busy, noisy class. They sat quietly near the front, watching the children around them chat and play. Eunice was also in that class, but because she was in grade two, she sat on the other side of the room with the older children.

Their teacher was Margaret Sigfusson, a tall, attractive, 31 year old dark-haired woman who was well-liked by her students. She noticed how inseparable the twins were and that they couldn't speak English. She couldn't tell which boy was David or Dennis, and both were too shy to say a word to her. She knew these were the poor little bushed kids who'd come to Ashern from west of Moosehorn. She wanted to help them fit in with the rest of her students, but needed their cooperation. At the end of the third day, she called Eunice to her desk.

"Eunice could you come here please," Mrs. Sigfusson said. "Please give this note to your mother."

Eunice nodded and took the slip of paper. She ran home and watched her mother open the note and read it slowly. Caroline had received many notes before, usually about the older boys day dreaming or not completing their assignments on time. She went to the school the next morning to meet with the teacher about the twins.

"Hello, Mrs. Pischke," Margaret said, extending her hand. "It's nice to meet you."

Caroline smiled and looked around her. It had been years since she had been in a school. The smell of chalk dust brought back harsh childhood memories about the years she spent in class.

"I've asked you to come to discuss the twins," Margaret began. "I'm having a hard time understanding them. What language do you speak at home?" Most children in the school spoke either English, German or Icelandic.

Caroline felt her face begin to flush. She was embarrassed because she couldn't understand everything the twins said either and didn't want to admit it to the teacher. She had hoped that the boys would have outgrown their speech problem by the time they started school. She had been so preoccupied with her own life that she'd forgotten about their quirky language.

"Eunice understands them," she said, avoiding the question. "Can she help out?"

"Well, I guess it's possible. The boys really aren't learning anything right now," she said. "They are so far behind the other students their age that if they don't learn to speak and start communicating with the rest of us soon . . ." then Margaret stopped. She could tell by the look on Caroline's face that she was very uncomfortable discussing this issue. "Well, it's too soon to tell," she said. "We'll teach them English and then see what happens. They may have to do some practicing at home, but we can discuss that later."

Caroline nodded, feeling like a little girl again. The air in the school room suddenly became suffocating as she tried to hide her panic.

"Can I go now?" she said, immediately hating herself for feeling intimidated.

"Certainly," Margaret said her voice softening. She was genuinely concerned about the twins and had not intended to make their mother feel inferior. "We'll talk again."

Classes began and Eunice's desk was moved to the front of the room beside her brothers. This embarrassed her since she had already spent two years in grade one. It didn't take her classmates long to notice that she was having to interpret for the twins.

"Retards!" a few of the older children taunted during recess. "The twins are retards!"

Eunice was embarrassed by the comments and pretended not to notice. The twins, of course, were oblivious to what was going on. They didn't care much about what other people said or thought of them. Most of the time they were in their own little world and the only person who invaded their consciousness was Domko. As far as they knew, he was out of their lives for good.

* * * * *

"You's be tellink Carlorka," Domko said, as he scooped a spoonful of stew onto his plate.

Walter knew that he was being asked to relay how good Domko was and how things had improved at the farm. Walter thought for a moment. Things certainly had improved. Since returning in mid-May, Domko hadn't lost his temper or threatened to hit him once. Walter craved male attention and had concluded that this man might be able to take the place of his beloved father.

"I'd l-like to go see Mom this Sunday," Walter said. "W-ill you take me?"

Domko smiled as he spooned the chicken and vegetable mixture onto the 13-year-old's plate.

"I's be brinkink you ant some cream," he said. "Ve visit ant brink potato ant carrot."

Walter was also anxious to have his mother and siblings return to the farm. He missed his brothers and needed help with the chores. He and

Domko had put in long days to get the summer work done and now it was time for him to return to school. He didn't like attending class, but was looking forward to socializing with his friends, most of whom he hadn't seen in a year.

"M-maybe you want to come back?" Walter asked his mother on Sunday afternoon as he stood with her in the kitchen. "Domko's better, a lot better than he ever w-was."

Caroline thought for a moment. Domko was sitting in the living room reading a farm paper he had brought along. Kathy was playing with a small toy at his feet while the other children played loudly in their bedrooms. The twins came running out, one behind the other, screaming loudly with Eunice in hot pursuit.

"Gimme that!" she yelled, pulling a doll out of David's hand. "Get your own toys." Turning she flipped her nose into the air and marched back into the room she shared with her mother. Caroline was quick to notice that Domko seemed oblivious to the noise.

"I don't know Walter," she said furrowing her brow. "I don't know if I want to go back. I like living in Ashern."

Walter worked on his mother for most of the day. Caroline was wavering since Domko had been quite charming lately. She did a mental calculation of the pros and cons of returning to him.

"I'll think about it," she said to her son who smiled and gave her a brief hug.

For the first time since Caroline had moved to town, she allowed Domko to spend the night in her bed. Eunice and Rosie were sent to sleep with the boys and instructed not to disturb the adults once the bedroom door closed.

The following morning during breakfast, Caroline announced that they would be returning to the farm.

"No," Eunice whispered, in the hope that Domko wouldn't hear. "I want to stay in Ashern!"

The twins and Rosie started to cry.

"I won't go back!" Norman yelled directly at Domko who was sitting at the table stirring his coffee. The 11year-old then turned and ran out the door.

Ignoring the children's pleas, Caroline began packing their clothes and toys into crates. Domko seemed very pleased as he loaded their belongings into the borrowed pick-up truck parked in the driveway. Since Caroline had already paid the current month's rent, there were two weeks to remove the remaining furniture that couldn't be taken on this trip. Within a few hours, the children were sitting sadly in the back of the truck and travelling north on the highway to Moosehorn.

It wasn't so much his actions but rather his words the night before that had convinced Caroline to give their relationship another try. Domko had promised that he would be more supportive of her religion and that he would also become a Jehovah's Witness. He'd had numerous visits from a member of Caroline's church named Nick Skleparik during the past few months, and said that his words had helped to change him. Nick was a well-respected Witness that many people admired. Domko had quoted bible passages and asked her forgive him for being so harsh in the past.

"I's be but a some goot father," he'd said.

The children remained wary of Domko, even though it appeared he was a changed man. They had been back at the farm for nearly a week and were planning to return to Bayton school on Monday morning when David and Dennis made a startling discovery in the barnyard.

"Hey Davey," Dennis said, pointing towards a haystack. "What's that?"

David stopped and looked at what appeared to be a big rag doll lying on the ground a few feet away. Curiously, he took a few steps forward, then turned to Dennis and motioned for his twin to join him. They took a few more steps and saw it was their little sister lying face down at the edge of the stack. Both boys stopped.

"It's Rosie!" Dennis exclaimed.

"I think she's dead," David said seriously. "You touch her an' see."

"I ain't gonna touch her, you touch her," Dennis said.

"I think we gotta tell momma," David said. "C'mon."

The twins ran quickly to the house. They burst through the door to find their mother arguing with Domko.

"You's be beechin' around!" he screamed, standing in the middle of the kitchen floor. His back was to them and they could see their mother's face over his shoulder. She was crying and trying to defend herself. There were no other children in the house except Kathy who sat quietly in the front room.

David and Dennis turned quickly and ran back outside. They kept running into the bush and stayed there for the rest of the afternoon. Just before dark they crept into the yard. They hadn't eaten since breakfast and were weak from hunger.

Opening the kitchen door a sliver, David peered inside. He could see straight through to the front room where Eunice and Walter sat solemnly on the chesterfield. Kathy babbled and walked around them, trying to persuade an older brother or sister to play with her. Their mother walked from one bedroom into the other.

"He's gone," David said, sensing the serenity in the house meant Domko was not there.

They went inside to find Norman and Steven playing cards at the kitchen table. The twins went straight to their mother.

"Momma," David whispered. "Where's Rosie?"

Caroline walked past her sons to the other room. She was gathering up clothing and toys the children had brought with them from town. Caroline's face was purple in places and her arms were full of bruises.

"Me an' Denny saw Rosie by the haystack," he said. "She looks dead."

"Hush!" Caroline scolded. "She'll be alright. You go and get into bed now."

"But Momma," Dennis protested. "We're hungry."

"Never mind, just go to bed. You won't starve before morning."

The boys were surprised at their mother's indifference towards their sister. They began to whine but stopped when she raised her hand.

"Go now," she said, her voice breaking as she fought back tears.

The boys scurried into the bedroom and jumped onto the bed. Seeing their mother so unhappy confused them. Life had been so good in Ashern and the boys wished they were still there.

Domko drove the tractor in high gear all the way to Moosehorn. He had left the house in a jealous rage after discovering that Caroline had been seeing a few men while living in Ashern. He had naively believed that he had been her only suitor the entire time she had been away.

His anger rose as he envisioned Caroline being intimate with another man. He cursed out loud as he drove towards the residential section of town. Pulling up to a row of houses, he halted the tractor abruptly in front of a small house. Jumping down from the tractor, he reached back and grabbed the rifle he had brought along. Striding up the front walk, he lunged onto the porch and began banging loudly on the door. When nobody answered it immediately he shoved the door open with his shoulder, almost taking it off its hinges.

"Julius?!" he screamed into the house.

A man emerged from the front room where he'd been reading. His face was fearful as his eyes darted from Domko's angry face to the gun he carried in his hand.

"Vere be some Julius?"

"Julius doesn't live here," the man said cautiously as he raised his hands into the air. "And I don't know where he is. You've got the wrong house."

He recognized the intruder as Bob Domko, Caroline Pischke's lover. Domko eyed the man suspiciously. He looked around for a moment then stormed out as quickly as he'd arrived. The man ran to the door and locked it. Then he went to the telephone to dial his neighbour. The phone rang twice before there was an answer.

"Is Julius there? Well, you'd better tell him to get out the back door. Bob Domko was just here and the crazy ass is looking for him and he's carrying a rifle!"

He slammed down the phone and ran to look out a side window, which gave him a clear view of the neighbour's house. He'd heard that Domko was crazy and that he'd threatened to kill Jim Deighton many times. This was his first encounter with the man and hoped it would be his last.

The back door of the neighbour's house was flung open and Julius ran out. Glancing from side to side, he jumped off the porch and ran into the bush behind the house.

Rosie spent that night outside beside the haystack. The twins checked her in the morning to discover she was conscious and had covered herself with hay. She stayed outside alone all that day and again that night. Caroline didn't dare check on the girl, fearing it would send Domko into another rage.

The following morning, Walter snuck the girl back into the house. When Domko went outside to check the cows to see if they'd been milked properly, Caroline signalled the children and within less than a minute they were all running down the road towards the Harwart house. Unfortunately the neighbours were not home, so the family was forced to continue to Ashern on foot. They made it to the Township Line then heard the rumbling of a vehicle approaching from behind. Caroline's first thought was that Domko had noticed they were gone and had come looking for them. The truck slowed as it approached then pulled up beside Caroline.

"Do you want a ride?" the man in the driver's seat asked.

Thankful it wasn't Domko, she smiled in relief. The man was a large Indian fellow with long thick hair and a few missing teeth and warm, sincere eyes. His young son stood on the front seat beside him, while his wife smiled in a timid but friendly way.

"We're goin' to Ashern," Caroline said. "Which way are you goin'?"

"We're goin' to Fairford," he said. "We'll take you to Moosehorn if you like."

As the children climbed into the back of the truck, Caroline thanked the friendly man whose last name was Woodhouse. It was a cold, bumpy ride to Highway No. 6. The small boy in the front watched the kids through the rear cab window. At first he peered through the window, then turned and buried his face shyly in his mother's hair. Gradually, he began to warm up to the strange faces smiling back a him.

Caroline could see the man and woman talking in front. The vehicle came to a stop at the highway intersection then turned south towards Moosehorn. Instead of slowing as they approached the town, the truck accelerated and it became obvious that the Indian family planned to take them all the way to Ashern before making the 35-mile trip north to the Fairford Reserve.

Once in town, Caroline leaned towards the driver's side window and gave the man directions to the little house which had sat unoccupied for the past week. As she and the children climbed out of the truck, Caroline offered to pay the man, secretly hoping he'd refuse since she had very little to offer.

Smiling he shook his head 'no'.

"Sometime when somebody needs help, you help them," he said quietly. "That will be payment enough." Waving, the man backed out of the driveway and Caroline watched the native family until they were out of sight.

The children were happy to be back in Ashern.

Life fell into a routine for the family and the children began attending school regularly. They'd fallen behind in their studies but didn't seem too concerned about the consequences. Walter was able to earn money as a newspaper carrier for the Winnipeg Free Press and Tribune. Soon he'd earned enough money to buy a gun he'd admired at Thorkelsson's store. He joked that if Domko came around, he'd shoot him. Afraid of Domko again, he secretly hoped for the opportunity to protect his mother and siblings.

Living in town wasn't without its difficulties. Caroline's aborted attempt to reconcile with Domko and his pursuit of her friend in Moosehorn had caused wild speculation about the woman. It was embarrassing for the older children who were teased at school and Caroline found it difficult to face people in town. Pressure from the Witnesses added to Caroline's problems as they made it clear that her behaviour was unacceptable.

She began to rebel and again pulled away from her religion. Remembering her own neglected childhood, Caroline began to give in to the pressure from the children to celebrate special occasions such as Christmas and birthdays. The twins turned seven years old February 8 and much to everyone's surprise, Caroline baked a birthday cake for them.

One afternoon a member from the church showed up at the door to guide her back onto the right path. This man continued to visit regularly for the next few months. Soon Caroline was attending meetings again and reading the bible. Sometimes the man would bring his briefcase and they would discuss religion, but sometimes he would not. The children usually had to stay outside for many hours while they had a private visit. They didn't mind since he wasn't very nice, criticizing them whenever their mother couldn't hear him.

On a sunny Saturday afternoon in February, the children decided to go for a walk while they waited for the man to leave. The children chatted to each other as they pulled Kathy on a small sleigh west along the road toward the school. It had snowed the night before and they met a neighbour shoveling his driveway.

"Hi kids," he said with a smile. "Where are you off to?"

"We're going for a walk," Norman said. "We gotta stay outside until the man from the church leaves."

The neighbour frowned as he looked at the children, then towards their house. He had heard rumours about their mother's promiscuity and wondered if they were true. The women in town had been gossiping viciously about Caroline and her choice of men. It appeared to him that no matter what Caroline did, she just couldn't keep herself out of trouble.

The children walked to the school grounds where they played until their hands and feet started to freeze. They arrived home to find the man had left. They were glad to see their mother was in good spirits.

Heavy snowfall that winter kept Domko isolated on the farm. As soon as the spring thaw arrived, so did he, bringing gifts and apologies like he did the year before.

He began pressuring Caroline to move back to the farm. She suspected that he only wanted her and the children to return for work, she vowed not to fall victim to his cajoling again. She decided against sending Walter to the farm since he was a good worker and could easily earn money for the family by getting a job with a farmer near town. She and the children were so much happier in Ashern that there was no reason to move back to the farm.

Unfortunately, saying 'no' to men wasn't easy for Caroline. She had been raised to believe that husbands were heads of the household and that wives obeyed orders. She was expected to bear children, care for them and do all the housework and half the farm work.

Caroline didn't mind hard work, but despised being beaten. In an effort to placate Domko, she allowed him into her bed and gave him money from her mother's allowance whenever he asked. As long as she stayed away from the farm, he treated her well. She had always wanted a better life and now she had one. Besides, she was enjoying the attention of a few men who were adding spice to the doldrums of having to care for eight children. There was no doubt that Caroline was driven by drama. If there was nothing exciting going on in her life, she managed to create something to keep her in constant turmoil.

One evening while Domko was visiting, there was a knock at the door. Caroline answered to discover a local drunkard who had been dared by a few men at the tavern to ask her for a date. Once Domko realized what was happening, he flew into a rage and attacked the man. Neighbours telephoned police but by the time they arrived, Domko had already beaten the man unconscious. Police intervened and to the children's delight, Domko spent the night in jail.

* * * * *

Over the next year Domko continued to visit and pester Caroline to go back to the farm. She continued seeing him and a few others, refusing to give Domko an answer. The children were settled nicely in Ashern, enjoying the freedom of town life. They made friends and even went to the Ashern theatre a few times. Not one of them wanted to go back to the farm, not even Walter. He was older, more confident and had been accepted by his classmates.

* * * * *

"I'm pregnant," Caroline said to her neighbour one afternoon in May 1956. Given her marital status, nobody dared ask who the father was. Caroline knew herself, but her options would be fewer if she told. She held her cards pretty close to her chest and decided she would tell people when the time was right.

This latest pregnancy did not please members of her church. To have a child out of wedlock was barely forgivable once, but twice? During the next few months, she received pressure from both the Hilbre and Ashern Witness groups to reveal the name of the father of the baby. The older children listened as the Witnesses advised her to repent and ask forgiveness. She was also told to return to the farm and marry Domko. She refused and found herself alienated from the groups that had been her family for the past ten years.

Soon afterwards a social worker arrived from Winnipeg.

"Where's Martha Jeske?" Caroline asked after she invited the man in.

"She's married and moved to Selkirk," the social worker said. "I'm her replacement."

He asked Caroline a few questions, meticulously writing her answers in a file. She could sense that something was wrong by the tone of his voice.

"Caroline," he began, "We have received an anonymous letter saying that you have had regular visits from your common-law husband. Could you please explain this?"

Caroline's mouth dropped open in shock. She was aware that the rules stipulated she could not have a man living in the house while she was receiving mother's allowance payments. She knew that overnight visits would be frowned upon by welfare officials, but could see no other way to keep Domko from harassing her endlessly. Her mind whirled as she realized that someone was watching her closely and hated her enough to report her to the authorities.

Names of the people she suspected began to enter her mind, including the father of her unborn child.

"He comes to visit his child," Caroline said innocently. "He doesn't come very often."

The man met her gaze and held it until she turned away.

"I'm afraid that we have a handwritten report that Mr. Domko has been staying overnight on a regular basis, showing that the two of you are behaving as husband and wife," he said curtly. "Since it appears that you and he have worked out your differences, you will no longer be receiving mother's allowance payments."

Caroline was stunned. She couldn't even argue with the man's logic because it was true. Recklessness had cost her freedom.

Chapter 9

Norman's surprise

MARJORIE HARWART'S FAVOURITE JOB was driving the team of horses. She loved the feel of the reins in her hands and the power of her father's brown and black Bays. These were beautiful, cooperative work horses who enjoyed putting in a full day's work.

Marjorie sat on the seat as the tines of the hay rake rattled noisily behind her while the horses trotted down the road. The sun was beginning to cast a shadow in front of her as it set behind the tall trees lining her route.

At 13, Marjorie was quite a tomboy. Her hair, cut short, was held off her face by a hat that also protected her from the sun. Her thin arms and legs were tanned brown and a light sprinkling of freckles lined her nose. She liked haying season best since it gave her the opportunity to be with the horses. The days were long now and she had spent that afternoon raking hay in the north quarter. Her father had left her there alone while he cut hay in another field.

It had been a wet spring but June and early-July had been warm and dry. Now, farmers in the area were concentrating on harvesting hay on the high ground. A few more weeks of sunny weather and they would be able to cut the low spots. If the weather held out, Marjorie would be raking again the following day, then helping her father stack the day after that. It was never a good idea to cut and rake too much before stacking, since it would sometimes rain and spoil the hay before it was piled.

The grumbling in Marjorie's stomach told her it was long past supper time. Mosquitoes swirled up from the grass as the horses rumbled along, so she kept the pace brisk in a bid to outrun the hungry insects. It had been a hot day, so the cool evening breeze felt good on her sweaty skin.

As she approached the Pischke farm, she could see there was more activity in the yard than usual. She reflected that life had been different for her since Caroline and the children had left. She had friends at school, but none lived as close and she missed the daily visiting that took place as she chased the cows morning and night.

This evening, it looked as though Domko had visitors. As she got closer, she could see they were children. Standing up, she recognized Walter and Norman. Then she noticed Eunice pumping water from the outdoor well while the twins stood beside her watching.

"Hey you guys!" she yelled, waving one hand high above her head as she snapped the reins to hurry the horses. "It's me! Marjorie!"

Eunice looked towards the road and waved excitedly. Walter and Norman also began waving as all of the children stopped what they were doing and ran towards the road. Marjorie slowed the horses to a stop as she passed the barn. Jumping down, she ran towards her friends. They stopped within a few feet of each other and stared.

Her friends were back.

The twins had grown quite a bit since Marjorie had last seen them. For a moment she couldn't tell them apart. Then the more aggressive twin took a step forward and she recognized him as David.

Eunice had also grown. She was 10 now and just as talkative as ever. Walter was still skinny and awkward at 15. She glanced at Norman then looked away quickly. The 13 year old caused her heart to skip a beat. He was still the most handsome boy she knew.

After a few awkward moments, the children were laughing and joking as always.

"What are you guys doin' here?" Marjorie asked.

"Uncle John brought us back" Eunice answered. "We're gonna live at the farm again."

"Yeah," Norman added. "Mom said Domko has changed, but he's makin' us work already and we just got back."

"Our Mom's gonna have another baby," Eunice said quickly. "Isn't that exciting?"

Marjorie nodded. She knew that Domko was mean to the kids but didn't know to what extent. Rather than thinking about him, she concentrated on how happy she was to have her friends home.

"She's back with Domko?" Emma asked incredulously. "When?"

"They came back today," Marjorie said, as she removed her shoes at the door. "Isn't that great?"

Emma didn't answer. She was glad to have her neighbour back for selfish reasons but knew it was not in the best interest of the children.

Gus shook his head. Domko had been crazy as ever since Caroline's departure two and a half years ago, and showed no signs of improving. Gus had hoped that Caroline was gone for good after the botched reconciliation in the fall of 1954.

"I don't know what to think about this," Emma said to her daughter. "Here's your supper."

"Oh yeah," Marjorie said, taking the plate from her mother. "Caroline's going to have another baby."

Gus and Emma looked at each other. Emma rolled her eyes, then slipped on her shoes.

"I'm going over to talk with her myself," she said.

Gus nodded, then stared silently out the kitchen window.

Domko was quite pleased with himself when Caroline decided to return to the farm. In his mind, he was the centre of the universe. He seemed to believe that every decision or action taken by his family and neighbours was for his benefit or detriment. There were no grey areas as far as he was concerned and as time wore on, this character trait was becoming more pronounced.

Now that the children were back on the farm there would be plenty of hands to help harvest hay. Caroline would cook and milk the cows, two jobs he detested. She was pregnant again, but that didn't matter as long as she continued to work. At this point, he didn't care if the child was his or not. He only wanted Caroline and the older children to be at home to help him with the work.

Emma had been over that night to talk to Caroline. The neighbours were always interfering in his business and he didn't like it. He made sure he stayed in the kitchen so the women wouldn't have time alone together. Emma soon tired of his presence and left.

All the children except Rosie and Kathy were expected to work long hours in the fields. Their days began when Domko rose with the sun and started barking commands at them. They would rush outside to milk cows, and feed and water livestock, pigs and chickens.

Soon they were in the hayfields cutting and sweeping hay. This was a long, laborious job that took most of the summer to complete. Because Domko's equipment was so antiquated, haying was much more labour intensive than on land where farmers had tractors and modern haying equipment such as metal rakes and stackers. This bothered Domko who liked to think that the way he did things was best.

Haying with horses and old fashioned mowers and rakes was a dangerous job for children. A runaway team or miscalculation on the part of a young farmhand could cause a tremendous amount of damage or cost the young worker his life.

Fortunately, for the Pischkes they managed to squeak through the early years as farmhands virtually unharmed. The dangerous elements to the job involved the mechanized cutting blades that pulled behind the team. The farmhand worked between the horse and the mower that there was always a chance that the unit could upset if the team turned too sharply.

Careless young farmhands sometimes lost a limb after falling off the seat and landing in front of the mower. Another piece of equipment to be taken seriously was the multi-tined rake which had a row of curved tines which gathered the hay into windrows. A worker could easily become tangled in the tines and dragged along the ground if not careful.

The children were aware of the precautions they needed to take. Unfortunately, they were often tired and dizzy from overwork. Any hesitance to continue was interpreted by Domko as laziness.

"I think he wants us to fall an' chop off our feet," Norman said one hot afternoon.

"Yeah, but I don't know who he'd get to do the work. It sure wouldn't be him," Walter added.

Sometimes in the afternoon, Domko would take a nap after going back to the house with a load of hay. This lightened the children's load as they were able to play for a while or stop for a drink of water.

Walter was responsible for keeping the younger children on track, a job he did well. Sometimes he and the children would come across a patch of ripe wild strawberries or Saskatoon berries. Walter always let them stop for a while to eat. Often it was all they had to eat the entire day.

After working for two solid weeks without a break, all of the children were hoping for rain. One evening while they were resting in their bedroom after a particularly long day, Domko called to them from the kitchen. His voice was soft, almost kind. They looked at each other and then slowly filed into the kitchen to see what he wanted.

Sitting in his usual spot, Domko had eight chocolate bars sitting on the kitchen table. The bars were lined up in a neat, tempting row.

"Kathy," Domko said in a soft voice. "I's be givink you some chocklit bar."

Kathy toddled over to her father following the sound of his voice. Domko had been giving her lots of treats lately, so she came whenever he called. He took one bar from the table and pulled back the wrapper. He put the bar in the two year-old's hand. Her eyes stared aimlessly, but she had no trouble getting the candy into her mouth. The other children looked on in amazement. There were seven bars left.

"Who's I's be givink but a some chocklit bar?" he cooed. The children looked at each other again in amazement. Walter was impressed. This was the same man who had treated him kindly the summer before.

If only we could work harder and do a better job, he would treat us like this all the time, Walter thought. He looked at Dennis who was asking for guidance from his eldest sibling. Walter smiled at the boy. The children had worked hard this week and it looked as if Domko would be rewarding them for it.

Dennis loved sweets and he missed his father so much. He believed what his mother said, that Domko would treat them better if only they would be good. Dennis had tried especially hard these past few weeks, and hadn't received a beating for a while. Maybe his mother was right. All he had to do was to be a good boy. Stepping forward, he gave Domko a wide smile.

The man could see the eagerness in the youngster's eyes.

"Here Dennis," he coaxed. "I's be givink you some."

Dennis walked slowly towards him. The man took a bar from the table and held it out to the boy. Just as he reached out to take it, Domko let out a roar.

"Fraa!" he screamed, flinging his right arm into the air over his head.

Lunging forward, he grabbed the youngster by the arm. The rest of the children realized what was happening and ran in all directions. Caroline came from the front room in time to see Domko slip off his belt and begin strapping Dennis.

"Chocklit bar?" he taunted, each time the belt whipped across the boy's backside. "I's be givink you some!"

Domko held the boy by one arm, and Dennis screamed every time the belt snapped against his legs. Dennis could hear his mother yelling in the background, and felt Domko's body jolt back a few times as she pulled at him, but his anger was ferocious. He hadn't beaten any of the children for a few weeks. He turned and slapped her with the belt until she ran from the house.

Soon the beating stopped and Dennis lay in a heap on the floor, unable to move. Tired and out of breath from the effort, Domko stood over the boy for a few moments, his chest heaving. In one swoop, he gathered the chocolate bars and stormed past Dennis into his bedroom. He hid the bars in a dresser drawer which was off limits to the children. He then sat in his usual spot and lit a cigarette. He chuckled, as he usually did after beating one of the children. This time he sounded particularly satisfied with himself.

It was a quiet, cool night and the mosquitoes were heavy. The children lay in the fresh hay stacked in the field a short distance away. They looked silently up at the stars. A cow mooed in the distance and the sound of crickets chirping interrupted the silence.

The children buried themselves in the hay to protect their bare limbs from the mosquitoes that buzzed overhead. David's legs were sore as he often suffered sympathy pains when his twin was beaten. He sensed the beating was over and Dennis was lying somewhere in the house all alone. It pained him that he couldn't go to his twin, but knew from experience that there was nothing he could do.

Norman was the first to speak.

"You know there's this great place not too far away," he began. "It's across the lake by the beaver dam. It's a place where there is lots to eat and dads are good to kids."

The children liked it when Norman told stories. He had a great imagination and always knew what to say to make everyone feel better.

"I'm gonna build us a plane and fly us across the beaver dam," Norman announced. "I got it started and it's in the bush where Domko can't get it."

They were amazed by Norman's revelation. They knew he meant flying over Pischke lake, two miles directly east on their mother's land. The children had noticed that Norman was sneaking away from work and even got a beating for it one night from Domko. His siblings had no idea he was putting his time to such productive use.

They began asking questions at once.

"Where is it?" Steven asked.

"What colour is it?" Eunice asked.

"You don't got a pilot license," Walter said. "You can't fly without a pilot license."

"Do we all gets to go? Me an' Denny an' Rosie too?" David asked.

"Ssshhh!," Norman commanded as he raised his hand. He looked at Steven but was hesitant to say where the plane was. His brother might tell Domko in a weak or vengeful moment.

"It's in the bush but that's all I'm sayin'" he said. "It's just wood colour since it don't got to be no colour to fly. I don't care 'bout no pilot's license. I been readin' how to do it and I'm gonna fly whether they like it or not an' I'd like to see the police try an' stop me."

The children listened as Norman's confidence in the plan grew.

"When I get the plane finished we'll all fly away," he said. "First me an' Walter will go, then Steven, then I'll come back an' get the twins."

"What 'bout me an Rosie?" Eunice asked quickly.

"You can't come 'cause you talk too much."

"Hey!" she laughed, throwing a clump of hay in his direction.

"Just kiddin', I'll get you guys too."

Norman talked for a while about the plane and how wonderful life would be for them once they got over the beaver dam.

"H-how long will it take?" Walter asked.

Norman thought for a moment. "Well, I gots directions in a book I stole from school," he said. "I think it'll take about another week or maybe a day more."

David looked at his older brother. His heart swelled with pride. He could count on Norman to get them off the farm.

Morning came and David could hardly wait to find Dennis to tell him the great news. The gregarious twin jumped up and brushed the hay off himself. He could hear Domko yelling from the barnyard, a signal to the older children that their work day had just started.

David trotted to the house and went inside. His brother was lying quietly on the bed. There were beads of sweat on his forehead and wide, purple blisters had swollen his legs. Blood had dried on the places where the belt had cut through his skin. Flies buzzed around the youngster's wounds.

"Dennis," he whispered. "Get up Dennis. I gots great news."

Dennis slowly opened his eyes. The sight of his twin made him smile. Their secret language was a welcome sound in contrast to Domko's ravings. David and Dennis shared a bond that was difficult to explain. Surprisingly, Dennis didn't resent that he was usually the one who got caught by Domko rather than his brother. He honestly didn't know what he'd do without David.

"What?" Dennis asked through parched lips. His head pounded with pain.

"C'mon Dennis," he said, gingerly pulling his brother's arm. "Let's go 'fore Domko comes back."

Dennis thought groggily back to the night before. David was right. They should probably get out of sight, just in case Domko came back and wanted to beat him again. He sat up on the bed then swung his legs over the side. Carefully he stood, leaning on David for support. Glancing around nervously, he hobbled to the door. Opening it he could hear Domko yelling from inside the barn. Hurrying in the opposite direction, the boys disappeared into the bush.

Following one of their trails, the twins walked for about twenty minutes before deciding on a hiding spot. They thought it would be best to stay there for the day, rather than risk facing Domko again. Sometimes after he had beaten a child, he would challenge them as soon as they were on their feet. Norman and Walter were able to ignore the man, but Dennis or David would begin to cry. That was interpreted by Domko as a sign of weakness, and he'd usually beat the child again. It was best that they stayed away until Dennis felt stronger.

Being in the bush during the summertime was pleasant. Except for the insects, the boys enjoyed the serene setting. Birds chirped and the sun shone through spaces in the trees. It was an old bush full of oak and poplars, so undergrowth was minimal. It was a perfect place for youngsters to hide. Leaning up against a fallen poplar, the boys began daydreaming out loud.

"Norman's makin' a plane and he's gonna fly us outta here," David said, pleased that he had waited for the right moment to tell his brother the plan. "Norman says over the beaver dam it's like Ashern an' he's gonna fly us there."

Dennis was impressed with the idea. "Who's gonna go?"

"Us all," David said. "Except we can't tell momma 'cause she might tell."

Dennis nodded. "Where we gonna live?"

David thought for a moment. "Maybe with some nice people like ones with the big car," he said, remembering the time he and Dennis were nearly put into a foster home.

"It don't matter," Dennis added. "Long as Domko ain't there."

The rains finally came in early late July. Domko rose early, looked out the window and grunted. The children were careful not to let their happiness show as they looked forward to a day off work. The younger children played quietly in the bedroom, while Caroline and the older children milked the cows. Domko ate, then shaved, a sure sign that he would be going to Moosehorn for the day. The children were so happy they could hardly contain themselves.

Caroline came in shortly afterwards and spoke to Domko in Polish.

Eunice nodded a happy nod to her brothers and Rosie. She knew that her parents would be taking the cream to town, and then doing some shopping. All the children would stay behind except Kathy.

When the older boys came in the house, they were instructed to pull the cream can up from the well and load it in the back of their uncle's truck, which Domko had borrowed earlier in the morning. Domko hoped to buy a car soon because he was embarrassed to travel to town with the horses or by tractor. He borrowed the truck from Caroline's brother whenever he could, but wanted a car of his own.

Caroline agreed that they needed a vehicle. She and Bill had had a car, but there was a lien on it, so it was repossessed shortly after his death.

Soon Domko, Caroline and Kathy were on their way to town. The children were left with a list of chores that had to be completed before sundown. It sounded as if Domko and their mother would be gone all day. As soon as they were out of sight, the kids began running and playing in the rain. It had been so hot that this rainy morning felt like a holiday.

Norman ran into the bush behind the barn with his siblings close behind. They knew instinctively that he was going to work on the plane and were eager to help. They hadn't seen it yet and were anxious to catch a glimpse of their salvation. The path was well worn from Norman's numerous trips. They came to a small clearing and situated behind an old rock pile in a clearing at the edge of the bush was the makings of Norman's plane.

The youngster had nailed together three wooden apple crates and was fashioning a pair of wings that were attached to the sides. The wings were made from the box tops, nailed together end to end. Norman had painted a big number 8 with a circle around it on each side of the 'fuselage'.

The children watched in awe as he explained exactly how it would work. Holding up a prop he explained that it would propel the plane into the sky.

"We gotta wait for a windy day to go," he said. "That way the prop will turn fastest."

Walter and Steven were skeptical. They moved closer to the plane to take a better look.

"It don't got no w-wheels," Walter said. "How's it gonna take off without wheels?"

"It don't need wheels, stupid," he answered quickly. "It's like a glider, but with a prop so it can go on wind power, like I told you. We'll put it on the barn roof an' the wind will take us up." Picking up the book he had been using to build the model, he wiped a wet page across the back of his pants and pointed to the picture in the middle of the page.

Walter and Steven looked at each other then shrugged their shoulders as they turned to go back to the house. The twins, Eunice and Rosie stayed behind. They thought the plane was a good one and told Norman so.

"We'll go without 'em," Dennis said, trying to patch Norman's damaged ego. "We ain't got no room for them anyhow," he added.

Norman started fiddling with what would soon be the tail of the plane. Even though he didn't show it, he appreciated his brother's faith. He could always count on Dennis to say a kind word.

By afternoon, the skies began to clear. The sun came out so Marjorie came over to play for a few hours. The children finished the chores, then went home with Marjorie, hoping Emma would feed them. As usual, the older woman obliged. The children played outside until they saw the car coming from the south.

Quickly, they ran into the bush just north of the Harwart house. They watched quietly as their mother and Domko got out of the car sending Steven to check whether Domko was in a good mood. The boy returned a few minutes later to say it was safe to go home.

Domko was often pleasant when he returned from town as the trip gave him the chance to get away from the children, cash the cream cheque and pick up a few supplies. He'd buy treats for himself and Kathy, behaving generously in front of towns people while privately begrudging Caroline every cent used for her children. He'd show off and brag about the number of cattle he had to anyone who'd listen, usually the men at the creamery. They were polite but then criticized him the moment he left.

"A dog!" Dennis exclaimed, as he pointed towards the back of the truck. "Look Davey, a dog!"

A medium-sized male dog with brown blotchy, wiry hair watched the children carefully as they approached. His ears perked and tail wagged gently behind him as his tongue hung heavily out of his mouth. He looked to be full grown and reasonably good natured. The children could not understand why such a nice dog would be a stray. Norman began coaxing the dog to jump out of the truck.

"What are we gonna name him?" he asked, just as his mother came from the house to get a bag of flour. The children started suggesting names but nothing seemed to fit the dog's appearance.

"When I was a girl, I had a dog that looked like him an' I called him Bruno," Caroline said, as she motioned for Walter to help her carry the 100 lb. bag into the house.

"Bruno?" Norman pondered, looking from his mother to the dog.

Timidly, the dog edged his way to the truck tailgate, then cautiously jumped down. Immediately the kids gathered around him, their dirty hands roughly grabbing his fur. The children squabbled to be the first to hug the dog who rolled onto his back and stuck his feet in the air.

"C'mon Bruno," Norman called. "I gots a stick for you."

The dog watched the boy carefully. Norman pointed the stick towards him then threw it into the yard. Recognizing the game, Bruno jumped and ran for the stick, bringing it back and dropping it at the boy's feet.

"Hey, I trained him already!" Norman exclaimed. A look of pride came over his face as he announced that Bruno was the smartest dog that had ever lived.

That evening the children sat and watched as Domko opened a package containing a cake he'd bought in town. He cut a huge piece for himself, then called Kathy over to give her some. The other children sat in a line on the floor watching, as the two year old fumbled with the cake. Their mouths watered as they watched her smear rich icing all over her hands and face while she stuffed the gooey chocolate into her mouth.

David watched carefully as Domko wrapped the remainder of the cake, then put it on top of the cupboard which sat along the wall in the kitchen. The cupboard was a green two-piece unit that held towels, dishes and jars. The children sat on the floor and stared hungrily at the cake until bed time. They were fortunate to have eaten that day at Harwarts, but hadn't had a treat in a long time.

Domko watched them with a satisfied expression on his face. He enjoyed taunting the children and took great pleasure in seeing them suffer. He believed that money earned on the farm should be used to support him, Caroline and Kathy. He didn't mind if the other children ate leftovers, but they were never allowed to eat something that had been bought at the store.

Caroline had argued with him about this, but finally gave up trying to make him see reason. Whenever she brought up the subject, he would criticize and demean her to the point that it wasn't worth the effort. Luckily the children were able to scrape together enough to get by on from the generous Harwarts and Deightons. Caroline watched silently as she saw no reason to irritate Domko needlessly.

The next afternoon the children worked in the field while Domko took a nap. Because the ground was still soft from rain the previous day, Caroline and the twins went to the garden to pick weeds and vegetables.

The boys filled a five gallon pail with new potatoes, carrots and beets, then carried the pail back to the yard to clean the vegetables. Dennis busily scrubbed dirt from the vegetables while David used his weight to push the handle on the outdoor water pump. The boys were cheerful as they thought of the supper they would enjoy thanks to Walter who had butchered a chicken that morning.

Carrying the vegetables into the kitchen, David couldn't help but notice the cake that Domko had put on top of the cupboard the night before. His body ached for the taste of chocolate as he looked up at the package sitting seductively on the top edge of the cupboard. He took a bite from a carrot hoping to fool his stomach, but within a few moments he realized this wasn't going to work.

If I eat the cake, Domko will never know, he thought, glancing up at it again. He calculated he could get the cake, eat it and be in the bush within a minute. He looked at Dennis who was diligently dropping potatoes into their mother's large pot.

Of course I'd have to give some to Dennis, he thought. He decided to enlist his brother in the plan, realizing that half the cake would be better than nothing.

"Hey Denny, look," he whispered, pointing to the cake.

"What?" Dennis said, smiling mischievously.

"Should we?"

"Who's gonna get it?"

"You go check Domko," David said pointing towards the front room. His heart was beginning to race in his chest.

"No!" he protested in a loud whisper. His eyes widened. "If he sees me, I'm dead!"

"Sssh an' he won't. Hurry 'fore he wakes up."

Dennis scowled at his brother then tiptoed towards the front room door. Slowly craning his neck around the corner, he could see Domko asleep on the couch. The man's arms were across his chest as he snored and muttered quietly. Dennis shuddered, then looked back towards his brother. He signalled David to get the cake.

David slid a small stool in front of the cupboard, then quietly climbed on top of the stool. Gripping the side of the cupboard, he braced one foot on the edge of it then stretched to reach the cake but found he was too short. Looking back at Dennis for encouragement, he saw his brother motion to hurry up so he hoisted himself up onto the cupboard edge. With both feet on the ledge, he stood on his toes then reached overhead to grab the cake. As he tried to get back onto the stool, he lost his footing and clutched the side of the cupboard in an effort to regain his balance.

Suddenly the top half of the hoosier pitched towards him. David tried to hold it back, but the doors swung open and everything from inside began crashing to the floor. He lost his footing and fell to the floor with the cupboard crashing down upon him. The thin shelves jabbed into his chest as the weight of the heavy wooden box began suffocating the thin boy. David struggled to breathe as panic overtook him.

The commotion woke Domko who jumped from the couch with a roar. Dennis froze near the doorway, receiving a backhand across the face as Domko stormed past him. The blow sent the boy sliding across the floor. In one motion, he righted himself and scrambled under the table, just as their mother came in from outside.

"You soneebeech bastard!" he screamed, lifting the cupboard off David's chest. "You's be breakink it! You's be goot for nuthink!"

A vein on Domko's forehead protruded and the area near the scar turned white. His eyes flashed white as he picked up a block of wood from beside the cookstove. David covered his head with his arms as he struggled to catch his breath. The wood crashed down on his arms and chest as Domko swung hard, the momentum lifting his feet off the floor. David screamed in pain as pieces of bark flew in all directions. Still not satisfied with the beating, Domko began kicking the boy with his heavy boots.

"Boleslaw!" their mother yelled. "That's enough! You're gonna kill him!"

Caroline grabbed Domko by the arm, distracting him enough that the disoriented boy was able to scramble towards the door.

"Ruch a muchtork booken," David yelled in the secret language to his twin as he ran out the door.

Their pregnant mother was flung backwards as Domko turned and landed a karate style kick directly on her abdomen. She flew across the room, crashing into the milk pails piled near the door. She laid on the floor in a heap with her arms curled protectively around her stomach as her attacker kicked her twice in the back then stormed outside.

When all was quiet, Dennis crawled out from under the table then over to his mother. She was lying on her side, with her back to him.

"Momma," he sobbed. "Get up Momma, 'fore he comes back."

Caroline slowly pulled herself up then staggered to the bedroom. Crumpling on the bed she rolled towards the wall.

"Go hide Dennis," she murmured. "Go hide with David in the bush."

Dennis stared longingly at his mother's back. He didn't want to leave her but he was too afraid to stay. Turning, he ran into the kitchen and grabbed the squashed cake that was sitting in the middle of the floor. Dashing out the door he knew which direction to run since his brother had told him in their language where he'd be hiding. After running into the bush beside the house, he turned east. Within a short time he caught up to his brother who was sitting on the path talking to Bruno while he was waiting.

"I gots the cake," Dennis said trying to sound cheerful. "That ole' devil ain't gonna get none tonight!"

David laughed, then grimaced in pain. Holding his chest he stood then limped further into the bush, this time behind Dennis. Within a few minutes, they had divided the cake. Both began eating slowly, knowing they wouldn't be eating much else in the days to come. Bruno followed closely on their heels as they disappeared into the thick foliage.

Caroline laid on the bed and slept for the rest of the afternoon. Domko came in later and was openly ashamed of his earlier actions. He began apologizing to Caroline who groaned in pain as he stood solemnly beside the bed. Usually she enjoyed the attention, but not this time.

Domko put the cupboard back in place then stacked all the items inside. As evening wore on, he quietly ordered the children to finish the chores. Eunice cooked supper while Steven kept Kathy from bothering their mother. Caroline laid on the bed all night and the younger children slept on the floor mattress while Walter and Norman slept outside in the hay. Nobody knew where the twins were.

Chapter 10

Norman's first flight

DO COYOTES EAT KIDS?" Dennis asked his brother as they lay side by side at the edge of the east bush with coyotes howling balefully nearby. Dennnis was afraid of coyotes and sometimes dreamed that they were attacking him. In spite of this, he still believed it was much safer outside than being inside with Domko.

"Nope, they only eats mice an' skunks," David said. "We don't gots to worry anyhow 'cause we got Bruno here."

The dog lay beside David's side, looking up and perking his ears occasionally. Bruno felt as safe with the boys as they did with him.

"Do you 'spose that ole Satan is ever gonna go away?" David asked as he casually patted Bruno's rough fur.

"I dunno," Dennis answered. "It don't matter no more 'cause we's gonna fly over the beaver dam with Norman."

"Think we should tell momma?"

"No, 'cause Norman said so" Dennis warned. "An' it's Norman's plane."

David felt horribly guilty that his mother had received a beating for defending him. He tried hard not to let Dennis sense his remorse and vowed that she'd never receive a beating on his account again.

The following morning Caroline barely stirred. Sweat poured from her body as she trembled with fever. She groaned as the children gathered around her. Domko ushered them out of the house to do chores, leaving only Kathy and Rosie behind. The girls played quietly in the front room, sensing that something was seriously wrong with their mother.

Caroline's water broke about 1 p.m. After that, the contractions were fast and hard. Rosie wanted to go see her mother who was crying in pain, but Domko was in the room as well. The painful cries turned to an angry whisper a short time later. Soon, her mother was in the kitchen. She and Domko were discussing something and he was begging for forgiveness. Rosie crept quietly into the kitchen to see what was wrong.

A round white wash basin sat on the kitchen table. It was filled with blood and fluid and a bloody, slippery looking mass. Laying on top was a small baby - it's knees pulled up tightly to it's chest. It looked stiff and cold, its face a deep blue colour. Rosie was just a child but she understood with just a quick glance that the baby was dead.

The gasp that escaped her lips caused Domko to turn and find her staring at the scene from the kitchen doorway. Instinctively, he grabbed a cast iron frying pan from the top of the stove and lunged at her. Rosie cowered in fear, her arms covering her head.

"No, Boleslaw!" Caroline pleaded. "She's too little. She'll never remember this."

Domko's guilt over what had happened to the baby stopped him from hitting the girl. Rosie glanced up to see a look of anger and confusion in his eyes. His arm shook as he lowered the pan, dropping it on top of the stove. He let out a faint growl, which she knew was her cue to run. She realized it might be her only chance to escape unharmed, so she took it without hesitation.

"Norman, when is we gonna fly across the beaver dam?" Dennis asked two days later as he and David tagged behind their older brother. Their stomachs growled loudly with hunger, but neither dared to suggest eating since it was their first day back after stealing the cake.

"If it's windy, we can go tomorrow," Norman said, sticking one finger into his mouth then pointing it solemnly into the air as he gazed into the sky. "Yep, the wind's comin' from the right direction."

The twins were impressed with Norman's knowledge of the technical aspects of flight.

"Domko's inside, so we'll work on the plane tonight," he said. "You gonna help me?"

The twins nodded in agreement, eager to do whatever Norman asked. Flying over the beaver dam was all the boys could talk about since Norman confided the plan to them a week earlier.

"C'mon let's go then," Norman said, leading the twins into the bush behind the barn. "I need help gettin' the plane into the clearing over there." he said. "You guys grab one end and I'll take the other."

Turning the plane on its side, they were able to carry it down the path, stopping for periodic rests before finally reaching the barn. Setting it down beside a haystack, they decided that it would be best to cover it with hay for the night so Domko wouldn't see it. They avoided his gaze as they crept into the house and past him while he sat reading at the kitchen table. Their mother was already asleep in the master bedroom, while the girls whispered to each other on the bed in their room. The twins were famished but ignored the pangs and even smiled. They believed that after the next day, they would never be hungry again.

Morning came and the twins jumped out of bed. Looking out the window, they were pleased to find it was warm and windy. Glancing up, they could see the nearby tree tops wavering in the wind. Looking at one another, they smiled.

Norman, Walter and Steven were already outside milking the cows. It promised to be a good drying day, so Domko would expect them to stack hay by late afternoon. Wouldn't he be surprised when they flew past him and over the beaver dam!

When milking was finished, Domko assigned a chore to each child, then went back into the house. As soon as he was gone, the children ran to the back of the barn where they found Norman. Rosie tagged along, hoping that the big kids would finally explain to her why everyone had been whispering so much lately.

Norman was trying to figure out a way to hoist the plane onto the barn roof. The wind was blowing heavily from the west, exactly the way he wanted. Tying a rope around the plane just behind the wings, he gave it a little tug. Satisfied that the rope was tight enough, he disappeared around the corner of the barn.

The twins chattered excitedly and within a minute, Norman was on top of the shanty-style barn roof. Walter and Steven emerged from the barn a few minutes later, curious to see what was making so much noise.

"Throw it up to me," Norman said pointing to the loose end. Walter grabbed the rope and threw it up a few times before it was caught.

"Lift up the plane," he yelled, pulling the rope taut. Walter and the twins got underneath and lifted the plane as high as they could. Soon it was dangling six feet off the ground as Norman held it steady from the roof.

"C'mon up an' help me," he called as he struggled to keep his balance.

Walter climbed the loft ladder and hurried to the top of the roof. His bare feet gripped the wooden shingles as he hauled on the rope and helped his brother pull the plane higher. Eunice, Rosie and the twins watched from below as the plane balanced precariously on the edge of the roof. Norman and Walter were able to pull it the rest of the way, and together dragged it to the highest roof point which faced north.

The wind was strong and the children's spirits were high. The plane was placed on the very edge of the roof with the front end hanging over. The twins wanted to get a better view of the take-off so they stood on the manure pile directly under the plane. Dennis stood as he usually did on David's right hand side. Looking up, they could see the bottom while Norman and Walter climbed in. As the pilot, it was Norman's responsibility to crank the prop while Walter pushed with his arms to coax the plane closer to the edge.

"What about Rosie and Bruno?" Walter asked pointing to his sister who watched from a short distance away. Bruno watched thoughtfully as Rosie held her cat.

"I'll come back for them later," Norman said nervously. "We'd gotta go."

The boys tried to coax the plane closer to the edge by rocking their bodies back and forth. Soon, the plane began to inch its way forward. Suddenly, the apple crates tilted forward and the heavy makeshift fuselage plunged nose first towards the ground. Norman and Walter let out a yell and the twins screamed in bewilderment as the plane crashed less than a foot from them on top of the manure pile.

Walter banged his face on the back of Norman's head on impact, then the brothers rolled down the six foot pile. They laid on the ground stunned for a few moments.

"What happened?" Dennis asked David. "I thought they was gonna fly?"

Surrounded by debris from his plane, Norman jumped up and kicked what remained of the fuselage. He had known deep in his heart that the plane wasn't going to fly, but so desperately wanted to leave the farm and take his brothers and sisters with him.

"Stupid thing!" he said, kicking the box again. "One of these days I'm gonna get a real plane an' I'm gonna fly wherever I want!" The twins watched as their brother stormed down the hill and disappeared into the north bush.

"Hey, Davey," Dennis said, his voice rising in optimism. "He almost flew."

Norman received a whipping that day after Domko discovered the remnants of the plane in the manure pile. The boy took the beating well, barely crying as his siblings hid nearby.

The children lost all hope of escaping the farm as the summer wore on. Each day was a horrible routine of work, beatings, criticism and starvation as Domko treated the children worse than animals. The younger children could not remember life before him and sadly were becoming accustomed to the poor treatment they received.

Domko's rages were emblazoned in their memory like a wildfire scorching the prairie land. The more he beat them, the more they ran away. The twins spent as much time as they could in the bush less than a half mile directly east of the house. It was a good place because they could see the house and activity in the yard, making it difficult for Domko to sneak up on them.

The twins would slip into their own world of make believe to shield themselves from the cruel reality of life. They could play for hours with very little - twigs, leaves, stones and David's wee-wee. Each day they would hope that Domko would miraculously disappear and each day when they awoke to found him still on the farm, they would console each other and hope the next day would be better.

One afternoon David and Dennis dragged old pieces of wood to a hiding place in the bush and built themselves a crude fort. They made it comfortable with eating utensils, old dishes and the occasional tin of canned food they were able to sneak from the house. Nobody, including their mother, seemed to care that they spent most of their time in the bush.

One late August afternoon, the twins were playing near their fort along the edge of the bush when David discovered an interesting hole near the base of a poplar tree. The hole was big enough to house a large rodent, possibly a rabbit or skunk.

"Hey, Denny, look" he said. "What does you think lives in there?"

"I dunno," his brother said, bending close to examine the hole.

"Stick your arm in an' see," David coaxed.

Dennis looked at his brother then fearlessly knelt beside the hole and stuck his arm inside. He got in up to his elbow before noticing something was blocking the way. He peered inside, but couldn't see anything. He reached in again and touched something that had been stuffed in the hole. It felt like a box.

Thinking that they had stumbled across treasure, Dennis grabbed the end of the box and pulled. A piece snapped off in his hand. The twins could tell it was part of an apple box, similar to the one Norman had used to build his plane, only smaller. Reaching in a third time, Dennis tugged on soft material, pulling out many pieces. Examining it, the boys recognized it as the cotton filling from an old quilt. Curious, he continued to pull and became excited at the prospect of finding something valuable in the hole. Being engrossed with their discovery, the twins didn't hear Domko approach from around the edge of the bush.

"Fraa!" he yelled.

The twins jumped to their feet in fear and noticed that Domko seemed to recognize their find.

"You's be gettink away!" he roared. "If I's be seeink you, I's be killink you soneebeech bastard!"

The twins turned and ran into the bush. Once out of reach, they stopped to watch as Domko knelt and began stuffing the cotton material back in the hole. Then, he carefully filled the hole with dirt he dug with his hands.

"What's he doin'?" Dennis asked.

"I dunno. When he's gone we'll go get our fort an' move it over here."

Later that afternoon, they cautiously returned to their hiding place to discover a pile of rubble.

A few days later, the twins helped their older brothers pick rocks on a piece of land that Domko hoped to seed the following spring. It was heavy work since he made the children fill five gallon pails by hand, then carry the pails to a wagon. Once the wagon was full, it was pulled by horse to the edge of the field. The children had to empty the wagon by hand into a rock pile while Domko sat on the horse barking instructions.

The boys worked in silence until Domko went back to the house for lunch. The twins listened intently as Walter and Norman discussed shooting Domko and burning his body. Walter had hid near a rock pile the day before with the gun he'd bought in town. He didn't have the courage to shoot.

"*I* shoulda done it," Norman boasted. "I ain't no chicken like you." Taking that as a challenge, Walter wrestled his brother to the ground. He was bigger and stronger, but Norman had a wild mean streak that made him difficult to beat in a fight. They wrestled for a while then agreed to a truce.

Domko returned shortly afterwards and the children went back to work. Later that afternoon, David and Dennis slipped away from their siblings and hid in the bush beside the church. They discussed at length their brother's plan to kill Domko.

"Somebody's gotta kill him before he kills us," David said. "D'ya think Norman will?"

Dennis thought for a moment. "If he don't, then I will."

David looked at his brother in surprise. He had always thought of Dennis as too timid to do such a thing, but staring deep into his brother's eyes he could see that he'd changed. There was now a hatred that David hadn't noticed before.

"I'll help you," he said.

While they laid beneath the stars that night, the twins planned how they would kill Domko at first opportunity. David encouraged Dennis, hoping that his brother wouldn't change his mind. Early the next morning, they snuck into the grainary to get a gun. Both were experienced with low calibre rifles and shot guns, having hunted with their mother since they were four years old. Nobody seemed to worry that they might shoot each other's heads off, so they didn't worry about that either.

They chose an old .22 calibre rifle that had belonged to their father. David grabbed two shells from the box on the shelf, then cautiously the pair ran from the grainary north into the bush. When they were out of sight they checked to see if they'd been followed. They hid the gun, then went to get the cows from the east pasture.

Each boy's stomach turned into knots as they chased the cows into the yard. Domko was standing in the barn waiting for them. He smirked, thinking the only reason the boys had come home that morning was for something to eat. When the older children had finished milking the cows, the animals were chased back through the fence. Later that afternoon, the twins returned to the field to bring the animals home. They hated chasing the cows through the knee deep water that virtually surrounded the farm. Sometimes Domko allowed them to take a horse, but only when he was in a good mood.

The twins could hear barking coming from a field to the north. Squinting, they could see their neighbour's dogs chasing the cattle home. David and Dennis watched as the large dogs chased the cows through the water, nipping at their heels.

"Look at that," David said in amazement. "They gots cattle chasin' dogs." He had heard from the boys at school that there were special dogs trained to chase cattle. David hadn't believed them since any dog they'd ever owned had chased cattle with less noble intentions. He watched intently as the long-haired, golden-coloured animals chased the herd out of sight.

"Did you see that Denny?" he said. "We gotta gets some cattle chasin' dogs too!"

Dennis agreed and they discussed at length how much better their lives would be if they had dogs to help them do the work. As they sloshed through the wet grass, they imagined the many ways that their lives could be made easier.

"Do you think they have dogs that pick rocks too?" Dennis asked, feigning ignorance. Both boys burst into laughter then suddenly stopped. The wind was blowing gently from the south, bringing a foul smell with it.

"I think the devil's comin'," David whispered. "C'mon let's hide."

The twins ran quietly into the bush and crouched down. They waited a few minutes then sure enough, Domko emerged from a bluff of trees into the clearing where they had just been. The man stopped with his hands on his hips, then looked from side to side. He looked directly towards the bush where they were hiding. They must have been daydreaming too long so Domko had come looking for them, suspicious that they had been playing instead of working. As he continued along the path, David and Dennis took off through the thick bush towards home.

"Where's the gun?" Dennis asked.

"Just up here a ways," his brother said as he ran ahead.

The boys ran through a clearing into the last clump of trees closest to home. Making their way towards the edge of the bush, they could see the cattle continuing their journey. Domko would soon give up searching for them and come along the path.

The rifle was sitting where they had left it, leaning against a fallen oak. David grabbed the gun, then nervously took the bullets from his pocket. He loaded one in the chamber, then handed the gun to Dennis. Both boys crouched down behind the tree, facing the path.

"I dunno if I can do it," Dennis said weakly.

"Sssh!" David whispered. Straining he could see Domko in the distance, coming into the bush. The man glanced from side to side as he crept quietly, hoping to catch the twins off guard.

"He's coming!" David whispered, pointing over the tree. "Aim for his head 'cause you gotta kill him."

Dennis rested the barrel of the gun on the tree. Taking a deep breath, he shut one eye then peered with the other through the sight.

"Tell me when to shoot," he whispered. His heart was pounding so hard that he was momentarily surprised that neither David nor Domko could hear it. He cocked the gun.

Domko continued to move closer and when he was about 100 yards away, he started to turn away from the boys.

"Now," David said.

Dennis's finger shook as he took careful aim. He could see the side of Domko's head through his sight. Finger vibrating on the trigger, he closed his eyes and squeezed.

Click.

The gun had jammed. It sounded like a clap of thunder in the boys' ears, as they froze, expecting Domko to see them in their hiding place. Domko heard the sound and turned back towards the boys.

"Try again, Denny!" David rasped, now lying on his back behind the tree.

Panicking, Dennis cocked the gun again. This time he aimed quickly and pulled the trigger again.

Click. The gun had jammed once more!

The twins looked at each other in disbelief. This time Domko stopped and looked suspiciously around. He had heard something, but wasn't sure what. They boys kneeled frozen on the ground for what seemed like an eternity. Then, satisfied that they were not in the area, Domko turned and walked out of the bush.

Jumping up the boys ran in the opposite direction from Domko. Branches whipped their faces and legs as they veered off the trail into the thick bush. Tears of frustration streamed down Dennis' face as they ran into the clearing and fell to their knees on the ground. Without a word, Dennis pointed the gun towards the sky and fired again. This time the gun went off.

The brothers looked at each other and their eyes locked. Just what they had suspected was true. Domko was the devil. A feeling of hopelessness washed over them as they realized that no matter how hard they tried, they'd never escape his grasp.

Chapter 11

The Bayton School

IT WAS ALMOST TIME FOR another school year. Mrs. Louise Collier, settled into the teacher's cottage behind the school just prior to the Labour Day long weekend.

At 66 years of age, Louise had worked most of her adult life as a teacher with an old school attitude to her job. This short, stocky teacher believed that discipline and learning went hand-in-hand.

Before accepting the position at Bayton school the year before, she had worked near Lundar, approximately 40 miles south of Ashern. She preferred smaller district schools to the multi-classroom facilities in urban centres.

Louise was pleased to be back at work, the summer break finished. Cobwebs waved lightly as she opened the windows to let in fresh air. She brushed dead flies from the sills as she went, dusting off desks before she swept the floor. When she was finished, she sat down to review the registers from the previous year.

Herbert Metner, secretary-treasurer of the local school board, told her to expect approximately 20 pupils, in grades one to eight that year. She worked all afternoon preparing lesson plans for the first week. Taking a short break, she decided to go through mail that had accumulated during the summer. There were numerous advertisements for teachers supplies plus books, contests and transfer slips for what looked like a family of six children named Pischke. Louise had heard rumours about the family that lived less than a quarter mile from the school. She wondered out loud if Mr. Metner's estimate included these children. One family could make a huge difference in a school this size.

The last piece of mail she opened was a white envelope addressed to the teacher at Bayton school. Since Mr. Metner had already gone through the pile, she decided this piece must be for her. Tearing open the envelope, she pulled out a sympathy greeting card. Puzzled, she opened it. The card read: "To the teacher at Bayton - Our sincerest condolences on the return of the Pischke children." It was signed by a few teachers at the Ashern school.

Six hellions, she thought to herself as she tossed the card into the trash. *Just my luck.*

School began a few days later. Mrs. Collier was curious to see who these Pischke children were. Unfortunately, they were easy to pick out. While most of the children were clean and well dressed for the first day of school, the Pischkes were not. Cow manure covered their ripped clothing and it looked as if they hadn't bathed in a month. They were obviously very poor and neglected since their clothing was torn and poorly fitted.

The oldest boy Walter stuttered badly and was the only one in the family wearing shoes. Men's dress shoes, to be exact, and they looked rather odd on a teenager.

Eunice, the little girl, talked so fast she was difficult to understand. Mrs. Collier had to tell her to slow down numerous times. She was a cute little thing, but jumpy and nervous.

Norman and Steven were unusually quiet for their ages, preferring to sit together which worked well since they were in the same grade.

Then there were the twins. There was something wrong with those two boys who seemed to be in their own little world. They spoke a language that Louise had never heard of before, partly explaining why they had failed grade one twice already. When she addressed the twins, they cowered and said nothing. At eight years-old, they were much too big to be in first grade but she had no other choice but to place them there.

Her first battle with the Pischke children came sooner than she had expected. During opening exercises, they would not stand to sing God Save the Queen, nor did they say the Lord's Prayer. Mrs. Collier took a long ruler and slapped it down on Norman's desk, but the boy refused to stand.

"Our Momma says we don't got to stand up," Norman said. Walter and Steven nodded. They remembered the licking they had received from their mother after she found out they had stood for the exercises at the Ashern school. They weren't going to risk that again.

Mrs. Collier was not amused. Exasperated, she smacked the ruler on the desk a few more times, then across the older boys' knuckles. The other students sat silently as she argued with them. Fearing they'd also be hit with the ruler, the twins slid underneath their desks.

At the end of the day, Mrs. Collier prepared a note which was sent home with Walter. The following morning, Caroline Pischke arrived at the school with her children. Classes were delayed while everyone waited outside and the two women had a discussion.

Caroline explained the religious philosophy of the Jehovah's Witnesses to the teacher, saying that her children did not have to take part in opening exercises. Mrs. Collier finally conceded that while she was opposed to treating children from one family different than the others, since Caroline insisted, she would do so against her better judgement.

It was a heated argument between two strong-willed women, one that even the toughest man on the school board would have shied away from. Everybody knew one thing about Caroline - when she was undecided, she was easily swayed, but once she made up her mind about something, she never changed it.

Caroline marched victoriously out the door as classes began. The Pischke children were instructed from that day forward to stand in the cloakroom during opening exercises. This embarrassed the older children, since their classmates giggled, underlining that the Pischkes were were different from everybody else.

In spite of her disagreement with Caroline, Mrs. Collier softened towards the children. She now understood what the sympathy card had meant - it wasn't that the children were bad but their situation was impossible. It was obvious that these children were neglected and it appeared that Caroline had fallen under the spell of some ridiculous cult. Mrs. Collier was too old to change her ways, but decided to make concessions as far as these poor children were concerned.

It didn't take David and Dennis long to figure out that the more time they spent in school, the less time they spent near Domko. The older boys were forced to stay home from school on many occasions to pound fence posts, shovel manure or pick rocks. School was not important to Domko who bragged that he had only a grade four education and was "but a some goot."

One afternoon the twins decided to talk to their mother about the dogs they had seen chasing cattle. They described the animals to her, asking what type of dog they were. Caroline told the boys that they were called 'Collie' dogs.

"Momma, can we gets a collie dog?" David asked.

"No, those dogs cost too much money," Caroline explained.

"Maybe if them dogs have pups, we can get one?" Dennis asked. "Dogs are always havin' pups and they get drowned."

Caroline smiled but said nothing. Later that evening she told Domko about the conversation, thinking he would find it amusing. Instead he became angry. The next day he cornered the twins in the barn.

"Dennis be some goot for sheet," he sputtered, as he closed in on them. Grabbing the boy by the shirt, he pulled him close. "Yous be vantink collie dogs, eh? I's be showink you collie dogs." He backhanded the boy across the face, sending him flying into the barn wall. David crouched as Domko kicked him in the hip. He strode out of the barn as quickly as he had come in.

"Don't be sayin' no more about Collie dogs," Norman admonished. "You know the ole bastard hates anything he ain't got."

Dennis and David nodded. They were going to have to be more careful about what they said to their mother.

* * * * *

It was a warm September weekend morning when Emma Harwart received a frantic knock at her back door.

"Mrs. Harwart, you gotta come quick!" Eunice panted. "Domko

smashed Rosie an' she's lyin' on the floor!"

Emma slipped on her shoes then grabbed her first aid box. Marjorie, who had been mending at the kitchen table, followed her mother and Eunice as they ran the short distance to Caroline's house.

Now what has he done? Emma asked herself. *That poor child has been through enough.* Rushing through the door, Emma could see the girl lying crumpled on the floor beside the woodstove. There was a fresh bloodstain smeared on the wall above her body.

"She's dead," David said casually as he paced back and forth. "Rosie's dead."

"Yep, she's dead," said Dennis.

The boys' indifference toward their sister unsettled Emma.

How much have these children seen that they are so callous towards another's suffering? she asked herself.

Caroline was kneeling by Rosie, her cheeks stained with tears.

"What happened?" Emma asked as she felt Rosie's neck for a pulse.

"I don't know," she answered weakly. "I was outside in the barn and when I came in found her like this."

"Where's Domko?" Emma asked angrily. "He's the one we should be asking."

Caroline shrugged her shoulders.

Emma turned her attention back to the injured girl. Gently, she began feeling the child's body for broken bones. Bruises in various stages of healing covered her body. Her face was covered in blood form what appeared to be a bleeding nose.

"Rosie," she whispered. "Can you hear me?"

The girl didn't move. Dark bruises were starting to appear on her face and neck.

"I think we should get her up off this cold floor," Emma said, gingerly picking up the limp child. Rosie flinched as Emma carried her to the bedroom with Caroline and the rest of the children following closely behind. Lying Rosie on the bed, Emma turned to Caroline.

"I think we should get Doc Steenson to come see her," Emma said. "Being unconscious like this is a bad sign."

Caroline looked at her daughter lying motionless on the bed. She knew that Domko would not approve of the doctor visiting the farm. "Can we wait awhile and see how she does first?" she asked.

Astonished at Caroline's answer, Emma made no comment. She then turned her attention back to Rosie who began to stir and moan in pain.

"I'll stay with her then," Emma said, ushering everyone else out of the room. "Marjorie, you go home. Caroline, get me a cool, damp cloth."

It was evening before Emma arrived home. Gus and Marjorie met her at the door with a barrage of questions.

"Well, it looks as if Rosie is going to be alright," she said. "I'm going to town tomorrow and I plan to report this to the police."

"If you do that, then Caroline will be in trouble too," Gus said, trying to calm his wife. "If the social workers start coming around, she'll lose those children for sure."

"Well, maybe it would be the best thing for them," she said. "She must know that too. You should have seen Caroline. She was so scared of Domko that she wouldn't even call the doctor. A mother shouldn't have to put up with watching her kids get beat up like that."

Gus took the first aid kit from his wife and motioned for her to sit at the table. Marjorie sat down beside her mother, anxious to hear what they were saying.

"Did you ever find out from Caroline anything about Domko being deported?" Gus asked. "He's not a Canadian citizen you know, and I'd heard that after beating up that fellow in Ashern that the police came down pretty hard on him. Did she ever mention it?"

"All I know is she could have signed a paper to get deportation started but she refused," said Emma. "No doubt they asked her to sign while Domko was sitting there. That would be just like those police, you know. They expect her to stand up to him while they are there and then fend for herself as soon as they leave."

The Harwarts continued to mull over Caroline's situation well into the night. They sided with Caroline, but found it difficult not to question her motives. They found the whole situation puzzling and frustrating.

"The less we see Domko the better," Emma said. "And you," she said pointing her finger at Marjorie, "you stay away from him. He's crazy and one of these days he's gonna kill somebody."

Marjorie nodded solemnly. Staying away from Domko would not be a problem for her.

* * * * *

It was an unusually warm and dry fall. Walter spent one mid-October afternoon out by the grainary where he repaired and greased his muskrat traps, for the winter trapping season. He had more than a dozen traps that would provide him with an opportunity to make extra money. He had trapped a few years earlier, but had abandoned the hobby when the family moved to Ashern. He daydreamed as he tested the traps, remembering everything his father had taught him. Now his father's traps belonged to him.

I'm gonna make enough money to buy myself a motor scooter, he thought. A friend from the church had a nice scooter that Walter had been eyeing for some time. Now it was for sale and Walter had asked the man to hold it for him until he earned enough money to pay for it.

Domko stood in the kitchen and peered out the window. He watched Walter working diligently by the pumphouse. They boy had been there most of the afternoon, but Domko was too lazy to go and find out what he was doing.

"Vat Valters be doink?" he asked Caroline in a gruff voice.

"Getting his traps ready."

"Vat he's be doink?"

"He's going to start trapping again," Caroline said. "There's good money in fur."

Domko thought for a moment, then stared out the window with no expression.

"Mooney?" he asked quietly.

Caroline nodded. "Lots of farmers around here trap."

Lighting another cigarette, Domko stared out the window again. Since there was money to be made, the idea suddenly appealed to him. He decided that he should encourage the boy's hobby and maybe buy a few traps for himself.

When there was enough money to buy rolled oats, Caroline cooked a big pot of porridge in the morning.

Then while she and the older children milked the cows, Domko would eat his breakfast and appear in the barn when finished. Once the chores were done, the older children were allowed to eat while the younger ones fended for themselves. Sometimes the porridge they were able to scrounge in the morning was all they ate the entire day.

One morning the twins waited patiently for Domko to go to the barn before appearing in the kitchen. They jumped from bed as soon as they heard the outside door slam shut. Hungrily, each grabbed a bowl from the cupboard, then began spooning big globs of porridge into them.

"Hey Denny," David said, pointing to the shelf by the door. "Want some cream?"

Dennis' eyes widened. Domko only allowed the family to use skim milk for their porridge. The cream from the daily milkings was saved, cooled, then taken to town and sold. Domko kept the cream can up high so that the children couldn't get at it. The boys had taken cream once before and had been caught. While David had escaped, Dennis received a severe beating for the theft.

"C'mon Dennis," David said. "You watch at the window an' I'll get it."

The thought of cool cream on his porridge was more than Dennis could resist. Agreeing, he ran to the window, looked out and signalled David that nobody was coming.

Grabbing a cup from the counter, David pushed a stool under the shelf, then stood on it. Reaching up, he had to stand on his toes to get the cup into the can. Dipping it into the cream, he was careful not to spill any of it as he hurried back to the table, pouring it on Dennis' porridge before running back for more.

Dennis grabbed the bowl and ate hungrily, hoping Domko wouldn't come back before he finished. Dave reached into the cream can once again, but this time had a difficult time dipping the cup into the can. He pushed down, but felt resistance. Standing on his toes, he tilted the can slightly towards him and peered in. Floating on top of the cream was a large, black rat. It must have fallen into the cream and drowned overnight.

Startled, David pushed the can back and jumped down from the stool. Wiping his hands feverishly on his shirt, he ran to his brother.

"Dennis!" he choked. "There's a drownded rat in the cream!"

"Wha?" Dennis said, stopping in mid-sentence. Disgusted, he spit the porridge onto the table then stuffed his shirt into his mouth to wipe it dry. The thought of the rat turned his stomach. Within a few seconds, he was gagging and vomitting on the floor.

David grabbed Dennis' bowl and scraped the remaining porridge into the slop pail. He shuddered to think what Domko would do if he saw the wasted porridge and cream, so he took the spoon and stirred the contents of the slop pail until the cream disappeared.

Taking his own bowl, he scraped the porridge back into the pot. The mixture had cooled and fell in a congealed glob in the bottom. Dennis cleaned up his vomit, while David returned the stool to the corner. They could hear their mother and siblings coming in from the barn.

Caroline and the boys stepped into the kitchen, each carrying a pail of milk. Pouring it into the separator, Eunice sat down at the machine and began turning the handle. The older boys grabbed a bowl of porridge and ate quickly before going back outside to finish chores.

The twins sat solemnly at the kitchen table. Once the initial shock of the rat began to wear off, both boys began seeing some humour in the situation and were beginning to find it difficult not to laugh.

Domko came in and sat at his usual spot in the corner. Wet manure dripped from his boots, as he stirred sugar into a fresh cup of coffee. He called the twins 'goot for sheet' then reaching across the table, backhanded David across the head for giggling. Abruptly, he got up from his place and went to the wash basin at the far end of the kitchen. He and Caroline began conversing in Polish. Domko splashed some fresh water on his face and then covered it with shaving cream. He took a straight razor and began shaving off two weeks growth of beard.

The twins looked at each other and smiled. Domko was going to town and it was as if a tremendous weight had been lifted from their shoulders. They waited in silence for what seemed like hours before he was ready to go. Disappearing into the other room, he came back a few minutes later wearing his 'town clothes'. He didn't bother to bathe but simply slipped the clean clothes over his dirty long underwear.

Caroline got Kathy ready to go, then disappeared outside. Domko went to the shelf and reached up for the cream can. Placing it on the floor, he grunted as he looked inside. The rat was floating on its side.

"Greedy bastard," he said. Reaching into the can he grabbed the rat with his dirty hand then threw it on the floor. Hoisting the can onto his shoulder, he carried it outside to the waiting tractor. He returned a few moments later, kicking the rat aside. Yelling at the twins, he told them to get into the crawlspace under the house, through the hole in the living room floor.

Domko glanced around for the girls, but couldn't find them since Rosie had snuck under the bed and Eunice had darted out the door and ran to school. He wasn't too worried about the girls, but was concerned that the twins might eat something while he was gone.

The boys cowered from Domko as he pulled back the door covering the dark hole. He grunted at the boys, commanding them to climb inside. The cool draft on their feet made them instantly regret that in their eagerness to eat that morning, they hadn't taken the time to find socks. They also wished they had run to school with Eunice.

Dennis climbed into the hole after David, then Domko slammed the lid shut overhead. It took a few minutes before the boys' eyes adjusted to the darkness. The crawlspace was cold and damp and the smell of rodent feces permeated the stale air. The space was filled with dirt and scraps of building material had been discarded when the house was originally built. There was only about three feet of headroom so the twins had to crouch to move around. After their encounter with the dead rat just a few hours before, each jumped nervously at every noise.

"Do rats live under houses?" Dennis asked.

"I don't thinks so," David said looking nervously around.

The boys amused themselves by reminiscing about the enjoyable times they had while living in Ashern. Sitting on the damp ground, they waited patiently for one of their siblings to open the door. As usual, their conversation was about survival.

"Dennis, you gots to run faster from Flatfoot. He gets you all the time."

"I know," he said. "But I can't move when he yells."

"Yeah, but he smashes you even when it ain't your fault," David said remembering the first serious beating. "Dennis, how come you said you took the chocolate anyway when everybody knows Rosie did it?"

Dennis thought for a moment. "I didn't want Satan to kill her."

It was dark outside before Domko and Caroline arrived home. Walter had let the twins out of the hole in the late afternoon, but only after they promised to jump back in before Domko got home. Eunice kept watch and when they heard the tractor coming, the boys scrambled back into the hole. The children sat quietly as Domko, their mother and Kathy came in. Domko was in a reasonable mood which helped lift everyone's spirits. A large bag of flour, sugar and rolled oats was unloaded from the wagon. Domko called Walter outside. He was beaming when he returned a few minutes later.

"Domko b-bought me some traps," he said slyly to Norman, raising his eyebrows. "I'm gonna trap all winter an' s-spring. Maybe I won't h-hafta go to school."

"Where are the twins?" Caroline asked.

Eunice pointed to the front room. "In the hole," she said quietly.

Caroline got up and went to the front room. Lifting the lid she peered in. "What are you boys doin' down there?" she asked.

"D-domko p-put us here," David stammered.

"Well, come on out," she said, extending her hand.

Caroline considered confronting Domko about putting the twins in the hole, but decided against it. He was in a good mood and she didn't want to risk making him angry. It was a cool night and she didn't feel like sleeping in the barn again. Besides, whatever they'd done to cause his anger was long forgotten. She encouraged the boys to mix with the rest of the children, but to be quiet and not draw attention to themselves.

The following morning before school David finished feeding the chickens and pig, then decided to find Dennis, who had disappeared before breakfast.

David skipped along the trail through the bush towards school. He'd wanted to find his only toy first, which he had hidden along the path. It was the front wheel from an old wheelbarrow that he'd found one day out behind the barn. It was about 18" in diameter with a wide spoke sticking out of the center on both sides of the wheel. David found he could push the wheel along the ground by holding the spoke. It was fun to run with the wheel, but Domko had seen him playing once and threatened to destroy it, so David was careful to hide it after that.

He called the toy his 'wee-wee' and thought about how he seldom let Dennis play with it. His twin had been sad lately, so David decided that he'd let Dennis push the wee-wee home after school. He'd hidden it just off the path, close to the church. As he hurried along he recalled how Domko had bought Walter traps a few days before. He couldn't understand why nice things like that were never done for him and Dennis.

As David rounded a small bend in the path, he suddenly sensed that something was drastically wrong at this usually safe spot. He came to a full halt, then threw his arms over his head as he jumped off of the path. He could senses there was something in the trees above him. David looked up and screamed in horror. There, hanging over his head along the path, were three full grown dogs. Each had a rope tied around its neck. The rope had been strung over a pole that was suspended horizontally between two trees. The ends of the ropes were tied neatly to the trunk of one tree.

David stared at the animals in disbelief. Although he had never seen the dogs up close before, he knew these were the neighbour's prized Collie dogs that he and Dennis had been talking about. They were the same golden colour and looked to be about the right size. Their eyes bulged with death and their tongues hung loosely out of their mouths.

David turned and ran back towards the house, his mind numb with horror. He remembered hearing dogs barking nearby the night before, but had thought nothing of it. Domko must have caught the dogs then led them to the spot and strangled them. That's what he'd meant when he'd said, "I's be showink you but a some Collie Dogs!" Only he could be that cruel.

David ran through the yard into the house. "Momma!" he yelled as he stepped into the kitchen. "You gots to come!"

Caroline was standing in the kitchen chastising the older boys who were as visibly upset as David. She was telling them to be quiet and not tell anyone what they'd found. Domko was always fighting with one neighbour or another and suspected these might be George and Nina Kiesman's dogs. Caroline told the boys that she didn't want any more trouble with the neighbours and that they should keep quiet.

Domko sat chuckling at the table.

"That means you too," Caroline said turning to David. "Now I don't want to hear another word about no Collie dogs."

David began crying as he ran out of the house. At that moment he needed his mother to wrap her arms around him in comfort. Instead he'd been admonished. David suddenly realized how much he needed Dennis. Instinctively he reached out with his right hand, but Dennis was not there. Panic overtook him.

Where's Dennis? he asked himself as he looked frantically around the yard. He felt lost without his twin and wondered if Dennis had met the same fate as the dogs. The thought of Dennis hanging by his neck somewhere sent David running down the road in blind panic. He glanced nervously into the bush as he went. His heart pounded heavily in his chest as visions of trying to survive without his twin raced through his mind.

He ran up the school room steps, then burst through the door, interrupting a story Mrs. Collier was reading to the class. David could hear nothing but a hollow ringing in his ears as the students turned to face him. The children were startled by his panic, but soon began to giggle as the teacher scolded him for being late and disrupting class.

There sitting at his desk at the very front of the room was Dennis. He'd come to school early, along the road so he hadn't seen the dogs. A wave of relief passed over David as his twin smiled brightly from the front of the room.

Chapter 12

Walter's Christmas

"I CAN'T NEVER UNDERSTAND WHAT that stupid bastard is sayin'," Norman complained one day. "He beats the shit out of me an' I never know why."

Walter nodded. "M-me too. We're not goddamned Pollacks, how are we s-s'posed to understand him?"

It was a cool, November day and the pair were in the field forking hay onto the hayrack. It was the first of three trips from the field to the barn they'd have to make that afternoon. Old enough to understand that the living conditions at the farm were deplorable, the boys were beginning to rebel against Domko's tyranny.

"I'm gettin' outta here as soon as I can," Norman said. "I'm gonna move away an' get a plane."

Walter nodded. He believed that Norman would move away someday and become a pilot since he was plane crazy. Walter wished he could be as tough spirited as his younger brother.

"H-hey what did old Squeezer get you for yesterday anyway?" he asked. The older Meisner boys nicknamed Domko 'Lemon Squeezer' or 'Squeezer' because he liked to squeeze lemons into his tea. It was an odd nickname and one that was never said to his face.

"He wanted me to get eggs but I thought he said 'axe'," he explained. "So I walk over holdin' this axe and he gets so made he almost shits himself. I shoulda smashed him over the head with it."

Both boys laughed and began shoving each other into the hay. Walter pushed his cap back and began sneering at his brother.

"Yous be goot for sheet!" he said, pretending to hit Norman who laid laughing in the hay. Their antics pleased Bruno who began running around the boys, barking excitedly. Norman reached out and grabbed the dog, pulling him into the hay. Bruno's big wet tongue lapped his face.

"He sure is a good dog, eh?" Norman said stroking the animal's head. "We don't need no collie dog as long as we got Bruno."

Remembering the dead dogs suddenly took the fun out of their play. The boys sat and stroked Bruno somberly as he watched the boys with thoughtful eyes. Always in-tune with the children's feelings, Bruno would frisk and play when the children were happy and sit quietly beside them when they were sad. He was a devoted companion to Kathy, who grabbed him by the fur as he led her around the farm.

"Well, we'd better get finished before he comes back," Walter said.

"Where's momma?" Dennis asked his twin.

"Don't know," David answered.

Caroline had disappeared early that morning and nobody seemed to know where she had gone. Their older brothers were outside and Domko had gone to check on them.

"The lamp don't got no fuel," Dennis said. "D'ya think we should fill it up?"

David examined the oil lamp sitting on the kitchen table. Pulling off the top, he stuck his finger into the lamp and found there was no fuel. The inside of the small house was dark as the weather was dreary that day.

Picking up the lamp, he carried it to the door where there was a large metal kerosene can. Bending, he unscrewed the cap from the can. Then, he tilted it, peering in, in an attempt to see how much oil there was.

"Lemme do it," Dennis said, grabbing a box of matches from beside the cook stove. "I'll look inside."

Standing beside his brother, Dennis lit a match then stuck it inside the can. Suddenly, there was a bright flash of light and an explosion that sent both boys sprawling across the room. Dennis screamed in pain as flames from the can seared his face and burned the front of his hair. Both boys lay on the floor stunned for a few moments before realizing what had happened.

"You o.k. Dennis?" David asked as he crawled across the floor.

"My face, it's burnded," Dennis said. "Is it gone?"

David pulled his brother's hands down and examined the injury. Black soot covered Dennis' face and his hair was still smoldering. The injury didn't look that bad, but David could tell by his brother's expression that the damage to the outer layer of skin, especially on his forehead and nose, stung horribly.

"We gots to get the doctor," David said. "'cause your nose might fall off."

Dennis began to cry. The initial shock was beginning to subside and the injury to his face was becoming quite painful. Also, he didn't want to lose his nose.

"Where's Momma?" he asked.

The boys sat helplessly on the floor in the kitchen. Within a few minutes Domko came inside, towering over them as he surveyed the scene. The matches had spilled beside the mis-shapen can and the oil lamp had rolled to the middle of the floor. It took only a few moments for Domko to realize what had happened. David braced himself for the worst as Dennis cried nearby.

Suddenly, Domko threw back his head and roared with laughter. He looked back at Dennis' burned face, then laughed heartily again.

The twins sat stunned on the floor. It was the first time they had ever seen the man laugh. Dennis whimpered in pain and humiliation as Domko stood above him mocking the injury.

"Dennnnis," he cooed. "Hows be but a some face? It's be oogly."

For the rest of the day, Domko sat in his usual spot, smoking and chuckling to himself. The older boys came in late that afternoon and their mother returned shortly afterwards. The suggestion that the boy be taken to the doctor was met with more laughter from Domko.

"I's not be spendink mooney on Dennis," he said sarcastically as he dismissed the idea outright.

By early December, everyone in the community and members of her church knew that Caroline was expecting yet another child in the spring. Nothing more was said about the earlier pregnancy which Caroline dismissed as a miscarriage. Some people knew that she'd carried the baby almost to term. They also suspected that it was a beating from Domko that caused the early delivery and subsequent death of the child.

The Harwarts and Deightons were disgusted because Caroline remained with Domko, in spite of how badly he treated her and the children. Most other neighbours refused to get involved in the situation.

Caroline's common-law relationship with Domko prompted senior members of the Witness congregation to pressure her marry and live in accordance with the Bible. Weekly visits by church members turned into pre-marital counselling sessions with the entire family being required to attend. The children were expected to sit quietly for up to two hours as passages from the Bible were read. Caroline was asked to acknowledge and repeat the passages many times over.

One evening the conversation became more personal. Problems that the couple expected to face were raised by church members. Domko was at his solicitous best.

"The problem be her," Domko said in his most innocent voice. Sucking on his cigarette, he then pointed to Caroline. "She's not be lookink after some keets."

Domko said that he wanted to marry Caroline so they could raise the family together, but her reluctance to discipline the children bothered him. He was upset that the children didn't listen and that he had to be the disciplinarian. He went on to explain that the plate in his head caused him grievous headaches, saying that the children's unruly behaviour was affecting his health to the point where it was hard for him to work.

The children sat solemnly at the table and listened. David and Dennis looked at each other in amazement. Both turned to their mother who watched without expression as Domko continued to criticize her and the children. The man from the church listened intently then looked at each child. As his eyes met theirs, they sank one by one in their chairs and lowered their eyes to the floor.

To the Witness member, it was obvious that Domko was paying the price for Bill Pischke's lenience. The man could understand Domko's point of view - after all he wouldn't have wanted to raise these children either, especially the twins who were so backward they refused to speak English. Caroline was fortunate to have Domko in her life and the man told her so. Nowhere else would she find someone to take on the responsibility of such a huge, unruly family.

The following week, the children sat for nearly two hours listening to recitations from the Bible. Bored by the monotony of the lessons, the older boys started horsing around. Tilting their chairs back, they began a secret contest to see who could tilt his chair back the farthest without falling over.

Dennis was sitting closest to the door with David on the left of him and Steven on the right. Eager to be in the game, Dennis tilted his chair back as well. He started to teeter and before he could regain his balance, Steven reached out with his foot and kicked his brother over. Dennis and the chair slammed against the door, and the boy rolled outside. The children burst into laughter, but the adults were not pleased. Domko jumped up and confronted him as he sprawled on the ground.

"You's be goot for nuthink!" he whispered, kicking Dennis in the side as the boy scrambled to get up. Domko stormed back into the house and Dennis followed meekly behind.

David shook his head.

Poor Dennis, he thought. *Dennis always gets it, no matter what.*

In spite of his erratic nature, Domko made a few friends in the area. These were people who either did not realize how he treated Caroline and the children, or people who did not like the family and believed they deserved the treatment they received.

Each fall and spring Domko went to Winnipeg with one of these friends. His two day absence meant the children were able to relax and enjoy themselves. Caroline also seemed relaxed when he was gone, which made the older children wonder why their mother didn't kick him out of the house for good.

When he returned, Domko brought a large cardboard box full of clothing home with him. The clothing had been purchased from a second-hand store. While some of it was ugly or worn out, the children didn't dare complain for fear he'd become angry. They scrambled for mitts, coats and sweaters. There were enough shoes and boots in the box for each child and everyone received a matched pair, except for David who ended up with one running shoe and a black rubber boot.

When the clothes were handed out, the children were made sit on the kitchen floor and watch while Domko called Kathy to his side. He pulled a brand new coat and warm, felt-lined boots from a bag. He tried the items on his daughter who was then told to walk back and forth so everyone could look at her.

"See," he cooed to Caroline. "I's be but a some goot father."

The biggest event of the year was fast approaching. The annual school Christmas Concert brought all members of the community together. It was anticipated with excitement by children and adults alike.

Preparations began in late November, for the big event which was to be held a few days before Christmas break. There was a tremendous amount of pressure on the students to prepare their costumes and memorize their lines. Concert preparations occupied most of the day as the date drew closer.

The Pischke children were not allowed to participate since their religion forbade them to acknowledge such pagan rituals. According to their religion, Christ was not born in December and even if he had been, celebrating his birthday would be considered inappropriate.

Instead, the children were segregated in a corner of the room and given extra mathematics and spelling assignments. This made them feel badly as they watched the other children excitedly painting murals and singing Christmas carols.

Walter was particularly interested in the idea of Christmas. He discussed the concept secretly with his classmates, then passed the information on to his siblings. What they were told conflicted drastically with their mother's beliefs, but Christmas sounded so wonderful he wanted it to be true.

The day of the concert finally arrived. Every family would be there except the Pischkes and this bothered Walter. That evening he snuck out of the house and ran to the school. As he neared the old building, he could see warm lights shining festively through the windows. The resonant sound of singing followed by laughing and clapping grew louder as he approached. He climbed the steps to the school and quietly opened the door to the cloakroom. A mixture of different colognes greeted him from the many coats hung along the wall.

Walter watched silently from the small vestibule as his classmates acted out a scene. A chorus of giggles erupted from the audience as one small shepherd adjusted the towel on his head, then waved and smiled a wide toothless grin to his parents. Then suddenly all was silent as Marjorie stepped out from behind a handmade tree dressed as an angel.

"Fear not," she called out. "I bring you tidings of great joy. For tonight born unto you in the town of Bethlehem is a child and his name shall be Jesus Christ."

The choir of older girls standing on a bench behind the scene began singing, their voices quiet at first but then growing stronger as parents gave approving nods. A few of the mothers dabbed the corners of their eyes with handkerchiefs.

"Hark the herald angels sing," they sang sweetly. "Glory to the newborn King! Peace on earth and mercy mild, God and sinners reconciled."

Walter stood and watched while a warm feeling came over him. He could feel the love in the room and had a sense of what this celebration was all about. The concert was almost finished when a large man in a red suit walked through the door. Hearing the noise behind him, Walter turned and recognized the white bearded fellow as Santa Claus, the man his classmates had told him about. Santa had come to the concert just as the children had promised! He gave Walter a nod and a wink, then carrying his sack burst in, bellowing a chorus of 'HO HO HO's'. The boy watched in amazement as the children gathered around and Santa Claus handed out candy and small toys to the children.

Marjorie noticed Walter standing at the end of the room. She caught his eye then gave him a timid wave. Marjorie looked truly beautiful in her costume and he smiled meekly at her. Then, he slipped out the door, realizing it was time to go before others saw him there.

During the walk home, he became convinced that Christmas was a wonderful thing. After seeing Santa Claus face-to-face, he decided that this year he would hang one of his socks by the woodstove on Christmas Eve so that Santa would fill it with toys and candy. Then his mother wouldn't be able to deny this was all true.

The following day he told his siblings about his plan. Steven and Norman scoffed at the idea but Eunice and the twins listened intently. They were too frightened to discuss this with their mother who had disapproved of such ideas in the past .

Christmas Eve arrived and both Caroline and Domko were in a pleasant mood. Although he was careful to not let the Jehovah's Witnesses know, Domko was a devout Catholic who had no intention of giving up his religion.

Remnants of Catholicism also remained deeply instilled in Caroline. As much as she hated to admit it, the holiday season still made her feel warm inside. She cooked a nice supper and the entire family ate well that night. The children played quietly while Walter worked diligently to make a hook to attach to one of his largest, cleanest socks. Steven and Norman chided him as he prepared to hang his stocking by the woodstove.

"You guys will see," Walter said. "I'll be the only kid here who'll get candy an' toys from Santa Claus."

The boys laughed. Domko listened but said nothing while Caroline watched her eldest son. She did not discourage the boy from hanging his sock on the woodstove before he went to bed. This surprised the twins who had been warned strongly against believing in such paganism. They had been taught that other religions were evil and that the people who believed them were wrong. They were discouraged from associating with people outside their religion because of the bad influence it created. Here Walter was behaving exactly as they had been told not to.

On Christmas morning, Walter awoke and jumped from the bed. He ran to the front room to find his sock still hanging by the stove. He stood for a moment, his eyes wide with wonder as he looked at the long black, bulging sock.

"See!" he said to his siblings, who were gathering around to look. "I told you!"

Grabbing the sock from the hook he excitedly stretched open the top and stuck his hand inside. Freezing for a moment, his mouth dropped and his face reddened. Pulling his hand out he stared in disbelief at a fistful of potato peelings. Emptying the contents of the sock on the floor he found three rocks. Steven and Norman couldn't help themselves and began laughing at their brother. Walter looked from his siblings to his mother then at Domko. Tears stung his eyes as he ran past his brothers who were now laughing so hard they rolled on the floor. As he grabbed his coat and stormed out the door, Domko sat chuckling quietly at the kitchen table.

Caroline knew that she should chase after Walter, but couldn't bring herself to find and comfort the boy. She thought back to her own childhood and shook her head. Believing in the Catholic God had never done her any good.

It is time Walter toughened up, she thought. *Life is miserable an' the sooner he realizes it, the better off he'll be.*

Walter didn't return to school that January. He was determined to make money on his trapline and spent most of his time in the bush. His spare moments were spent stretching and curing the skins in preparation for sale in the spring. Domko and Caroline supported his decision to work instead of going to school.

Since Christmas, Walter had withdrawn somewhat from his siblings. He preferred to be by himself now. Since he was trapping most days, Norman and Stephen had to do his share of the chores. Walter kept it a secret that as soon as he had enough money saved, he was going to move away from the farm.

They should get used to me not bein' there, he thought to himself. *I won't be around to do no more chores or make fun of. Then they won't be laughin' at me no more when I got my own place."*

Meanwhile, the other children were expected to behave and work like grown-ups. They never went to town so school was the only contact they had with other children.

They had little idea of the world outside their parcel of land. The longer they lived away from Ashern, the more backward they became. Visitors to the farm were rare, so the appearance of a strange car sent the children running into the bush.

The younger children feared all men, except Jim and Gus. As time wore on, basic survival instincts began to rule the children. They ate greedily at their siblings expense and became desensitized to each other's suffering.

Domko's constant belittlement stripped them of their confidence and self-worth.

After a particularly terrifying week in early January, the twins fled in the evening and ended up on the Harwart's doorstep. Emma answered a vigorous knock to find Dennis and David standing there without coats or mitts. Dennis was wearing a short sleeved shirt, pants and a pair of dress shoes that looked too big. David had on a sweater, thin pants and a rubber boot on one foot, running shoe on the other. Their hair was matted and their faces were dirty.

"Domko k-kicked us out," David said. "C-an we come in?"

Emma opened the door wide and hurried them into the house. The days had been relatively warm, rising up to 10 degrees Farenheit during the day. At night, though, it dropped way below zero. This was unseasonably warm for January and Emma knew it wouldn't last. These children would not survive if Domko kicked them out during a cold spell.

Marjorie was completing her homework at the table. The look of terror on their faces soon vanished as they stood and talked to the patient girl. Their speaking skills were improving as they learned more English at school. Other people were beginning to understand them when the boys made the effort and took the time to speak real words. Mrs. Collier was surprisingly patient with the boys and even put them in grade two for the second term.

Emma fed the twins, then sent them to the front room where their chattering wouldn't interrupt Marjorie. They sat on the chesterfield and looked around. To them, the Harwart's modest home felt like a palace. The sight of Gus sitting contentedly in an easy chair made them long for a real father figure.

"Hey Dennis," David said, pointing to a pair of stereo speakers mounted on the wall. "Look."

Puzzled, Dennis looked at the small brown boxes and shrugged his shoulders. David began explaining what he guessed the boxes were for.

Gus peered over his glasses and began watching the boys. He listened as David pointed to the radio and speakers. Getting up off the chesterfield, the twins went to the wall to examine the boxes that had been crudely fastened to the wall. Their eyes were wide in amazement. They spoke to each other as if nobody else was in the room while their hosts listened intently.

"Big shots," David said in an admiring voice. "They gots radio all over the place!"

Dennis seemed very impressed as he looked around him. This truly was the best house they'd ever been in. They remembered being here before when they were younger, but had been too small to notice their surroundings.

"Well, it's time to go to bed," Emma said, interrupting their conversation. "You all have school tomorrow and I don't want Marjorie failing her test by stayin' up too late."

Emma cleaned the boys up as best as she could, then sent them into Marjorie's bedroom. They went willingly, anxious to sleep in the bunk beds again. Emma followed soon afterwards and tucked Dennis into the top bed while David crawled into the bottom bunk. Marjorie came in a short time later, crawling into her bed along the opposite wall. The three talked for awhile until Marjorie drifted off to sleep.

Dennis brought the sheets and quilt up to his nose and took a deep breath. The blankets smelled so clean and warm a feeling of joy passed over him. This bed was comfortable and he loved being in it all by himself. In the silence he could hear David breathing quietly below him.

Dennis knew that when morning came, he and his brother would have to go back home. He thought long and hard for a reason not to leave. How badly he wished he had been born to Gus and Emma!

"Gus, I don't want to send the twins home tomorrow," Emma said as she climbed into bed. "I'll never forgive myself if anything happens to those boys."

Gus thought for a moment. "We've fought enough with Domko about his treatment of the family," he said. "If we try to keep those boys here, can you imagine what will happen?"

"Yes," Emma agreed, "But if we involve a social worker, maybe they can step in and do something to make it legal. It would be good if they lived here with us, then they could visit their mother whenever they wanted but still be away from Domko."

The couple discussed Caroline's life and her children's future well into the night. They concluded it was Caroline's responsibility to kick Domko out of the house. How much could they interfere when the children's own mother seemed indifferent about their care? Neither wanted hard feelings with their neighbours, but they felt guilty about not doing more to help the children.

"Besides Emma," Gus said, "I'm getting too old to start raising two young boys. Our family's all grown and it's almost time for us to retire."

Emma agreed that the children weren't her responsibility. Why did she feel such a need to help when her efforts seemed so unappreciated by Caroline?

"If only Bill were still alive this wouldn't be happening," she sighed. "If he knew what was going on in that house, it would break his heart."

Chapter 13

A night in the bush

CAROLINE ARRIVED THE FOLLOWING AFTERNOON and persuaded the twins to go home with her. Emma could overhear her telling the boys that things were going to be better as they pulled on the jackets she had brought along. The twins were apprehensive, but wanted desperately to please their mother. Caroline gave Emma a timid wave then left.

A few nights later, the children were asleep in bed with their mother when Domko stormed into the bedroom. He and Caroline had argued earlier in the day about the Harwarts, so she had refused to sleep in his bed. Domko was angry about this, warning the children that he'd kill Gus if they ever went to Harwart's house again. The children awoke with a start to find Domko attacking their mother. The older boys ran out the kitchen door towards the barn with Eunice and Rosie close behind, while the twins lay trapped between their mother and the wall.

Domko yelled at the twins. He began punching them with his fist as they tried desperately to get to the end of the bed. He was angrier than they'd ever seen. He seemed fueled by passion as he threw his entire body on top of their mother. It appeared to the twins that he was smothering her and they ran quickly out of the room.

"Get your coat Denny," David said as he pulled on his boot and shoe. Reaching up, he grabbed a coat from the hook and ran out the door with Dennis on his heels. Nervously, they looked around. It was a dark, cold night and they weren't sure which direction to go.

"Should we go to Harwarts?" Dennis asked his brother who was leading the way.

"No, goin' to Harwarts makes Satan mad an' he said he's gonna kill Gus," David reasoned. "Let's go to Deightons."

Dennis nodded as they started the long walk across the fields and bush to Jim's farm. He laboured to keep up with his brother since his leg was still healing from a bad beating he'd received earlier that week. Both boys found it difficult to make their way through the snow banks which had drifted three feet high in some places. Fortunately, the recent warm weather followed by a cold snap had created a thick crust on top of the snow, so the boys were able to walk on top. Occasionally one of their feet would break through a soft spot and a leg would plunge deep into the snow. David had to stop to empty his rubber boot many times, while

Dennis' ankles were rubbed raw.

Fortunately for Dennis, he'd grabbed Walter's coat which was too big so the arms hung down past his wrists. David's coat was too small so he tucked his arms high up in the sleeves to prevent his hands from freezing.

After more than an hour of walking south-east through bush and frozen swamp, with no hat or mitts, David couldn't go any further. Both boys had lost all feeling in their frozen toes and their fingers were so numb from the cold that they could no longer bend them. They could see a light in the distance, but had no idea how much further it was to the neighbour's farm.

"Denny, I think we gotta stop," David said as they trudged through the bush.

"We gots to keep going 'cause I think we're almost there," Dennis said.

"I'm mixed up," David said. "I don't know if we're going the right way no-more. I think we shoulda got there already."

"But I don't wants to sleep in the bush," Dennis said. "It's too cold out."

"It'll be o.k.," David said reassuringly. "I gots matches so we can make a fire."

Having experienced a few cold nights alone in the bush in early fall, David had snuck a box of matches from the kitchen drawer which he kept in the breast pocket of his coat. Domko noticed the matches were missing, but so many things had being taken from the house lately that he didn't know who to blame. The children were stealing supplies in order to survive. Learning to live in the bush had become a matter of life and death for them. Domko was at his worst in the dead of winter, the most dangerous time of year. During January, it wasn't uncommon for temperatures to dip to 35 degrees below zero farenheit.

The twins marched about 100 yards into the bush until they came to a trail that ran east to west. It looked like a reasonable spot to spend the night. They gathered some deadfall and piled the branches and logs against two trees that were growing close together. Using their feet, they cleared snow from the ground to make a modified fire pit. They peeled the damp bark from the fallen branches exposing the dry, seasoned wood. It took nearly a dozen matches before their kindling sparked a good fire. Taking sticks, they scraped the ground close to the fire until most of the snow was pushed aside. They sat on the ground side-by-side, slowly adding wood to the fire until it was burning well. They warmed their hands and feet, then gradually laid down on the ground. Pressing their bodies close together they tried to sleep. The sharp cracking of tree branches was the only sound to interrupt the cold, clear darkness of night.

The boys slept fitfully, waking many times to add wood to the fire and warm their freezing hands and feet. The coldest part of the morning came right before dawn.

"Davey, I'm hungry," Dennis said, no longer able to sit still. Pacing in front of the fire, he turned to his brother. "What are we gonna do?"

"I'm hungry too," David replied. "We'll wait here 'til almost lunchtime then go to Deightons."

"Why don't we go now?"

"If we go too soon they might make us go to school," he reasoned. "Then Domko might see us."

Dennis agreed that it would be best to wait.

Jim shivered as his bare feet touched the cold floor. The fire in the house had gone out a few hours ago so the room had cooled considerably. Making a fire in the big wood stove in the living room was the first thing he did each winter morning. Before long, the house would be warm and cheery. Ruby would make coffee and breakfast while he milked the cows. He would then return to eat before the morning chores. It was a morning ritual he shared with most farmers in the district and one he enjoyed.

Jim opened the outside door, the brisk air striking his face like a slap. The thermometer nailed to the side of the house read 18 degrees below zero farenheit. It was a typical January day, cold and clear. As he walked toward the barn, Jim could see the sun beginning to rise in the east. Beyond it, he spotted a thin cloud of smoke rising in the bush about a mile away. He stopped and squinted.

"What would be burning in the bush?" he asked out loud as he reached down to pat his dog who was awakening in a nearby pile of hay.

The most likely possibility, he thought, *is that a plane has crashed in the night.*

There was a lot of aviation activity in the area since the Canadian Forces Base Gypsumville, about 35 miles north of Moosehorn was in full operation. He often saw planes flying low overhead, sometimes three a day. He could think of no other reason for a fire in his bush during the middle of winter.

Quickly, he ran to the barn to harness the horses thinking he might have to rescue someone from the bush. He hitched the horses to the sleigh and within a short time, the team was pulling him along the familiar path he used weekly to bring hay in from the field. The animals lowered their heads as they ploughed a fresh trail through the deep snow. They came to the trail that ran through the bush. Jim hoped that whatever was on fire was close by since it was the only part of the bush that was accessible.

The team was less than a half a mile into the bush when Jim saw something along the path ahead. As he got closer, he could could make out the forms of the Pischke twins sitting around a fire.

The first thought that came to his mind was that the kids were up to mischief. Rumours and accusations had been rampant in the community about the children and the trouble they had been causing. Most of the accusations were coming from their own house as Domko cast blame on the children for everything that went wrong on the farm. Not that Jim had much respect for Domko's opinion, but many people in the community thought the kids, especially the twins, were incorrigible. Jim couldn't help but wonder if he was the one who'd been wrong all this time.

"What are you kids doing?" he asked as he halted the horses and jumped down from the sleigh. "Trying to burn down my bush?"

The children cowered.

"N-n-no Jim," David stammered. "We had to make a fire to stay warm."

"What for?" Jim asked, his hands on his hips. "How come you're not at home."

"Satan kicked us out," David said.

"How long have you been here?"

"All night," David answered.

Jim could hardly believe what he was hearing. Looking around, he saw evidence that the boys had been there for some time. There was a pile of wood stacked neatly by the trees and the snow had been pushed away and packed down to make a clearing. There was a thick pile of ashes in the fire, indicating it had been burning for quite some time.

"You been here all night?" he asked.

"Y-yes," David said through chattering teeth.

"He b-b-beat us up and we got lost and couldn't go no further," Dennis explained. "We was comin' to your house."

It was a miracle the boys hadn't frozen to death and Jim knew it.

"C'mon," Jim said, kicking snow into the fire. "You kids are comin' back to my place."

The twins got up stiffly. Their young voices were suddenly full of enthusiasm, although it would take a while before their limbs thawed. They had made it through the night and now Jim was going to take care of them. They couldn't have asked for a better person to come along. They knew Jim wasn't afraid of Domko and believed that he wouldn't let him hurt them.

They unhitched the horses and turned the sleigh around. Within a few minutes, the sleigh was gliding briskly to Jim's home. The boys took turns telling Jim what had happened the night before. David started a sentence, then Dennis would add to it, and David would finish. It was the way they always spoke, and those who knew them had grown accustomed to it. The boys were conscious they had to speak slowly so that Jim could understand them. Their stuttering and poor pronunciation made it difficult for strangers and they knew it.

Jim shook his head in wonder. He was ashamed of his momentary distrust of the boys.

"He doesn't know his arse from a hole in the ground," Jim said.

The twins looked at him in surprise.

"A farmer I was talkin' to," he explained. "He said you boys are the bad ones, always givin' Domko a hard time."

The twins looked at each other, astonishment showed in their large eyes.

"No Jim," David begged, not wanting their friend to turn against them. "It's not us, we's not the bad ones. Ole Satan just tells everyone we is."

Jim and the twins stepped into the house, greeted by the smell of breakfast cooking and Ruby's warm smile. Jim explained to Ruby what had happened while the twins took off their coats. The boys immediately went to stand by the woodstove in an effort to warm up.

Ruby and Jim talked in hushed tones in the kitchen. Ruby shook her head in amazement then went to talk to the twins. At her request they lifted up their shirts and pulled off their pants. Bruises covered their bodies, some old and some new.

Dennis showed Ruby, who was obviously sympathetic to their plight, where his leg was sore. David interjected to describe the beating a week ago that had left him unable to raise his right arm higher than his shoulder. Jim poured himself a cup of coffee while he watched.

"We don't gots to go to school do we?" David asked.

"No, not today," Jim said. "We're gonna go to Ashern. There's somebody else who should see those bruises."

Ruby fed the children then Jim finished his morning chores. He took the car battery from the house and started the car. By early afternoon, they were on their way down the road.

Jim's heart softened as he glanced over his shoulder and looked at the twins sitting solemnly in the back seat.

Why Caroline had returned to the farm in the summertime he couldn't understand. He had heard that she had been cut off welfare because Domko was spending the night. That was something else he couldn't quite understand.

How could such an attractive woman have a relationship with such a crackpot, he asked himself. He hadn't seen much of Caroline and the children since they had moved back to the farm, but had heard rumours that Caroline was associating mostly with Witnesses. This made her non-witness friends and family feel uncomfortable, particularly because Caroline's seclusion was encouraged by members of her church.

The twins became excited as the car approached Ashern. Jim followed the highway through town, and the boys pointed excitedly at a house, showing Jim where they had lived while in town. Turning again, Jim stopped in front of the RCMP office. Jim led the twins into the building. An officer was sitting at a table drinking coffee. Jim thought he must be a new officer in town since he didn't recognize him. Jim explained what had happened that morning and told the children's story from the night before. The officer listened quietly as Jim described Domko's erratic behaviour. The boys stood quietly as the officer studied them closely.

"Leave the boys with me," the constable said. "I'll talk to my superiors and see what we can do."

Satisfied with the arrangement, Jim extended his hand to the man in friendship. He was confident that this officer would see to it that Domko was jailed. Turning to the twins, he assured them that they were in good hands then left the office.

Jim drove back to Moosehorn, stopping at the supply store. He loaded the car with groceries then went to the cafe. There he had coffee with a few people from town, relaying the amazing story to all who'd listen.

"I swear that if something isn't done about that Domko, he's gonna kill one of those kids," Jim said, shaking his head.

The men at the table listened intently. They were anxious to hear gossip about Caroline whose relationship with Domko was often a topic of conversation.

It was early afternoon when Jim started home. Turning onto the Township Line, he glanced in his rear view mirror and noticed a police car approaching from behind. Slowing down, he pulled far to the right to let the car pass. Snow swirled in front of his car as the cruiser went by. Once the snow had settled, Jim could see the outline of the officer and two little heads in the back seat.

There were certain families in the area that weren't considered 'normal', and the Pischke family was one of them. The officer glanced in his rear view mirror to watch the twins for a moment. The boys talked hurriedly among themselves, pronouncing words that he couldn't understand. He couldn't help but like these strange little characters but had been warned that their mother's common-law husband was a bit odd. He'd have to get a complaint registered from the mother to do anything and had been warned that she wasn't likely to cooperate. The police certainly couldn't take Jim Deighton's word that the children were being beaten. After all, everyone knew that Deighton and Domko hated each other and that they fought over land all the time.

These domestic cases are such a waste of time, he thought to himself.

Usually the mother would end up defending the husband, so it was seldom the father was ever charged. Often, women like Caroline did nothing to help themselves. Removing the children was an option, but not one the police were authorized to do by themselves unless the situation was immediate or life threatening. How could they take the word of two little boys? This would have to be channelled through the provincial child welfare department. The officer decided he'd check out the situation and if warranted, file a report in Winnipeg.

The twins sank down in the seat as the cruiser turned north toward the farm. Domko was going to be very angry that the police had been summoned to the house. They hoped that Jim's story had been convincing enough and that the sight of bruises all over their bodies had made an impression on the officer. The boys were confident that the officer would arrest Domko and take him away like the time in Ashern after he beat up that drunk man.

"Is this your house, boys?" the officer asked, slowing and pointing to his right. The twins nodded that it was. The car turned into the driveway and the officer got out. The twins waited in the car until they were told to follow him into the house. A scowling Domko answered the brisk knock at the door. He invited the policeman in, while the twins followed close behind. They didn't look at Domko but kept their eyes glued to the floor.

The officer asked Domko a few questions, then asked where Caroline was. Domko replied that she was visiting her father and brother near Faulkner. The officer looked around the house and it was obvious to him that the family was very poor and backward. Kathy and Rosie played quietly on the floor. Eunice and the older boys were at school. The officer asked about the boys and why the neighbour had brought them to the police.

"They's be runnink away," Domko explained. "I's not be knowink vat to do."

Domko explained the bruises on the boys' bodies by saying that they were always playing and fighting with their older brothers. Because the officer couldn't question Caroline and felt uncomfortable waiting for her to return, he soon left the house.

The sight of Domko glaring at them in anger caused each boy to wet his pants. Domko waited until the car had pulled out of the driveway before turning on the twins. They stood frozen on the spot as Domko slid off his belt. The boys screamed in pain as he whipped each one. He continued beating them until they couldn't scream anymore.

Chapter 14

The yellow dress

IT TOOK THE TWINS NEARLY A WEEK to recuperate from the beating. Their mother knew that Domko had injured them, but was too afraid to say anything to him about it.

After the beating the twins lost all confidence in the police's ability to help them. They decided that if they went to the neighbours again, they would ask that the police not be called.

Caroline and Domko married secretly January 26. Her father and members of the church seemed satisfied with the union. They hoped that her life would straighten out and she wouldn't be as much of an embarrassment. Those from the old school believed that the man was the head of the household and that Caroline might start obeying Domko now that he was her husband.

Domko had pushed for marriage since the summer before when he'd been threatened with deportation. Now that he was married to a Canadian citizen, he could stay in Canada for good.

Soon after the wedding, Caroline and Domko paid her father a visit. They desperately needed money to renovate the house and update the farm equipment. Domko pressured the old man by complaining that he was having to support another man's children. Old Walter agreed with his new son-in-law, since supporting Bill's children wasn't something he wanted to do either. Not wishing to upset the man who had accepted his daughter and her brood, Walter gave them a substantial loan with an open re-payment date.

He was hoping to keep Domko happy, so that his daughter would not shadow his doorstep any longer. He was tired of giving her money and kept careful track so that if it was never repaid, the loan could be subtracted from any inheritance that he would leave for his three children. Over the years, Caroline had used up a good portion of her share.

* * * * *

Winter turned into spring. The twins escaped to Deightons and Eunice ran to the Harwart house at every opportunity. The older children continued to work hard before and after school, while 15 year-old Walter ran his trap line, accumulating a healthy pile of furs in the process. He found it impossible to check the traps in mid-March when a four day storm dropped more than seven inches of snow in the area. By the end of the month, Walter trudged through the snow and brought the majority of his traps home. He had been trapping muskrats since February and by the beginning of spring thaw, he had more than enough furs to pay for the motor scooter he'd been dreaming of all winter.

After the last of the muskrat skins had been stretched and cured, Walter asked Domko to take him to Winnipeg to Sidney I. Robinson, a fur buying company that would purchase the furs. Domko agreed to go later that week when he could sell the cream at the same time. Walter looked forward to the day with anticipation.

Walter bounded out of bed Friday morning to find Domko getting ready to go. The man turned to the boy and informed him that he decided to go with his friend, Hugo Russell instead, and that Walter would have to stay at home. Walter protested, but Domko held firm. He joined his brothers in the barn as Domko drove out of the driveway with Walter's furs piled high in the back of Hugo's truck.

"I thought you was going to Winnipeg?" Norman asked as Walter picked up a milking pail.

"No, the old bastard changed his mind," he said. "But I guess it don't matter if I buy the bike now or next week 'cause it's too wet to drive it anyhow."

His spirits lifted as he talked about the furs and how much money he anticipated receiving for them.

"I'm gonna buy the motor scooter an' then get Mom whatever she wants with the leftover money," he beamed, whistling as he thought about how his new motor scooter would make him the envy of the neighbourhood boys. "I think Mom wants a new dress. Hey Norman, what would you do if you turned rich?"

"Whatta ya mean IF I turned rich?" Norman laughed. "I'm gonna be rich someday and I'm gonna buy a plane. I've been readin' about 'em and I'd buy one I could give people rides in." Norman cheerily discussed his plans for the future as Walter's mind wandered back to what he would do if he had a lot of money. He decided that after he bought the motor scooter and a new dress for his mother, he would build a brand new house then kick Domko off the farm. He'd buy up land from the neighbours and have at least 200 cows. He figured he'd continue to trap even if he was rich.

"Yeah, and I'd buy a car so we wouldn't hafta go to town with the horses no more," he said interrupting Norman's description of plane engines. "Yep, If I was rich I'd buy you all whatever you wanted."

Domko arrived home early that evening in an excited mood. As the children filtered outside to unload the truck box which was piled high with tin sheeting. Domko bounded through the house as the children scavenged through the clothes box he brought full of pants, shoes and shirts.

"Punks! Punks!" he said. "I's be givink but a some punks sheet!"

"What are you talking about?" Caroline asked in a puzzled tone. She had never seen him so excited before.

As the children came into the house, he told them to sit at the table and listen to his story. His eyes flashed as he acted out the scene that had taken place that afternoon.

Apparently while in downtown Winnipeg, he had been accosted by two young men. Domko was carrying the clothes box and had a wad of cash in his coat pocket. The 'punks' wanted the box and threatened him with pocket knives. They told him to hand over the box and the money.

Pretending to oblige, Domko sat the box down then had reached into the breast pocket of his coat. Instead of giving them his money, he pulled out a hunting knife with a six-inch blade. He let out a roar and began to chase the would-be muggers down the sidewalk. The young men ran for their lives as Domko slashed the air behind them.

He puffed out his chest as he told the story, predicting that he would be the last person those punks ever tried to mug. Caroline and the older boys laughed as the twins and girls sat in total silence. David was afraid of the knife, knowing that Domko carried it all the time.

Domko must have sensed the boy's anxiety as he suddenly smiled a sinister smile. Reaching into his pocket he pulled out the knife. David let out a small gasp as the razor-sharp blade shone in the dim kitchen.

"Punks!" he said, making eye contact with David. "I's be givink you some!"

Walter had listened to the story long enough and could hold back his excitement no longer.

"So how much money did I get for my furs?" he asked.

"Fur?" Domko chuckled as he began filling a plate with stew from the pot that sat on the stove. "Vat fur?"

"The furs you took today, t-they were mine," he said.

"You?" Domko asked innocently. "They's be mine."

Walter was stunned. "B-ut I spent all winter trapping them," he said slowly, not understanding what his stepfather was saying. "T-those were my furs."

Domko spooned food into his mouth while Walter waited patiently for an explanation.

"Who's trap they's be? Marjie?" he said as he chewed. "They's be my trap."

"Y-you gave me those traps," he stammered as his face began to flush in anger. "The f-furs were mine and the m-money is mine."

Domko looked up from his plate. His eyes flashed and the area near the scar on his temple turned white.

"Who's food yous be yit?" he said, standing up to face the boy. "I's be buyink you pant and coat, and yous be trowink it in the bush!" Domko continued to berate the boy, calling him stupid and useless.

Suddenly the picture became crystal clear to Walter. Domko had planned to keep the money right from the start. How gullible he felt! He'd been trapping all season, foolishly believing that he'd be allowed to keep the money.

He stared at the deceitful man before him and shook his head sadly. As soon as Domko sat down, Walter turned and walked out the door. The cool evening wind whipped across his face as he walked towards the bush path that headed north.

He'd had enough. Walter walked away from the farm vowing never to return.

* * * * *

As the snow melted, the water in Lake Manitoba and its tributaries began to rise. The farm became an island, surrounded by water in every bog, ditch, dugout and low spot on the land. One afternoon Caroline called the children together to warn them about the dangers of deep water, especially Pischke lake. She told them that the bottom of the lake was soft and that there were many deep spots where adults wading through the water would suddenly disappear when the lake bottom caved in. She gave a strict warning that the children were to never cross the beaver dam.

The twins looked at each other then at Norman. They had discovered the deep water just days before when they had been playing on the ice Norman had pushed a six foot-long stick through a hole, moving water underneath had caught the limb and wrenched it from the boy's hands.

* * * * *

Caroline had heard through the grapevine that Walter was living with George and Nina Kiesman a few miles away. Domko had told her to go and pick up the boy and bring him back to the farm, but Caroline had refused since she had heard that the Kiesmans were moving to Winnipeg and had offered to take the boy along. There was a job opportunity for Walter as soon as he turned sixteen, just a few months away.

In the battle of wills between the couple that followed, Domko insisted then that the twins begin doing morning and evening chores with Eunice and the older boys. Caroline gave in so the nine year-olds were then expected to work daily in the barn yard.

One afternoon in mid-April the children returned home from school to discover their mother was gone. Domko was there and seemed distracted. Not feeling well, Caroline had apparently been taken to hospital by Gus and Emma. The children asked when their mother would be returning home, but Domko didn't answer them.

It started raining that morning and by the end of the day, the already full ditches were overflowing with several more inches of water. Frustrated that they couldn't do any work outdoors, Domko flew into a rage and the children raced to the barn to escape his grasp. The floor in the loft of the old barn creaked and groaned as the children scurried to the far corner where the roof didn't leak. The tin that Domko had bought with Walter's fur money was intended for the sides of the barn, still sat in a pile outside.

The youngsters slept in a stack of old hay as rain pounded on the roof. They awoke the following morning to find it still drizzling. They did their best to stay out of Domko's way as they completed the morning chores. He paced the kitchen floor, muttering to himself about the hay crop as another five inches of rain fell that day.

Caroline wasn't gone long before Domko began feeling sorry for himself. He was a poor cook who was almost helpless in the kitchen. He instructed Eunice to go to the barn and bring him some eggs. She did so and the children watched in amazement as he cracked the shell on the edge of the table, then threw his head back, sliding the raw egg into his mouth. He swallowed in one gulp then reached for another egg. After repeating this six times, he belched then wiped his face with the back of his hand. The children looked at each other in disgust but said nothing.

The following morning the entire family went to the barn to do chores. The children went willingly since it sometimes gave them the opportunity to sneak food. Domko wasn't able to watch them all the time, so they soon learned to use their time alone effectively.

While milking the cows, the older children often took milk when he wasn't watching. Domko followed a strict routine which included going back to the house once the children had started chores. Eunice gave each child a knowing look as they waited until he left. As soon as he was gone, she ran to the far corner of the barn and dug a tin cup out from under a stack of hay. Norman watched from the door as Eunice dipped the cup into the milk pail. She drank the warm milk hungrily, then dipped it again and handed it to Rosie. Then it was the twins' turn, and finally Steven and Norman. The milk helped ease the knawing pain in their stomachs and lifted their spirits. When Domko returned, he found the children diligently milking and never noticed the missing milk.

That morning, Rosie's cat paced and meowed by the barn door. The cat had almost starved over the winter, but had grown fat that spring from mice and other rodents. She found a comfortable spot on the floor between the two rows of cows and watched thoughtfully as the cows waited patiently to be milked.

The cat turned her head to listen as the children squirted milk into the small tin pails. She knew that if she waited long enough, Rosie would sneak her some milk too. She meowed and purred softly each time the girl walked by. Rosie's job was to hold each cow's tail and then take the filled pail and carry it carefully to to the door. She'd pour the milk into the larger cans without spilling a drop, then return the pails to the older children. She'd stop to pat the cat each time she went by as the cat arched her back in appreciation.

Domko never approved of having a cat in the barn and would kick it out of the way if he saw it near the cows or milk pails. Since pets were of no value to him, he thought the children shouldn't have them either. While the children watched, he would drown or bludgeon newborn puppies and kittens regularly and without emotion.

Caroline had saved Rosie's cat's life more than once by removing it from his sight and the animal had become less cautious in his presence.

Domko supervised the milking by standing in the middle of the barn, leaning on a shovel handle. He watched Rosie's exchanges with the cat then smiled menacingly. Without warning, he suddenly lunged forward, pinning the cat to the barn floor with the sharp edge of the shovel. The cat screeched in pain, startling the children who turned to see what had happened. The animal struggled out from under the sharp edge, its back end almost severed from its body. It looked around helplessly, as its intestines spilled out onto the floor.

The cat dragged herself past the cows into the feeding stall as a crying Rosie ran close behind. The girl crawled into the manger and cradled her pet in her lap until it slowly died. The other children looked on helplessly but didn't dare stop milking to console their sister. Domko watched them carefully to be sure nobody went to Rosie's aid. Then apparently quite pleased with himself, he grunted softly and carried the milk can to the house.

A week later, Domko went to the hospital to pick up Caroline. Complications at the end of her pregnancy meant she had had to spend a few weeks in hospital before the birth. She and the baby recovered from the premature birth, arriving home weak and tired to find the house and children in an awful mess. Manure had been tracked across the floors and the dishes hadn't been washed since the day she had left. The house stunk badly and the children were dirty and hungry. Her first inclination was to go back to the hospital, but instead she went to the bedroom and called the children to come and look at their new baby brother.

Domko beamed with pride about his new son who looked very much like himself with his dark skin and slavic appearance. They named him Raymond.

A month after Caroline arrived home, the public health nurse came to visit. Margaret Burnett was surprised to see that although the farm seemed to be better managed, the children appeared as neglected as ever.

"How come you kids aren't in school?" she boomed at the twins in a thick British accent.

David hesitated for a moment. This woman had a loud, strange voice, one like he'd never heard before. She was a big woman with dark hair and assertive mannerisms.

"W-we had to do c-chores," he stammered, looking at the ground. "We're g-goin' n-now."

The nurse watched as the boys walked past her car, then into the bush towards the school. They carried no books or lunch and their feet were bare.

She shook her head. She had heard that Caroline had returned to the farm from Ashern after her mother's allowance payments had been cut off. She had also heard many stories about Caroline's infidelities and Domko's rages and wondered if they were true. Apparently the children were thieves who couldn't be trusted. Margaret knew all about small towns and how the rumour mill turned. She decided she would see for herself once she got to know the family better.

Her first impression of Domko was not good. He sat at the table holding a grimy coffee cup in one hand and a cigarette in the other. He smoked during the entire visit, eyeing Margaret suspiciously as she examined Raymond.

Caroline loved babies and was proud of her new son. He was a stocky, contented child who nursed well and had put on just the right amount of weight. She beamed when Margaret gave the baby an excellent bill of health. Glancing over her shoulder, Margaret asked to speak with Caroline privately. Caroline nodded and the women moved into the bedroom. She raised the issue of birth control, as Dr. Steenson had advised Caroline that she should not have any more children since this ninth pregnancy had taken a toll on her health. Caroline smiled sheepishly and nodded. When she finished, Margaret wasn't sure how much good the talk had done.

The nurse noticed a big difference in size between Kathy and Rosie . The blind girl was almost as tall as the six year old and appeared to be much heavier. Caroline had told the nurse that Kathy had been blind since birth, but rumours in the community were that Domko had blinded her in one of his rages.

Kathy didn't appear to be neglected, but Rosie looked thin and gaunt. Margaret made a note that the twins looked awfully thin too, but because she hadn't seen the older children, she was unable to make a full assessment. Their differences could be attributed to their very different looking fathers. Margaret remembered how tall and thin Bill Pischke had been compared to short and stocky Domko. She made a few notes then left the house. She was relieved to be out of the confines of the dirty, cramped space and into fresh air. She decided to return in the fall, but intended to arrive late in the day so she could see the older children. If there was something wrong, she believed they would tell her.

* * * * *

Farmers were just beginning to nourish hope of getting into their fields when it started to rain near the end of May. By the end of the month, more than 14 inches had fallen. Domko was fit to be tied as he paced the house all day long. He had just bought more cattle and was worried he'd have no hay to feed them that winter.

The children listened intently as Domko and Caroline discussed plans for an addition to the house. It was a promise he had made to her before they were married and she was holding him to it. He also wanted more space and a bedroom for himself, Caroline and his two children. He'd never felt comfortable in the house and hoped that by changing it, he could erase all memories of the children's dead father.

Crude plans were drawn and the project began a week later with the help of local carpenter Henry Herzog. Henry arrived one morning with his tools and began measuring and discussing the renovations with Domko. Lumber was purchased with the money they had borrowed from Caroline's father earlier that year. Soon the kitchen area was removed from the east end of the house and dragged over the well and outdoor pump to make a pumphouse. A lean-to style addition was built on the north side. The attic was opened as part of a plan to build a stairway to an upstairs bedroom for all the children except Kathy and Raymond.

One evening when the job was half finished, Henry met Gus on the road while he was on his way home. They exchanged pleasantries then Henry described the work he was doing on the house.

"Why would you want to help that miserable old son-of-a-gun?" Gus asked, surprised that the quiet, kindly man appeared to like Domko.

"Why not?" Henry asked. "He seems alright to me."

"Well, what I know of him I don't like," Gus shot back. "and the way he treats those kids is a disgrace."

Henry thought for a moment. "I think he's doing a good job with the kids. He's straightening them out, that's all. Domko told me all about those kids and how they run away when they have to work."

Stunned, Gus shook his head in disgust. Now he understood why so many people didn't seem to understand when he complained about Domko's treatment of the children. Likely they believed that the children deserved the beatings they received and were unaware of the severity of Domko's treatment. He was poisoning the community against the children by telling people they were like little animals. It seemed there was nothing anybody could do about it.

Gus decided that arguing with Henry wasn't worth the effort. It was obvious the man had made up his mind and nothing Gus could say would change it. The men waved to each other, as Henry left without fully realizing how disappointed Gus was.

* * * * *

For Eunice, the best thing about having Marjorie as a neighbour was that she was three years older and only one size bigger. This meant that each spring and fall when Emma cleaned out Marjorie's closet, she'd pass clothes on to Eunice. One afternoon Marjorie brought over a box full of clothes. Eunice became excited as the box was dropped on the floor of the front room. Together they went through it as Eunice thanked her for t-shirts and each pair of shorts.

"They are all freshly washed and pressed so you don't have to worry about them smellin' like they've been in storage," said Marjorie, whose mother had insisted that the clothes be in good shape. Emma didn't want Eunice to feel bad about accepting charity.

Eunice smiled as she pulled more items from the box, then let out a delighted gasp when she reached the bottom and discovered a dress. Eunice's eyes glowed as she pulled out the shin length, yellow crepe dress. It had puffy short sleeves and a low neckline. Small bows adorned the front and the sleeves. It was the most beautiful piece of clothing Eunice had ever seen.

"Thanks Marjie," Eunice exclaimed, pulling it close. "I love it!"

"You're welcome," Marjorie said, glad her favourite dress was being appreciated. "It's gonna look real good on you."

Eunice was anxious to put on the dress, but Domko was sitting nearby watching the exchange take place. The idea of undressing near him made her feel uneasy since he had been looking at her in a strange way lately. Instead, she took the dress and placed it at the bottom of the box and covered it with the other clothes. She didn't want Domko to be able to find it easily, just in case he felt it was too frilly for the farm and destroyed it. She would show it to her mother, though, since she could appreciate a girl's desire to own a beautiful dress.

The following afternoon, Caroline and Domko had to go to Moosehorn to pick up more building materials for the house. As soon as they were gone, Eunice ran to the bedroom and dug through her box of clothes. She pulled out the yellow dress and marvelled at how lovely it was. Stripping off her dirty slacks and t-shirt, she pulled the dress over her head. Looking at herself in the full length mirror on her mother's bedroom wall, she could tell the dress was a little big, but it was still the most wonderful thing she'd ever owned. Cinching it in at the waist, she stood on her toes. Tossing her chin into the air, she tried very hard to look grown up.

Pretending that she was Cinderella, Eunice twirled in the dress. Closing her eyes, she visualized a handsome prince riding up the driveway to take her away to his castle. Then suddenly, Domko appeared in her fantasy, causing her to frown. Domko would never let her leave the farm to be happy. He began yelling at the prince who jumped down from his horse. The prince showed no fear as he pulled a long sword from a sheath at his waist and swung it at Domko who stood in stunned silence. The sharp blade sliced easily through his neck and Domko's head dropped to the ground.

The prince then took two steps forward and kicked Domko's head into the bush! Eunice giggled out loud at the thought. Then she visualized the prince turning to her, saying that she was the most beautiful girl he'd ever seen. He helped her onto the back of his big, white horse where she sat side-saddle like the fancy ladies in books. She wrapped her arms around his waist as they galloped down the road to live in a big castle. She sighed as she played the scene over again in her mind. Flopping on the bed, she closed her eyes and dreamed of the day she would be able to leave the farm. How truly wonderful it would be to live in Moosehorn with a handsome husband.

The sound of Henry pounding nails on the roof brought her back to reality. The noise reminded her that Domko would be home in a few hours. The cows needed milking soon, and it was her job to bring them from the pasture. She decided to leave the dress on a little longer, but hoped her brother's wouldn't see her behaving so silly.

The sight of herself in the dress, combined with her earlier fantasy, helped lighten her step as she skipped outside. It was a sunny warm day and for the first time in a long time, she felt good to be alive. She skipped past the barn onto the well-worn path to the pasture, her bare feet squishing on the cool, wet grass. She picked up a piece of twine and wrapped it around her waist.

Her brothers were supposed to help her, but they were nowhere in sight. She didn't care, though. Without them around, she could be whoever she wanted to be. At first she hummed a tune silently then she began to sing outloud as her confidence soared. Twirling, she looked down to see the dress flowing and twisting as she changed directions. She was truly giddy from the dress, as she rounded the bush dancing and singing.

The cows were relaxing in the shade of the trees a short distance away. The sight of Eunice skipping and singing in the flowing dress startled one of the younger animals. It took off in the opposite direction from where Eunice was planning to lead them. The other cows, skittish from Domko's harsh and erratic behaviour, also took one look at Eunice and began bawling. Within a few seconds, the entire herd was up and running full speed away from the singing girl. Eunice stopped and watched in dismay as the cows disappeared along the path into the next bush. She began chasing after them, slipping on wet grass and cow manure as she ran. It took more than an hour before the cows were calm enough to chase home.

As the barn came into view, the cows began to bawl and trot towards the familiar building. Eunice's daydreaming had been spoiled by the ruckus with the cows, but she had been very careful to ensure that no harm had came to the beautiful yellow dress.

Chapter 15

The Health Nurse visits

AFTER SCHOOL FINISHED AT THE END OF JUNE, Steven went to live at Elmer Ruchotzke's farm west of Ashern. With the two older boys gone, this put a lot of pressure on Norman and Eunice, though they never complained about the workload for fear of receiving a beating.

No matter how hard they worked, Domko berated and criticized them at every turn. Their only break was walking the seven miles to Mooschorn to pick up the mail. Since Norman was the oldest living at home, this privilege was usually reserved for him.

Renovations to the house were finished by mid-summer. The family was pleased with the new living quarters. The addition to the east end of the house plus the opening of the attic made their home more than twice its original size. The children were happy to move into the attic bedroom, while Domko moved his belongings into the large room in the far corner of the house. He bought himself a double bed and chest of drawers. Nobody was allowed in his room except Caroline and his two children. The twins were happy about this, aiming to stay as far away from him as they could.

The children moved their meagre belongings and the double bed from downstairs to the attic. The bed was placed along the east wall. A small window in the west let in fresh air and afternoon sunshine. Buffalo board had been nailed from the ceiling to the floor, making the room smaller than the actual size of the attic. This was to provide ventilation and air movement in the eaves behind the walls.

One evening after a long day of mending fences, Domko came storming up to the attic bedroom in the middle of the night. The children were awakened by his ravings as he held a kerosene lamp at the foot of the bed. They were too frightened to move as he lifted up the blanket and stuck the lantern underneath.

"I's be lookink at but a some feet," he bellowed. The children quivered as he examined their feet. David and Dennis' were caked in blood as they had been forced to fence a strip that bordered a neighbour's oat field. Since the boys had outgrown their shoes, they were working in bare feet. Normally they had tough callouses, but because it had been such a wet spring, their feet were soft and susceptible to cuts. It was worse because coarse stubble had been left behind from threshing the previous fall.

Domko looked at the blood, then moved to examine Eunice's feet, making her feel very uncomfortable. When he finished, he turned and went downstairs. The children were unsure of his motive, guessing that he may have been checking to see if their feet were clean or dirty, a possible indication whether they had been working or not. The next day they reported this bizarre behaviour to their mother but she offered no explanation.

"He's been doing a lot of strange things," she said. "Keep out of his way."

The feet checking continued nightly for almost two weeks.

The added space in the house seemed to satisfy Domko who still spent most evenings reading at the kitchen table, but it didn't stop the beatings. One night the children were in bed when a cow began to bellow outside. The children listened intently as a calf, who must have been separated from its mother, answered somewhere in the distance. The sound of the cow and calf bellowing back and forth, was enough to send Domko into a fit of rage. He came flying up the stairs, removing his belt as he ran. He began telling the children that it was their fault that the cow and calf had been separated and that one of them must have left the gate open. They cowered in the bed as he made these illogical accusations.

Tearing back the blanket, he began strapping them viciously. No parts of their bodies were spared as they fought to escape his grasp. Within a few seconds, all but David had scrambled out of the bed and down the stairs. He hunkered down in the corner between the bed and the wall as Domko stood on the floor kicking him him with his heavy boots. Each time he kicked the sobbing youngster, he would let out an exuberant grunt. David was older now and beginning to realize that Domko's rages were more than just a reaction from a throbbing head. It appeared the man took great satisfaction from beating the children. David vowed that Domko would never trap him in bed again.

* * * * *

"You's be chasink into some Deighton," Domko ordered as he pointed to the south where their farm bordered Jim's oatfield. It was now late summer and Jim's oats were heading nicely and on the verge of ripening.

Dennis and David looked at each other. Usually their job was to keep the cows off of the neighbour's land. Now they were being told to purposely allow the cattle to graze in Jim's field. Sixty-five cattle could do a lot of damage in a short time.

They protested until Domko picked up a heavy stick and began chasing them. David ran in one direction while Dennis headed the opposite way, a trick they'd learned after they got caught more than once when they ran together. Domko could run incredibly fast for a short distance as long as he kept a straight line. The boys learned quickly that if they split up and zig zagged, he could never catch them. This time, though, he picked up a stick and flung it as hard as he could, catching Dennis in the back of the head and knocking him to the ground.

"What if Jim comes?" David asked, distracting Domko from his fallen brother.

"Vat? Yous be scared of your daddy?" he spitted sarcastically as he referred to the neighbour.

David shrugged as Dennis wobbled to his feet. Domko motioned for the boys to get the cows. They reluctantly chased the animals through their meadow and onto Jim's land. As they walked slowly behind one old, lame cow, Domko snuck up on the boys and smacked each one of them on the head. It was a familiar warning, telling them that if they didn't do as they were told, they were in line for a beating. The boys shrunk as he glared at them.

"You's be bringink some out later," he said. Turning on his heel, he strode back to the house. David and Dennis sat and waited as the cows greedily chewed and trampled Jim's oats.

Before long, the twins noticed a tractor appearing from the south. It accelerated when the driver saw the cattle spreading far and wide in the field. The boys could tell it was Jim as he stood up and began waving his hat in anger. The twins had mixed feelings about their neighbour's timing. On one hand, they were glad that Jim's field wouldn't be totally destroyed, but they were embarrassed to have to explain this mess to their friend.

Their faces flushed as Jim jumped off the tractor.

"What the hell is this?" he yelled. "Get your goddamned cattle out of my field!"

"Domko m-made us do it," David said. "He made us chase the cows in here."

Jim looked at the hapless youngsters trembling in fear. Each had huge bruises on their legs and arms. Dennis had the telltale signs of a black eye.

"Well at least help me get them off here," he said softening. "Then I'll go talk to that stupid ass."

The twins obliged, running in opposite directions in a wide circle to pen the cattle and chase them out of the field. It was a difficult job because the cows were enjoying the fresh oats.

Jim followed on the tractor as the boys chased the cows back into their pasture. Then he turned and accelerated towards the farm as the boys ran behind. The twins were afraid to be near Domko when he was mad, however, they couldn't resist the temptation of seeing Jim yell at their stepfather. After all, he was one of the few people in the community with enough guts to stand up to him.

Jim cursed as he drove along the edge of Domko's pasture.

We didn't need fences in this part of the country until that fool arrived, Jim thought to himself. *Most the farmers around here are too proud to steal from one another.*

The problem was that Domko didn't have enough land to support the number of cattle he had acquired. He wanted to fatten the animals on neighbouring land in case he was short of hay that coming winter. Jim hadn't been at all surprised to find Domko's cattle in his field.

As a matter of fact, he expected it.

Late one night a few weeks earlier, he'd seen Domko chase his cows into neighbour Herman Gall's field. As a precaution, Jim had been checking his own fields regularly since the middle of summer.

That Domko's a curse, Jim thought. *He thinks he owns the entire countryside.*

Jim drove his tractor straight from the field onto the grass in Caroline's yard, jumping off in front of Domko who was standing by the chicken coop. They argued for a few moments, then Domko pointed to the twins who had stopped to listen a safe distance away.

"I's not be doink it, they's be," he said innocently.

"That's bullshit and you know it," Jim argued. "If those boys chased the cattle into my field, it's because you told them to."

"They's be vatchink but a some cow," Domko explained. "They's be goot for sheet!"

"You can't fool me with that innocent act," Jim replied. "I can see right through you so don't waste your breath lying to me."

Domko threw his arms up in the air in anger. He screamed at Jim to leave the property, threatening to kill him if he didn't.

"I's be killink lots of men," he said. "I's be shootink but a some Deighton!"

"You're gonna shoot me?" Jim asked sarcastically. "I'm not afraid of you, you stupid sonofabitch. I've got a gun and I'm not afraid to use it either!"

Domko stepped back and stared in astonishment at the neighbour. Usually his threats were met with fear.

"I've shot lots of men too," Jim lied. "You keep your cattle off my land or I'll shoot you!"

With that, Jim turned and climbed back on the tractor. He roared through the yard, past the house and accelerated south down the dirt road.

Impressed with Jim's spunk, the twins laughed and ran into the bush towards the beaver dam. Glancing over their shoulders as they went, they saw Domko punching the air in frustration as he swore vehemently that he was going to kill both Jim and the twins.

Dennis and David stayed in the bush near the lake for a few days. By the end of the second day, they were tired of foraging for berries and decided to try and catch a rabbit. Walter had taught them to set snares, and luckily, Dennis had a piece of string in his pocket that could help them with their quest. David took the string and deftly fashioned a snare. Examining the ground closely, he spotted a rabbit run and tied the snare to a branch. The twins crept out of sight and watched for a while, expecting a rabbit to appear immediately.

"We got to catch one soon," Dennis said, his stomach growling. "I'm hungry."

David was hungry too. He'd lost track of time and couldn't remember the last time they had eaten. Bored with sitting and waiting in the bush, the boys decided to go to the lake. They pondered their future as they walked along.

"Do you think old Squeezer's gonna kill us?" David asked.

"I dunno," Dennis said. "He sure hates me. He hates me the most."

"Nope he hates Rosie most," David laughed, trying to reassure his brother. Domko did hate Dennis with a passion, but David didn't want to make his brother feel worse than he already did.

"What 'bout Norman?" Dennis added, playing along with the game. "He don't like Norman at all."

"Yeah, poor Norman," David said, remembering a beating his brother had recently received for neglecting to close a gate behind the cows. "He hates Norman almost as much as taking a bath!"

The twins laughed and pushed each other in fun. They climbed the bank of the lake where they could see a wide expanse of dark watter, stretching more than a mile wide before them. Tall reeds, growing close to the shore blew softly in the wind. The sun reflected brightly off the shimmering water, causing the boys to squint.

"Have you seen how funny he looks at us?" David asked. "Like we're evil or somethin'."

"Yeah, an' he never talks to us, just yells," Dennis added. "He thinks we're like them negro slaves, eh? I read 'bout 'em at school.There ain't no such thing as havin' slaves anymore, is there?"

David shook his head. "Nope."

"Hey Davey," Dennis said, his voice softening. "What do you 'spose people is like over the beaver dam?"

"I dunno," David replied. "Maybe they're good like in Ashern."

"Too bad Norman's plane didn't fly us there, eh?" Dennis asked. The boys sat on soft grass under a line of oak trees and stared across the water.

"When I'm a big kid, I'm gonna make us a boat so we can float across," Dennis said dreamily. "Then Domko can't get us no more."

David smiled at the idea. He looked at his brother and tried to imagine life without Dennis, shuddering at the thought.

"C'mon," he said, knocking his brother down the bank and into the sand. "Let's go swimmin'."

The boys fell asleep under the stars that night without having eaten anything but berries that day. They hadn't caught a rabbit so the snare was moved to a rabbit run along the fence. In the morning, they woke early to find a fat rabbit hanging by its neck.

"Yippee!" David yelled as he jumped up and down. "I knew this was a good spot. See Denny? I told you!"

Dennis eyed the soft, furry animal. At first, he felt sorry for the rabbit, but once the shock of seeing the dead animal wore off, his stomach began growling with hunger.

David skinned and gutted the rabbit, a skill his brother Walter had taught him. At the same time, Dennis made a fire, then poked two sticks into the ground to make a spit. David speared a sharp stick lengthwise through the rabbit carcass. Carefully, he hung the carcass over the fire and within a few minutes, the smell of roasting rabbit permeated the air. The fire sputtered as juice from the meat dripped into the flames.

"Is it ready?" Dennis asked impatiently.

"Almost," David said optimistically. He too, could hardly wait to sink his teeth into the roasting meat.

"We'll split it half an' half, right Davey?"

"Yep, I'll take the big half an' you can have the little one."

The brothers grinned at each other as they sat on the ground, waiting patiently for the meat to cook. Suddenly a rustling in the bush behind them caused them to look around. Domko towered above their heads. Usually they boys could smell his foul body odour as he approached, but the smell of the cooking rabbit had confused their senses. Domko must have seen the smoke and smelled the rabbit cooking.

"Vat?" he seethed. "You's be yitting ant peesing ant sheeting and doink nothing all day long."

Domko was too close for the boys to run away and both of them knew it. David gave Dennis a sideways glance, and instantly knew that it would be better to go back to work on the farm than to receive a beating for trying to escape.

Domko kicked dirt into the fire, then grabbed the stick that held the rabbit.

"Fraaa!" he yelled, pointing towards home.

The boys jumped up and started walking out of the bush with Domko close behind. They glanced nervously over their shoulders, hoping he wouldn't kick them from behind, a favourite trick of his. Chuckling, Domko slipped the rabbit off of the stick and began ripping it apart. He greedily stuffed the steaming meat into his mouth.

"Hey," Dennis said quietly. "That's ours."

Domko smiled and then with a whining voice, mocked Dennis. When the boy wasn't looking, he kicked him in the back, sending Dennis sprawling to the ground.

"Denny," David cautioned, grabbing him by the arm. "Don't turn your back like that!" he said in their twin language.

Dennis scrambled up and said nothing more as they walked home.

The twins spent the rest of the day pitching hay into stacks, working with Norman and Eunice. In the evening they had to get the cows from the pasture and chase them back to the barn for milking. After completing evening chores in the barn, they were allowed to eat whatever super was left by Domko, Caroline and Kathy. All the remaining children fought over the leftover pieces of boiled pork and potatoes.

That night the twins wearily climbed to the attic bedroom and fell onto the bed. They could hear Domko chastising Caroline downstairs for something she had forgotten to do that day.

"Hey, Denny I don't think we should sleep here," David whispered. "What if Flatfoot comes up?"

"I'm tired," Dennis said, closing his eyes.

David lay on the bed unable to fall asleep. Quietly he got out of bed and looked around the room for a place to hide. He noticed a six inch space along the north end wall where the builder had run out of buffalo board. Examining it closely he could see that if he pulled the piece of the wall back, he'd be able to squeeze in behind the wall. Remembering the beating he had received a few weeks ago, David began searching for something that would pry the nails out of the wall. Norman noticed what he was doing and came to his aid.

"Never mind the nails," he said, gripping the edge of the board with his hands. "Just do this."

With Norman pulling hard, the board snapped in half where the nails held it to the wall. The children now had enough space to crawl in if they turned sideways.

Eunice and Rosie followed Norman and David into the hiding spot. Sticking his head out, David called to his brother who was snoring quietly on the bed.

"C'mon Denny," David whispered harshly. "Come hide in here."

Dennis was enjoying having the bed all to himself and muttered that he wanted to be left alone.

"Denny! C'mon!" David said again.

Rolling over, Dennis turned his back on his brother. Finally David gave up and found himself a spot to sleep on the eaves. Within a few hours, the children were startled awake by the sound of Domko's feet pounding up the stairs. Disoriented from sleep, David jumped up to find a place to hide, forgetting he was already behind the wall. Relaxing slightly, he hoped that Domko didn't figure out where they were and come barreling through. His heart raced as he heard Domko approach the bed.

"Huh?" the man said, clearly surprised that everyone but Dennis was gone. Incoherent from sleep, Dennis looked around, not knowing where his siblings were either.

Domko began taunting and slapping Dennis until the slaps turned to punches. The boy wailed each time Domko's fist crashed into his face. David cringed as he heard his twin choking back tears and blood.

Dennis wimpered as Domko lifted him up and threw him against the wall. David could sense his siblings were also listening, but nobody dared say a word. The fact they had knocked a hole in the wall would be enough to send Domko into a bigger rage. It was very important for them to keep this hiding place a secret.

Domko soon stomped across the floor and down the stairs, satisfied that he had given Dennis a good beating. For some reason beating the children always made Domko feel good about himself. He didn't need a reason to exert his control over them.

The children could hear their brother sobbing softly on the other side of the wall, but nobody dared move to comfort him for fear their stepfather would hear and come back upstairs.

Summer wore on and the children continued to work long hours in the hayfield. They didn't mind this except that their stepfather constantly criticized their work. They looked forward to the few hours that he would leave them alone while he went in for meals or coffee breaks.

Bruno the dog tagged along wherever the children went, barking and running in circles around them. When Domko allowed it, the younger children rode the family's horse, a black mare named Dolly. The children loved this horse who would accept riders without a saddle or reins. Dolly followed voice commands and seemed to know intuitively where the children wanted to go. If a child slid off her back, the horse would stop and wait patiently for the child to climb back on. She had been relegated to the worst corner behind the barn since Domko's horses, Queenie, Jack and Darby, had arrived. Dolly allowed the children to nestle beside her at night when they weren't able to sleep in the house.

Domko disliked Dolly because the children were fond of her and because she was able to outsmart him most of the time. After being beaten by Domko a few times the horse became wary of her attacker. It was seldom that he could catch the bright mare who would take off running whenever he came near.

Dolly was too valuable to dispose of, so Domko reluctantly kept the horse, using her for the most miserable chores such as cleaning out the barn or working in the rain. He fed her only the bare minimum and trimmed her hooves only once, impatiently cutting too far into the pulp of her foot. Dolly walked with a limp for months after that, so he'd whip her to keep her going. She never became stubborn, but would flatten her ears and whinny whenever he came near.

Domko's horses were just the opposite to Dolly. They had wicked dispositions which he encouraged. Working with them was difficult as they were easily spooked, running away at every opportunity. The children could not control the beasts many times found themselves facing Domko's wrath if the sleigh would tip or the horses pulled the wagon too fast. Darby and Jack would bite the children if they came too close.

Late one afternoon, the twins rode Dolly to the east pasture to bring the cows home. They found the animals spread over a wide distance and started to search for the lead cow who carried a bell around her neck. Usually, the rest of the cows would follow if the leader could be steered in the right direction. However, there was a problem because this particular leader was by far the most uncooperative and bossiest of the bunch.

"I bet ole' Satan made her the lead cow just to bug us," Dennis said.

David nodded as the twins rode Dolly through the cows looking for old bossy. They had already been gone for a long time. Finally the lead cow lifted her head and her bell clanged loudly, just as Domko came riding around the corner on his horse to find them.

"Yous lazy soneebeech bastards," he seethed as he rode up beside them. "I's be waitink ant you's be playink some!" Pulling a 12 inch two-by-two out of his back pocket, he cracked it over their heads. Dolly whinnied and snorted at Domko as he smashed her over the head as well. The horse took off running which frightened the cows and they scattered throughout the field.

No matter how hard they tried, David and Dennis couldn't please Domko. The boys were beginning to feel useless and trapped under his iron hand. Their mother wasn't helping matters much, since she'd been brainwashed into believing that she and the children were to blame for Domko's behaviour.

* * * * *

One afternoon the twins were sitting in the grainary straightening used nails that Domko had bought at an auction sale. They banged the nails into shape for hours, a boring way to spend the final day of the summer holidays. They heard a car pull in the driveway, and stepped out of the grainary. It was Mrs. Burnett, the health nurse.

"Come here boys," she called as she walked across the grass towards them. "I want to talk to you."

The twins looked at each other and for a moment considered running into the bush. What would Domko do if he saw them talking to this stranger?

Shyly the boys stood up. Dennis looked at David for guidance.

"Bays Bickt?" he asked in their language.

David wasn't sure if she was a 'bad person' or not. He remembered the whipping they had received when the police brought them home from Ashern. He didn't want another beating like that. He looked the woman over carefully then told his brother to be quiet.

"What are you boys doing?" the nurse asked glancing into the old pail.

"Straightnin' nails," David said shyly. He stared up at the tall woman who in his eyes was resembled a dark haired angel.

"Where's Bob Domko?" she asked.

David shrugged his shoulders. He liked her strange voice and hoped she would talk to them more.

Mrs. Burnett looked at the twins carefully. They were dressed in ragged clothing and covered with dirt. Both boys had matted hair and snotty noses from summer colds. They eyed the woman shyly as she knelt to their level.

"There have been calls to the police about you children" she said. The neighbours are saying that Domko hits you. Is that true?"

The twins said nothing. It was so seldom that anyone outside the family spoke to them that they weren't sure how to answer. They knew they were difficult to understand and most outsiders didn't like them very much. They were also afraid that if they told this woman about their stepfather's rages, the police would come and Domko would beat them again.

"It's o.k., I won't tell him what you say," Margaret said. "I can only help you if you tell me what happens."

The twins stood for a long time before Dennis decided this woman could be trusted.

"S-satan smashes us all the t-time," he stammered.

"Who?" she asked.

Dennis looked towards the house.

Margaret glanced over her shoulder to be sure nobody was watching, then asked the twins to lift their shirts. The boys looked at each other then slowly complied. The nurse looked at their rakish bodies and shook her head. The boys were obviously malnourished and large bruises covered their backs and arms. David had open sores on his legs from a serious poison ivy infection that was never treated. Dennis had patches on his head where his hair had been pulled from his scalp. Margaret suspected that repeated beatings on their faces were even beginning to alter the twins once identical appearance.

It's high time for somebody to do something about this," she thought to herself.

Chapter 16

A three cent apple

MRS. BURNETT FILED A REPORT asking for a social worker from the Manitoba Child Welfare Department to investigate a case of child neglect at the farm. It took a few weeks for the social worker to arrive unannounced, for a visit.

While the health nurse was welcomed by families in trouble, social workers were seen as adversaries. Families were embarrassed to have them come to the house, since it usually meant there was serious trouble.

Because they had a full caseload of clients, the workers didn't have a lot of time to spend with the families they visited. In this particular area, the northwest Interlake, there were a lot of families requiring attention. Over time workers sometimes lost track of their cases. They didn't know if a file had been closed because they'd helped resolve the conflict or if the parents and children had simply learned to keep their problems quiet to avoid awkward visits.

It was a difficult, sometimes thankless job and staff changed regularly. Workers seemed to stay in one area for a few years before transferring.

Caroline was relieved to see that the social worker who'd cancelled her mother's allowance payment was not the same one visiting that day. The man pulled a new, clean file out of his briefcase.

Glancing around the house, the visitor did a quick assessment and wrote a few things in his file. While Caroline and Bob didn't appear to be a loving couple, most poor families he'd seen weren't very happy. It was obvious that their lives centered on making a living and it wasn't an easy life. She could see that Caroline was a textbook case of a poorly educated, backward woman with little experience outside of becoming a mother at a very young age.

Bob Domko was difficult to assess. His grasp of the English language was so poor that the social worker was unable to carry on a conversation with him. One thing was obvious, though, he loved Kathy and Raymond.

Domko played the model father as he held Kathy and lovingly glanced at Raymond. The social worker could see that this love was sincere. The two children appeared to be well cared for and neither feared their father. Kathy climbed willingly onto his lap and Raymond giggled and cooed when he came near.

"Would you mind taking the children into the other room?" he said to Domko. "I'd like to speak with your wife alone, please."

Domko eyed the social worker suspiciously, but then gave a gracious smile. Picking up Raymond, he led Kathy into the front room. The worker watched until he left then turned to Caroline.

He asked Caroline a few questions about her husband and their relationship before stating the reason why he was really there.

"Does Bob mistreat the children from your first marriage?"

Frightened by the prospect of having her children taken away, Caroline denied that this was the case.

"The boys are having a hard time believing their father's gone," she said. "I've been too easy on the kids and now they don't want to work or listen to Bob. It's not his fault that they run away, they just do, and the neighbours take them in. The neighbours don't like Bob much and listen to the lies that the kids tell. They're just kids telling stories, that's all."

"What about reports that the twins have bruises all over their bodies?"

"They are always fighting with their older brothers and the big boys are too rough," she lied.

"They also appear awfully thin," he asked. "Why are they so skinny?"

"Bill was thin like that, and besides they don't eat for days when they run away. There's nothing I can do about that if I can't find them to feed them."

"What about their school attendance? I've been told that the boys are forced to work instead of going to school?"

"The kids have chores before and after school, just like all the kids around here. They'll never learn to work if we don't make them. They miss school only when they run away."

The social worker believed Caroline's answers were not entirely true. Unfortunately, with the being his first visit, he didn't have enough family history to make an informed assessment. These children were likely neglected by the standards of others, but unless they were in immediate danger, there was nothing more he could do.

No judge in the country would support an order to apprehend the children after only one visit. The social worker would be reminded that his job was to help families resolve their problems not pluck children from a familiar environment and place them in another. It would be best for everyone if the situation could be resolved here. Taking the children should be the last option and it would take much paperwork and red-tape.

The social worker decided that putting the fear of God in Domko would be the children's best chance. He had a lengthy discussion with him, then put the family on probation. He informed him that if there were more complaints from neighbours, there would be a further investigation.

Whatever the social worker said to Domko seemed to work for a little while. He was deathly afraid of anyone who worked for the government and easier on the children for the next month. The twins overhead their mother and Domko talking about the social worker one evening while the boys sat near the top of the stairs in the bedroom.

"Hey, Denny," David said. "That man's gonna help us."

"Yeah, an' Domko's scared of him." Dennis said. "When do you think he's gonna come again?"

"I dunno. He gots to come all the way from Winnipeg an' that's a long ways."

"Yeah," Dennis said sadly. "I wanna be home next time he comes."

The following afternoon Caroline was sitting alone in the kitchen. She called the twins to sit with her because she had something to discuss. The boys were eager to talk with their mother. It wasn't often that she paid attention to them.

"I have an idea that I think will be good for both you boys and Domko," she said.

The twins listened intently.

"I've been thinking that maybe we should change your last name to Domko," she said, adding, "and that you boys should start calling him 'dad'. He might consider you his children and not be so hard on you."

David and Dennis' hearts sank. They were hoping that she had another foster home in mind. When the realization of what she had said sank in, both boys recoiled.

"No!" David screamed. "We can't do that! We don't wanna be no Domko!"

"Yeah," Dennis interjected. "An' I'd rather be dead than call Satan 'dad'."

Exasperated, Caroline shook her head.

"What's wrong with calling him dad?" she asked.

"He ain't our dad!" Dennis argued. "He's nothin' like dad, nothin' at all. I hate him an' I wish our real dad was still alive."

"Well he's not, so just quit talkin' about him," Caroline scolded. "Because you miss your real dad you don't wanna give Domko a chance."

"No, Momma that's not why," David argued. "He's mean to us, that's why we don't like him. We just can't call him dad."

"I'd rather be dead," Dennis said emphatically.

The twins sat with their arms folded tightly across their chests. Their expressions were identical and Caroline could see that there was no way she'd be able to convince them it was a sensible thing to do.

"Fine then," she said angrily. "But I don't want to hear you mentioning your father ever again then, do you hear?"

Her nine year old sons stared at her - but neither would agree.

* * * * *

Domko was definitely going to be short of hay this winter. He wanted to fatten his animals on the neighbour's feed before the snow fell. On the first of October, following afternoon chores he told David to take the horses and let them into the hay field where Gus had four large stacks of hay waiting to be hauled home.

Reluctantly, David took the four horses by the reins and led them just north of the barn to the section of crown land just north of the barn that Gus leased. David opened the gate and watched helplessly as the horses trotted in, knowing that Domko was somewhere in the bush watching him. He sat on the fence as the horses eagerly ate Gus' hay. They had been on thin pasture all summer long and welcomed a change to fresh cut hay.

The horses fed for about 10 minutes before Gus and Marjorie arrived pulling the hay mover behind the tractor. Gus became angry when he saw the horses and was surprised to see David sitting on the fence.

"I'm s-sorry Gus," he apologized in hushed tones, glancing over his shoulder. "Domko m-made me chase them in h-here." David hated doing Domko's dirty work, knowing that his stepfather was trying to create bad feelings between the neighbours and the children. David couldn't explain this to Gus, though. Instead he grabbed the horses reins and led them out of the field.

"Well, I'm sure glad we came today to haul this hay home," Gus said angrily. "Otherwise, Domko would have you in here with his animals every day until the snow flies."

David could hear the exasperation in the older man's voice. Gus tried hard not to show it, but David knew that his sympathy to the children was wearing thin. Domko already controlled much of their lives and was also trying to ruin the only decent relationships they had.

Marjorie stood by the tractor frowning. She didn't like seeing her friends in trouble, but her dad's livelihood depended on having enough hay to feed the cows. There was no doubt in her mind that this was not David's fault.

David led the horses home and then reluctantly told the story to Domko who laughed and spit on the ground at the mention of Gus' name. Later that afternoon, Marjorie and Gus hauled most of one, four ton stack home making three trips that day. They usually left the hay in the field and went for it as needed, but felt they could no longer trust their neighbour who might steal from them. So far, it had been warm and dry all month so they hoped to haul all of hay home by the end of that week.

The twins had spent the next two days picking rocks in a field that Domko had cultivated earlier in the year. Domko wanted to seed it to oats the following spring, but the rocks had to be picked first. He pulled the stone wagon behind the tractor while the twins carried rocks until they were too weak to continue.

Still insulted that their mother would suggest they take Domko's name, the twins dragged themselves upstairs without speaking to her. They'd had little to eat and were dehydrated from being in the sun all day. Both boys fell into bed without a word. Neither enjoyed going to school, but they were both looking forward to it next morning. Anything was better than the manual labour they were forced to do at home.

The next morning they finished their chores then ducked off to school before Domko noticed they were gone. Mrs. Collier was their teacher again this term. Although the boys were still in grade two, she had promised that if they worked hard, she would move them to grade three for the second term which began in January.

Gus stuck his head through the door just as Marjorie was almost finished washing the supper dishes.

"Fire!" he yelled. "The hay's on fire!"

She dropped a plate on the floor then ran out the door after her father. Emma came bounding out of the bedroom, pausing for a moment to slip on her shoes by the door. She ran as fast as she could down the driveway behind Marjorie. Gus signalled them to hurry as he climbed on the tractor waiting by the road. A few pails and shovels were strewn on the hay mover which was luckily still hooked to the tractor. Gus frowned as he looked to the north.

Emma and Marjorie jumped onto the hay mover then motioned for Gus to go. They held on tightly to the edge of the wood wagon as he accelerated past the Pischke farm. The wind, blowing briskly from the south was beginning to pick up speed. The Harwarts could see thick, billowing smoke rising in the north a short distance away. The smell of smoke permeated the air and they wondered why they hadn't smelled it sooner.

As Gus sped past the bush to the edge of Caroline's quarter section, he came to a clearing where they saw what was happening. Flames from a grass fire at Pischke's had spread to their land. The fire was engulfing the base of one of their haystacks that Domko's horses had been eating two days before. The flames crackled as the fire spread quickly up the sides of the dry hay.

Gus halted the tractor on the road, then the three of them jumped off and began running towards the fire. Using shovels, Gus and Emma began beating the flames, while Marjorie filled two pails with water from the ditch. She had a difficult time running without spilling water, but kept going because she was a strong, capable girl who never lost her cool.

She threw water on the stack then ran back for more. After nearly a dozen trips it became apparent to Marjorie and her parents that they would be unable to save the stack. The flames grew overhead and Gus and Emma were forced to back away from the heat.

"We'll keep it from spreading to the other stacks," Gus said, pointing to the remaining hay in the field.

They ran ahead and beat out the fire as it crept forward. Flames licking the dry ground, fueling themselves on small clumps of hay that were left behind when the stacks were built. Marjorie continued to carry pails of water and dumped them on the ground in big circles around the stacks. Her dad didn't have to tell her how important it was to save this hay. She had worked beside him long enough to know.

"That sonofagun!" Gus suddenly yelled. Looking at her father, she could see he was pointing south. On the other side of the fence, not more than 100 yards away, stood Domko. He was watching and laughing as the Harwarts struggled to save the hay.

"He did this, I just know it," Emma yelled, choking from the smoke. "He can't have it so he doesn't want us to have it either!"

Gus and Emma beat the ground even harder. The sight of Domko standing across the fence laughing at her and her parents caused a knot of hatred to swell in Marjorie's stomach. She hated Bob Domko for what he was doing to them and for causing harm to her friends. His presence caused her to work even harder to prove that he couldn't beat her. Tears of frustration welled in her eyes, ironically helping to relieve the stinging from the smoke.

The blaze was almost under control when neighbours arrived. Domko disappeared into the bush without being seen when the men from a neighbouring family joined in to help. Fortunately, only one stack was lost. It continued to smolder while the men assessed the situation. It was apparent that the fire had been started on the Pischke quarter before spreading to Harwart's hay. Gus was thankful that he had placed stacks far enough apart so that he didn't lose the whole field.

Fed up with Domko, Gus went to the neighbours to borrow their telephone. He wasn't going to let his adversary get away with it this time.

That following morning there was a knock at the school room door. The students all turned and began to chatter when they realized there was a visitor at the school. They gasped then became very quiet as two RCMP officers stepped into the room. For some of the younger children, it was the first time they had seen a police officer face-to-face.

Mrs. Collier talked to the uniformed men for a moment, then called for David and Dennis. The children let out another gasp, as the boys walked slowly to the back of the room.

"You're goin' to jail," an older boy taunted as Dennis walked past.

"Shut up," Norman said in a threatening tone, poking the boy in the arm with his pencil.

The twins were taken outside and the teacher followed. The older children jumped up and ran to look out the school windows. As they watched, the twins were taken to the police car and put in the back seat. Mrs. Collier returned and ushered everyone back to their seats.

"See what happens when you're bad?" she said cooly.

Norman gave her a disapproving look, but said nothing. Rosie , who was in grade one, was frightened because her brothers had been taken by the police. Eunice hunkered down in her seat, hoping that nobody remembered that she too, was a Pischke.

Dennis and David sat quietly in the back of the cruiser. Out of the corner of his eye, Dennis could see some of his classmates staring and pointing from the school windows. The officers sat in the front seat, questioning the twins.

"Did you boys light a grass fire yesterday afternoon north of your house?" asked one of the officers sternly. David recognized he was the same officer who had brought them back to the farm last winter.

"No, sir," he stammered.

"Are you sure?"

"Hey, Denny, we didn't light no fire did we?"

"No, sir," Dennis said emphatically.

"Your stepfather said that you boys lit a fire in the bush then went to school while it spread to Gus Harwart's hay. Do you know anything about that?"

The boys looked at each other in astonishment. Domko had blamed them again!

"No sir!" David said. "Ole' Squeezer just says we does stuff like that."

The officers turned and began talking quietly among themselves. David strained to hear what they were saying. Then the policeman drove the car out of the school yard. The boys thought for sure they were going to jail, but then the car turned towards the Pischke farm.

"Oh no," Dennis groaned. "Not again!"

Both boys began to cry as the officers turned in the driveway. Glancing in his rear view mirror, the officer at the wheel could see the boys hugging each other in fear. Reluctantly, the twins followed the officers out of the car but refused to go in the house. Domko came outside and frowned when he saw the boys standing quietly behind the police officers.

"Mr. Domko I'm afraid that we're going to have to charge you under section 9 (a) of the Fire Prevention act for letting a fire get out of your control and damaging another person's property.".

"I's not be doink it," he said pointing to the boys. "They's be!"

"I'm sorry, sir, but since they are your children and this is your farm, you are responsible for what goes on here." the officer said. "You are responsible for them."

Domko glared at the twins who looked silently at the ground. The officers discussed the charge with Domko a little longer then got back in their car. Before the cruiser had backed all the way out the driveway, the officers caught a glimpse of the twins running frantically into the bush.

"They probably lit the fire and are now in trouble with the old man," one said.

The other officer wasn't so sure.

"It was no accident," Gus said to the officers sitting at his kitchen table. "Domko set that fire on purpose to burn my hay."

They looked at the thin, old man and smiled. The officers had seen plenty of feuding neighbours before.

"I'm sure he didn't mean to burn your hay, Mr. Harwart," the older officer said. "He's blaming those twin boys and the boys are blaming him. There is certainly no proof that he set fire to your hay with intent, not unless you saw him do it?"

Gus frowned. "Of course I didn't see him do it, but I know he did. And you're only charging him with letting a fire get out of control? What about arson or willful damage to my property?"

"We'll admit he's a strange guy," said the younger officer. "But you can't prove he did it on purpose."

Gus laughed sarcastically. "I understand now," he said standing up. "You're afraid of him too, aren't you?"

The officers looked at each other and shook their heads.

"That's why nobody ever does anything about those kids," Gus continued. "He works his stepchildren like they are in a concentration camp. The wife and I can see it, so can Jim Deighton. Can't anybody else see how Domko manipulates everyone?"

Emma stood silently with her hands on her hips while the officers left the house. Gus didn't speak up often, but when he did he was usually right.

Caroline and the children stayed far away from Domko for the next few days. He was so angry about being charged with burning the Harwart hay that he threatened to shoot everyone in the house. He paced back and forth, glancing out the window while sucking on his cigarette. He dropped the ashes on the floor and ground them into the linoleum as he murmured to himself.

By now, Caroline was realizing that there was something seriously wrong with her husband. His behaviour was becoming increasingly irrational as he lamented that Gus was trying to destroy their farm. She suspected that he had set the hay on fire during one of his rages. She wondered if he had forgotten all about it? She sat at the kitchen table and listened, but dared not say a word as he paced back and forth.

She had hoped that their marriage and the addition to the house would give them a fresh start. For a while, his temperament had improved, but soon he had fallen into his old pattern. His constant rages and belittlement of the children caused her to become depressed. She was finding it hard to stay optimistic for the children's sake. She began looking for answers in the Bible, and immersed herself deeper in the church, the place she had always been told was a pillar of comfort and advice. She hoped that her friends could give her support during this troubling time. Now that the busy summer months were over, they would begin visiting again, bringing Watchtower magazines and news from the annual Jehovah's Witness gatherings. She hoped to go to a Winnipeg meeting the following spring to participate in what she'd been told was an enlightening experience.

* * * * *

"I's be goink to town," Domko said, grabbing his coat and storming outside.

Caroline hoped that Dennis was not around since Domko had been constantly picking on the boy. For some reason, poor Dennis was always in the wrong place at the wrong time.

Opening the door quietly, Caroline could see her husband marching towards the lean-to against the side of the grainary. He emerged a few moments later with the tractor. She lifted the cream can down from the shelf and met him at the door. Smiling weakly, she held the can out for him. His eyes were cold and unfeeling as he roughly took it from her. Within a few moments, he was gone.

That's another cream cheque I'll never see, she thought.

That afternoon the twins played happily in the ditch near the front of the house. The mud was thick and sticky, perfect for molding small figurines. Rolling the clay in their hands, they made cars, tractors, farm animals and buildings. Marjorie watched in amazement as Dennis took two small pieces of wire and poked them through the bottom of a tractor he was making. Rolling four balls into perfectly even wheels, he placed the wheels on the ends of the wire, then added a small piece of clay on the ends to keep the wheels from falling off.

Few people recognized the twins' capabilities, but Marjorie knew they had special artistic talents and that the boys were meticulous in their work. As each figurine was completed, it was carefully set on a piece of wood to dry in the sun.

Dennis and David spent most of the afternoon dreamily making toys until the sound of a tractor from the south jolted them back to reality. Marjorie had left a few hours earlier. while Eunice and Norman were bringing in the cows for the evening milking. The twins could hear the lead cow's bell as she made her way into the barn. Bruno jumped and barked as Norman threw a stick for the dog to retrieve. The twins lay flat in the ditch, hoping that Domko wouldn't see them.

The tractor turned into the driveway and stopped by the house where Domko unloaded a few supplies into the kitchen. The twins watched carefully as he got back on the tractor and drove it to the lean-to. He strode into the barn and suddenly there was an outburst of yelling. Norman came flying out of the barn and slid under the fence, running as fast as he could towards the bush by the church. Domko was on the boy's heels, catching him near the house, just out of the twin's sight.

"C'mon," David said, crawling out of the ditch. Hunched over, the boys ran stealthily to the corner of the house. The could hear their brother screaming in pain around the corner from them. Peering around, they saw Domko towering over Norman.

"Vas it goot?" Domko yelled as he beat the boy with a stick. "You punk!"

"No, no!" Norman lied as the stick smashed down on his body. "I didn't do it."

"Vat?" Domko roared. "Who's be doink it? Marjie be doink it?"

Eunice stood by the barn, her hands drawn up to her face. She flinched every time the stick smashed her brother's limbs. The twins watched sadly from a safe distance as Domko continued to beat Norman, putting the entire weight of his body into the effort. His feet came off the ground as he struck the child who was begging for mercy.

A growl began deep in Bruno's throat as he lowered his head and tail. Stealthily, he approached Norman's assailant from behind, baring his teeth in warning to the man. Domko didn't notice the angry dog because of his own rage. Bruno crept closer, the hair on his back now standing straight on end. Suddenly he lunged at Domko, digging his teeth deep into the man's forearm. Domko let out a scream as he knocked the growling, snapping animal to the ground.

"Fraa!" he yelled as the dog placed himself in front of Norman. Bruno's eyes remained lowered as he continued to growl deep in his throat.

"I's be showink it some!" Domko roared as he strode through the yard towards the grainary. He emerged seconds later carrying a .308 calibre rifle, snapping the clip in place as he walked.

Norman, who was disoriented from the beating, lay on the ground while Bruno stood protectively over him. It was then he realized what was happening.

"Bruno, get outta here!" Norman yelled. "Run, Bruno, run!"

The dog turned to the boy and his tail began to wag softly. He pressed his wet nose on Norman's face then this thick, soft tongue lapped the boy's cheek.

"Go away!" Norman said pushing the persistent dog away from him as he struggled to sit up. Once he realized the dog wasn't going to run, Norman turned to Domko who was quickly approaching.

"Please don't," Norman begged. "It's not his fault, it's my fault."

Without a word, Domko cocked the hammer. He smirked as he took careful aim, then pulled the trigger. Norman jumped in surprise at the sound of the bullet.

Startled, Bruno yelped and fell to the ground as the bullet pierced his abdomen. He lost control of his back limbs and began pulling himself along the ground with his front paws. In desperation, he crawled towards the bush, his brown eyes wild with fear and shock. Norman covered his eyes and began crying as his stepfather walked slowly behind the mournful animal. The dog wimpered as it looked sadly at the chuckling man above. Domko took his time while the dog struggled valiantly to escape. He waited a few moments before placing the gun six inches from the dog's head. Bruno panted softly and wimpered in pain as Domko slowly pulled the trigger.

Caroline was bagging carrots in the far garden when the first gunshot rang through the air. Turning toward the house, she could see Eunice in the barnyard and the twins at the corner of the house. Domko was standing near Norman who was lying on the ground. Caroline could see her husband raise the gun again.

"No!" she screamed, running through the pasture towards the house. Her heart raced wildly as she waved her arms. "Norman!"

Another shot rang out and Caroline screamed in anguish. She could see the twins running around the side of the house and Eunice turn quickly towards the barn. Norman was struggling to stand up, supporting himself by leaning on the side of the house. Domko turned and walked slowly back to the grainary.

Running through the field, Caroline experienced a wave of relief as she realized that Domko hadn't shot her son after all.

"What's going on?" she demanded breathlessly as she ran into the yard.

"I's be shootink that soneebeech," Domko said, pointing towards the brown lump of fur lying beside the driveway. The look of pleasure on his face made Caroline angry. She had liked the dog and was tired of Domko killing all the children's pets.

Domko explained that he was punishing Norman for stealing when the dog attacked him. Caroline eyed him suspiciously, but said nothing. Relieved that it wasn't Norman who had been shot, she decided it was best to forget the episode.

"Take into some bush," Domko ordered Norman, pointing at the dead dog. The boy leaned against the house and said nothing. The twins waited until Domko was gone before going to aid their brother, whose face was stained with tears. Norman's body was bleeding and swollen from the beating. He left the twins and hobbled down the driveway, his eyes filled with pain.

"Me an' Davey will do it," Dennis called out as he watched his brother walk into the bush across the road. The twins picked up the limp body of the dead dog and carried it into the bush by the church . They selected a spot near where they had buried Rosie's cat. David went back to the barn to get a shovel and together they dug a shallow grave. Kneeling beside it, they covered the hump with sticks and leaves.

"What did Norman do?" Dennis asked.

"He went for the mail an' put an apple on the bill at the Co-op," David said. "It costed three cents."

Chapter 17

It's a twelve foot drop

DOMKO CONSIDERED NORMAN'S LOVE for Bruno a weakness. He had enjoyed killing the dog and wanted to exploit the boy's love for the animal even further.

"Norrrrman," Domko would taunt. "Where's be Bruno?"

Norman would continue working without answering. For the next week he was called a thief and liar and berated for charging the apple at the store. Norman listened silently to Domko's ravings, not once making eye contact. He knew that the man was searching for an excuse to beat him again. He also knew that he would be the object of Domko's anger until one of the other children did something wrong, then Norman's misery would end.

That Friday night after chores, the twins saw Norman sneak out of the house. They knew better than to follow the fourteen year-old who was likely going somewhere to meet friends. Early the next morning, Eunice and the twins noticed that their brother hadn't come home the night before. When they chased the cows into the barn to start milking, Norman came down from the loft.

"What's wrong?" Eunice asked.

Norman's skin was grey and he smelled awful.

"Nothin," he said. "Where's the ole' black bastard?"

"In the house."

"Oh," Norman groaned as he went outside. Falling down on his knees he vomited beside the barn door. He came back in holding his head with his hands.

"Do you want some milk?" Eunice asked trying to console her sick brother.

"No!" Norman said wincing at the sound of his own voice. "I don't want nothin'."

The children were quiet as they continued to milk the cows. Norman grabbed a pail and stool.

"Guess what I did last night?" he said casually.

"What?" Eunice asked, peering around her cow.

"I got drunk," he said proudly. "Last night me an' the Meisner boys drank a whole pile of home brew."

Eunice laughed and the twins were shocked.

"Don't tell no one," he warned. "I don't want the ole' bastard to know."

Unable to finish milking, Norman crawled outside and vomited again.

"I can't do no more," he said. "I'm gonna sleep for a while."

He climbed back into the loft and fell asleep in the soft hay.

"Where's be some Norman?" Domko asked a few minutes later when he came into the barn to check on the children.

"I don't know, he didn't sleep upstairs last night," Eunice lied as her heart pounded heavy in her chest. She was never sure if Domko was asking a sincere question or if he knew the answer and was trying to trick her.

"Huh!" Domko grunted as he turned and went back to the house. He was clearly disappointed that the boy wasn't there to tease.

Later that morning, the twins were in the yard when Domko came from the barn, pushing Norman in front of him. He handed the boy a potato fork and they walked to the garden. He needed help digging a half acre of potatoes and Norman was the biggest and strongest of the children. The twins hid in the bush and watched while Norman dug as Domko stood nearby. The boy's pace began to weaken and he had to stop to vomit again. Domko laughed as he taunted the boy.

"Seek?" Domko teased. "Vat, yous be some seek?"

Norman nodded that he wasn't feeling well as he leaned against the fork. Domko told him to keep digging. Norman staggered and fell to the ground.

"Lazy!" Domko roared as he strode across the potato hills to the boy. Swinging his leg back, he kicked Norman hard in the stomach.

"Now you's be seek!" he said.

When the boy didn't move, he kicked him again. Then Domko took the potato fork and smashed the handle across Norman's back.

He strode back to the house and yelled into the bush for David and Dennis to finish digging the potatoes. Otherwise he was going to kill Norman if he came back and the work was not done.

Once Domko was in the house, the boys ran to the field, examining their older brother closely to see if he was dead, before they started digging. Within an hour, Norman staggered to his feet and began walking over the rows of potatoes drying in the sun.

"I ain't comin' back no more," he said to his brothers. He walked silently past the house then turned and began staggering north along the road.

Norman ended up at Bert and Hilda Nachtigall's in Steep Rock. When Domko heard about this, he went wild. The Nachtigalls and Caroline were good friends and they had offered to help in any way that they could. Caroline had once told Norman that if things got too bad on the farm, he could go there and the Nachtigalls would take him in.

Domko was furious about this and demanded that Caroline go get the boy and bring him home. Caroline tried, but Norman refused to return to the farm. She decided not to push the issue, fearing a ruckus would alert the social worker who would then begin an investigation that could lead to all of her children being taken away.

She returned home without the boy, hoping to explain to Domko. She tried to console her husband by saying that Eunice and the twins were old enough to work. Rosie was only seven, but she was a strong girl who would be able to help with the haying the following summer.

It took all of Caroline's courage to reassure Domko that the neighbours and members of her church were not trying to thwart his plan to build a successful farm.

Life for the twins and Eunice changed drastically after Norman left. Keeping up with the chores seemed almost impossible and they were forced to work long hours before and after school.

By early November, there was no meat left in the house and Domko was tiring of potato soup and holopchi. It was time to butcher one of the pigs, a job usually accomplished with the help of Norman. David and Dennis were bringing in armfuls of wood when Domko summoned them.

"Yous be come" he said, getting up from his chair. "You's be helpink me some."

The twins followed him outside, dreading the job ahead of them. Domko stopped at the pumphouse and got his gun while the boys continued walking to the pig pen beside the chicken house. The pig, thinking it was time to be fed, snorted and looked at the twins expectantly. A wave of sadness washed over Dennis as he looked at the animal they had fed since it was a weanling. David felt they were betraying the pig and turned away so that he wouldn't have to look at its face.

"I's be shootink ant yous be catchink it some," Domko instructed, pointing towards the pig. The twins stepped forward reluctantly and stood at the edge of the pen as the pig waddled over and began rooting the ground near their feet. Domko walked to the opposite side of the pen, and taking careful aim, shot the pig behind the front right leg. Squealing, the animal began running around the pen, it's short legs giving way to the sudden weakness on one side.

"Fraa!" Domko yelled, pointing at the pig. The twins jumped into the pen and slid around in the mud and manure until they were able to corner the pig and wrestle it to the ground. By now the animal had lost a lot of blood from the gunshot wound, and it was beginning to weaken. Domko jumped into the pen and knelt beside the boys. Reaching into the breast pocket of his coat, he pulled out his sinister looking hunting knife. Grinning at the twins, he grabbed the pig's head with his left hand and wrenching the animal's head back, he sliced through the pig's exposed neck in one swoop.

The animal's squeals became fainter, as it began to choke on its own blood. Domko continued to hack away at the dying animal's neck. suddenly, the pig convulsed violently and blood squirted all over the boys.

Seeing their disgust with the job, Domko reached out and grabbed David by the front of the shirt. He pulled the boy's face close to his and chuckled as he held the knife at eye level.

"I's be cuttink Pischke neck," he seethed, eyes full of hatred.

David held his breath and dared not move. His eyes darted from the knife to Domko, then back to the knife again. He was always threatening to kill them. Would this be the time?

Domko relaxed his grip on the boy. Slipping the bloodstained knife back into his pocket, he ordered the boys to drag the pig's carcass to the barn. At the barn, the animal was placed on a board above a barrel of boiling water. It was the twin's job to scrape the hair from the animal before it was gutted. The pig was then hoisted overhead with a pulley where it hung before it was cut into large chunks and stored in the grainary.

School was let out for the holiday season less than a week before Christmas. This meant that the children had no place to go during the day where they could escape Domko and his cruel verbal and physical abuse. With Norman gone, there had been a dramatic increase in the number of times a week that Domko would seek out the twins, taunt them and give one of them a whipping. They avoided him by going upstairs early at night to sleep in their hiding spot behind the wall.

Domko now had an obsessive dislike for Dennis. This was putting a tremendous amount of pressure on David to protect his twin. The boys sat for hours and talked in their own language, deliberately using many of their strange words when Domko was around. The language irritated Domko who couldn't understand what they were saying. The twins were able to squirrel away food and establish hiding places in the bush without him knowing. His lack of comprehension enabled them to yell warnings to each other without Domko understanding. He complained to Caroline that he wanted the boys to learn to speak Polish. The thought of this repelled the twins who flatly refused to learn Domko's mother tongue.

The twins sat on the bed and listened as Domko went outside for his evening check of the yard. They knew that if he found anything out of place, one of them would be in trouble. Getting up from the bed, the boys went and sat quietly at the top of the stairs. David stood and opened the bedroom window. He didn't think Dennis could take another beating so the window might have to be their escape route. Staring at the ground 12 feet below, he could see a light sprinkling of snow on the ground. Travel wouldn't be difficult and both were wearing their outdoor clothing, a practice they started after spending a few nights in the cold. David made up his mind to jump if he had to.

It didn't take long before Domko was back in the house, raving to Caroline about the children.

"Tramps! They's be some goot for nuthink!" he yelled. "They's be playink some not workink!"

Domko held up a handful of the mud toys the twins had made the afternoon Bruno was shot. They'd hid them in the barn and had been playing with them that afternoon. Listening upstairs, David realized that Domko had found the little toys he'd forgotten to hide. He knew from experience that their little farm scene had been smashed by now.

"C'mon!" he whispered in panic to Dennis. David swung one leg out the window and then the other so that he was sitting on the sill. He could hear Domko yelling and the rest of the children scrambling to hide from him. Closing his eyes, David jumped from the window sill, landing feet first on the frozen ground. He lost his balance, rolling back towards the house. A second later, Dennis tumbled to earth beside him.

"Are you o.k.?" David asked.

"Yeah, I'm o.k., how 'bout you?" he replied, trying to stand up.

"I'm o.k. Where are we gonna go now?"

"Let's go to Deightons," Dennis suggested.

The twins ran into the bush and followed the trail through the churchyard before turning abruptly east to their neighbour's house.

"What's he barking at now?" Jim said to Ruby as he got up from his chair to look out the window. The dog was standing and barking loudly at the edge of the yard. Jim could see two figures coming across the field. The dog seemed to recognize the pair and ran to greet them.

"It looks like the Pischke twins are here again," he said.

"Well, let them in," Ruby said as she looked up from her knitting.

Jim opened the door just as David lifted his hand to knock. The twins appeared slightly startled as the door opened.

"C-can we come in?" David asked. "The Devil's after us again."

Once they were warmed up, Jim demanded a detailed explanation of what had happened. The twins described how Domko had been on a rampage the past few weeks. Ruby listened in horror as David described how Bruno was killed and how Domko had butchered the pig.

Not wanting to be outdone, Dennis lifted his shirt to show his back to the woman. It was covered in huge, purple bruises.

"I gots those when Domko got mad 'cause I didn't 'member which horses bridle I hung up. I mixed 'em up an' it took me too long to get the horses ready in the morning."

Ruby gasped and shook her head.

"Yeah, an' he says we're good for nothin'," David said, craving sympathy from the woman. "He calls us tramps an' hobos an' soneebeech-bastards."

Ruby raised her eyebrows. She was surprised to hear foul words coming so innocently from such a young mouth.

"What happened the last time I took you to the police?" Jim asked.

"They took us back," Dennis began. "Satan told 'em a big story about us bein' bad all the time."

"Yeah, an' he got us again," David added. "Denny peed his pants."

"You peed too!" Dennis said, his face flushing.

David smiled and gave his twin a little shove. Then David gasped.

"Denny, look!" he said in amazement, pointing to the front room. "They gots a Christmas tree."

Ruby and Jim watched as the twins moved closer to the tree and began talking to each other in their language, as if nobody else was in the room. They boys pointed to the glass ornaments and gingerly touched the home-made decorations hung neatly on the tree.

It was obvious that they had never seen a Christmas tree before. Jim got up and quietly opened a box of matches. The twins watched in wonder as he lit the candles standing tall on the ends of the branches. They stood quietly, examining every inch of the tree as the flames flickered.

Ruby prepared sandwiches for the boys who ate hungrily, only glancing away from the tree to take another sandwich from the plate. Each drank a glass of milk and belched loudly. Ruby tsked and Jim laughed. The twins were totally unaware that their naive wonder about the tree was being enjoyed a great deal by their hosts.

"Well it's getting late," Ruby finally said, not wanting to interrupt their fascination but anxious to get to bed.

Jim blew out the candles as Ruby led the twins into the kitchen. Taking a washcloth she scrubbed the hands and faces of both boys.

"I'm going to get you some fresh clothes," she said, disappearing upstairs. She returned with a clean pair of underwear and pyjamas for each boy. "Put these on."

The boys stripped off their clothes and left them in a heap on the floor. Ruby picked up the smelly clothes, which were stained with pig manure and blood, depositing them in the porch.

"I'll burn those in the morning," she laughed, then her voice softened. "Now, it's time to go to bed.

Her son were home visiting for the holidays and was reading in the upstairs bedroom, so Ruby led the twins to the extra bedroom off the kitchen. David and Dennis climbed into the bed as she tucked the covers up under their chins.

"Good night," she whispered.

"Good night, Aunt Ruby," they said in unison. They watched as she turned and left the room. The boys stared quietly at the ceiling for a few moments.

"Someday I'm gonna get me a Christmas tree," Dennis said dreamily.

David had also been thinking about Christmas. He hoped that he and Dennis would be able to stay at Deightons until the holiday was over. He listened to the baleful howls of coyotes and was thankful that he and his brother weren't in the bush.

Soon Dennis was breathing heavily, but David found it difficult to fall asleep. He could hear Jim and Ruby talking quietly in the kitchen. He wondered if the Deightons were always this nice or if they just pretended to be that way when he was there.

He'd seen Domko behave in a deceptive manner, to the point where most people in the area thought he was providing well for his family. 'A good man,' his grandfather and uncles had said. David wondered if Jim treated his family poorly when nobody was around to see. He pushed the thought from his mind and chastised himself for betraying one of their few friends.

It must be late now, David thought. He could hear Jim and Ruby getting ready to go to bed. Footsteps came quietly towards the room, so he closed his eyes and pretended to be asleep. Ruby's feet padded softly across the floor into the room. She stopped beside the bed and kissed Dennis' forehead. David breathed slowly and deeply, hoping Ruby wouldn't realize he was still awake. Next, she pushed back David's dirty hair, then leaned down and kissed him softly on the cheek.

"You're good boys," she whispered softly, "always remember that."

Ruby quietly left the room. David's heart swelled as his cheek burned from the warmth of the kiss. He didn't dare open his eyes or touch his face for fear the sensation would disappear. He played it over many times in his mind until he drifted off to sleep, vowing to remember the gentle kiss forever.

No effort was made to send the twins home in the days that followed. The children happily played with Ruby's teenage son Charles, skating on an outdoor rink and building forts in the snow. The twins happily helped with the farm chores, embarrassing Jim with their eagerness.

"Hey Jim, who lives over there?" David asked pointing to a farmhouse across the road. He and Jim had just finished shoveling out the barn.

"That's Newman's place," Jim answered.

"Are they nice?"

"The mother and girls are nice, but don't ever go there in the middle of the night. That old buggar Henry is almost as bad as Domko. When he gets drinking, he loses his mind."

"How come?"

"Hard to tell. People are funny, you never can tell what they'll be like until they take a drink."

"Domko never drinks at least not what I seen," David said. "D'you 'spose he'd be worse if he drank?"

"Knowing Domko, I guess you could say that," Jim laughed. "What do you think? Can he get any worse?"

"I hope not!" David exclaimed. "That black bastard is mean like the Devil already." Then David looked at Jim admiringly. He seemed to have experience in these matters and David trusted his judgement.

Jim smirked as the boy looked back toward the Newman house. It seemed hard to believe that there was another person who was almost as bad as Domko living so close. David was thankful that his friend had warned him. He realized that he and Dennis would have to be more careful about who they trusted in future.

"I don't want people to think we're takin' advantage of those boys," Jim said the following day to Ruby.

"You don't have to worry about that," she said. "Everybody knows."

Just then the four boys came into the house for lunch. After the meal, Dennis offered to help Ruby with the dishes. He and David had to talk and decided it was time to ask Ruby an important question.

"Aunt Ruby," Dennis asked. "Are you gonna get us anything for Christmas?"

"No sir!" Ruby joked, hugging the boy affectionately. "You won't be here on Christmas will you? Don't you want to go home?"

"No, ma'am," he answered. "We're gonna stay here. We don't got no Christmas tree."

Ruby smiled at the quiet twin. She'd noticed how much more outgoing he'd become in the past few days with her encouragement.

"What do you want for Christmas?" she asked in a serious tone.

"Don't matter," he said, smiling. "We like everything."

Ruby nodded with approval.

These children were thankful for the simple things that most youngsters took for granted, like a meal or a pair of mittens. She felt bad that she'd taken the boy's question so lightly.

"You'll find out tomorrow," she said.

The children bounded out of bed early the next morning. There were nearly as many presents under the tree for Dennis and David as there were for Ruby's son. She was thankful she had a surplus of knitted mitts and socks to give the twins. She had one knitted sweater on hand, so had quickly made another to match. She had worked late into the night Christmas Eve to finish the project, but felt it was worthwhile since it was important to her that the boys each have decent gifts. Ruby had even insisted that Jim make a quick trip to town to buy the boys each a toy.

She smiled as she watched the twins open their stockings, both filled with fruit, chocolate and hard candy.

That day they sang Christmas carols, ate a turkey dinner and spent the day playing games. The twins were in a state of blissful shock the entire time, barely able to comprehend that life could be so good.

Word soon spread through the community that the twins were at Deighton's farm. Shortly after Christmas day, Caroline arrived to take the twins home. Fearing the social worker would come again, she hoped that the latest incident hadn't been reported to the police by Jim.

Jim stood in the kitchen and watched disapprovingly with his arms crossed across his chest as Caroline stood in the doorway persuading the boys to go home with her.

Tears came to Ruby's eyes as she noticed an immediate change in the boys' posture. Dennis began to withdraw while David's shoulders slumped as they listened quietly to their mother.

Caroline said that Domko was sorry he had chased them out of the house.

"You don't live here," she whispered emphatically. "You don't want Ruby and Jim to get sick of us, now do you?"

The twins started to cry as they gathered up their gifts. Caroline gave Ruby a disapproving look when she noticed the wooden cars each boy grasped tightly. Ruby guessed what Caroline was thinking and was quick to answer.

"Well, I couldn't very well give my son something and not the twins," she said. "Besides, the mitts and sweaters will come in handy."

Caroline nodded. At one time she also knitted for her family, until Domko criticized her for wasting time making things for her children. He even burned a few of her projects.

"Thank you but it wasn't necessary," Caroline said.

"Yes, it was," Ruby said cooly. She had qualms about interfering with Caroline's religious beliefs, but stubbornly believed she was justified in giving gifts to the boys. Her icy gaze defied Caroline who said nothing as she turned and left, pushing the crying boys ahead of her.

Chapter 18

The Lutheran Church

A WEEK-LONG COLD SNAP kept the family close to home in the middle of February. One afternoon while the twins were sitting on the front room floor drawing, David ripped his pants on a nail in the floor as he stood up. The tearing sound caused everyone to look at David who began trembling as he tried to hide the tear. The sound was also heard by Domko who dropped another log in the wood stove.

"Fraa!" he yelled. "See! I's be buyink some pant ant he's be breakink it!"

Caroline scolded David for his carelessness. She told him to fetch her mending kit from the bedroom. David skittered past Domko, returning with the kit tucked under his arm. His mother handed him a needle and thread, telling him to fix the tear. He avoided walking near Domko as he sat down in the far corner and easily threaded the needle.

He began sewing the same way he'd watched his mother many times. He sewed for over an hour, making small, precise stitches while Domko watched from across the room. David avoided making eye contact with his stepfather, hoping he'd become distracted by someone else, but the other children had the good sense to keep quiet.

When David finished, he stuck the needle in the spool of thread then hurried to his mother's side. Just then, his stepfather's voice boomed across the room.

"I's be lookink at some pant," he scowled.

David cringed. He dreaded having to stand within inches of Domko while his pant leg was examined. Slowly inching over, his mind went numb as he silently prayed the mending job would be judged suitable. Keeping his body back as far as he could, he stuck the offending pant leg forward. Domko leaned down to look at the stitching then let out a roar.

"Vat? You's be playink!" he yelled.

David squirmed out of reach and ran towards the door. His siblings scattered and Dennis bolted outside.

Domko screamed obscenities as he ran after the boys, knocking Kathy to the ground as she became entangled in her father's legs. This caused him to stumble, giving the twins the opportunity to escape.

Running along a path in the snow to the chicken coop, the boys quickly darted inside. David pulled the outer door shut but left the inside door open. The twins hid behind the door since there was no time to think. They could only hope that Domko wouldn't look there.

Suddenly the outside door swung open.

"Daaaavid. . ." the familiar voice cooed. " Dennnnis . . . I's be givink you pie."

The boys stared straight ahead as Domko looked through the hen house. The birds squawked nosily as he knocked over chop pails and checked the roost. The twins held their breath as their pursuer neared the door. Grunting, Domko stood for a moment, wondering where to look next. He opened the outside door, then pulled the inside door closed behind him as he stepped outside. Eyes squeezed shut, the boys each let out a tiny gasp of relief. David opened one eye to discover that the boys were alone.

"C'mon," he said to Dennis as he tip-toed to the small window. Looking out he could see Domko sneaking towards the barn. "As soon as he's inside, we gotta get our coats."

Dennis nodded in agreement. They waited until Domko vanished into the barn then flung open the door. The boys ran into the house, each grabbing a coat. Dennis' hands trembled as he pulled on his boots.

"Now where do we go?" he asked his brother.

Caroline appeared from the corner of the kitchen."Run!" she said. "He's coming back!"

The twins dashed out the door just as Domko came through the barn yard fence.

Confused, he stood watching for a few moments then angrily started to chase them. He hated playing cat and mouse and didn't like it when the boys tricked him.

The boys ran into the bush near the church. Soon they could hear Domko's feet pounding on the snow behind them. They came to the church yard fence where snow had drifted higher than the top wire and formed a snow bank. Scrambling up the bank, they slid on top of the snow and rolled down the other side. They scrambled to their feet and continued running through the deep snow towards the cemetery.

Domko was only a few feet behind, but suddenly stopped. David glanced over his shoulder to see their tormenter kicking the snow on the other side of the fence. He shook his fist in the air and swore at the boys. Had he continued chasing them for a few more yards, he would have caught them. David felt buoyed by the discovery that Domko wouldn't step onto the church grounds for some odd reason.

"C'mon," he said as he ran to the far side of the church. "He can't see us over here."

Panting, the boys fell in the snow. Out of sight, they stared at the sky as they listened to Domko cursing.

"Ah, shuddup you ole' Flat Foot," Dennis said under his breath.

David looked at him and laughed. They'd escaped!

The twins waited by the church until they were certain Domko was gone. The sun was beginning to set and soon they'd need a place to sleep.

Dennis followed David up the cement steps at the front of the church.

He pulled on the door which was padlocked shut.

"How do you s'pose Norman got in here anyway?" Dennis asked.

"It never used to be locked 'til Norman got in an' crapped on the floor," David said. "Then the church people had a meeting and locked the door."

"Oh," he said. "That darn' Norman wrecked it for us."

"Maybe we can get the lock open," David said. "Gimme the wire that's holdin' up your pants."

Dennis opened his coat and slid the wire from his belt loops. With one hand clasping his pants, which were at least two sizes too big, he used the other to hand the wire to his brother.

David stuck the end of the wire into the key slot then pulled down. "This is called pickin' the lock," he said with a worldy ring to his voice. "I read 'bout it in one of Walter's comic books. You watch that nobody's comin'."

Dennis nodded, looking to the south and then north. He was impressed that David had thought of the idea of forcing the lock. But after five minutes with no success, Dennis suggested that they climb in a back window.

David pulled on the lock again. Giving up he tucked Dennis' wire in his pocket and the boys jumped from the church steps to the ground. They walked around the building, agreeing that their best chance to get inside was through the back window. As they looked up at the small glass panes, it seemed like an impossible task to them.

"It's so high," Dennis said looking around. "We got to get somethin' to stand on."

"I gots somethin' to stand on," David said, pushing his twin down. "You."

By climbing on Dennis' back, David was able to reach the window sill. There were no handles, but he was able to coax the window open by pinching the wood dividing the panes and then pushing upwards.

"Is it almost open?" Dennis asked meekly from his bent position on the ground. He tried to tuck his hands into his jacket sleeves. "My back's gettin' sore an' my han's are cold."

"I think I got it, Denny," David said as the window rattled slightly. "Now you gotta stand up so I can get in."

Dennis wobbled up slowly as his brother balanced on his back. David pushed up the window the rest of the way then reached inside. with his arms. Holding onto the sill, he swung his legs from his brother's back and gained a foothold on the wood siding. Dennis watched as his twin wiggled his way inside, his legs suddenly disappearing from sight. David landed with a thump on the floor, then stood up and smiled as he appeared at the church window with a small wooden box.

"Here stand on this," he said tossing it into the snow.

Dennis stood on top of the box and with David's help, he was able to shimmy through the window. The boys found themselves in the church's small storage room. Opening the door, they peeked out, half expecting someone to be there to confront them. Stepping out, they found themselves at the front of the church near the organ. A large storage box covered with a red velvet cloth sat in the middle of the floor directly behind them. Candles in brass holders sat importantly on top. Opposite the storage room was the minister's vestibule and inside hung the minister's cloak. The vestibule opened onto a raised podium which had a large, thick bible open in the middle, waiting to be read.

Two rows of empty pews faced the front and a large wood stove sat at the back of the room by the entrance.

"I guess we'll get in trouble if we get caught here," Dennis whispered, his voice echoing as it bounced lightly off the high ceiling.

"It don't matter as long as we don't crap on nothin'" David said.

"Should we make a fire?"

David thought for a moment. "No. If the neighbours see smoke at the church, they'll come an' take us back home. The candles will keep us warm," he said, lifting the holders down from the table. He lined them in a row on the carpeted floor, then lit the candles with matches he found in the storage room.

Dennis sat down in front of the small fires and stared into the light. It was almost dark and the temperature was dropping. He stared into the lights and shivered as David appeared from the vestibule wearing the minister's cloak.

Dennis was shocked at the sight. "Take that off before Momma sees you!" he exclaimed.

"She ain't gonna see us here," David said confidently. "It's real warm - feel it."

Dennis grabbed a corner of the red velvet cloak and stroked it. As David sat down, the cloak brushed against one of the candles knocking it over, but the boy was able to grab it before it did any damage to the rug.

Dennis snuggled close to his brother and pulled the cloak around himself. "Wouldn't Momma be mad if she saw us in this?"

"Yeah, an' wouldn't Satan be glad if we just did nothin' an' froze in the snow," David mocked. "We gotta take care of ourselves 'cause nobody else is gonna."

The boys relaxed against the wall while they listened to the wind whistling softly through the bell tower. The old rafters groaned and floorboards creaked from the cold. They sat quietly for a long time until David finally broke the silence.

"What if one of us turns blind like Kathy?" he asked.

"We won't," Dennis said quickly. "She was a baby when he made her blind an' we're big already."

"Yeah, but Denny he can make you blind too," David said. "You gots to cover your head when he hits you."

"I do!"

"No, you gots to do it like this," David continued, wrapping his arms in front of his face and over the top of his head. "'Cause if Flat Foot smashes you an' you turn blind, you won't be able to work no more. You know what'll happen then."

"Yeah, he'll shoot me like he shoots the dogs," Dennis said.

David nodded. Domko had stolen many dogs from neighbours then callously shot them if they misbehaved. The boys had watched this and reasoned they could be next. "What do you figure it's like to be dead?" said David.

"Momma says that when we die, we'll be in the new order and things will be be better."

"What about the ole Devil?"

"He ain't good enough to make it to the new order."

"Are we?"

"Ruby says we're good. An' Momma used to say we was good until Satan kept tellin' her we're bad. The people from the church don't think we're good, but they don't decide who goes to the new order."

"You've been listenen' too much to momma and the church people."

"Yeah, you're right," Dennis said. "But maybe we're wastin' our time tryin' to live. Maybe it would be better if we just died and went some other place."

"All I know is that I can't just stand there like you and let Satan kill me. I gots to run and you gots to run too," replied David.

"I know, but I freeze up," Dennis explained.

David shook his head. Yawning, he stretched his legs and Dennis examined the careful stitching that David had done earlier.

"How come he got so mad 'bout your pants"?

David snickered. "'Cause I stitched 'em to my long underwear too!"

Dennis laughed and gave his brother a shove.

"Hey!" he said pointing to David's waist. "How come you didn't use your wire 'stead of mine?"

David gave him a sly look. "'Cause I didn't want my pants to fall down."

Within a few hours, the twins fell into a fitful sleep. The drafty old building continued to echo softly through the frosty, clear night. David woke shivering many times and worried that if he slept too deeply, he'd freeze to death. Each time he woke, he nudged Dennis who muttered and turned away.

As long as he keeps movin', then I know he ain't dead, David thought.

Morning came and the frigid church became secondary to the gnawing in their stomachs.

"I'm hungry," Dennis complained. "I didn't get to eat yesterday."

"Me neither," David said.

"What should we do?"

"It's too cold to go far. Maybe we should go to Emma's?"

"Is it a school day?"

"I dunno. What day is it?"

"Friday?"

"Just as long as it ain't Sunday, we can hide here after we eat."

The boys stood and stretched their stiff limbs. The candles had burned low so David plucked the stubs from the holders and tossed them in the corner. He returned from the storage room with a handful of long, thick candles. Pressing them into the holders, he tidied their sleeping area.

A few minutes later, the boys climbed out the storage room window and fell into the hard snow.

"Let's go to Emma's," David said as he hid their stepping stool in a small drift at the back of the church. "She'll give us somethin' to eat."

The air was crisp and the snow crunched noisily under their rubber boots. Peering around the front of the church, they instinctively checked to see if Domko was by the road. The morning was quiet as the sun rose in pink rays behind them. They hurried past the school to the log house ahead. The lights were warm and inviting in the window. Smoke from the chimney lifted gently into the sky, freezing mid-air in the stillness.

"It's c-cold," David said as a chill wracked his body. "Prob'ly the coldest day yet."

"Uh-huh," Dennis agreed as he tucked his chin into the top of his coat. His breath froze on the metal zipper instantly, forming little frost buds that grew as he watched. It was too cold to breathe through his nose so he took short breaths through his mouth to force air into his lungs. He was glad they didn't have to run.

The twins glanced toward the open barn door and saw a lit lamp hanging at the entrance. They hurried to the familiar house and rapped on the old wooden door. Marjorie answered and without hesitating, let the boys inside.

"Can we stay for awhile?" David asked. "Ole Satan kicked us out again."

Emma bustled towards them.

"Of course you can come in," she said. "It's much too cold for children to be outside."

Dennis stood behind his brother shyly. Emma pulled out two chairs and motioned for the boys to sit down. They slid off their frozen boots.

"Now, what's this about Domko kicking you out again?" she asked. Before they could answer, she told Marjorie to get the boys some slippers. "We can't have their feet on this cold floor," Emma said.

"This floor is good 'n warm, not like the church," Dennis interrupted.

Puzzled, Emma eyed the twins. "What do you mean?"

"We ran out yesterday afternoon," David explained. "An' crawled into the church an' stayed there over night."

"You slept in the church?"she asked. Her tone was angry and for a moment the boys thought they had done something wrong.

"We didn't break nothin' an' we shut the window when we left," David apologized.

"That's not what I meant," she said softly. "I mean, children shouldn't have to sleep outside in the dead of winter. You boys could have froze to death. Did you make a fire?"

"No, ma'am, we was too scared," Dennis said.

Just then the door opened and Gus came inside. He was bundled in a thick coat, felt hat and heavy mitts. He pulled off his boots and unwrapped the scarf covering his face.

"Forty-four degrees below zero - the coldest day yet," he said. Then he noticed the twins sitting at the table. "By jimminy, what are you boys doing out in weather like this?"

"They slept in the church last night," Emma scoffed. "Can you believe it?"

Gus shook his head. He poured himself a cup of coffee and sat down. "Hope you boys didn't make a big mess in the church."

"No sir," David said seriously.

"That's good because people will be arriving for services soon, and I don't want to see you boys getting into trouble."

David looked at his brother. It was Sunday after all!

Emma served a breakfast of eggs and toast. The twins ate hungrily but tried their best to be polite.

When breakfast was finished, Marjorie disappeared outside to do chores. The twins took this as their cue to leave since Gus predicted the temperatures would rise once the sun was high. It had been a long, lonely winter and Emma was looking forward to an afternoon of visiting in town.

The twins thanked the Harwarts for breakfast then began walking home. Gus had been right. It was already beginning to feel warmer outside.

As they walked down the road, they noticed a car parked in front of the church. A member of the congregation had arrived early to light a fire to warm the building before the service began. The man left the church, but the twins decided to wait outside until the service was finished. Pushing snow off a fallen tree, the boys sat patiently while cars filled with families arrived and people began filtering into the church.

Soon afterwards, singing could be heard, and while the boys couldn't understand the words, they knew that the hymns were being sung in German.

"We wa, we wa," Dennis sang quietly. Soon David joined in and the boys swayed back and forth as they listened to the hymns echoing in the still afternoon.

It was a long time before either boy spoke.

"Gus an' Emma are Lutherans, you know," David said. "An' they're not bad. How come Momma's church says that all other religions 'cept the Witnesses are bad?"

"I dunno," Dennis said. "But momma understands an' she tells us the truth because Witnesses never lie."

"Jim Deighton never lies an' he's not a Witness," David argued. His brother read more than he did and understood their religion much better.

"Maybe he's good alright, but he ain't goin' to the new order like us."

"What's gonna happen to him?"

"He'll just turn to dust."

The twins waited quietly as they watched people leave the church. They sat in the bush until the sun was low in the sky. Making their way through the snow, they climbed in through the window again. David tossed another log in the wood stove reasoning that if anyone saw the smoke, they would think it was still burning from that afternoon. It was beginning to get dark inside so the boys lit the candles once again.

"It ain't so bad in here," David said. "An' I don't care what no Witnesses say, the Lutherans ain't bad people."

Dennis couldn't argue with that statement. "Do you think that God cares us Witness kids are in his Lutheran church?" he asked.

David mulled over the question as he took the minister's robe from the vestibule once again. "There ain't no God," he said matter-of-factly.

Draped in the robe, the twins huddled together once again on the cold floor. Soon they fell asleep.

Hunger drove the boys home the following afternoon. They crept in the house while Domko was outside. Since there was nothing else to eat, they each grabbed a handful of rolled oats. Stuffing the oats in their pockets, they quickly ran upstairs to hide.

The following morning they came down quietly in time to help with the milking. Domko watched them suspiciously as they each picked up a pail by the door. He never beat them when they came home, unless they brought the police. He would taunt them, though, about where they'd been and call them lazy. Domko never understood they ran away because they feared him.

When morning chores were finished, they walked to school with Eunice and Rosie.

"Thanks a lot for goin' an' leavin' me with Domko and the chores," Eunice said sarcastically. "Next time take me too. Where did you guys go anyways?"

"We hid in the church an' had breakfast at Emma's," David said. "But don't tell Momma or we'll get in trouble."

"I think she knew anyways," Eunice said. "You shoulda seen how mad Domko was yesterday. He came stormin' in the house complainin' about havin' to listen to all them Germans singing at the church."

"Good!" the boys said laughing. "We wa, we wa!"

After school that day, Domko was waiting on the road to make sure the children didn't run away.

"Hitchink a some horse," he said to Dennis and David as they neared the barnyard. "Bringink but a some hay."

The boys hated going for hay in the middle of winter since it was a cold job and Domko's horses were miserable. The horses would often rear and upset the sleigh with hay rack on it, and the boys would have to stop and fork they hay on again.

Domko stood in the doorway watching as the boys led Darby and Jack through the barn yard. Darby reared and when Dennis tried to bring the horse under control by pulling on the reins, the horse turned and bit him hard on the forearm.

"Ouch!" Dennis cried. "He bit me! That stupid horse bit me!"

Thinking the whole scene was quite humorous, Domko let out a roar of laughter. This sudden outburst startled the horses, sending them running towards the barnyard fence, dragging the twins behind. Both boys let go of the reins as the horses galloped through the yard.

"Dennnnis!" Domko yelled, pointing towards the running horses. "Fraaa!"

The boys knew this was a signal to catch the horses, and not to bother returning home until they had the animals under control. They ran after the horses, which had turned north on the road. As the boys chased the frantic animals, they glanced back to see Domko standing in the barnyard. He was shaking his fist and cursing at them.

After the boys had pursued the horses down the road for a half mile, the animals veered into a neighbour's field.

"We'll get behind 'em and chase 'em back to the house," David said.

The horses paused while the boys walked past them and tromped through the heavy snow in the ditch. The animals raised their heads and pawed the ground as the boys approached them from behind. Spooked, they ran once again, this time towards the south, trotting past the farm yard with David and Dennis running breathlessly behind. The horses continued down the road, past the school and into Harwart's yard.

Marjorie noticed the horses as she walked from the barn to the house. She could see David and Dennis creeping up behind the animals, so she positioned herself between the sweating and breathless animals and the barn. The horses' eyes rolled far back as they stood quietly watching the twins. Suddenly, they bolted into the field.

"Satan's gonna kill us," Dennis fretted as the boys struggled to keep up to the horses who ran easily through the deep snow. "We can't go back without them."

"I can help you," Marjorie offered.

They continued chasing the horses around the field, then fell exhausted in the snow.

"Maybe if we just wait, they'll go into the barn," Marjorie suggested.

"We got to get them horses an' get hay before dark," David said.

Marjorie looked at her young friend and saw true fear in his eyes. "Maybe my dad can get them. He's got a way with horses."

They sat and watched as the animals finally walked slowly towards the open barn door. The children approached cautiously. Marjorie grabbed a small pail and filled it with oats from the nearby grain bin.

"Here, take this," she said handing it to Dennis.

Within a few minutes, the horses were calm enough to be led home. Domko stood in the doorway of the house and barked instructions for the twins to get a load of hay. Eunice followed and together they hitched the horses to the sleigh and rode to the east hayfield. It was after 10 p.m. before they returned to the house after loading, hauling and unloading the hay at the barn. The twins crawled into their hiding spot behind the wall in the eaves of the attic.

"I hate them horses," Dennis said, inspecting the tender spot on his arm where the horse had bit him. "How come ole' Squeezer makes us use Darby an' Jack when Dolly is good to us."

David looked at his brother.

"Whadda you think? He hates us and so does his horses. He likes watchin' us fight 'em."

Eunice crawled in beside her brothers with a book. She loved to read, but had to do it without Domko knowing. He disapproved of the children drawing, reading or playing. Whenever he caught her reading, he'd grab her by the hair and lead her to wherever there was work to be done.

Eunice had waited weeks for this novel from the school library. She was told it was quite good and she didn't want to be disturbed.

"Be quiet 'cause I'm gonna read," she said as she made herself comfortable in her usual spot.

Her eyes adjusted quickly to the dark as she leaned close to the edge of the eaves. A tiny beam of light shone in from downstairs. It came through a small hole she had scraped in the sawdust insulation at the point where the roof and floor met.

Being the oldest, she was able to take the best spot for herself. The twins and Rosie were relegated to an area near the outside walls. Dennis, who was not as hearty as his twin, sometimes complained that he was cold, so David would silently switch spots with him.

The next morning the twins awoke to find their hair stuck to the frost that had accumulated on the inside wall the previous night. David noticed his head and face were numb from being pressed against the cold wall. Reaching up, he gently pulled his hair free.

Domko allowed Rosie to go to school that day, but Eunice and the twins had to stay home. He said that because they had wasted so much time the afternoon before, they could redeem themselves by cleaning out the barn.

The children were disappointed since they would rather have been at school. Still they were thankful for a breakfast of porridge and skim milk.

They ate as much as Domko allowed, knowing they had a long day of manual labour ahead of them.

Hauling manure from the barn was the worst job a horse could be assigned to. The boys weren't surprised when Domko insisted they harness Dolly for the job. Since she reared whenever Domko was near, the boys had to hitch her to the stone boat, a platform of boards on heavy wood runners.

They coaxed her along after going around to the back of the barn where Dolly stood patiently most of the winter. The horse placidly went along and stood patiently while they hitched her up. They led her into the barn and she waited without complaint as Eunice and the twins began shoveling manure into the old wagon. They started near the back of the barn where the strong, ammoniated smell nearly overpowered them.

Since the departure of the older boys, the children were finding it difficult to keep up with chores. The manure had piled up fast since the last time it was hauled, so it would take many trips before the children would be finished. They filled the wagon then led Dolly out of the barn to a near-by field where they stood on top of the pile and forked it onto the ground.

Domko checked on the children a few times that morning. Satisfied with the job they were doing, he went back into the house. The children worked hard all day, then late in the afternoon just as they were finishing Domko came out to make another check. This was the last load and the manure was piled a little too high in the wagon. Since they were near the end of the job, they saw no harm in this but Domko noticed and called them 'lazy'.

Grabbing the horse's reins from David, he tried to lead Dolly out of the barn. After realizing who was in command, the horse suddenly got stubborn and refused to move. Angry at the horses defiance, Domko began cursing at her. He picked up a shovel and hit the horse over the head. Dolly reared slightly, which made him angry and forced him to back up.

Dropping the reins, he smashed her over the head again. Then he went past her into the barn and picked up a pitchfork. He barked commands at the children, telling them to get the horse out of the barn. Dennis and David grabbed the reins and tried to coax Dolly who did what they said and started to move. She jolted the stone boat forward and slipped on the icy, wet cement near the doorway. The boys knew they had filled the wagon too full and began apologizing for Dolly who was struggling to her feet. Her back end banged into the stone boat, causing her to stumble again.

"Lazy beech!" Domko screamed. With all the force of his weight behind him, he rammed the pitchfork prongs into Dolly's rump. Pulling the pitchfork out, he jabbed it in again, this time pushing it as far as it would go. The horse screeched in pain as she struggled to stand.

Grunting and swearing, he jabbed her again, this time enjoying a perverse pleasure as he penetrated the delicate area beneath the horse's tail.

"Dolly, get up!" the children begged as tears streamed down their faces while they pulled the reins. The horse's back legs were trapped underneath the stone boat and her front legs slipped on the cement. She whinnied in pain and fear as Domko continued to impale her.

"Lazy, beech bastard!" he swore as he strode to the doorway and pounded the shovel down on the horse's head once again.

He continued to beat her as the children stood crying nearby. He smashed her head one more time, then threw down the shovel and stormed towards the house.

Once he was gone, the children gathered around the horse. Unhitching her from the stone boat, they were able to coax her to stand since Domko was out of sight. Blood streamed down her back end and she whimpered in pain as the twins lead the limping horse to her bed behind the barn.

Eunice gathered hay in her arms and after a few trips, had enough to soften the bed. Dolly wobbled as she struggled down on her uninjured side. Eunice and Dennis stroked the horse's sweaty neck as David snuck to the grainary and returned with a can of forbidden oats. Carefully pouring the oats on the ground by her head, he rubbed her nose gently. Glancing quickly at the horse's rump, he had to turn away from the sickening sight of frozen blood congealing in long streams down her leg.

"Oh Dolly," he said his eyes full of tears. "We're so sorry."

The horse whimpered softly as the children nestled closely. Too afraid to go inside, they slept huddled beside the horse who looked lovingly back at them. David could see Dolly's eyes wet and shining in the moonlight. As she whimpered, he could tell that Dolly was also crying.

David and Dennis at 18 months.

Caroline as a teenager

No. GEN.322/2/48.
Date 11th September, 1947.

Authority issuing certificate:—HOME OFFICE.
Indication de l'autorité qui délivre le certificat

Place of issue of certificate:—LONDON.
Lieu où l'on délivre le certificat

CANADIAN IMMIGRATION
OCT 22 1947
LONDON—ENGLAND

CERTIFICATE OF IDENTITY.
CERTIFICAT D'IDENTITE.

Valid until 10th September, 1948.
Valable jusqu'

The present certificate is issued for the sole purpose of providing the holder with identity papers in lieu of a national passport. It is without prejudice to and in no way affects the national status of the holder. If the holder obtains a national passport this certificate ceases to be valid and must be surrendered to the issuing authority.

Le présent certificat est délivré à seule fin de fournir au titulaire une pièce d'identité pouvant tenir lieu de passeport national. Il ne préjuge pas la nationalité du titulaire et est sans effet sur celli-ci. Au cas où le titulaire obtiendrait un passeport national, ce certificat cessera d'être valable et devra être renvoyé à l'autorité qui l'a délivré.

Signature of holder,
Signature du titulaire,
Domko Boleslaw

Surname / Nom de famille: DOMKO
Forenames / Prénoms: Boleslaw
Date of birth / Date de naissance: 14th August, 1914
Place of birth / Lieu de naissance: Dobromil, Poland
Nationality / Nationalité d'origine: Polish
Surname and forenames of Father / Nom de famille et prénoms du père: DOMKO, Wojciech
Surname and forenames of Mother / Nom de famille et prénoms de la mère: MIKODEN, Katarzyna
Name of wife (husband) / Nom de la femme (mari): -
Names of children / Noms des enfants: -
Occupation / Profession: Farmer
Former residence abroad / Ancien domicile à l'étranger: Poland, Russia, Palestine, Italy
Present residence in the United Kingdom / Résidence actuelle dans le Royaume Uni: Withybush Camp, Haverfordwest, Pembrokeshire.

DESCRIPTION.
SIGNALEMENT.

Age / Age: 33
Height / Taille: 5' 3"
Hair / Cheveux: Dark Blond
Eyes / Yeux: Grey
Face / Visage: Oval
Nose / Nez: Normal
Special peculiarities / Signes particuliers: -
Remarks / Observations

Le soussigné certifie que la photographie et la signature apposées ci-contre sont bien celles du porteur du présent document.

Signature of the issuing authority,
Signature de l'autorité

Bob Domko's passport

Bill Pischke

The farm view from the south bush where the children would hide

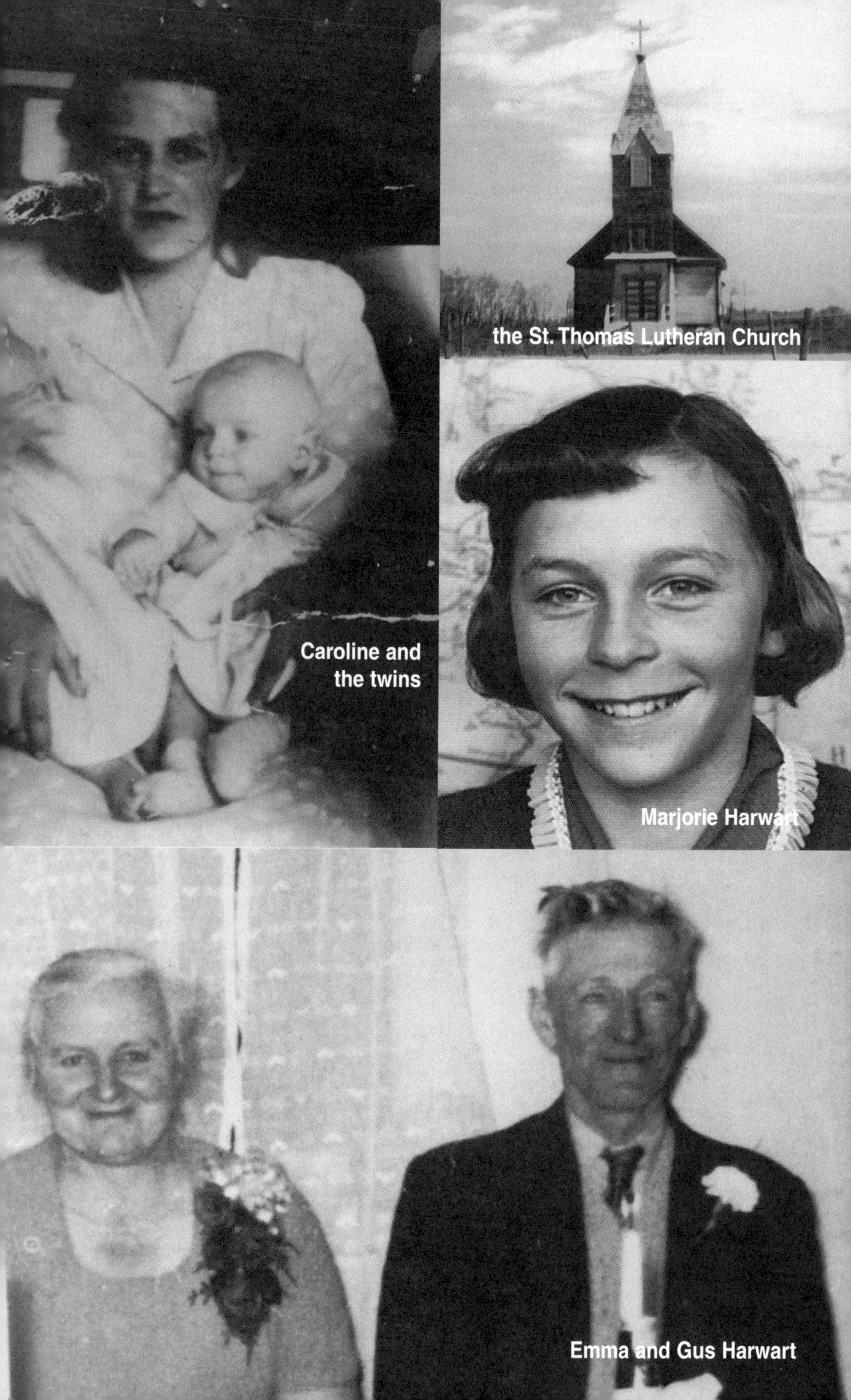

the St. Thomas Lutheran Church

Caroline and the twins

Marjorie Harwart

Emma and Gus Harwart

Ruby and Jim Deighton

Mrs. Louise Collier

Jim and Ruby Deighton's house

Miss Leah D'Hoore and the class from Bayton. Dennis and David are in the back row wearing white toques.

The inside of the Pischke barn. Taken in 1996.

Gus and Emma Harwart's house. Taken in 1996.

Mrs. Marion Gering

Margaret Burnet

A view of Pischke (Reed) Lake from the bank where David and Dennis walked in the middle of the night.

Anna and Leon Koch

Kenny and Alvin Koch

Dennis, David, Eunice, Caroline, Rosie, Kathy and Raymond in front of Domko's car

Jim Deighton

Ruby Deighton

Frederick's old barn

Dennis and David in front of school

Chapter 19

Boiling the chop

DAVID'S NIGHTMARES BEGAN SOON AFTER he saw the dogs hanging from the tree. They started as small, frightening scenes that would wake him almost immediately. As his stepfather's behaviour continued to get worse, so did the nightmares. By springtime, not only was Domko terrorizing the children day and night, but also in David's dreams.

Severe hunger pangs in a growing boy's stomach didn't help matters during the day. The twins snuck small tins of food into the bedroom hiding place behind the walls whenever they could. Sometimes the boys would split a can of sardines between them and it would be all they ate for three days.

Now there was even less money to spend on groceries. Domko had bought two quarter sections of land and a car. Fortunately, fish spawned in nearby creeks each spring and the twins became experts at fishing with a spear. They brought home mullet and walleye on a stick they carried between them. Domko sent them back to their fishing holes many times since the fish made good feed for the pigs and chickens.

"I don't wanna feed this to no pig," Dennis said under his breath as he and David stood in the kitchen cutting mullet.

"Me either," David said chopping the head and tail off of a still-wriggling fish. He then cut the body in half.

Domko brought a full can of skim milk inside and poured it into a large pot. He told the twins to place their cut fish, including entrails, in the pot as he disappeared back outside. The twins were scooping armfuls of fish when Domko returned carrying a sack. He poured in a quarter of a bag of crushed grain, then stirred to see if it was enough to thicken the mixture. Satisfied, he started a fire in the cookstove and placed the pot on top. Soon the mixture began to cook and to the starving children, it smelled incredibly good.

When their stepfather went back outside, Eunice, David and Dennis decided to taste the chop intended for the pigs and chickens.

Pushing a chair in front of the wood stove, Eunice stood on the seat and peered into the pot. The twins climbed beside her, Dennis was also on the chair and David leaned against the counter top.

"Yuk!" Eunice said as she poked a swim bladder with her finger. The sausage-shaped white bags ballooned to the top and bounced as the mixture cooked. With a big spoon, she scooped some of the chop into her mouth. Although she made a face at first, she took a second spoonful.

Dennis reached in and plucked out a piece of fish, careful not to burn his fingers. He cleaned the tender white meat from the bones before sticking them back in the pot. It didn't take long for the children to become accustomed to the taste of the chop. They ate the mixture at every opportunity for the rest of the morning.

"Satan's coming!" Eunice whispered as she looked out the window. David jumped off the chair and darted to the table. The children sat and waited innocently, hoping Domko wouldn't notice how bloated they were. He eyed them suspiciously the rest of the morning but said nothing.

The chop was still cooking in the afternoon. The children were pleased that they hadn't been caught and helped themselves to more while he was outside.

"I wonder what it's like to eat good like this all the time," David said, spitting fish scales into his hand and then flicking them into his pant pocket. He smiled at Eunice as they watched Dennis take a big handful of fish and put it in his mouth. Parting his lips, he pulled out a few large bones and put them back in the pot.

When the chop was cooked enough, the fire in the stove was allowed to die. As the pot cooled its contents began to settle, Domko came inside and gave a low grunt when he peered in the pot. He glanced at the children who stood solemnly in the kitchen. Placing his thumb on one nostril, he blew one side of his nose into the mixture, followed by the other. Turning to the children, he smiled and wiped the back of his hand across his dirty face.

They stood in stunned silence as he strode outside.

"Bleeeccch!" Eunice said, her whole body convulsing in disgust.

"Well, I guess we won't be eatin' that no more," Dennis said as he gagged.

* * * * *

Domko openly bragged about his new car to anyone who'd listen. A 1949 Ford, to the children's knowledge it was the first vehicle he'd owned since coming to Canada. The cream-coloured car helped elevate his status, in the area which pleased him greatly. He bragged to Caroline and the children, saying what a good farmer he was and how more productive the farm had been since his arrival.

"Momma says he's a lousy driver," Dennis confided to his brother one evening as they climbed into bed. "She says that he's gonna kill himself or somebody else if he don't learn how to drive."

David smiled. "Maybe he will an' we don't got to think about shootin' him no more!"

The twins laughed. They listened to Domko talking peacefully with their mother downstairs. She had been disappearing a lot lately, leaving the house early and not coming back until after supper. It sounded like

Domko was trying to make amends out of fear that she might leave him for good.

The following morning the twins tackled their their early morning chores. On their way in from the barn, they noticed that Domko was not watching them as usual. They went into the kitchen where they found him shaving in front of the mirror. The glanced at each other and smiled. Hoping he hadn't noticed, their expressions then became serious. The boys sat mesmerized at the table as their stepfather carefully used a straight razor to slowly remove his beard. David shuddered as the keen blade scratched across the man's neck.

Domko turned to face the boys and the sight caused them to look away. They fought the urge to laugh as he grunted, in satisfaction that he'd done a good job shaving. When he went into the bedroom the boys giggled softly at the contrast of his clean cheeks and mouth with eyes and forehead that were still black from weeks of filth he hadn't washed off.

"I's be takink the cream," he announced as he returned from the bedroom and lifted the cream can off the shelf. The children relaxed only after his car started.

"I ain't never goin' anywhere with him in the car," Eunice said, directing her comment mostly towards Rosie. "I don't wanna be alone with him an' you can't run away if you're in the car."

The twins nodded and Rosie listened solemnly. Eunice had become very good at avoiding Domko, so they paid attention to her advice.

Suddenly, the children heard a tremendous roaring noise that could only have come from Domko's car. It was followed by a horrible crashing sound. Running to the window in the front room, the children could see that Domko's car had smashed into a tree at the edge of the driveway. He was sitting in the front seat absolutely still, his chest against the steering wheel.

"He's dead! He's dead!" Dennis said jumping into the air. "Satan's dead!"

The children began cheering and laughing as they watched from the window, rejoicing in their good luck. Cheers gradually began to diminish as they noticed him begin to move slowly.

"Oh no!" David cried. "He's not dead, he's just pretendin'."

Dennis didn't want to believe this. He blinked his eyes and watched for some sign of impending death. He could see a huge gash on Domko's forehead and hoped this could be life threatening.

"Maybe he's hurt and will die later," he said hopefully, looking at Rosie. She stared up at her big brother, wanting him to tell her what she desperately wanted to hear. "Sometimes people don't die right away, they die later when you take 'em to the hospital," Dennis added.

The children watched quietly as Domko opened the door and slowly stepped out. Still dazed, he walked to the front of the car and began examining the damage.

"No, the ole bastard isn't gonna die," David said sadly. "We better get outside 'fore he comes in."

"Yeah," Eunice agreed. "He's gonna be real mad, 'specially if his car is wrecked."

The children scurried outside and stood on the driveway. They stayed far away and watched as their stepfather cursed his bad luck.

"Bring a some pail," he yelled at nobody in particular.

Eunice ran to the barn and returned with a small can. She approached him cautiously then hurried back to where her siblings stood. Domko muttered to himself as he placed the can under the front end of the car to catch coolant that was flowing to the ground.

"Bring a some horse," he said to David who hurried towards the barn and returned with Darby. Domko took the reins and attached a chain between the horse's harness and the car's back axle. The children watched silently as he commanded the horse to pull. Darby struggled forward, pulling the car slowly away from the tree. Domko motioned for David to take the horse back to the barn. Then without a word, he strode to the shed and returned on the tractor. He loaded the cream and held it between his knees as he set out on the drive town.

After he left, the children examined the car and shook their heads.

""Do you think it's wrecked?" Eunice asked.

"It looks like it to me," David said. "It don't drive no more."

Domko returned later that afternoon followed shortly afterwards by a tow truck. The children watched as the truck drove slowly into the driveway. A man stepped out and walked around the crashed car while Domko parked the tractor in the shed and returned to the accident scene. The children knew the man's name was Kurt because it was written right on his shirt. They watched as the tow truck driver as he looked at the tree and then at the broken branches lying on the ground. Small twigs and leaves lay scattered across the hood and roof of the car.

"So, what happened here?" he asked.

"The horse be kickink it some," Domko answered in a serious tone.

Kurt raised his eyebrows as he looked at the car then at Domko again.

"Eh?"

"The horse she be kickink it some," he explained, pointing to the mangled front end of the car.

Kurt looked at him in disbelief but said nothing. He began chewing absentmindedly on a toothpick which had appeared from somewhere inside his mouth.

"Whatever you say," he muttered under his breath as he got back in his truck and backed it towards the rear of the car.

The twins watched and giggled quietly.

"The horse?" David whispered.

"Be kickink it some?" Dennis imitated.

They both began to laugh, which caused Domko to glare at them. Kurt fastened the tow truck hook to the car's undercarriage and the men spoke for a few moments. They agreed that it would be best to tow the car to town for repairs. Domko watched sadly as his prized car was towed down the road.

The children took that as their cue to get the cows for evening milking. They hurried towards the wintering area just north of the barn.

"Did you see that's guy's face when ole' Squeezer said the horse did it?" David laughed.

"Yeah, where'd that horse go anyhow, you know, the one that's got branches for legs," Dennis said sarcastically.

"Yeah," David added. "That's one damn funny lookin' horse."

* * * * *

Always looking for ways to expand the farm, Domko had bought a truckload of bred beef cows which had arrived in fall and calved in February. Instead of removing the calves from their mothers as he did with milk cows, he decided the calves would be raised by the cows then sold for slaughter as feeders the next fall. He believed beef cows were a much easier way to make money than expanding the milking herd. He also wanted to keep current with other farmers in the district.

The twins were kept home from school one day to help with the miserable job of castrating the young bull calves. Each spring the pail fed bull calves were castrated and now it had to be done before the beef cows and calves were turned out to pasture.

First the cows had to be separated from their young ones, which resulted in a huge commotion. The cows bawled constantly on one side of the fence while the calves, which were put in a large holding pen, struggled to get out.

Dennis was given the job of chasing the calves from the holding pen into the long chute where Domko's knife awaited them. Dennis had to block the calves from turning and running back into the holding pen. David waited part way down the chute where his assignment was to let one calf through, while stopping the remainder. Domko stood at the end of the chute and with a sharp knife, removed the trapped calf's testicles. This was a gruesome job which caused David and Dennis to cringe each time a calf would bawl in pain as the knife sliced through the soft skin. The job didn't appear to bother Domko, who threw the bloody sacs on the ground with little thought.

Controlling the smaller calves was not difficult, but a few of the early-born calves weighed more than 200 lbs. At one point, two calves running and kicking pushed their way past David. Domko sneered at him and David was relieved that he was able to hold onto the second animal.

"You's be holdink it some!" Domko yelled.

David struggled, then released the second calf once the one ahead wobbled out the end of the chute.

There were only five calves left in the pen when all of them suddenly decided that they wanted to go down the chute at the same time. One calf kicked Dennis so hard in the leg that it knocked him to the ground. He writhed in pain as David tried to stop the charging animals. Domko was just reaching under a calf's tail when two more barreled into his arm, startling the first calf. Bawling, the animals pushed their way to the end of the chute and forced the end gate open. All the calves ran out, kicking and bawling.

Furious, Domko turned to David.

"Vat? You's lazy goot for nuthink bastard," he screamed as he strode towards the cowering boy. Pointing the bloody knife at David's groin, he sneered.

"You's be doink it or I's be cuttink it some!"

David cringed at the thought of Domko slicing through his pants and queasily assured his stepfather that he'd be more careful. They and chased the calves back into the holding pen as Dennis limped to catch up.

David shut his eyes each time Domko sliced off a calf's testicles but continued to guard the chute carefully. He was weak with fear and nausea by the time the job was finished. Domko wiped the knife across his pants to remove the blood then put it back in his breast pocket. He went to the house after instructing the boys to chase the calves back through the fence into the wintering area where the cows waited impatiently.

"What did he say to you?" Dennis asked, noticing how sick his brother suddenly looked.

"He said he's gonna cut it off," he whispered weakly.

"Cut what off?"

"You know," he said lowering his eyes. "It."

"What?"

"My putz," he whispered.

Dennis gasped. "He wouldn't! Would he? What are you gonna do?"

"I don't know. I sure don't wanna go in there," he said gesturing towards the house.

The boys decided to stay in the barn for the rest of the afternoon. They hoped Domko would cool off. They knew from experience that he would be primed to beat one of them and now David was the most likely target.

The boys climbed into the loft and sat on a pile of soft hay. Tiny streams of sunlight shone through thin spaces between the barn walls.

"It's almost like he's gotta beat us or somethin'," Dennis said.

"Yeah, the same way he's gotta eat an' sleep an' smoke," he added.

"Yeah, then he's happy again until he gets worse and he smashes one of us again."

They thought about Domko's rages and tried to guess his motivation.

"Do you think he wants to kill us?" Dennis asked.

"Yeah, prob'ly. He hates us 'cause we're German. An' we're not his. I heard him talkin' to Momma an' he thinks we're gonna take the farm."

"Then how come he don't just do it?"

"'Cause he don't wanna go to jail. He's tryin' to make it look like we kills ourselves."

Dennis thought about his brother's answer.

"Do you think he's nuts?"

"He's smart enough to make himself look good. He tricks everyone an' knows how long he can smash us before killing us. Does that sound nuts to you?"

"I dunno."

* * * * *

The social worker made another surprise visit to the farm. This time it was Martha (Jeske) Patterson again. She was filling in until the department found a replacement for the area. Martha brought along a male colleague from the child welfare department. As the car pulled into the driveway, the twins ran into the bush.

"Did you see that?" she said to her co-worker.

Stepping out of the car, Martha walked towards the the trees. She'd dealt with other bushed families before, but was surprised the twins would run. She remembered them as being very outgoing while living in Ashern.

"Come out of there boys," she yelled. "I want to talk to you."

Slowly, the boys edged their way out of the trees.

"How come you boys aren't in school?" she asked.

Neither said a word. She looked carefully at the boy's poorly-fitted, torn clothing and dirty faces. They were awfully thin and neglected looking. The health nurse had told her that she suspected the Pischke children were being neglected. Martha remembered a look of sadness in the woman's eyes when she spoke of them.

"Where did you boys sleep last night?" Martha asked.

They looked at her solemnly.

"Do you understand English?"

David nodded yes.

"I asked where did you sleep last night?"

"In the barn," David said.

"How come you're not in school?"

David shrugged his shoulders. "We don't gotta go," he said.

"Yes you do," she replied. "All kids have to go to school. How old are you?"

David looked at Dennis who began counting on his fingers.

"We's 10," Dennis answered.

"How come you run into the bush when visitors come?" she asked.

David kicked the ground with a bare toe.

"Are you afraid?"

He refused to look at the woman. He wasn't sure he could trust her to say nothing to Domko. He was likely standing at the window watching.

If Domko became angry, then David would be blamed.

"That's alright," Martha said. "You don't have to tell me everything right away. I want you to know that I'm here to help you, not to make things worse."

David nodded and looked deep into the woman's eyes. They looked vaguely familiar and like eyes he could trust.

The kitchen door opened and Domko and Caroline came outside. Trying to sound polite and unrattled, they invited the social workers into the house. Caroline told David and Dennis to stay outside, which they happily agreed to do. They were glad for the opportunity to examine the social worker's car. When they finished, they disappeared back into the bush where they felt safe.

"There's nothing we can do," Caroline said despondently. "They run away."

"But why do they run away?" Martha asked.

"Because they don't want to do chores or go to school."

"The neighbours say the boys are frightened of Mr. Domko," the social worker said. "Is that true?"

Domko scoffed as Caroline tried to sound composed.

"They miss their father and treat my second husband badly because of this," Caroline said. "We can't control them no more."

"Well, running away from home and a loss of control by parents can be classified as incorrigibility as far as our department is concerned. If an investigation proves the boys are incorrigible, we can obtain a court order to have the children removed from the home and placed in foster care."

This explanation seemed to upset Domko. Caroline was confused because she knew he hated the boys. She thought he might like to have them living elsewhere. But then who would do the chores?

"We only remove children as a last resort," Martha explained. "But we have to think of what's best for the boys. Something will probably have to be done if they are uncontrollable . . ."

"We'll start controlling them," Caroline said defensively. "They're good boys, just full of mischief that's all. We'll make sure they go to school more."

"You've said that before," Martha interrupted. "The files shows school attendance has been a problem since before your first husband died. I have copies of their school records which show they missed eight days in the first term and have already missed 10 this term."

"Well, David was sick a bit, and Dennis doesn't like to go anywhere without him," Caroline lied, her voice trailing off.

"We need to find out why these boys keep running away," Martha said, looking at Domko who sat and smoked with a silly grin on his face. He seemed to enjoy watching while Caroline scramble through her lies.

Martha stared at him. There was no doubt in her mind that something was wrong with this man. Based on the assessment by the health nurse and Doctor Steenson, Martha was certain Domko had a mental problem.

"Have you thought about seeing a doctor?" she suggested to Domko. "I can arrange it if you like."

"He's been to see Doctor Steenson and there's nothing they can do about the headaches," Caroline interjected.

"I'm not talking about the headaches," the social worker said in simple, straightforward fashion. "I mean about his temper. There are doctors who specialize in problems of the mind."

Suddenly Domko began paying attention to the conversation.

"Vat?" he spitted as he stood up. "I's be crazy in but a some head? I's not be, she's be! Ant they's be!" he said pointing in the general direction of the Harwart and Deighton farms. He began pacing up and down the kitchen floor as he raved that the Harwarts and Deightons were conspiring to ruin his farm.

Caroline tried to persuade him to sit down, but finally just stared at the table. She knew he was making matters worse by showing his angry side to the social workers. Martha and her co-worker watched carefully as Domko ranted and raved. Then he stopped as quickly as he had started. He eyed Martha suspiciously and quietly put an end to the meeting by opening the door and suggesting it was a long drive back to Winnipeg.

Reluctantly the social workers got up and left the dark, dirty house. Caroline followed them outside while Domko slammed the door behind them. Caroline apologized saying he had a headache as the social workers climbed into their car.

Since the children were in no immediate danger, there was nothing more the government visitors could do. Martha sat for a moment and made notations in a file that was filling with information. Where it all would take her she wasn't sure, but she had a gut feeling there would be a confrontation soon. The car backed out of the driveway.

"How can children survive under those circumstances?" her co-worker asked.

"You'd be surprised," she said. "There are a few around here who do."

Caroline fell into a deep depression after the social workers left. She looked around her unkept house and at herself in the mirror. Why had her life turned out like this? Why didn't she have a nice job? More than anything Caroline had wanted to be a nurse, just like Margaret Burnett, but she had to leave home at a young age. She often thought what a glorious job nursing would be - to travel around and visit new mothers and babies, give shots and help those in need.

Caroline hated her life and didn't want to be surrounded by nine children any longer. She had tried running away many times, but always returned home when she ran out of money.

And what about the children? The twins and Eunice were old enough to fend for themselves and they took care of Rosie. She didn't worry about Domko hurting Kathy and Raymond since it was obvious he was very proud of his own children. She believed that if she was successful in finding a new life somewhere, she could send for the children later. It was finding the new life that made her despondent and she spent the next week in bed.

She listened to Domko berate the children, but felt helpless to do anything about it. Sometimes Domko would come into the bedroom and force himself on her. She accepted this the same way she allowed him to beat her with his fists. She was too frightened to stop him. Afraid of what he'd do, afraid of how strong she would have to be to change her life, she looked at the ceiling,and daydreamed of a better life.

Sometimes he would come into the room and argue with her. He became suspicious of her motives for refusing to leave the bed. She did no house work or chores, and nothing he said could force her out of the shell she'd built around herself. He called her lazy and good for nothing, but she just listened then turned her back. If he hit her, she just covered her head and said nothing until he was finished.

For the children, this was especially frightening. They hated seeing their mother in this condition. It was as if their real mother was gone and a stranger had entered her body.

"Don't worry, boys," she said one evening. "Justice is right around the corner. Don't be afraid of dying, since we all die sometime. It looks as if we'll be dying on this farm, likely by Domko's hand. But death isn't something you need to be afraid of. It is something to welcome. I've done all I can here and am ready to go to heaven."

"But momma," Dennis cried. "We don't want you to die. We don't wants to die. We wants to live in Moosehorn some day."

"Maybe that will happen, but maybe it's not meant to be."

"But I don't want to go to heaven yet," David said.

"Don't worry, son, it's wonderful there. You children won't have to worry no more about Domko. It is a place where everybody loves everybody and only the special people get chosen. You are such sweet boys, you'll be there with me and it will be wonderful because there are beautiful animals and there's lots of food for everybody."

They listened to their mother and before the end of the evening, David and Dennis wanted to die also.

Although still depressed, Caroline came to her senses within a few weeks. She began moving around and was able to carry on a normal conversation. It wasn't the first time she'd been depressed, but this bout had definitely lasted the longest. She emerged from it a slightly different person. Now she seemed to accept her lot in life. She told the boys she was going to fight no longer, and her fatalistic attitude remained in place.

Domko had arranged to have a local electrician, Mr. Milner, come to the farm to wire the house and barn. This seemed to brighten Caroline's spirits, especially when Domko said he'd buy her some electrical appliances.

Because school was out for the summer, Mr. Milner brought along his son, Walter, as a helper. Walter was a few years older than the twins and big for his age. David and Walter became friends and soon found themselves roughhousing like most young boys. Dennis watched from the sidelines as Walter wrestled David to the ground. Domko also watched and one day after David had conceded defeat once again, Domko called him to the house.

"Vat you's be losink again?"

David was stunned. "We're just playin'. Nobody's gettin' hurt."

"You's be hittink some bastard like this," Domko said, making a quick kicking motion towards David's groin. He then showed David how to punch an opponent in the nose with the palm of a hand, a karate move he'd learned in the army.

Embarrassed, David looked, around hoping that the Milners couldn't hear what Domko was saying. "I don't wanna hurt him - we's just playin."

"You's not be playink no more!" Domko threatened.

He told David that if he saw Walter win the wrestling again, he'd beat David until he couldn't walk.

Red-faced with humiliation and anger, Dave went back outside. He made an excuse that he had to do chores and stayed away from the spot where the father and son were working until they left for the evening.

The following day, David avoided Walter. He knew that he couldn't beat Walter at wrestling and feared that if he lost again, Domko would keep his promise to beat him. Later that afternoon, he approached Walter.

"I don't want you to be comin' around no more," David said to his friend. "Me and Denny don't like you so don't come back."

Walter was stunned. His 12 year-old face reddened as he struggled to gain his composure.

"Don't worry," he said, voice quivering. "I won't."

Disappointed that the fight between Walter and David had failed to materialize, Domko taunted David for weeks. He called him a coward and tried to goad him into doing something foolish so that he could beat him. David ignored him and eventually Dennis did something wrong and Domko responded by beating him instead.

* * * * *

One morning Domko got up and told the boys that they would be going to an auction sale that day. With the exception of hiding at the neighbours, it had been almost a year since the boys has been off the farm. They became rather excited about the prospect of an outing. They'd never been to an auction sale before.

They climbed into Domko's car and drove the five miles to the farm where the sale was being held. When they arrived, the boys became frightened by the many strangers there and refused to get out of the car. Domko scowled at them until they timidly got out of the back seat. They followed Domko as he looked at the things that were being offered for sale that day. There was old equipment, household items, lumber and some junk.

Soon the twins felt relaxed and were able to look around on their own. People at the sale watched, as the twins examined items and talked animatedly between themselves. Many residents of the district believed that the Pischke children were thieves, David and Dennis were being watched especially for that reason, although they didn't know it.

Glancing around, Dennis noticed two strange men pointing and talking about him and David. This made him feel self-conscious so he persuaded David to move with him to the centre of the crowd. The sale had just begun and they were interested to see what might happen.

The boys listened as the auctioneer spoke very fast while he worked to get bids from the audience. At first the buyers were quiet and careful, but as the sale progressed, they began bidding aggressively. The boys watched as Domko bid on a bundle of lumber and got it. At least three more bundles of approximately the same grade and size were sold to other men. The crowd gradually moved down the field, coming to a selection of guns.

Domko told Dennis to bid on the next gun. Dennis was too frightened and shook his head no. He couldn't stand to have all eyes on him and he knew that trying to bid quickly would be much too difficult. He and David weren't able to answer fast because of their stutters, a condition that worsened when they were nervous.

Domko glared at Dennis. He didn't want to buy the gun himself because of all the rumours he believed Gus and Jim were circulating in the neighbourhood. He motioned for Dennis to bid then stood with his arms crossed and waited.

The gun was held high by the auctioneer's assistant and the bidding began. Dennis' heart beat fast in his chest as he stared at the ground. He couldn't bring himself to bid even once on the gun. It sold for approximately $8 to a young man from Ashern named Gilbert Geisler. Gilbert took the gun proudly as Domko glared at Dennis.

"You's be tellink him I's be givink him one dollar more," Domko said, pointing to Gilbert. Domko made a hitting motion which meant if he didn't approach the man, he'd get a beating.

Dennis shrunk from the idea of talking to a total stranger, especially on Domko's behalf. Slowly he made his way over to Gilbert and tried to offer him $1 more for the gun. He stammered so bad, the man became uncomfortable as Dennis tried to spit out the offer. Finally he was able to make himself understood, but the gun had been a good deal and Gilbert wasn't willing to part with it.

Dennis turned and slowly walked back to Domko, who glared at him and called him 'useless' under his breath. Tired of having the twins around, he told them to go home and get the tractor and the wagon so they could load the lumber.

Thankful to be allowed to leave, Dennis turned and ran as fast as he could away from the crowd, while David followed close behind. A few men snickered at the sight of the children who scampered like frightened rabbits. Wanting the men to know he also thought the boys were like animals, Domko shook his head in disgust.

"Strange little buggers," one man said.

"That's for sure," the other agreed.

The twins arrived back at the sale a few hours later. The crowd had moved around a bluff into another field, nobody was around except Domko. Nervously, he told the boys to quickly load the wood. Jumping to the ground, the boys could sense the urgency in his voice and within a short time had all the wood loaded on the wagon. Thinking it was time to go, David got back on the tractor while Dennis climbed on top of the pile.

"You's be takink some pile," Domko said quietly, pointing towards another stack.

"That's not ours," David said.

Domko gave him an icy stare then reached over and hit David on the head with his fist. He pointed towards the pile and motioned for them to hurry. He then walked back towards the crowd which was steadily moving in the opposite direction.

"Should we?" Dennis asked.

"We gotta," David reasoned. "Or he'll kill us for sure."

David drove close to the other pile and jumped off the tractor. As fast as he could, he handed wood planks up to Dennis who stacked them neatly on top of their pile. Soon the wagon was overloaded with wood.

"Hurry up!" Dennis whispered. "We gotta go before they come back."

David jumped on the tractor and drove quickly through the field. He passed by the farm house and accelerated, driving top speed all the way home. His stomach turned over a few times at the thought of what they had just done.

Domko arrived home later that afternoon in an incredibly good mood. He went out to the back of the barn and inspected the huge pile of wood. He strutted through the kitchen, bragging about how smart he'd been that afternoon and how the other fellow hadn't had the good sense to stand guard over his wood.

The twins listened in disgust then went outside to do evening chores. Soon, a truck pulled into the driveway. It was the man who had bought the wood after Domko. He'd found it missing when he wanted to load and go home. Someone had suggested to him too look at the Pischke farm.

Domko did a very good job of looking surprised.

"They's be takink it some," he said pointing towards the twins.

Motioning for the man to follow, he walked to the barn and then acted surprised to see such a big stack.

"I's be tellink but they's be stupid soneebeech don't be doink some," he explained. "I's say one pile, they's be takink two."

Domko told the man to bring the truck into the barnyard, then instructed the twins to load half the amount into the man's truck.

The man watched suspiciously as the boys once again loaded the wood, this time for the rightful owner.

Chapter 20

He wasn't much of a father

WITHIN A FEW DAYS, everybody in the district had heard about the stolen wood. The twins were branded as thieves and they and their stepfather were watched carefully from that day forward.

Domko arrived home from town one afternoon a few weeks later, ranting and raving that he'd been discounted at the creamery for having too much milk in the bottom of the cream can. It was a trick he pulled most of the time, pouring in milk to top up the can, but this time he'd been caught during a random check.

Employees at the Co-op were also watching Domko. He'd been caught stealing goods by stuffing them inside stove pipes, then only paying for the pipe. He also lined his coat pockets with chocolate bars and small tools. Sometimes they caught him, sometimes they didn't.

One evening while the children sat quietly studying, Domko tried the coax them into taking a chocolate bar. It was an old trick that they all knew and no longer fell for.

David and Dennis had put in a long day haying and sat quietly at the table drawing. Dennis became so involved in sketching an elaborate farm scene that he absentmindedly began banging his foot against the wall. Domko listened to the sound for a while, then suddenly flew into a rage.

Marjorie had gone for a walk down the road that evening.

A teenage girl sometimes needed to be alone with her thoughts and Gus and Emma didn't mind as long as she finished her chores first and returned home before dark. The sun was setting behind the west bush and the mosquitoes began buzzing in the damp grass. Sandy ran ahead, then doubled back, sniffing the ground and chasing anything that moved. She'd pick up the fresh scent of a rabbit and run happily into the bush.

Marjorie thought about her life and future. A few children in school tried to embarrass her by reminding everyone that her parents were poor. Her mother always told her to be thankful for the things she did have and to keep in mind that there were always children less fortunate than herself. Of course, that's when the Pischkes came to mind.

As Marjorie walked down the road, she could see Caroline's newly renovated house. Things certainly appeared to have improved since Domko's arrival at the farm. The house was larger, there was hydro and a car. The barn was being fixed with tin siding and Domko had bought more cattle. He even acquired more land.

Marjorie remembered overhearing a discussion about Caroline by a handful of women in the community. They had said she should be thankful for a husband like Domko, especially since she had seven children when they met. The women also complained that the twins were spending too much time in the church and making a mess. One woman said that a box of candles, which should have lasted two years, needed to be replaced at the end of the winter because the children were breaking into the church and lighting the candles. They also played with candle holders and took things from inside the church and left them outside. The women agreed, though, that this should not be mentioned to Caroline in case the boys might burn the church out of spite.

Marjorie remembered looking at her mother during the conversation. Emma bit her lip as she listened and scoffed quietly a few times. She had told Marjorie many times that it was pointless to argue with a group of stubborn, old German women. Then she'd laugh, saying that she knew this first hand because she was one herself!

When Emma could listen no longer, she stood up and said, "The good Lord put that church beside the Pischkes for a reason." She then strode out of the room. The women sat silently, not knowing what to say. Marjorie's heart was bursting with pride as she ran to catch up with her mother.

"Let that be a lesson to you, Marjorie Harwart," her mother had said seriously. "Just because a person has money in his pocket it, doesn't mean he has kindness in his heart."

Marjorie continued walking down the road and was soon within a few yards of the Pischke house. Suddenly, she could hear a commotion coming from inside. She could hear Domko yelling and smashing things against a wall. Her friends were screaming and crying. Horrified, Marjorie stopped to listen. She had never heard anything so heartwrenching in her whole life. She stood on the road listening helplessly.

Sandy came out of the bush and bristled at the sound of Domko's voice. She barked sharply a few times before sitting at the feet of her mistress. Marjorie listened to the sound of her friends begging and screaming as the man raged through the house.

Then Marjorie began running towards home. The sound of her friends' pleas began to fade and were replaced by the chirping of birds and crickets. It seemed so unfair! How could such horror be happening in such an idyllic setting? Tears stung her cheeks as she tried not to imagine what her friends were facing. She ran up the driveway and burst into her house. Out of breath she wept as she told her mother what she'd heard.

The children screamed as Domko cornered them in the kitchen. He began strapping whomever he could reach and soon, all but Dennis had escaped from the room. The boy received a vicious beating as he lay on the kitchen floor. When Domko was finished, he sat grunting at the table. Dennis crawled towards the attic stairs and David helped him climb into bed. Too stiff to move, Dennis fell on the bed while David took a thin blanket and covered them both.

The following night, the entire family was awakened by David's screams. Sitting up straight in bed, the boy screamed as loud as he could. His siblings became frightened and moved to the other side of the room when they were unable to wake him. Caroline dashed up the stairs and grabbed her sweating son and held him down. David continued to thrash around, his wide, unseeing eyes witnessing something terrible somewhere in his mind. Eventually he stopped screaming, but began trembling as he fell back to sleep.

David's nightmares continued all week. Caroline began sleeping upstairs in the children's bed in an effort to wake David before the screaming began. Domko soon tired of this. He became jealous that Caroline was paying so much attention to her son. One night as the children were going to bed, he decided to go upstairs and talk to David about the nightmares.

As he began making his way up the stairs, the children panicked and ran to hide. Dennis ran to the window, but wasn't able to get it open. Two huge spikes had been nailed through the base of the window into the sill. Domko had nailed it shut!

Dennis' struggles drew a wide grin from Domko who soon he'd forgotten he'd come upstairs to harass David. Instead he began beating Dennis who cowered in a corner.

"We-wa!" David yelled as he ran down the stairs and out the kitchen door. In bare feet, he ran into the bush and along the path to the church. Out-of-breath but confident he was safe, he sat down to wait for Dennis at the back of the building. Dennis would know where he was hiding since "we-wa" was their secret word for church. His body ached in sympathy as he watched the bush for over an hour. He kept pushing the thought from his mind that one of these times Dennis might not arrive.

He began to doze. The sound of someone approaching woke him with a start. He looked towards the bush and saw his twin hobbling towards him. Dennis staggered, then fell on the grass.

David cringed at the sight of his brother. Dennis' eyes were swollen shut and his lip was cracked and bleeding. There was blood all over his chest and arms, likely from a bloodied nose. Dennis reached into his mouth and winced as he checked a loose front tooth. He wiped a bloody hand on his pants.

"You strong enough to climb in?" David asked motioning towards the church window.

"No," Dennis slurred.

"O.k., we'll sleep here then."

David rested on the grass for a few moments.

"Hey Denny," he said.

"What?"

"You look awful."

"I know," his brother answered then cried himself to sleep.

"It's a miracle he made it this far," Ruby said as she wrung a cool cloth in the wash basin. "That boy's half dead."

Jim watched as his wife wiped blood from the face of Dennis who winced in pain.

"Well, this time the cops are gonna have to listen," Jim said. "One look at that boy and they'll realize what a crazy fool Domko really is."

Within an hour, Jim and the boys were on their way to Ashern. The twins sat quietly in the back seat while Jim watched them carefully in the rear view mirror.

"Hey Jim," David said softly. "What if the police are gonna take us back to the farm?"

"That's not going to happen this time, I promise you that" Jim stated matter-of-factly.

"Why not?"

"'Cause it's pretty obvious how beat up your brother is. The police can't ignore it this time. They will have to do something."

The boys trusted Jim. They knew he would keep his promise. Soon they pulled up in front of the police station and the boys reluctantly followed Jim inside. They waited in the porch while their protector went in to speak to the officers.

Jim poked his head around the corner. "C'mon in here," he called to the boys.

Timidly, the twins went to his side. An older officer towered over them in the middle of the floor. They were relieved to see that he wasn't the same officer who had taken them back to the farm a few years earlier. And he wasn't the same one who'd charged Domko after he set fire to Gus' hay. This was a big, rather ugly looking man who showed no emotion as he looked at the boys. Another younger officer sat a short distance away.

"That ain't so bad," the older officer said, looking from the twins to Jim. "My dad used to beat me like that all the time."

The room fell silent. The twins watched as Jim's neck began to redden and the colour spread across his thin face.

"Well then," Jim said angrily, poking his chin towards the man. "I don't think you had much of a father."

Turning, he grabbed the twins by the arms. "C'mon boys, I'm not leavin' you here with an asshole like that." Jim stormed out the door as the boys struggled to keep up.

"Where we goin'?" David asked as he and Dennis climbed into the car.

"I'm takin' you home," he said. "To my place."

As Jim drove out of town, the young officer made a discreet call to the child welfare department in Winnipeg.

That evening Ruby and Jim invited the Harwarts over to discuss Caroline's family and the plight of the children. All of them agreed that something had to be done about Domko. They decided they would have to convince Caroline to either leave Domko or make him leave. The difficult part was deciding who would talk to her.

"Well, I know I can't," Ruby said. "We were good friends, but she doesn't have much to do with me since she became involved in the church and since I gave toys and clothes to the boys at Christmas."

Everyone agreed. "I can talk to her," Jim piped up. "I can make Carrie listen."

Ruby tsked. "You're far too easy on Carrie and you know it! She's not going to listen to you any more now than she ever has."

Sheepishly, Jim agreed. Most of what he said to Carrie went in one ear and out the other.

The group looked at Emma who shrugged her shoulders.

"Well, I suppose I could talk to her," she offered. "Gus and I will do it."

"It's not going to be easy," Ruby warned.

"I know, but if she has a mind to, she can get rid of him," Emma said. "That's her house and her quarter of land and I say she has a right to it."

"Yes, but Domko paid for all the renovations to the house and owns all of the cattle. He's not going to want to go . . ."

"I'll kick him off!" Jim offered. "Hell, I'd kill the bastard myself except I've never killed anybody and don't want to get thrown in the hoosegow for the rest of my life."

Gus laughed. "Yes, if Domko turned up dead, everybody would know who did it! How would you plead anyway?"

"Guilty! And I'd be damned proud of it, too. I'd say that I was doing a community service," Jim laughed, banging his hand on the table for emphasis. "I'd be doing everybody a big favour."

The four adults chuckled at the off-colour joke, which helped ease the tension that was building. They didn't like talking about anybody in such a disrespectful way, but Domko had pushed them too far. They discussed the issue long into the night and the Harwarts promised they would talk to Caroline at the first opportunity.

The following morning, while Jim was out mending fences a half mile away, Domko arrived to pick up the boys. The twins hadn't seen him approaching as they quietly played outside. They turned around to find Domko standing in the yard. Reluctantly, they climbed into the back of his car. By the time Ruby saw the boys leaving, it was too late. She ran to the door in time to see Domko wave and drive out of yard and turn towards the Pischke farm.

"That coward," Jim scoffed later. "Just like him to turn up and take them when I'm not home. Did he say anything to you?"

"Nothing. He just waved politely and left."

"Polite my ass. That Domko can be a charmer when he wants to be."

Late that afternoon, Emma invited Caroline to the house for coffee. The women chatted for a while before Emma was able to work her way around to the real reason for her invitation.

"It must be hard for you," Emma said. "Raising the children without Bill. How are you doing?"

Caroline eyed her friend suspiciously. "What do you mean?"

"Well you know, kids never like a stepfather as much as their real father," she said. "How's Domko managing?"

Just then Gus came in the house. He'd been in the yard pretending he was doing something important while he waited for the women to get through the idle chit chat. He sat down at the table as Emma got up and poured him a cup of coffee.

Enough beating around the bush, he thought.

"So, how's he doing?" Emma asked again.

"Alright, I guess," Caroline said quietly. "He's a little hard on the kids but they need disciplining."

"How come your boys have been sleeping in the church?" Gus asked.

Caroline was stunned. She stammered and looked at the table as she searched for an excuse. "They run away. We've tried to keep them at home but there's nothing we can do."

"How come they run away?" Gus asked.

"I don't know," Caroline replied, thinking how familiar this conversation sounded.

"Are you sure? I remember how badly Domko was treating you and the kids before. That might be enough to make them run away," Gus suggested.

"Well he's the head of the house and the boys just can't accept that," Caroline said.

"What about the girls?" Emma interrupted, then in a hushed voice added, "are you sure he's not, you know, bothering them?"

"No!" Caroline insisted. "He wouldn't do that."

Gus shook his head. "I wouldn't be so sure. The longer he stays, the harder it's going to be to make him leave. We've talked to Jim and Ruby about this and we all agree that if you need help, we're here to give it to you. Heck, Jim even offered to help kick him out if you like."

Suddenly Caroline's back stiffened as she realized what was happening. She hadn't been invited over for coffee, this was a plot to get rid of her husband! She couldn't believe that Emma, Gus, Ruby and Jim had been conspiring behind her back. The people from her church were right after all - she couldn't trust outsiders.

"I have no plans to kick my husband off the farm," she said emphatically. "And I don't want to hear any more about it."

"What about the kids?" Gus asked.

"What about them?"

"Well, they are turning up hungry and beat on everybody's doorstep. Doesn't that matter to you?"

"Of course it matters but there is nothing more I can do."

Exasperated, Gus stood up and paced across the floor.

"Caroline, we've heard that the social worker has been coming to your place and we both know that's not good news," he said. "If you're not careful, she'll take those kids away from you and put them in a foster home. Do you want that?"

"Of course not,"

"Well then? You're going to have to make a choice," he said. "Either Domko or the kids, otherwise I can see that you just might lose Bill's kids."

"The kids can look after themselves," Caroline said curtly.

Stunned, Gus and Emma stared at her. "What?" Gus asked.

"The boys can look after themselves, but Domko needs me. He loves me and can't manage on his own. If they were better, he wouldn't get after them so much. The kids will be grown soon and then things will be better for us."

"So you're saying that if given a choice, you'd pick that old coot over your own children?" Emma asked.

"Yes," Caroline said. "But it won't come to that."

"It will!" Emma retorted.

"No it won't, because I won't let it."

"Well what are we supposed to do?" Gus asked. "Mind our own business?"

Caroline looked at the ground as she stood to leave.

"When the boys come here, you could send them home," she said.

"To what? More beatings?"

"I can take care of my children myself," she said.

With that Caroline turned and walked out the door.

Emma and Gus sat in utter disbelief for a moment. Was this the same Caroline they'd always known? It couldn't be! They concluded that she'd been beaten and harassed so much that she was beginning to side with her tormentor.

"She'd better not show up on my doorstep again," Gus said angrily.

The twins sat upstairs and listened to their mother and Domko discussing all that Gus and Emma had said that day. They overheard their parents fuming about the neighbours interference and talking about ways to even the score. The boys listened with growing fear as their mother began to sound almost as unravelled as Domko.

The following morning, the twins had just finished feeding the chickens when they noticed a familiar car pull into the driveway. Frightened, they ran into the bush.

Martha Patterson stepped out of the car.

"Come on over here boys," the social worker yelled. "Come out of the bush."

The boys cautiously edged their way into the yard. It was Martha coming to visit them again.

"You don't need to be afraid of me," she said in a forceful voice. "I just want to talk to you again."

Just then Domko came outside to see what the commotion was. He took one look at the social worker and began to pace back and forth.

"Vat?" he seethed. "I's not be vantink you here. I's be callink the police."

"I came to check on these boys, and it's a good thing I did," she said. "I'm here in response to a call from the police. They told me the neighbours brought the boys into the station again."

Domko flew into a rage at the mention of his neighbours. "They's be not tellink the truth!" he yelled.

He complained that the neighbours were conspiring against him to ruin the farm. He said they were mean, spiteful people who were jealous of him and his possessions.

Martha let him complain for awhile then interrupted his ravings. "Why does this boy have bruises all over his face?"

"He's be fallink down," Domko said innocently.

"With a little help from you?"

"Vat?"

"Why do you beat these boys?" The question came out a little blunter than Martha had intended. She regretted it immediately, but didn't waver.

Suddenly, it appeared that something in Domko's head had snapped. He began growling viciously and screaming at the social worker.

"They's be lazy German bastards," he yelled.

His eyes darted in anger and the scar on his forehead began to turn white as the blood drained from his face. The gold tooth shone menacingly as he approached her. Martha refused to step back as the boys cowered behind her.

"If anything ever happens to one of these kids," she threatened, pointing her finger aggressively at him. "I'm going to know who did it and the police will haul you away for good."

Domko hated being challenged by this woman and began punching the air in front of her. He inched his way closer, screaming that he wasn't afraid of a fat, German bitch and that given the chance, he would show her who the real boss was.

Martha didn't back down. She almost wished he would hit her. At least then she could charge him with assault and he'd end up in jail. Her arms shook with anger as she faced him. There was no way she could leave the boys alone with him, knowing the pattern of his potentially violent rages.

"If you kill one of these kids, so help me God," she seethed. "I'll string you up myself."

Martha held her ground until Domko's pent up energy eventually got the best of him. Soon he became exhausted and surprisingly calm. Martha sent one of the twins into the house to get Caroline who appeared a few minutes later.

Unfortunately, Martha was not prepared to take the twins that day. She had no court papers and hadn't made arrangements for a foster home. She knew it would be horrible to split up the twins, especially since they were so ignorant about life off the farm. It would be better to return when prepared, but in the meantime she would try an old trick that often worked.

"Your husband is out of control and should not be left alone with these children," she said to Caroline. "You have a choice. Either he find somewhere else to stay, or I take them with me."

Caroline looked at Domko, then yelled at him to take his things, get in the car and leave. Much to the surprise of the twins, he went into the house quietly and emerged a few minutes later carrying his duffel bag. He threw it in the back seat and out of the driveway sped past Martha's car before turning north.

Caroline and Martha talked for a while, then it was time for her to go. She waved to the children and said good bye as she left to visit a family near Grahamdale. Wanting to be sure that Domko wasn't hiding somewhere along the road so he could return, she also turned north. She drove along the road for a few miles then satisfied that he was gone, turned west at the next intersection.

The children were surprised at how easy it had been to get rid of Domko. As they played and competed for their mother's attention, they noticed how preoccupied she seemed. Without her husband around, their mother had more time for everyone.

The children finished the evening chores, had supper and went to bed. The twins discussed the day's events until they fell asleep. They awoke a few hours later to the sound of laughing downstairs.

Creeping along the floor, the boys went to the top of the stairs to listen. They could hear their mother talking to someone in the bedroom. Then they heard it - Domko laughed. He was back! He'd come back in the night and their mother sounded glad. The boys could hear them laughing about the trick they'd played on the social worker.

Chapter 21

A puppy named Bo

CAROLINE WAS ABLE TO CONVINCE DOMKO that if the social workers took the boys, he would have a difficult time managing on the farm.

Reluctantly, Domko agreed to watch his temper if she would discipline the twins. The children noticed the positive effect Martha had on Domko and wished she'd visit more often.

Domko then transferred his anger from the boys to the neighbours. He now had an obsessive dislike for the Harwarts and Deightons and maligned them to other neighbours and friends whenever he had the chance. Word got back to Emma and Gus that Domko had been making threats in town. He said that if Gus didn't start minding his own business, he'd "show him what he could do to a young girl like Marjorie."

The threat again alerted the Harwarts to the grim reality of the type of person they were dealing with. They sat Marjorie down at the table and talked to her about the threat and explained that while they would continue to help Caroline's children, they would be more subtle in their tactics.

"We'll be telling the police anytime we see something out of place," Emma said. "Sooner or later, they'll have to do something, especially if we keep pestering them. I'm sure the social worker is pretty close to doing something, and I just might call her too. But you have to keep in mind that Domko's crazy and that he just might hurt you if he gets the chance."

Marjorie nodded in understanding. She was frightened by the thought of Domko anywhere near her .

"If he ever tries to catch you, run away as fast as you can," Emma warned. "Don't be afraid to scream or yell."

"O.k. mom," Marjorie said trying to hide the fear in her voice. "I know what to do."

* * * * *

The rest of the summer was filled with plenty of hard work. The boys and Eunice spent long hours doing chores and haying. Their farm had been very wet that year so the boys were kept home from school in early September to help clean up the fields. Many families in the area considered it socially acceptable to keep boys home from school to assist with farm work. At 10 years of age, though, the twins were considered a little young to be held out of school.

The boys were still in grade three and having difficulty in school. While they disliked staying home with Domko, and they didn't enjoy sitting in the classroom either. Because they were absent so many days, they were trapped in a never ending cycle. They would miss school, try to catch up, work late at night and then return to school tired and hungry the following day.

The return of fall sent Domko on his semi-annual trip to Winnipeg. He hired the local transfer owner, a man named Hugo Russell, to haul his cattle to the Winnipeg Stockyards. Domko was never confident enough to drive that distance himself, but he accompanied Hugo because he didn't want to miss the opportunity to go to Winnipeg. He came back late that afternoon from his one-day trip with a box of used clothing and a puppy.

"I's be gettink some goot Collie dog," he announced proudly.

The children were surprised and pleased to see the puppy. It was a big pup but they could tell it was young. It whined and cowered as the children gathered around. It was mostly white with brown and beige markings on its head and back. Domko explained to their mother that he'd seen the puppy playing in somebody's backyard in Winnipeg, so he'd called it over and taken it.

Caroline smirked but said nothing. The children didn't seem to care that the pup was stolen, they were just glad to have a dog that Domko found desirable.

He won't shoot a valuable dog like this, Dennis thought. Especially if it was trained how to herd cattle.

The poor little pup had been sick most of the way home so David hurried to get it something to eat. They decided to name him 'Bo'.

The puppy took an instant liking to the twins, which disgusted Domko. He watched unhappily as Bo followed closely on the boys heels wherever they went. The pup would happily run after the twins, hiding behind their legs when they tried to teach him to herd the cattle and to be brave.

"He's just too little yet," Dennis said. "When he's big, he's gonna help us good."

"Yeah," his brother agreed. "But we better not let Domko know it makes us happy 'cause then he'll kill Bo for sure."

One late fall afternoon, the twins took the shotgun to the beaver dam to hunt ducks. The old single barrel 10 gauge shot gun was a relic that would blow apart after each shot. The 'blunderbuss's' clips were worn out and had to be snapped together again before the gun would re-fire. This was a fun game to the pup who would bark at the loud noise of shot and get in the way as the twins scrambled to pick up the pieces. To the boys, shooting ducks was a matter of survival. If they didn't down a bird, they went hungry.

"O.k., you hold me while I shoot," David said.

Dennis nodded and braced himself against his twin's back while David took aim. They waited until a small flock of ducks which they could hear coming flew overhead. David closed his eyes and squeezed the trigger. The impact from the gun sent both boys backwards.

"You got some!" Dennis yelled as he heard the water splash when the ducks hit. He pointed towards the reeds. "Over there."

"Do you think Bo will be able to get the ducks outta the water next year?" David asked.

"Hope so," Dennis said as they waded up to their chests among the tall reeds to fetch the downed ducks. They shivered as they swam to shore. Within a few weeks the beaver dam would freeze over.

When they'd run out of shot and had a decent number of birds, the boys looked toward the sky. The sun was beginning to set and it was time to round up the cows for the evening milking. They chatted as they walked through the field to the spot where the cows were resting. Accustomed to a daily routine, the animals stood and began lumbering along the tree lined path to the barn.

"Give him one to carry," David said pointing to the pup

Dennis gave one of the ducks to Bo. The dog looked at it for a few moments then took it in his wide jaw and proudly carried it.

"Look, he thinks he got it himself," Dennis said.

The twins laughed at the sight of the puppy struggling to carry the big mallard. Bo watched the twins out of the corner of his eye.

Dennis noticed a strange looking calf among the herd.

"That ain't ours," he said. "Where do you think he came from?"

"I dunno," David said. "We better leave him here in case someone comes lookin' for him." The boys wondered about the calf's owner as they tried to separate it from the cows. The 400 lb. calf ran in circles around the boys as it kept returning to the herd.

"We better just let him go," David said. "Or Satan's gonna be here any minute lookin' for us."

Domko was waiting at the barn. The boys gave the ducks to their mother for cleaning, including Bo's which Dennis had to carry after all when the pup became bored and dropped it.

The cows moved into their familiar stalls leaving the stray calf to wander through the barn yard. Domko stood watching the animal as the boys approached.

"Who she's be?" he said pointing to the dark brown calf.

"Don't know," David said, lowering his eyes. "We tried chasin' him out but he kept comin'."

Domko cornered the calf long enough to lasso it. The calf bawled unhappily as he lead it into the barn then tied it to a back stall.

Later, the boys listened as their mother and stepfather discussed the stray calf. They said they would put word out to the neighbours over the next few day, hoping someone would claim it.

During the week that followed, Domko fed the calf hay and oats twice a day. The boys thought the treatment was odd since he never paid that much attention to the pail-fed calves.

Nobody claimed the calf for more than a week, then it was suddenly gone one day when the boys returned home from school. They asked their mother had taken it, but she didn't answer. They shrugged it off, assuming she was having one of her strange moods. Then they forgot about it.

A few days later, the boys came in late from doing chores to find a huge beef pot roast cooking on the stove. The smell was unbelievable! Their stomachs growled as they sat beside Eunice and Rosie on the chesterfield while waiting to be called to supper. Caroline hummed softly as she poured a generous helping of boiled potatoes and carrots into a bowl and then carried the meat and gravy to the table. Caroline and Domko were in exceptionally good moods that evening as he served himself a generous portion first, and then Caroline filled Kathy's plate. When they had finished eating, the other children were allowed to sit down.

David and Dennis gave each other suspicious looks as they took their slabs of meat. They had eaten beef many times at the Deightons and Harwarts, but never remembered eating anything but chicken or pork at home until now.

As they filled their plates, they expected Domko to reach across the table and take it away from them, but he didn't. Later that night in bed, they discussed the wonderful, but unusual meal they'd had.

"Whadda you think?" David asked.

"I dunno. Whadda you think?"

"I think we just ate that calf."

"Me too. Do you think momma knows?"

"'Course she knows. She cooked it."

"I mean 'bout it bein' a stolen calf."

David thought for a minute. "If she don't know, then she's pretty stupid 'cause we ain't never eaten beef before. We're 'sposed to think he's gonna start feedin' us good now?"

Dennis stared up at the ceiling. "It was good, wasn't it?"

"Yep, it sure was."

* * * * *

One blustery, cold November evening, members from the church came to visit. Caroline was still trying to prove that she was 'worthy' to the congregation so she behaved nervously when they came inside. They looked around the house for a few moments then sat at the kitchen table. The children were forced to sit still and listen through the small talk until the lecturing began.

"Caroline, you know that you must get your own house in order before you can begin spreading God's word," the man said. "The way you are living is not worthy of His approval."

Domko snickered and she shot him a disapproving glance. While the two of them were certainly getting along better, he still enjoyed watching her squirm.

They discussed how important it was for members of Jehovah's Kingdom to be honest, kind, upstanding citizens. They said church members must treat everyone with respect and never lie. Jehovah's children must be clean, respectful and well-mannered. Caroline knew that her family was falling short on all counts and was ashamed. She was going to have to change and so were the children to be worthy of representing Jehovah door-to-door.

Domko reached across the table and picked up the Bible. He began reading thoughtfully and shook his head in agreement. In a soft voice, he apologized to the church members, saying that his wife would try harder in the future and that he would also like to begin studying. To this, the witnesses nodded in approval. Having both Caroline and Domko practising the faith properly would be the key to straightening out this family.

David and Dennis looked at each other and made a face. They knew Domko well enough to know when he was lying, but the visitors were unable to see it. They giggled softly, much to the chagrin of their parents.

"And you musn't spare the rod," the visitor said as he looked at the boys. "Spare the rod and spoil the child."

The twins shrank in their seats. Domko had been tolerable since the social worker had visited, now he was being told to 'not spare the rod'? His chest puffed up as he listened to the visitors and eyed the children. As soon as the Witnesses prepared to leave, the twins slipped out of sight upstairs. Hiding behind the wall, they didn't want to be around if Domko decided tonight would be a good night to 'not spare the rod.'

The twins weren't exactly sure what the terminology meant, but to them a rod was a stick and they'd already received enough beatings to last a life time.

"Whadda you think it means?" Dennis asked.

"I think it means you gotta smash kids to make them good," David answered.

The following day the boys received a beating because the bull escaped through the fence and was found roaming among the neighbour's cows. This neighbour had heard that Domko allowed his animals to roam free on the land of other farmers.. He had had enough first hand experience with Domko to know the man had no respect for the property of others. The police showed up at the door and Domko was fined again, this time for $55, under the animal husbandry act after admitting it was his bull roaming the countryside.

The boys ran to Harwart's house. Nobody was home so they continued walking until they came to an old barn owned by the Frederick family. It had been used for many years, but was now abandoned. The boys went inside the clean building and David climbed halfway up the ladder to peer into the loft. The huge hip roof made the area very spacious and piles of soft hay covered the floor.

David suddenly felt a familiar feeling as he looked around. He sensed he'd been there before. A brief, fuzzy memory came to him as he remembered that he and his siblings had accompanied their mother and father to a community barn dance in the loft. David remembered was planks of wood sitting on top of bales along the sides of the barn, and he recalled the sound of adult feet stomping across the floor, to laughter and fiddle music. Children ran and played, darting between the dancing adults.

David smiled. This looked like a warm, safe place to spend the night.

"Gimme Bo," he said to his brother, who stood waiting below.

Dennis picked up the puppy and struggled to lift the growing dog over his head. Bo grunted softly as David grabbed him around the waist and continued up the stairs. Dennis followed and they decided to make themselves a bed in the hay.

They stayed in the barn until they got hungry in the early evening. Just as it was beginning to get dark, they peered out the window facing their farm. There was no sign of Domko so they decided to walk back to Emma's house. They were relieved to see a light in the kitchen.

"Can we have somethin' to eat?" David asked when Emma answered the door.

Looking at the boys, she shook her head in disbelief, then disappeared from sight. She returned a few moments later with a loaf of bread and a plastic container filled with jam. The boys nodded in thanks and gave her a timid smile then turned and walked back toward the old barn.

"Those boys are sleeping in Frederick's barn tonight, I just know it," Emma said to her husband.

"Well, at least they are nowhere near Domko," Gus said sarcastically. "And by jimminy, you heard what Caroline said - supposedly they can take care of themselves."

"Well, I don't care what she says or how much Domko threatens. I'll never turn those boys away," she said. "If they don't feel comfortable coming here to sleep no more, then so be it, but I won't send them out to starve or freeze."

The following morning, Emma asked a neighbour to phone the police. Since the phones were party lines, many people in the district listened to the conversations so the whole community soon knew what was going on. Luckily, Caroline didn't have a phone.

Not wanting to stay in the barn another night, the twins walked through the bush to Deighton's house. Ruby and Jim welcomed them so they stayed overnight while Bo was allowed to sleep in the outdoor porch.

During breakfast, Ruby and Jim watched as the boys slid down the wooden banister on the stairs which led to the attic bedroom. This was great fun for the boys who had never done anything like this before. Out of breath from racing up and down the stairs, they plopped down at the table. They happily ate a big bowl of porridge with toast. When they were finished, they fed their pup and went outside to help Jim with chores.

They stayed another night and enjoyed the time away from home.

The police cruiser drove slowly into Caroline's driveway. The officer glanced at Martha who sat beside him in the front seat. She gave him a weak smile as she rehearsed what she planned to say.

"How do you think this will go?" he asked.

"Hard to tell," she said. "No matter how bad kids are beat up, they seldom want to leave home. It's all they know. In this case, these kids are so bushed it could be difficult persuading them to leave. They might kick and scream and Mr. Domko isn't going to want to let them go either. Those kind of guys never do."

The officer nodded in understanding.

They got out of the car and slowly approached the house. Martha carried an apprehension order from a judge. It transferred the care of the children from their parents to the province. She had a foster home ready to take both boys.

"I gave their parents plenty of warning," she said defensively. Then her tone softened as she turned to the officer. "I hate doing this you know."

"I understand," he said.

The officer rapped quickly on the door while Martha prepared herself for the worst. Caroline answered and the moment she saw the social worker she knew why she was there. Caroline backed away from the doorway, allowing the pair inside. Martha wasn't surprised to see Domko sitting at the kitchen table. She knew that when she'd banished him from the house a few weeks earlier that he would come back. Maybe even the same night, but at least his short absence would have given him the chance to cool down before taking his frustrations out on the children.

"I know how much this is going to upset you but I'm here to pick up the twins," she said handing Caroline the court order. "I really think that it will be in the boys' best interest."

Domko looked at Martha and grunted. "They's not be here."

"What do you mean?" Martha asked as her heart beat heavy in her chest. "Where are they?"

"We don't know," Caroline said. "They ran away again."

Martha thought for a moment. These people were not going to tell her where the children had gone. She felt slightly embarrassed that she was unprepared for this. She watched Kathy and Raymond playing happily on the floor with their father's tools. She and wondered why it had to be this way. Why couldn't this man treat the twins with the same love and affection as his own children?

"Do you know where they are?" she asked.

"No," Caroline said, "try the neighbours."

"Do you mind if I look around?" the officer asked.

Caroline agreed as she wiped her hands absentmindedly on a dish towel.

The officer went into the front room, poked his head in the downstairs bedroom then went upstairs. He looked under the children's bed and whispered for them to come out if they were hiding. He returned to the kitchen and shook his head.

"Alright," Martha said. "We'll look elsewhere and before we go, we'll bring the boys back here. You do understand, though, that we will be taking them with us tonight?"

"Yes."

They turned and left the house. "Now what?" the officer asked as they stepped into a cool north breeze. The sky was overcast and it felt like it was going to snow.

"Do you think they're in the bush?" she asked.

"Not a chance. If they'd slept outside last night, they would have froze to death for sure."

Martha looked towards the east bush. "That's what I'm worried about."

They got in the car and drove slowly down the road. They checked the school house but the teacher and the boys' siblings hadn't seen them in days.

"This is the place where the call originated," the officer said as he turned in a driveway. "Mrs. Harwart might know something."

Emma invited them into the house and told them all she knew. The boys had come to her door a few days earlier and she had given them bread and jam. She said she suspected that the twins had spent the night in an old barn near the township line. Martha and the officer thanked Emma and drove until they came to the abandoned building. The big wide doors slid open easily and they stepped inside.

"Dennis! David!" Martha called. "You boys can come out now!"

Everything was quiet. The officer climbed the loft ladder and returned a few minutes later carrying the plastic container.

"Well, here's the jam container she told us about, so I guess they were here for at least one night. Where do you suppose they went after that?"

"Who else has been calling the police about these kids?"

"Well, I have a few names, but the main one who comes to mind is Jim Deighton. He and his wife live just a few miles from Moosehorn along the township line. He's brought the boys in quite a few times himself. They might have gone there."

If you boys are going to stay here much longer, I'm going to have to put you in school," Ruby said as the three of them sat together talking in the front room.

"We don't like school," Dennis said.

"Most boys your age don't," she laughed. "But you won't get anywhere in life if you miss school. You have to learn to read and do arithmetic."

"I don't wanna read an' add an' stuff," said David. "I just like drawin'."

"Maybe so, but you can't make a living drawing. What will you do?"

"I dunno," he said.

"Are you going to farm?"

"No!" he exclaimed. "Me an' Denny just wanna get away from the farm.

She chuckled. "I know how you feel."

"Walter's got a good job in the city, so we wanna go live with him," Dennis said.

Just then Ruby noticed a police car pulling slowly in the driveway. "Run upstairs and hide!" she said. "Don't come down until I tell you to."

Without looking out the window, the twins ran upstairs. Ruby remembered the twins telling her how the police always took them home. After the officers left, the boys always got a horrible beating. Ruby looked out the window and saw a police officer and a woman get out of the car. She tried to look casual as she opened the door.

"Hello," she said smoothly. "What can I help you with?"

Bo jumped up and down, scratching the officer's pants and forcing Martha to protect her skirted legs from his sharp claws.

The pair introduced themselves.

"Come in," Ruby said, pushing the large pup back. "Don't mind him, he's just very friendly."

"We're looking for Dennis and David Pischke. Do you know where they are?" the officer asked.

"Uh, no I don't," Ruby lied. "Why? Are they missing?"

"Yes," he said. "Miss Patterson needs to ask them a few questions."

"Is this about their stepfather?"

"We can't discuss the situation with anyone except family, Mrs. Deighton," Martha said.

Insulted that the woman would suggest otherwise, Ruby bristled."I am like family."

"Well, we seem to have a few people in the area who feel that way," she said. " They're laying claim to these boys, but all it does is get them in trouble at home." Martha was becoming frustrated because it was getting late and she hadn't found the boys.

"Are you saying that I should just turn them away when they show up here in the middle of the night?" Ruby asked. She didn't appreciate being scolded by strangers who didn't understand the situation, especially in her own home. She frowned at the officer.

"It's just that people sometimes mean well but say and do the wrong things," Martha explained. "I'm sure you're thinking of what's best for the boys."

"That's right. I think about those boys a lot," Ruby said her chin wavering. "Me and my husband think about those boys more than you'll ever understand."

"Do you mind if I look around?" the officer said.

Ruby hesitated. Her heart skipped lightly in her chest as she tried to look relaxed. She hoped that Jim wouldn't come in and spoil everything. "No, I don't mind at all."

The officer checked the spare bedroom off the kitchen then went into the front room. Martha continued to talk to Ruby, who was having a hard time concentrating while the officer edged his way through the kitchen to the stairs. His legs disappeared and she could hear his heavy footsteps above her as he looked around the attic bedroom. It was then she noticed the boys' coats hanging by the doorway. She was thankful that they were much too big for the twins and could pass as Jim's.

Ruby nodded as Martha said that she and the officer needed to take the boys back to the farm. Ruby's mind whirled as she wondered where they were hiding, hoping they didn't pick an obvious spot like under the bed. The thought occurred to her that if the officer did find the boys, she might be arrested for obstructing justice.

Justice, she thought to herself. *There is no justice for these boys! These people aren't going to help them now anymore than last time. The poor little beggars will probably get another beating as soon as they get home.*

The officer returned and Ruby breathed a sigh of relief.

"If they come, will you contact me please?" Martha asked handing Ruby her phone number.

Ruby nodded and within a few minutes, the pair were gone. She watched them drive away, then went quickly upstairs.

"Boys," she whispered. "You can come out now."

There was no movement for a few moments, then slowly two little heads slid out from under the bed.

Astonished, Ruby stared at them. "How come he didn't find you?" she asked.

"'Cause we're good hiders," David said proudly.

Martha and the police officer continued to look for the boys but found that people in the community were very uncooperative. Martha stayed in an Ashern hotel that night then returned to the farm the following day. Caroline met her smugly at the door offering no suggestions about the whereabouts of the boys.

"You're welcome to go through the bush if you like," she said. "And you can bring the cows home while you're at it."

Martha was angry and frustrated when she returned to Winnipeg that night. She'd spent two whole days looking and still hadn't found the children. She suspected somebody was hiding the boys, but wasn't sure which of the neighbours were the culprits. Martha guessed to find out she'd need a search warrant for every house.

Her caseload was piling up and she knew she wouldn't get an opportunity to go to Moosehorn for a few weeks. The police promised to phone her as soon as the boys were found.

Caroline arrived at Deightons the following morning to pick up the twins. Ruby was not pleased but felt very uncomfortable about keeping the boys from their mother.

"We need the boys at home to do chores," Caroline said coolly. "Why should they be here helping Jim instead of us?"

Tired of fighting with everyone, Ruby agreed to let the boys go. She knew she couldn't stop Caroline from taking her own boys and felt foolish thinking she could keep them. Besides, she had other things on her mind. Things that the boys, Caroline and Jim just wouldn't understand.

* * * * *

Domko never beat the boys when their mother brought them home, only when the police did. The twins got out of the car and went inside. Domko growled at them to get to work, so they ran out to the barn. He taunted them about going to Jim's house and worked them even harder than usual. About a month later, David received a bad beating and the boys ran to Deighton's house again.

"Where's Aunt Ruby?" David asked when Jim opened the door wide to let them in.

"She's gone," he said unhappily.

"Gone in town?"

"No, gone for good. She's not coming back to the farm," he said, his eyes filling with tears. "She just couldn't take livin' here anymore I guess."

The twins were shocked. "When did she go?" David asked.

"About three weeks ago."

David thought back to the day the social worker had come to the house and confronted Ruby. "Did she hafta go to jail?"

"Jail?" Jim asked, obviously distracted. "No, she didn't go to jail, she's living in Winnipeg."

The twins stayed overnight but found things weren't the same there without Ruby. Jim was very depressed and would cry a little bit, then become angry. Even though he only seemed angry at himself, he frightened the boys. They felt very uncomfortable and left the next day.

"Thanks Jim," Dennis said as they began walking through the snowy fields towards home.

They walked quietly for awhile then David broke the silence. "Why do you 'spose she left?"

"I dunno. Whadda you think?"

David hesitated. He looked at Dennis who walked naively beside him. He'd given this a lot of thought and was certain of the answer.

"'Cause of us," he said sadly. "Ruby left 'cause of us. Mrs. Patterson an' the police yelled at her an' got her in trouble. She didn't wanna have to hide us no more so she left."

"Do you think so?"

"I know so."

Dennis started to cry. "She musta got scared an' ran to Winnipeg so they wouldn't put her in jail."

"Yeah, I know. I'm glad she ran away 'cause I don't want Ruby to go to jail neither."

The boys decided not to go to Jim's anymore since they'd already caused him enough trouble.

They spent that night in the bush. They found a sheltered spot just off the trail and built a small fire so Domko wouldn't see it. They huddled close to the flames as the temperature dipped to about twenty degrees below zero. Bo had grown quite a bit in the last few months and slept beside them, blocking the cold north wind. The twins fell asleep that night nestled in the dog's warm fur.

Chapter 22

The car accident

IN THE WEEKS THAT FOLLOWED, no obvious effort was made by the police or the social worker to find the twins. A quick call by Martha to the Ashern detachment confirmed that the boys were at home and that there had been no additional reports of violence. The police assured her that things seemed to have settled down. They said they would call her immediately if anything else happened.

Martha was relieved to hear this because December was one of her busiest months of the year. Her replacement had been hired and she was in the process of training the young woman. She would brief the new social worker on family and leave implicit instructions that if the boys were brought to the Ashern detachment again, they should be apprehended.

Satisfied with the arrangements, Martha hung up the phone and opened another file.

Winter had set in. Domko's behaviour was worsening as it had in the past. He was most violent during the cold weather, ranting and raving that the neighbours were trying to ruin his farm and that the children were conspiring against him. He seemed obsessed with Gus and Marjorie, bringing them into conversation for no reason. As he demanded more affection and attention from Caroline, she faded in and out of her own depressed state.

Their relationship had become very one-sided and Caroline's need for affection, love and understanding was ignored by him. While caught up in their own wants and needs, neither thought of the children, whose lives were dismal. The children craved a life of normalcy which by now had become nothing but a faded memory.

Marjorie enjoyed being left at home alone. At 15 years old, she was quite capable of doing the chores while her parents went to town.

She hummed softly as she opened the barn door. The horses stood patiently in their stalls. Margie approached one and softly patted the animal on the rump.

"C'mon boy," she said. Pulling a harness off the hook, she put her knitted mitts on the horse's back then slipped the harness over the horse's head. It was time to lead him to the water trough outside.

Something caught Sandy's attention and the dog ran barking towards the house.

While this was happening, Marjorie hummed as she fastened the reins. This was her favourite horse, the quietest of them all. He whinnied softly, pawing the earthen floor and nudging his nose near the pocket of her work jacket.

"Nothing tonight," she said as he patted him gently. "I don't have any sugar cubes. Mom said she'll bring some from town."

Slipping her mitts back on, she led the horses towards the door. She stepped into the barnyard and turned toward the trough. Looking up, she came to a startled halt. Standing just a few feet in front of her was Domko. He wore a thick, buffalo hide coat. He wore felt rubbers on his feet - high felt insoles with a rubber shoe that covered the toe. Domko held a rifle stiffly at his side. Sandy was circling him angrily.

Marjorie took a step back. She tried to hide her surprise as well as her fear. Sandy growled deep in her throat as she stopped circling and stood in front of him.

"Vere's be Gus?" he demanded.

Marjorie hesitated. Her parents had gone to Winnipeg and weren't expected back until late.

"They're in Moosehorn," she lied. "They should be home any minute."

Domko's eyes narrowed. He stared intently at the girl then at the horse she was leading.

"I's be vantink to go huntink," he said. "You's be tellink him."

Marjorie nodded and swallowed hard. It struck her as odd that he would want to go hunting with her father since they despised each other.

Domko took a step closer and she let out a tiny gasp. She remembered what her mother had said: Run!

Sensing her fear, the horse pricked its ears back. With nostrils flaring, it began pawing the ground. It also reared slightly which was a sign for Domko to stay away. Sandy continued to bark aggressively while baring her teeth at the unwelcome guest.

Domko sneered as he looked at both animals. Marjorie fought to control the horse which seemed to sense the dubious intent of the unwelcome visitor.

"You's be tellink Gus," Domko said as he looked into the barn.

By this time, the animals had become so unruly that Marjorie didn't think she could control them much longer. They created a welcome diversion and it was the first time she'd ever been pleased to have a horse rear while under her control.

Domko stared at her with his flashing, angry eyes then slowly began to back away. Marjorie loosened her grip on the horse, and it took two steps towards Domko who turned and slowly walked towards the house. He looked over his shoulder at the teenager then strode down the driveway.

By now Marjorie's legs had turned to rubber. Her mind whirled as she led the horse to the trough, then quickly back to the barn. In panic, she ran on wobbly legs towards the house. Bursting through the door, she kicked off her boots and threw her jacket and mitts on the floor. Running to her parents bedroom, she pulled her dad's .22-calibre rifle from it's rack on the wall. Opening his bureau drawer, she took a handful of shells and with a shaking hand, pressed one into the empty chamber. She took the remaining bullets and put them in her pocket then paced through the house, jumping at every sound. Gradually as the evening wore on, a steely resolve replaced her initial fear.

If he shows his face here again, I'll shoot him, She thought as she sat at the kitchen table in dim light. He's not gonna hurt me.

She went to her bedroom and opened the window. Sandy was sitting watchfully which made her feel better. The dog's tail began to wag as Marjorie dropped some food into her bowl in the snow. When she'd finished eating, Marjorie told the dog to watch for Domko. The little dog seemed to understand what she was saying and looked cautiously toward the Pischke farm. Marjorie told her good night and lowered the window.

She climbed into bed that night with her clothes on. She placed the rifle on the floor beside the bed then eventually fell into a fitful sleep. She awoke each time Sandy barked or she heard a strange creak in the house. It was well past midnight before Gus and Emma arrived home.

Marjorie emerged from her bedroom to tell her parents what had happened. Trying to make light of the situation, Emma sent her back to bed, but not before Marjorie noticed her mother give an anxious glance to her father. There was fear in Gus' eyes although he tried not to show it.

* * * * *

Domko rejoiced when he heard that Ruby had left Jim. He ridiculed the twins about her sudden departure saying they were responsible. He could sense the boys were embarrassed and knew that if they didn't go to Jim's, there would be less interference by the police.

Caroline used this opportunity to tell Domko that the boys should be attending school regularly. This would keep the teacher or school board from reporting their absences to the social worker. Domko agreed, not wanting to face Martha again.

For the first time since they started school at Bayton, the twins were being encouraged to attend regularly. They'd missed so much already that year that Mrs. Collier could not promote them to grade four as promised. In January, they were still in grade three.

As their language skills improved, David and Dennis began enjoying school. While they mostly kept to themselves, they did make a few friends.

During recess and noon hour, their classmates would skate on a patch of ice in the school yard. The boys would use half the ice to play hockey while the girls twirled and jumped at the other end as they pretended to be world-class figure skaters. The twins, and a few other students whose parents could not afford skates, watched from the sidelines.

Mrs. Collier saw this and encouraged students with extra skates at home to bring them to school. Odd pairs were matched and the leftovers were kept at the school.

One day the twins were in the cloakroom.

"Hey, Denny look," David said. "A pair of skates!"

Lying on the floor were two skates. Dennis picked one up and examined it. It was a men's skate about size 10 and the other was a woman's figure skate about size six. Both were for the right foot. These were strays that had been too good to throw away. The teacher still hoped to find a match, but this hadn't happened as yet.

The boys watched the mis-matched skates sit unclaimed for a few days. They discussed taking turns wearing them during the noon hour so they could skate with their classmates.

"No, we better not," Dennis said. "We don't know how to skate an' we'll fall down. They'll make fun of us. "

David agreed. That Friday afternoon when school was over, the twins each tucked a skate inside their jackets and ran home. They darted up to their bedroom.

"Here, lemme put 'em on," David said, taking the girl's skate from Dennis. He jammed his right foot in the small space.

"Can you get it on?" Dennis asked.

"Yep. Hand me the other one."

Dennis gave him the man's skate which was much too big for his brother's foot.

"I'll get somethin' you can use," Dennis said, running down stairs. He returned a minute later carrying one of Domko's farm papers. He scrunched up a page and stuffed it into the toe of the boot. David slid his foot in and wiggled it around.

"It's good," he said, tying it before walking across the floor. "Here you try."

Dennis tried on the skates and agreed that they'd have no trouble skating like this.

The following morning they finished their chores and snuck along their path to the beaver dam with Bo on their heels. They were happy to discover enough clear spots on the ice so they wouldn't have to scrape it, which was fortunate since neither one of them had a shovel.

They decided that Dennis would try skating first. David walked along the ice in his rubber boots while Dennis clung to the back of his coat. They had a wonderful time sharing the skates, slipping and falling as the pick on the figure skate dug deep into the ice. It sent them reeling forward while the smooth men's skate caused them to fall over backward.

"Hey Davey," Dennis said. "If we get to be good skaters, we can go across the beaver dam an' never come back."

"Yeah," David said. "The ole Devil won't never catch us on these!"

The boys played and laughed. David was pretending to be Domko on skates when suddenly a strange noise coming from across the beaver dam caught their attention.

"What's that?" Dennis said, pointing to the east. Their eyes squinted in the bright snow as they watched as an unusual-looking vehicle crept along the snow. It turned and began coming across the ice. The twins listened and looked again as the vehicle turned in their direction.

David quickly untied the laces of the skates and pulled on his boots.

"C'mon, Dennis, " he said, whistling for Bo. "Let's get outta here."

The boys ran up the bank and paused on top to watch as the noisy vehicle crawled along. They ran as fast as they could along the trail as the noise grew louder behind them. They stayed on the twisting path, hoping whatever was coming wouldn't catch them.

"Do you think it's Martians?" Dennis asked fearfully.

"I dunno but it's gotta be some kinda space ship," David gasped. "I ain't never seen nothin' like it before."

Their hearts pounded loudly in their chests as they ran. For the first time ever, Dennis was happy to see the farm site as they emerged from the bush. As they ran into the yard, they yelled to Domko that something was coming. They hid behind the chicken barn as Domko strolled to the edge of the yard. The boys crouched on the ground and waited until they heard the noise come in the yard. Curious, David peeked around the corner of the barn. He could see two men standing beside a strange-looking tractor that had skiis instead of wheels. Domko was being friendly to them, extending his hand. It was now obvious to David that these were men and not martians but the twins were still too shy to leave their hiding spot.

David looked carefully at the interesting machine. Blue and silver , it was split in to two pieces. It had a seat, a bicycle steering wheel and skiis in the front. Domko was asking the men questions as they lifted up the steel hood.

"It's some kinda snow crawler," David said.

"Lemme see too," Dennis said, pushing his brother out of the way. "It goes pretty fast, eh Davey?"

"Yeah, but I don't know why it don't get bogged down in the snow."

"Me neither."

"Do you think they got more of 'em or do you think it's the only one?"

"I dunno but it looks fun to go over the snow like that."

The boys watched as the men climbed back on the snow machine and turned in a wide circle. They waved good bye to Domko then drove back through the bush. As soon as Domko went back into the house, the boys ran from the chicken barn over to the tracks. They were the strangest marks they'd ever seen.

"So how do they make it go?" David asked as he sat in the snow examining the tracks.

"I dunno. It looks like a big, bumpy snake trail," Dennis said.

The boys sat and looked at the tracks for an hour, trying to figure out how the machine was driven. As it began to get dark, the boys agreed they should preserve the tracks overnight. They went to the barn and brought back armfuls of hay.

"Here we'll cover 'em up an' then we can look at 'em later," David said.

That evening they overheard their mother and Domko discussing the men and their snow machine. They were from the Helm family who lived across the lake. They had been asking about a calf of theirs that had been missing since late that fall. They had noticed that the animal was gone and had thought it must be dead until they found a break in the fence. They decided to make one last try to find the animal by visiting neighbours who had land bordering their pasture.

The twins heard Domko and Caroline laugh. Dennis looked at David who had an 'I told you so' look which caused Dennis to scowl at his mother.

It was a few days before the twins' birthday in early February. It had been a warm, overcast day and evening was quickly approaching. Domko and Caroline decided to drive to Moosehorn to buy flour and pick up the mail. Domko told the twins they had to go along while the rest of the children stayed home with Eunice.

The twins weren't pleased that they had to go, knowing there was only one reason. Domko needed them to push if he drove into the ditch. He could not manage driving on slippery roads and got stuck in snow many times on the way to town. He began taking the twins with him so that they could shovel and push the car out.

The twins sat in the back seat as Domko drove slowly down the road. A three day storm near the end of January had dumped quite a bit of snow in the area, making the roads impassable until the plough had made a single passageway. The road was banked high with snow and it was quite exciting for the children who felt as if they were in a tunnel as the car crept along the road.

Dennis motioned towards the floor. David's eyes widened as he looked silently back at his brother. On the floor in front of them were a shot gun and steel whip. They knew Domko also carried a hunting knife in the glove box. No wonder Eunice refused to drive with him!

Dennis moved closer to his twin to avoid touching the weapons. It was already dark and they had passed Deighton's house when suddenly a set of lights appeared in the distance.

Domko kept driving but was becoming increasingly nervous. He knew he would have to pass very close to the other vehicle and his nervousness caused him to drive faster. This worried Caroline since the car was now less than 100 yards away. The boys were sitting on their knees watching over their mother's shoulder as the other car pulled over to the side of the road and came to a halt.

"Boleslaw, slow down," she yelled in Polish. "Slow down!"

Panicking, he suddenly slammed his foot on the gas pedal, then made matters worse by turning towards the other car instead of away from it. Domko roared and Caroline screamed as he drove head-on into the front of the parked car.

The impact caused him to smash his face on the steering wheel, and his door flew wide open. Caroline flew shoulder first into the dashboard then banged the side of her head on the windshield. Dennis hit the back of the seat with his chest, while David smashed his face against the top of the seat.

Their car came to an abrupt halt and everyone sat in silence for a moment as they gathered their senses. Then they all began groaning at once. The impact re-opened the wide gash on Domko's forehead from his accident earlier that fall. He wiped the blood from his forehead as Caroline massaged her ribs.

"Are you boys o.k.?" she asked.

Dennis said he was, but David cried hard since his teeth had been smashed in. Blood was dripping from his mouth, which also caused him to panic.

"I'm o.k., but I think David's hurt," she said to her husband.

Domko grunted as he stepped onto the road. The other driver got out and walked towards the front of the cars to assess the damage. Domko recognized the man as Henry Kort.

Caroline got out of the car and walked down the road in an obvious state of shock. The twins watched from inside as Domko began yelling at Henry. He accused the man of being a poor driver and claimed that he would have seen the car if both of Henry's lights had been working. Henry ignored Domko since he was mostly concerned about his wife who appeared to be injured.

Another car came along soon and Henry hitched a ride to phone the police and tow truck. He returned about fifteen minutes later and the twins watched as Mrs. Kort hobbled to a waiting vehicle, favouring a broken ankle.

"He really did it this time," Dennis whispered. "Maybe they'll take him to jail now."

David nodded. His mouth throbbed as he gingerly touched his front teeth. They'd been pushed all the way back and were still bleeding.

Soon afterwards a passing car stopped and the driver offered to take Caroline and David to the hospital. She refused, asking to be taken home instead. The driver nodded and before long they were back at the farm.

The following morning, Caroline was in so much pain that she sent Eunice to the neighbour's to ask for help. The girl returned with Herman Gall who offered to take Caroline to see Dr. Steenson in Grahamdale. Domko would not allow David to go.

Caroline arrived at the doctor's office and he was not surprised to see her. He'd treated Mrs. Kort's ankle the night before.

Dr. Steenson was of medium height and built stoutly. His chubby round head was topped by a thin layer of black hair and he sported a thin moustache. Underneath his extra weight, was a fine boned man with a soft, almost feminine voice and exquisite hands. He was confident at all times and moved at basically the same speed whether it was a routine check-up or an emergency. He was confident and knowledgeable - some say brilliant. He read extensively and was aware of all the new medical theories and treatments world-wide. Rumours circulated that he was indeed a genius and there were some people who swore he read minds.

Dr. Steenson had a somewhat gruff bedside manner, as gruff a a man with a soft voice could have. He finished most of his statements by asking a question. He also wasn't overly concerned about sterilization which he felt was the nurse's job. He thought nothing of appearing in the clinic waiting room in a blood-stained smock after removing an abscessed tooth from an old farmer's mouth. He'd call in the next patient then disappear.

Dr. Steenson was much too rough when he gave needles, but the sickest of babies would find comfort in his gentle embrace. How he found the time to raise a family with such a large practise, nobody knew, but the communities he served had great respect for his wife Ruth. She was a trained nurse who assisted him on many occasions.

In spite of Dr. Steenson's eccentricities, he was a trusted and respected physician.

Dr. Steenson examined Caroline then bandaged her rib cage. It was obvious that she'd cracked three ribs in the accident. He prescribed bed rest and reached into his pocket for a bottle of painkillers. He placed a dozen in a small envelope then handed them to her.

"How are things with you and Bob?" he asked.

Caroline looked at the floor. "Fine," she answered.

"I've heard rumours and think that he should come in for another check-up," the doctor said. "He probably should see a specialist, do you know what I'm saying?"

Caroline stammered. She hadn't expected to discuss her husband.

"Because if it is a mental problem, it isn't going to get better without treatment," he continued. "He has two personalities, doesn't he? One that he shows you and his his friends then one that erupts when he's angry, am I right?"

She didn't answer.

"Medical treatment has come a long way, do you know what I mean? There is medication that can help and it can be done quite discreetly at this stage. If things go too far, well then the whole community finds out."

Caroline nodded gently.

"It's not my place to make a diagnosis on the few times I've seen Bob, but he's displaying the symptoms of a disorder that will only get worse if left untreated. It's up to you to let me know if things get out of hand and we can force him into treatment if we have to. Do you know what I mean?"

Caroline nodded.

"Good," he said opening the examining room door.

The police came to the house later that afternoon. They needed to file an accident report and wanted to hear Domko's side of the story. As the officer got out of the car, Domko called the twins and told them to sit at the table.

"You's be sayink he's only be havink one light!" he whispered as Caroline answered the door. "It be his fault!"

The twins sat quietly and watched as the officer came into the kitchen. After they exchanged pleasantries, the officer asked Domko what had happened the night before.

He invited the officer to sit down, then explained that it had been dark and the snow was piled very high along the sides of the road. The wind was blowing snow from the tops of the banks, making it very difficult to see. He was able to make out a light coming towards him. He said that when the cars met, he noticed the other vehicle had only one light and it was on the far side. By the time he realized where the car was on the road, it was too late and he couldn't stop. He hit Kort head-on. He said it was Mr. Kort's fault.

The children sat quietly listening to the story. Domko looked at the family and nodded at them for approval. The officer watched as Caroline and the boys agreed that this is what had happened.

The officer made a few notes on his pad, then tucked it in his pocket. He said that since the two drivers had given different explanations about the accident, determining fault would be difficult. Domko insisted that he was not at fault, but was careful not to push the officer too far.

David's teeth were so sore that he was unable to eat. A week after the accident he walked to Herman Gall's and asked that he take him to see the doctor. Herman agreed and drove David to Grahamdale.

Doctor Steenson was surprised to see him.

"How come you didn't come in sooner?" he asked.

David shrugged.

"He wouldn't let your mother bring you, is that right?"

David looked at the floor then nodded in agreement. He stood in front of the chubby doctor who wore a stethoscope like a necklace. The doctor then instructed him to open his mouth wide. His small, warm hands prodded inside David's mouth.

"If you were a man, we' never be able to adjust your teeth like this," Steenson said as he pulled the jammed teeth forward. "But young gums are soft and the roots of baby teeth dissolve once a tooth comes out, do you know what I mean?"

David nodded yes.

"I get a lot of people in here needing dental work," he said, as he started an elaborate story. He pulled roughly on the boy's teeth and David's eyes began to water. He let out a small groan, but tried very hard not to offend the doctor.

"I once had a boy in here once who fell out of a tree and I had to pull all his teeth out," Steenson continued. "Lucky for you, we don't have to do that, isn't that right?"

David nodded again.

When Dr. Steenson finished he reached into his pocket and pulled out a small bottle of painkillers. He gave a few to David then patted him on the back and sent him on his way.

The twins decided that they needed a reliable place to hide from Domko with Ruby gone. They didn't feel comfortable at Jim's and their mother forbade them to go to Harwarts house. They stayed in Frederick's barn a quite a number of times, but Domko discovered this hiding spot and brought them home. They still spent many nights in the church but had heard from the kids at school that the congregation was becoming angry about this.

"They're gonna lock the window an' then we won't have no place to go," David said one day. "We got to make our own place to live."

Dennis agreed.

"Wouldn't it be great if we had a place an' Satan couldn't find us?" he asked.

"Yeah, we could do whatever we want," Dennis added.

The boys discussed the idea of building themselves a hut in the bush.

"Where would we build it?" Dennis asked.

"In the bush along the trail to Jim's," David said. "You know, where we slept with Bo. That's a good spot that ole Flat Foot's never found."

Dennis agreed this would be a good spot. "We can take some of them burned nails an' we can get wood from the ole barn."

The more they talked about building a hut, the more excited they became. It was spring, so the days were beginning to lengthen. The warm sun had melted the snow from their bush paths and along the road.

One afternoon when Domko wasn't home, the boys started gathering materials for the hut. Bo tagged along as they dragged old planks from Fredericks barn through the field into the bush. The boys chose a spot just inside the trees along the trail to Jim's. Domko never came this way so they felt they would be safe.

The twins made countless trips that day and the next. They filled their pockets with nails and took one of Domko's hammers. Carrying a piece of an old tire and some tin, they trudged into the bush to begin building.

"How big should we make it?" Dennis asked.

"Big enough for me, you, Bo an' maybe Beanie an' Rosie."

"That's pretty big. Are you sure we got enough nails?"

"Yeah, an' if not we can always get more. Ole Flat Foot will never notice."

Dennis nodded as he trudged along beside his brother. He could always count on David to come up with good ideas.

"I got it all thought out," David explained. "We'll make it with a leaning roof so the snow doesn't pile on top in winter. We'll make a door, that's why I brought this rubber, so it'll bend. You can do the hammering 'cause you do that good, while I hold on to the wood."

They discussed how the finished hut should look just to be sure they had the same building in mind.

The boys hammered boards together until dark. They crept to their bedroom that night, did chores in the morning and went to school. That afternoon, they finished chores then went to work in the bush for a few hours. They returned home hungry and exhausted. The following day they called Bo as they ran towards the bush and the dog came bounding down the path.

"We're almost done," Dennis said happily as they ran along. "Should we tell Eunice an' Rosie?"

"Not 'til we're done," David answered. "Today we can put the door on and it'll be ready for sleepin'."

The boys reached the familiar spot, but couldn't see their hut at first. Because of its colour, it blended well with the bush.

"Once the leaves come out, he'll never find us," Dennis said. "We can live here forever and he'll never know."

Picking up the last of the boards, they laid three of them on the ground horizontally then placed a fourth board crosswise. They pounded nails with determination. The building gave them hope that Domko wouldn't always have a hold over them. Flipping the door over, David cut the rubber into three big pieces and placed them along the edge of the door. Dennis nailed on the rubber hinges and together the boys put the door in place.

"Over more," Dennis said.

David held the door in place as Dennis began nailing the hinges to the hut. When he'd put five nails into each piece of rubber, they considered their place finished. The boys stepped back to admire their work.

The hut was about five feet tall and six feet wide. The boards ran horizontally between four well-placed oak trees. The front was higher than the back and the boys had planned it that way to allow rain to drain off the roof.

"Next we'll put on the tin," David said. "That way it won't leak.

"What if Domko sees it? He'll say we're stealin' again."

"Stealin' what? The tin? Walter's fur money bought that tin an' so really it belongs to him. Walter wouldn't mind if we used it."

Dennis laughed. His brother was right.

"Yeah, HIM sayin' we're stealin' is really stupid."

Pulling back the door, the boys stepped inside. The ground was still damp from the melting snow.

"We gotta get somethin' to make a stove," David said. "There's gotta be some old scrap around that we can use. Whadda you think?"

"Hmmm . . ," Dennis laughed. "How 'bout parts of ole Satan's car? It's not good for nothin' now!"

The boys laughed as they looked around the hut. Bo poked his head inside.

"We gotta get somethin' in here to sleep on cause it's too wet," Dennis said.

"Yeah, tomorrow we'll bring some wood an' some hay and we'll make beds."

The next day Domko was waiting on the road for them after school. Disappointed, the twins followed him home to do chores. He knew they had some fun planned so he kept them working until dark. He watched them suspiciously as they chatted to themselves in their secret language. They each ate a bowl of potato soup for dinner then went to bed. It had been a few days since anyone in the house had received a beating, which was a warning to the boys. They knew to stay far away from Domko since he'd be looking for an excuse.

The boys slept behind the walls of their room that night as a precaution. David was still plagued by nightmares about having his neck or private parts slashed. He was too frightened to sleep. There was always a chance that Domko would beat him because of the nightmares.

After tonight I don't have to worry about that no more, he thought happily.

The boys tried to hide their excitement as they finished milking the cows the following morning. The girls sensed something exciting was happening and pressed for answers.

"You'll find out," David teased. "When we're ready to tell ya."

"Yeah," Dennis added. "when we're ready."

As the boys carried the milk, Domko intercepted them between the barn and the house.

"We's be cuttink wood," he said handing David the old swede saw.

Reluctantly, David traded the milk pail for the wobbly saw.

"You's not be runnink away or I's be killink you bastards," Domko warned.

"We won't," David said as he stood waiting in the yard with his brother. Eunice came darting out of the house.

"Boy, I hate cuttin' wood," Dennis whispered.

"Yeah, me too."

Domko came out a few minutes later and they all went to the woodpile at the edge of the bush. The trees had been hauled in to dry the fall before.

Now they had to be cut into one foot lengths so they would fit in the stove firebox. The children knew this was an all-day project.

It would be Eunice's responsibility to hold the long end of the log across the saw horse while the boys sawed chunks off the other end. Draping her body over the log, she held it in place as David pulled one end of the saw and Dennis the other. They see-sawed back and forth until the one-foot piece dropped to the ground, then they started again. It was a long, boring job that the children hated. He always made them cut wood in cold weather which froze their hands.

Sunny breaks that morning were replaced by a strong north wind and wet snow in early afternoon. Out-of-breath, the boys listened as Eunice filled them in on what had been happening at the house when they weren't there. They continued working, punctuated at intervals by Domko returning to inspect the job they were doing. He often stayed for a long time and the children had to work quickly while he stood and watched. When he was satisfied the job was progressing, he went back to the house. This gave the children a break.

"I'm cold," Eunice complained as she pulled her sleeves over her hands. "My feet are cold too."

"Me too," Dennis said. "How long is he gonna make us work?"

"I dunno," she said. "He's mad at you guys for runnin' away."

Bo was scrounging food by the chicken coop and lifted his head to listen to the children.

"Here's how I stay warm," David said. "C'mere Bo. Here, boy!"

Hearing David's voice, Bo lumbered over to where the children worked. The dog, still at the clumsy puppy stage, almost knocked them over with his friendliness. David grabbed him and buried his hands deep in the dog's fur.

"Yuk! He stinks," Eunice said turning up her nose.

"He don't stink," David said defensively. "All dogs smell like that. Besides he don't smell as bad as ole Satan."

Eunice agreed and laughed. "Yeah, an' I don't go near him either!"

The dog enjoyed the children's laughter and barked a loud, deep bark. His mouth hung open loosely and drool dripped from his heavy jowls. He was mostly a dirty white colour, with big dark and light brown patches on his eyes, ears and across his back. He was growing to be a huge dog in spite of seldom being fed. By now it had become very obvious to everyone that Domko had mistaken his breed.

"That ain't no damned Collie dog," David said as he grabbed his end of the saw. "Ole' Squeezer was so proud of himself for stealin' a Collie."

Dennis laughed. "Yeah, do you think he's noticed yet?"

"I dunno, but Marjie says Bo's some kinda Saint Brenard."

"That's BER-nard," Eunice corrected.

"That's what I said," David argued. "Brenard."

Domko came back ten minutes later and the children began sawing quickly. The saw wobbled a few times then suddenly, the thin blade broke.

"You's be broken it some!" Domko yelled lunging towards them. Eunice darted into the bush as he grabbed David by the hair then knocked him to the ground. Dennis did not move quick enough and Domko grabbed him by the arm. He backhanded the boy hard, sending him toppling over the saw horse. He began punching and kicking the twins as they covered their heads with their arms. The boys held their breath against the blows, hoping it would hurt less.

They noticed he was alternating between boys so that neither of them could get away. The boys knew that this beating was for more than being there when the saw blade broke. They knew it was because they had a secret from Domko.

I don't care, David thought as he tried to ignore the heavy boots kicking his back. "We won't come back no more. We're gonna live in our hut in the bush an' he'll never find us.

Domko grunted each time his boot connected with the boys' backs and legs. He didn't care where he kicked them and lately had been trying even harder to injure them. The boys were twelve years old now, and beating them was hard work. Though Domko never admitted it out loud, the twins were tough as nails and had a stubborn survival instinct that made them hard to beat.

He kicked them until neither one was moving. Then he grabbed the broken saw and threw it in the grass. He picked up enough wood for the night and breathlessly laboured to the house. The twins laid on the wet ground for a while until they knew he wouldn't be coming back.

"He's gone," David groaned in the secret language. "You o.k.?"

"Yeah."

"C'mon, lets go to our place. We can stay there from now on."

The boys struggled to their feet and slowly walked along the bush path toward the church. They came out near Harwart's, then cut through the field to the old barn. David gathered an armful of hay while Dennis pulled two boards across the wet ground through the field to their hut. Bo followed closely behind as wet snow whipped against their faces. To get to the hut, they had to wade through ankle deep water and mud.

Dennis was beginning to tire and was disheartened from the beating. David did his best to keep his brother's spirits up.

"I got matches," he said. "Just think about how nice an' warm it'll be in there tonight. We don't got to worry about Squeezer no more. We even got Bo to sleep beside an' you know how warm he is. If we feel better later on, we can go to Emma's an' ask for bread. It'll be good from now on, Denny, I promise."

The boys walked through the last slough to the edge of the bush. As they walked into the bush, they felt the wind subside and suddenly felt heartened. They'd made it! Looking around in the dark forest, the boys were having a hard time finding their hut. David looked back for a moment and realized they had come too far south.

"C'mon, it's this way," he said.

Walking towards the north, the boys came into a small clearing where the hut was. Dennis gasped as he dropped the wood he'd dragged all the way from the barn. The twins stood in agonized silence as they looked at the charred remains of their hut.

Domko had burned it down.

Chapter 23

Norman comes home

THE BOYS SLEPT THAT NIGHT around a campfire beside the charred remains of their hut. They returned home two days later and nothing more was said about the hut.

Domko chuckled about what he'd done but boys refused to acknowledge that anything was wrong. The twins continued to go to school and work hard during evenings and weekends. If Domko beat them, they would run to where the hut had been since it was still an excellent hiding spot. They considered re-building but had used all the scrap lumber they could find the first time around. Besides, he'd just burn it down again.

Domko's cattle were escaping and travelling to the pastures of neighbours because his fences were in desperate need of repair. Domko feigned ignorance when the neighbours came to complain. He blamed the children - saying they'd left a gate open. The boys felt like yelling that they weren't responsible, but preferred the scowls of neighbours to Domko's fists. They continued peeling fence posts as he blamed them and their mother for everything that went wrong on the farm.

One afternoon David returned upset from school upset because Bo was not waiting in his usual place by the fence across from the school. David had a horrible feeling that something had happened to the dog.

"Ma, have you seen Bo anywhere?" he asked when he came into the kitchen.

Caroline didn't answer right away.

David became nervous as he watched his mother. He sensed something was wrong.

"Domko shot him about an hour ago," she said.

"What?" David yelled. "Why'd he do that?"

"I don't know," she said pointing east. "He's not dead. I saw him run that way."

Dennis stayed behind to milk while David took off running into the bush. Tears streamed down his face as he called the dog. He stopped to listen each time he thought he heard whimpering, but the sounds turned out to be splashing water or chirping birds.

David ran first through the bush to the beaver dam. Then he cut back through the east meadow towards home. He went to the church then to Harwart's house. He checked the abandoned barn and then went to Jim's house along the bush trail. He hoped that Bo had remembered going there as a pup, but Jim shook his head that he hadn't seen the dog

David looked in the barn and around the buildings. He went home on a different path, calling the dog as he went. It was late and dark by the time he got home.

Domko was chuckling in his usual spot David walked in the door. He avoided eye contact and went immediately upstairs to find Dennis who was crying limply on the bed.

"You o.k.?" he asked, realizing Dennis had received another beating.

Dennis nodded as he stifled back tears, his body tender and throbbing. "Did you find him?"

"No. I'm gonna look again tomorrow."

He sat down beside his brother.

"Do you think the coyotes will get him?" David cried softly.

"No," Dennis said bravely. "He's stronger than a coyote."

"Yeah, but he's hurt."

"He'll be o.k. David, don't worry."

The next morning David left fifteen minutes early so he could search for Bo. He met Dennis on his way home with the cows.

"Did you find him?" Dennis asked.

David shook his head 'no'.

That night he looked again and then again the next morning but still could not find the dog.

The following day the twins fled into the bush to avoid a beating. They ran to the spot where their hut had been. As they approached, a sickening smell permeated the air. The twins looked at each other.

Cautiously, the boys came around the edge of the bush and peered into the clearing where their hut had been. There, lying on the ground beside the campfire was a giant mound of fur.

"Oh no!" David exclaimed, covering his eyes. "He went here 'cause I told him it was a safe spot. I walked right by him an' didn't see him."

David was heartbroken that Bo had chosen to die in their hiding spot. He felt he'd betrayed the dog by not finding him. He remembered the night when Bo had sheltered them from the wind as they slept cuddling his fur by the campfire.

"We woulda died if it hadn't been for him," David whispered. "He was there for us, an' I shoulda been here for him."

Dennis didn't know what to say. He was accustomed to David having all the answers and being strong. He'd loved Bo too, but not as much as David. It hurt him deeply to see his brother in so much pain. Physical pain was one thing, but the feeling that someone is ripping out your heart is all together different.

"C'mon," he said. "We'll go some place else."

The school year finished in mid-April that year because of tremendous flooding. This pleased Domko who needed full time workers. One early May afternoon, he returned home from town with a load of poplar rails and the boys knew they were in for a long, hard job turning the logs into posts. They'd seen their older brothers do it a few years before and groaned as Domko called them over to unload the wagon.

While the boys worked, they noticed Gus walking down the road towards the farm. He hadn't been over in more than a year so they were surprised to see him. They stopped unloading the rails and gave him a faint wave. His angry expression softened slightly as he looked at the twins.

"Where's Domko?" he asked.

"Over there," Dennis said, pointing towards the lean-to where the tractor was kept. "He'll be back in a minute."

Gus watched the boys working as he waited. He hadn't seen them up close for quite awhile and was surprised at how much they'd grown. They were still awfully thin, but big boned and strong. He'd seen them many times trudging through the fields east of his house and wondered where they were going.

Domko's not going to be able to push these kids around much longer, he thought. *Hopefully he won't kill one of them first.*

Gus made small talk with the boys as he watched Domko approach.

"Domko, you're cattle are in my field again," he said. "I want them out of there right now."

"Vat?" he asked surprised.

"Don't give me that innocent look. You know what I'm talking about. It's the third time this week they've got in and I'm sick of it."

Domko laughed.

"Then you's be keepink them out," he taunted.

"Me? They are your cattle! It's your responsibility to keep them in."

Domko laughed and shook his head.

"You won't be laughing if somebody loads them up and ships them to Winnipeg," Gus warned. "You can start taking better care of them and while you're at it, you can take better care of these kids too."

The twins smirked at the comment. They had never heard Gus yell at Domko before and stopped to admire the man's nerve.

Having said all he came to say, Gus turned to walk out of yard.

"Fraaa!" Domko yelled as he lunged at the older man's back. He kicked Gus in the back knocking him forward. Shocked, Gus turned to face his assailant. A look of understanding came over his face. Now he fully understood the fear the twins lived with every day.

Domko continued to swear and chase Gus. At 67 years of age, Gus was no match for the 45 year old bully. Domko continued to push and kick his visitor down the road. Ashamed that they had witnessed such a disrespectful display by their stepfather, the boys hung their heads.

"We can't get Gus in trouble no more," Dennis said, understanding how it felt to be humiliated. "He's too old to fight Satan."

There were more than 100 poplar rails that needed to be peeled, sharpened and soaked in bluestone before they could be used for fenceposts. The boys worked on this day and night for more than two weeks.

"Why do you 'spose he never gives us nothin' to eat?" Dennis asked. He and David had snuck away from work and stood in the grainary flicking mouse droppings out of the handfuls of chop they ate.

"He don't want us to get strong," David said. "As long as we're skinny an' hungry, we can't fight back."

Dennis nodded in understanding.

"Wait here," David said. "I gotta go outside."

Dennis nodded and continued eating the chop.

David walked calmly into the bush and off the usual trail. He needed to go to the bathroom, and since Domko had never bothered to build an outhouse, there was a spot in the bush where everyone went.

David came quietly around the edge of the bush and saw Eunice crouching down. She finished and stood up, but didn't notice him standing there. She turned and went in the other direction.

David gasped. He forgot why he had come and turned, running as fast as he could back to the house. Out of breath, he burst through the door.

"Denny!" he yelled. "You should see what happened to Eunice!"

"What?"

His eyes were wide with fear. "He did it!"

"He did what?"

"He cut it off. Eunice don't got one no more."

Dennis couldn't believe his ears. "No! It can't be!" he said.

"Yeah, remember hearin' her scream?" he gasped. "An' notice how she's been arguin' back? An' sometimes she cries at night and we don't know why."

The twins ran to hide upstairs to finish discussing poor Eunice.

"Are you gonna look?" David asked as they sat on the bed.

Dennis nodded that he would spy on her the next time she went into the bush. The pair decided to stick together and if Domko ever had the other one trapped and brought out the knife, the other guy would have to do something to distract him.

"Are you ever gonna fight back?" Dennis asked.

"I dunno," David said. "I'm too scared to hit back."

"Me too."

"I'm scared he'll just kill us an' throw us in the beaver dam an' nobody would even know.

"Yeah, like that time when he took us fencin'," Dennis said. "He woulda killed us 'cept old Gus was sittin' there."

The twins remembered how one afternoon Domko told them they had to fix a fence near the beaver dam. The boys sat on the wagon as Domko roared through the field. They sensed something was odd about this because they had no fences along the beaver dam. They recognized the bags and hammer between Domko's knees as the same equipment he carried when he went to drown litters of puppies. The boys knew instinctively that they were in danger and planned to jump off the wagon and run into the bush the moment the wagon stopped . When they arrived at the lake bank, all were surprised to see old Gus Gall sitting fishing. Domko had become unnerved by this, turned the tractor around and took the boys home.

"There was no fence to fix was there?" Dennis asked.

"If there was," David said. "We never fixed it."

Caroline had been gone for over a week, then suddenly arrived home. She disappeared again while the boys were out mending fences so they weren't able to tell her about Eunice.

Suddenly the twins saw a familiar figure walking towards them.

"Who's that?" David asked, hope rising in his voice.

"It looks like Norman," Dennis answered.

The twins stopped working as their brother approached.

"Hey, Norman!" David called. "Whadda you doin' here?"

"I'm back for awhile," he said. "I'm sick of livin' with those people and mom came an' asked me to come back. She said you guys can't get all the work done. They're gonna pay me a dollar a day an' I'm gonna stay an' get my grade eight at Bayton."

The twins smiled, happy to have their brother home. Not only because he'd help with the work, but also because Norman was a lot of fun to be with.

In the time he had been away, Norman had grown about three inches and filled out nicely. At almost sixteen years of age, he was a formidable brother to have around. The twins suddenly felt a little safer.

"So," Norman said as he grabbed the heavy hammer. "How's the ole bastard been treatin' you?"

The twins groaned.

"Like shit," David said.

"So you haven't killed him yet?"

"Not yet. We're too scared," David said trying to sound grown up. "We tried but Dennis couldn't make the gun work."

"Me? It wasn't my fault. You was just lyin' there shakin' behind the tree. I didn't see you doin' no killin."

The three of them laughed as they caught up on each other's lives.

"Where is he anyway?" Norman asked.

"Dunno," David said.

"Who cares?" Dennis laughed.

They walked home and as they came into the yard, the twins noticed a shiny black motorcycle sitting near the house.

"Wow!" David yelled. "Is that yours?"

Trying to act nonchalant, Norman strode over to the bike.

"Yeah, I got it last month. Do you like it?"

"Like it? It's great," David said.

Dennis reached out to touch the seat.

"Don't touch it!"

He pulled his hand back. "Why not?"

"'Cause I said so. I don't want you to ever touch it without askin' me first, you understand?"

"O.k.," he nodded.

David walked around the bike, looking at it carefully. "Wow, this is great Norman, are you ever lucky. When I grow up I'm gonna get me a great bike just like this one."

One morning shortly after Norman's move back to the farm, the children were doing chores when a family from the church stopped by for a visit. They were on their way to the Jehovah Witness annual gathering in Winnipeg. The man and woman were dressed in their best clothes while their little girls wore dresses with ribbons in their hair. The older girls looked very pretty and turned up their noses as Caroline insisted Eunice and Rosie say hello.

The boys watched from a distance as Caroline invited the family in for coffee. They declined because they had a long drive ahead of them. David listened to them chatting to his mother and felt embarrassed for Eunice and Rosie who were dressed in their barn clothes.

"Hey Denny," he whispered. "See the rouge an' lipstick on them girls? All Beanie's got for rouge is cow shit!"

Both boys giggled half-heartedly. They felt ashamed that their family was so poor. They thought making light of the situation might make them feel better, but instead it made them feel worse. They knew Eunice didn't want to be standing there while the visitors compared her to their well-dressed daughters.

"Next year we're going to go too," Caroline sighed. "We just can't get away this time."

The families exchanged pleasantries and the visitors left for Winnipeg soon.

"Phoney bastards," Norman said under his breath to David. "It makes 'em feel good to come here 'cause you guys are poor an' it makes 'em feel rich."

"Are they rich?" David asked.

"'Course not, but they can point to the girls an' say, "see you girls are lucky, not like that Eunice and Rosie." An' don't worry, they don't like old Squeezer either. I know 'cause when I was livin' out I heard people talkin' 'bout you guys."

"People are talkin' 'bout us?"

"Yeah, you guys are pretty popular since you stole that wood," he said sarcastically.

"We didn't do it!" David protested. "He made us take it."

"I heard 'em sayin' that you guys are stealin' all the time. Some think you're drivin' poor ole Domko nuts. Poor Domko my ass! He was nuts long before he came here. Anyways that's why I came back 'cause you guys need help 'an I ain't afraid of the ole bastard anymore."

The twins looked stunned. "You're not?" they chorused.

"Nope. I'm almost as big as him an' I'm fast an' strong. I'm not scared of him no more."

David and Dennis stared at their brother in disbelief.

"Don't let him hear you sayin' that or he'll kill you," David warned.

Norman laughed. He looked into his brothers eyes and all he could see was fear.

"Christ you're bushed!" he said. "Do you ever go to town?"

David felt his face flush.

* * * * *

Summer came and soon haying began. Having Norman back was great for Eunice and the twins since it lightened their workload. They hayed the high spots early and worked their way into the low spots as the ground dried. There was a lot to do that year since because the land Domko bought the year before was also producing.

"So old Squeezer works you just as hard as ever," Norman said one afternoon. "Listen, I'm takin' off early so don't tell him where I went. Just pretend like I didn't say anything."

The twins nodded. They watched as Norman led the horses pulling the mower through the field towards home. There was only a little bit of stacking left to do that day and Domko was nowhere to be found, so the boys sat in the grass under a tree and took a break.

They sat chatting for a while then suddenly saw Eunice in the distance running through the field. Domko was right behind her.

"Look!" Dennis laughed. "His pants fell off!"

David also laughed at the sight. "He shoulda waited before he pulled off his belt."

Dennis stood up and watched as she disappeared into the bush. "Beanie will be o.k., she's a pretty fast runner."

The boys finished stacking then drove the horses home. It had been a long day and they were tired and hungry as they unhitched the team.

"Don't mix up the straps!" David warned.

Dennis fumbled with one pair but was careful to hang them in the right place. "Yeah, I remember what happened last time."

The boys strolled into the house where their mother was making supper. Raymond was crying because Kathy had taken something away from him. He let out a screeching noise that caused the twins to cover their ears.

"Let's get outta here," Dennis said. David nodded and they went back outside. They sat in the bush and talked for a while then decided to get a drink of water. David ran to get a sealer he had hidden nearby.

"We'll fill this up," he said.

The boys walked cautiously into the yard, looking over their shoulders for Domko. He wouldn't like it if he saw them taking a break and having a drink of water. They had to get to the pump house quickly and quietly without him noticing. The boys came around the corner of the house then stopped short. Domko was leaning over the water trough. They could see Eunice leaning over the water trough too, and he was holding her down. Her arms and legs were flailing and it was then they realized her head was being held under water.

Dennis turned and ran towards the bush while David ran into the house.

"Ma! Come quick," he yelled. "He's drowning Eunice in the trough!"

Caroline dashed out of the house then screamed. She ran over to her husband and pulled on his arm.

"Boleslaw!" she screamed. "Let her go! You're drowning her!"

Shocked by the intensity of his wife's voice, he let go of Eunice.

"She's be some moonkey," he spitted.

Caroline grabbed the girl and pulled her out of the trough. Eunice fell to the ground unconscious, her face a deep blue colour.

David stood and watched as his mother slapped Eunice's face and massaged her chest. She screamed for Eunice to wake up as she shook her. Within a few seconds, Eunice began to sputter and cough. She opened her eyes and it was obvious she was disoriented. She convulsed on the ground then turned over and vomited in the grass.

"What were you doing?" Caroline screamed at her husband. "You could have killed her!"

Eunice stayed limp on the grass for a few minutes as Caroline fussed over her. Domko stood ominously close by as Caroline helped Eunice to her feet. The teenager wiped her face with her hands then shot her stepfather a glaring look.

Neither said a word as Eunice went into the house and upstairs. After supper, Caroline followed and much to the displeasure of her husband, stayed in the children's bedroom that night. She had started doing that a few months before when she wanted to punish him. It worked well since he hated sleeping alone.

"What happened?" David asked Eunice that night when he climbed into bed. "What did you do to make him so mad?"

Eunice's face flushed and she was glad it was too dark for him to see. She turned on her side, away from the brother who had saved her life.

"Nothin'." she said.

The boys fell asleep, but Eunice was still awake well past midnight. She could hear Domko snoring loudly downstairs. The sound disgusted her and she shook with revulsion as she played back in her mind what had happened earlier that day.

She had been working in the hayfield when Domko approached her in an odd way. She had been sensing that he was looking at her differently now that she was maturing into a young woman. She knew enough about male-female relations to keep away from men with 'that look'.

He pulled off his pants and then tried to push her down. She'd squirmed free then ran into the bush. He chased her and caught her and that's when she'd lashed out at him in anger.

"Don't you come near me!" she'd screamed. "You touch me and I'll tell mom and the police." At that point he'd backed off but watched her suspiciously from a distance for the rest of the day. She'd been walking from the barn towards the house when he jumped out from behind the water trough and grabbed her. He must have been afraid that she was going to tell her mother what had happened. He pushed her head into the trough and just as she felt herself begin to float away, her lungs suddenly filled with air and there was a burning sensation in her chest.

Lucky for me the twins came along, she thought as she cried herself to sleep. *Otherwise I'd be dead.*

"You don't believe me, do you?" Norman said to the twins as they sat in the bedroom. "Not everybody's afraid of him like you."

"Well, he's crazier now, you just haven't seen him," David said. "He tried to drown Eunice a couple days ago an' you should see how he smashed Denny last week."

Standing up, Norman put his hands on his hips. "You guys look like you need a good laugh," he said. "Guess what I'm gonna do?"

"What?" Dennis asked.

"I'm gonna moon him."

"What??"

"I'm gonna moon him."

The twins jumped up. They had heard about mooning in school.

"No Norman, don't!" David begged. "Please don't do it. He'll kill you!"

"I'm gonna," he said as he strode toward the top of the stairs.

"Don't, or he'll cut it off!" Dennis warned.

Norman looked at him and smirked. "What the hell are you talkin' about?"

Dennis said nothing as he glanced over his shoulder at Eunice who was sitting on the bed reading. "Ask Eunice."

She looked up from her book. "Shhhh! I don't want him to know I'm up here."

Norman smiled then walked confidently down the stairs.

The twins followed their brother and when they realized he was serious, went to stand by the door.

Domko was sitting at the kitchen table stirring his coffee. He looked up suspiciously as the boys stood waiting by the door. Norman came around the corner, which startled him slightly. The teenager strode across the floor and stopped about ten feet from Domko.

"Hey, Domko," he said.

"Vat?"

"I'm gonna moon you."

"Vat be moonink?"

"I'm gonna show you my ass!" Norman yelled as he turned and pulled his pants down. He stuck his bare back end at Domko and gave a little wiggle.

"Fraaa!" Domko yelled as he jumped off the chair.

The twins ran out the door and split in different directions. Seconds later Norman followed as fast as he could with his pants down around his knees. Domko caught him three strides into the yard and the pair tumbled into the grass.

The twins grimaced as Domko beat Norman who was struggling to get his pants up. Instead of cowering as the boys always had, Norman stuck out his arms and legs to block a few of the blows. Domko beat him with a ferocity that the boys had never seen before. Soon, Norman was not moving on the grass and Domko's energy was spent. Satisfied, he grunted and went back into the house. When he slammed the door, the twins ran over to their brother who was lying flat on his back, panting.

"Oh, Norman we told you! He really got you this time," David said, looking at the stream of blood coming from his brother's nose.

Norman raised a hand and wiped his bloodied face.

"Yeah," he smiled. "But it was worth it."

Chapter 24

After the mooning

THE TWINS SAT AT THE KITCHEN TABLE that evening while their mother and Domko discussed Norman. Domko complained angrily about the boy's belligerence and disrespect.

With eyebrows furrowed, he paced the floor, angrily telling his wife what had happened that afternoon. Caroline glanced quickly at the twins to gauge their reaction to this outburst. The boys sat without emotion as Domko ranted and raved about their brother. He said nobody would be able to control Norman if he wasn't stopped soon.

"Ant then they's be doink it too!" he said, pointing at the twins.

David and Dennis shook their heads in disagreement. They were too afraid of Domko to do such a disrespectful thing as 'moon' him. They did admire their older brother, though, but kept that fact to themselves.

Caroline listened to her husband and agreed. Her support heartened him and he became even angrier. His eyes darted back and forth and he slammed his fist on the table. Their mother was beginning to think in a similar way to Domko and this frightened the twins. Caroline began discussing ways to keep Norman under control while Domko's solution was to work the children harder. The twins slowly slipped away from the table.

"Then he's not be moonink no more!" Domko yelled, thrusting his arm into the air.

The boys looked at one another in astonishment.

"More work?" Dennis whispered. "We can't work no harder than this!"

"I know," David said shaking his head. "How come ole Flat Foot always finds ways to make us pay, no matter what?"

"I dunno," Dennis said. "It ain't our fault Norman mooned him."

"Yeah," David whispered. "An' Norman's lucky he's got that motorbike so he can go whenever he wants."

Dennis agreed.

Norman returned late that night, humming to himself as he climbed into the bed. It was obvious he'd had a good time wherever he'd been that night. He chuckled to himself remembering the reactions of his friends when he told them he'd mooned Domko. Norman was an excellent storyteller who always had an audience. They'd thought it was hilarious! Norman fell asleep quite pleased with himself.

The following morning Domko glanced out the kitchen window and saw Norman's bike parked in the yard. With a roar, he woke the children and herded them outside to do chores. Instead of going back to the house as he normally did, he remained scowling in the center of the barn.

The children worked quickly and silently. Even Norman didn't have much to say. Then instead of allowing them into the house for breakfast, Domko made them hitch up the horses and go directly to the field to haul hay.

The children sat on the hay rack as it bumped across the field. Norman whistled softly as he held the reins.

"Thanks a lot Norman," Eunice said sarcastically. "Now 'cause of you, we gotta work even harder."

Norman looked at her as she sat beside him. Eunice was scowling for a reason unknown to him."Whadda you talkin' about?" he asked.

"Domko's mad 'cause you mooned him an' now we gotta work harder."

Norman laughed indignantly. "That's bullshit! That's just an excuse 'cause he's just turnin' mom against us, that's all."

"Yeah, well you didn't hear him last night," she said. "He's worried we're all gonna start moonin' him."

"He's full of shit an' so are you guys if you're mad at me 'cause of that," he said. "The ole bastard deserves more than to be mooned."

Dennis apologized for all of them. "We're not mad at you," he told Norman. "We just don't wanna have to work harder, that's all."

Norman laughed. "Well, I'm not worried. He's payin' me an' that's all I care about."

Domko kept his promise. During the next few weeks he worked the children hard from early morning until late evening. He watched them closely and used a heavy stick to beat all of them except Norman whenever they made a mistake. Soon the children were behaving like robots, methodically cutting, raking and stacking hay. They weren't allowed to talk, eat or take a break from the exhausting work as long as Domko was watching. Occasionally, he would go to the house, which gave them a short reprieve.

One afternoon Domko returned from lunch carrying a few pails. Caroline, Kathy and Raymond tagged along. There was a thick patch of Saskatoon bushes nearby. Sometimes the blossoms failed to survive spring frosts. But this year the wild berry bushes were heavy with berries that needed to be picked before they fell to the ground.

The children each took a pail and followed Domko and Caroline along the wooded trail. Stepping from the hot sun into the shade of the bush soothed their sunburned skins and raised the children's spirits. Raymond toddled ahead of them with Rosie. Kathy marched rather than walked to avoid tripping over roots and stones.

David looked around in wonder as if was seeing the bush for the very first time. A feeling of normalcy swept over him. This is how life should be all the time! The group came to the tall bushes and everyone instinctively spread out, each finding their own picking spot and declaring it better than the rest.

The children chatted quietly among themselves, pulling the branches down near their pails. They ran their hands along the small branches, gently stripping them of the luscious fruit. The first fat, dark blue berries made small popping noises as they dropped into the pails. Soon, many pails were lined with berries, until they were overflowing.

As David and Dennis picked, they scooped small handfuls of berries into their mouths when Domko wasn't looking. They were careful not to stain their lips. David wet the back of his hand with spit then rubbed it across his lips.

"Hey, Denny," he whispered. "Any on my face?"

Dennis looked carefully at his brother. "Nope. How 'bout me?"

"No, you're o.k. too."

The boys were the last to fill their pails, except for Kathy and Raymond who were eating heartily from the trees. Domko eyed the twins suspiciously as they tried to get Eunice, Norman and their mother to help them.

"Vat?" he spat. "They's be lazy hobos. See? I's be tellink you they's be goot for nuthink."

He walked towards the boys and made them face him.

"You's be eatink some?"

The twins shook their heads 'no'. Confident that their mouths were clean, they faced their stepfather as he looked them over carefully.

"Open but a some mouth!" Domko commanded.

The twins hesitated then began to shake as they slowly parted their lips. Domko's eyes bulged in anger at the sight of dark purple stains on their teeth and tongues.

"Fraaa!" he screamed. Reaching out he punched David in the face, sending him sprawling backwards and his berries flying through the air. Dennis fell to the ground anticipating a punch but received a kick instead.

Domko stood over them and screamed for Dennis and David to pick up their berries. Caroline led the rest of the children down the path towards home while the boys scrambled on the ground, scooping berries back into their pails.

"You's be some goot for sheet!" Domko fumed.

David could hear his twin crying. He wanted to explain to Domko why they had eaten berries, but knew his pleading would fall on deaf ears.

We're starving, he thought to himself. I'm so hungry my stomach feels like somebody is cutting it out with a knife.

"Fraaa!" their antagonist screamed again, this time thrusting his arm into the air towards home. The boys grabbed their pails and hurried down the path. Domko grunted as he followed close behind.

David sobbed unhappily as he trudged along. A knot of frustration welled in his stomach. All he felt towards his stepfather was utter hatred. He wondered if he would ever grow strong enough to escape Domko. The thought of how many years it would take sent a wave of despair through him.

The following morning Caroline and Eunice worked in the kitchen cleaning and preserving the Saskatoons. The mother and daughter chatted and gossiped as a breeze blew softly through an open window.

Eunice wanted to talk about Domko and how uncomfortable he made her feel. But Caroline was in such a pleasant mood that Eunice didn't want to spoil their time together. She tried to put her unhappiness out of her mind as she and her mother boiled the berry mixture over the wood stove. When it was thick, it would be poured for sealing into hot, sterilized jars that sat on the table.

The kitchen was sweltering from the heat of the stove so any excuse to stand by the window was welcome. Eunice paused as she listened to Rosie playing outside. It made her wonder if life was really as bad as it seemed.

Maybe this is just what it is like, she thought to herself. *Maybe this is what being a kid is about. When I grow up I can be or do whatever I want and that's not long off. I'm 13 now and in a year or two I can leave here for good.*

Eunice's spirits brightened as her mother sent her to collect eggs from the hen house. She grabbed the basket by the door and went outside. Not surprisingly, it was cooler outdoors than in.

She could see that Rosie had found herself a piece of rope and was skipping on the worn grass along the driveway. Rosie hummed skipping songs softly to herself, counting how many times she could skip before catching the rope on her foot. She loved to skip and lost herself completely in the activity.

Eunice sauntered to the hen house then stepped inside the dank building. The birds clucked noisily as the door shut behind her.

"O.k. chickens," she said. "I'm here to take your eggs."

The hens flapped their wings and tried to peck her hand, but Eunice reached deftly underneath the bossy birds.

"Blech!" she said as she tried to avoid touching the little pellets of manure surrounding the nests. "I hate chickens."

She finished gathering the eggs and started back towards the house. She stared into the basket and wondered how the contents of these strange little vessels turned into chicks. Looking up, she could see Domko walking from the barn to the house. He slowed almost to a full stop when he noticed Rosie skipping happily in the driveway. An all too familiar look crossed his face and Eunice knew what would happen next. Domko strode toward the unsuspecting Rosie who was skipping with her back to the approaching man. At the same moment, Eunice set her basket of eggs on the ground and began running towards her sister. She intercepted her stepfather just as he reached out to grab the little girl.

"No!" Eunice screamed frantically. "Leave her alone! Don't hit her anymore!"

Rosie clung to Eunice and buried her face in her sister's shirt. Eunice faced Domko.

"Huh?" he said. Surprised, he took a step back.

This was the second time that Eunice had stood up to him. She could sense his confusion and continued to scream until her mother looked out the window. To her surprise, Domko backed away. He went into the house and berated Caroline about the children's behaviour. He complained that they were conspiring against him and that Eunice had attacked him for no reason. Caroline listened as he alleged that the children were always together snickering and pointing at him.

The girls were shocked by what they overheard. They hoped their mother didn't believe lies. They also stayed outside the rest of the day.

Late that afternoon, Marjorie and her dog Sandy chased the Harwart cows down the road past the house, so Eunice and Rosie joined their friend. It was a twice daily ritual that gave the girls an excuse to visit.

Domko watched the children closely over the next few days. He tried desperately to listen to their conversations in hopes of learning how they were plotting against him. Perceiving a conspiracy, his only answer was to starve and mistreat them. He divided the children into work crews, believing that if he kept them apart, they would be less likely to turn against him. Whenever he was able to corner a child alone, he gave him or her a sound beating.

One evening after a particularly long, hot day, the children were relaxing in the kitchen before bed, when Domko singled out Dennis as the boy walked by. Dennis had become a favourite target since he was too frightened to run away.

"Dennis!" Domko said firmly. "Vy's you's be valkink like dat?"

Dennis stopped and looked at him then lowered his eyes to the ground. "I dunno."

"Vy's you's be doink it?" he said, swinging his shoulders from side to side.

"I don't," Dennis said meekly.

"You's be doink it!" he roared. Domko stood up and in an exaggerated fashion, strode across the floor imitating Dennis' walk. He made the other children watch as he wiggled his back end and swung his shoulders. This looked very funny to the children, but none of them dared laugh since Domko was deadly serious. He then turned to Dennis.

"Valk!" he commanded.

Dennis felt his face turn red as everyone's eyes were on him. He hesitated until Domko took a step forward, then he quickly walked to the other side of the room.

"See!" Domko said. "I's be tellink you. He's be valkink like it!"

Again he strode across the room, this time exaggerating the movements even more.

Raymond laughed at the sight of his father's silliness, while Norman scoffed. David and Eunice said nothing as they tried to ignore Dennis' embarrassment.

"I's vantink you's to be valkink like I's be," he said, strolling across the room in his usual stiff-legged gait. He stopped then motioned for Dennis to try it.

Dennis looked at him then took a few steps. Since he didn't know what was wrong with his walk, he found it very hard to correct. Stiffening his legs like Domko, he took a few more steps. This sent the children into a giggling fit because he looked so silly. Domko was not amused and continued to criticize Dennis who was so embarrassed that he wished the roof of the house would collapse on them.

For the next hour, Domko sat at the table and scolded Dennis as he practised walking across the kitchen floor. The other children tired of the spectacle and disappeared upstairs. Tears of frustration streamed down Dennis' cheeks as he tried to walk the way Domko wanted him to. If he didn't manage it, he knew he'd be beaten.

Domko teased Dennis without mercy for the next few weeks. He tried to change Dennis' walk to resemble his own stiff-legged stroll. If he caught the boy walking normally, he'd smash him over the head with whatever was near.

One evening Domko gave Kathy and Raymond a box of candy coated popcorn each. The children watched in envy, as they hadn't had a real treat since they lived in Ashern.

"Ant don't you's be giving the Pischkes none," Domko ordered.

Kathy and Raymond obeyed and smugly walked past their half-siblings. Raymond opened his box and stuffed the candy in his mouth. He then turned and clutched the box to his chest.

Dennis watched as Raymond dumped some of his popcorn on the kitchen floor. Out fell a toy whistle. Raymond ate the popcorn as he blew on the whistle, sending streams of pink spit out the end of the whistle. Walking past the twins, he blew the whistle directly in the boys' faces. David and Dennis sat unmoved as the two year old tried to elicit a reaction. When they wouldn't do anything, he moved closer and blew harder. The twins ignored him and eventually Raymond tired of the game. He put the whistle on the table and went into the front room.

The twins could hear Eunice and Rosie trying quietly to persuade Kathy to give them some popcorn, but the five year old refused. Kathy didn't want to do anything that might anger her father, since she'd lost a lot of his favour after Raymond was born. Raymond was by far Domko's favourite child and while he treated Kathy well, she could sense his discomfort with her handicap.

"No!" she whined. "Ta-Ta be saying no."

Rosie and Eunice tried to hush the girl as they hurried upstairs, fearing Domko might hear her whining and suspect the reason.

"Ta-Ta be saying no," Raymond mimicked.

The twins giggled in the kitchen. "He's just like ole Satan," Dennis whispered.

"The little bugger even talks like him," David agreed.

The boys moved to the table and Dennis noticed the whistle. He picked it up and wiped the pink saliva that covered it on his sleeve. It was made of bright blue plastic and had a tiny ball inside. Dennis raised it to his lips and exhaled. It tinkled softly and he watched with crossed eyes as the tiny ball bounced inside.

"Sshh!" David warned, as he looked towards the front room.

Dennis was enjoying the little toy and whistled again, this time a little louder. Their half brother and sister were making so much noise in the front room that nobody could hear the shrill sound of the whistle coming from the kitchen. Dennis played a quiet, unknown tune as he moved his head rhythmically from side to side.

Just then, Raymond came into the kitchen and noticed Dennis playing with the whistle. He opened his mouth as wide as he could and let out a screeching howl that could be heard throughout the house. Dennis threw the whistle down just as Domko came flying into the room. It was too late because Domko pulled off his belt when he saw Raymond standing in the middle of the floor pointing at Dennis and crying uncontrollably.

"Vat? You soneebeech bastard!" he screamed as he began whipping Dennis. David ran outside to hide, hollering in the secret language that he'd be in the barn.

Raymond continued to cry and feel sorry for himself as he picked up the whistle. Caroline came into the kitchen to see what had happened just as Domko finished beating Dennis.

"He's be hurtink Raymie," Domko sputtered as he picked up his son. The boy's expression by this time had turned from angry tears to spiteful indignation. He pouted and began acting very spoiled as his parents tried to console him.

Dennis waited until Domko was out of the room before he limped out the door. David waited for him near the barn and led him to a stack of hay.

"I'm scared he's gonna break your legs," David said. "An' then you won't be no good and then you know what'll happen."

"I ain't no good already," Dennis sobbed. The past few weeks had been particularly difficult with Domko teasing and hitting him constantly. "I wish I was dead."

"No, you don't," David admonished. "You don't wanna be dead. Just stay away from him that's all. An' run when he comes near you, don't just stand there."

"I told you before, I can't help it!" Dennis said, wiping the tears from his eyes with the back of his hand. "I freeze up."

The boys nestled in the hay, knowing that's where they'd spend the night.

"Did you see Norman watching him?" David asked, his voice thick with admiration for his older brother. "Did you notice how mad he looked? Norman didn't like him teasing you an' I figure one of these times he's gonna help us."

"Norman can't do nothin'," Dennis sobbed.

"He can too!" David said defensively. "He'll help us sometime, you'll see."

It was Friday morning and Norman had big plans for the weekend. He approached his mother and asked if he could be paid soon. He'd worked for six weeks and was anxious about his money.

"Ask him yourself," she said, motioning towards the table where Domko sat.

Norman looked at his stepfather. He preferred dealing with his mother. "Can't you just pay me?" he asked.

"I don't have no money," she said. "You have to ask him."

Norman dreaded the thought of asking Domko for anything. Even though they owed him the money, Domko went out of his way to make Norman feel uncomfortable about his paid position. The boy tried his best to look confident as he approached the table.

"Hey, I was wonderin' if I could get paid today?" he asked casually.

Domko looked up from his coffee cup. He stared at the boy but said nothing.

Norman waited for an answer, then asked again.

"Yeah, I'm goin' with some friends this weekend and need gas money for my bike."

Domko snickered. He took a long drag from his cigarette then blew the smoke towards the ceiling. He pushed his cup to the edge of the table then called to Caroline to fill it.

She quickly grabbed the pot from the stove and topped his cup then went back to peeling potatoes for the soup.

"You's not be done workink," Domko said as he stirred methodically.

"I know," Norman said cheerily. "But I'll be back and finish up just like I promised."

Domko took a gulp of coffee then sucked on his cigarette again. "If you not be vorkink, you be not gettink paid."

"But I need some money now," Norman said, his anger rising. "Nobody else would work for six weeks without gettin' paid. I'm almost sixteen an' I can get a job any place."

Domko grunted, thinking that Norman was more trouble than he was worth. He looked squarely at the boy in an attempt to intimidate him.

But Norman in response, folded his arms across his chest and stood his ground.

The veins in Domko's neck and forehead began to throb. The blood began to pool in the depression on his forehead, turning it a bright red colour. His eyes became riveted on the boy as his anger rose.

Norman knew his stepfather could explode at any minute. He tried hard not to let his fear show. "I want my money."

"Fraaa!" Domko yelled, thrusting his right arm into the air as he jumped off the chair.

Norman turned and ran out the door, slamming it behind him. He ran towards the bush but stopped once he realized Domko was not behind him. His initial feelings of fear turned to frustration and he began kicking the ground.

"I'm gettin' outta here," he said out loud as he stormed towards his motorcycle. He needed the twins to help push-start the machine but neither of them were nearby.

"Figures," he mumbled as he opened the lid of the gas tank and peered in. He knew the bike was low on fuel and even if he did get it started, he wouldn't get very far. He envisioned Domko standing in the yard laughing as he pushed the bike down the road.

"Damn it!" he said. "I'm trapped here with that sonofabitch an' a pile of work. The old bastard is likely never gonna pay me anyway, just like he gypped Walter."

The situation was humiliating and the more he thought about it, the angrier Norman became. He didn't like being taken advantage of. While his instincts had told him not to accept his mother's offer to work on the farm, he had gone against his better judgement because he felt sorry for her. She had begged him to come back and had been so very nice to him. Of course, once he arrived, she ignored him just like she always had. He'd been tricked, and he knew it.

"Oh yeah?" he spit. "I'll show him."

Turning, he strode towards the grainary. His mind whirled as he flung open the door. Grabbing his father's old rifle, he pulled back the bolt and looked inside. His hands shook as he grabbed a bullet from a box on the shelf. He loaded the chamber then snapped the bolt in place. He stood for a moment staring out the grainary door at the house. He swallowed hard as he thought about the humiliation, not only of himself, but also his siblings, especially Dennis. He recalled the many beatings they had all received and how downtrodden their mother had become. He thought about Bruno lying on the ground and how Domko had shown the dog no mercy.

"I'll show him how it feels," he said as he stepped out of the grainary.

Norman's mind was in turmoil as he walked towards the house with purpose. Just then, Marjorie chased the cattle down the road, waving as she went. He ignored her and hoped the sound her bawling cattle would muffle the gunshot.

As he walked towards the house, he formed a plan to confront Domko in the kitchen. He visualized shooting his stepfather in the chest to the accompanying screams of his mother. The police would come and take him away to jail. He knew that nobody would believe his reasons for doing it. Too many people thought the family was 'lucky' that Domko had rescued them from a life of poverty and unhappiness.

He reached for the door knob but stopped. Norman shook his head angrily. He'd never killed anything except for a few ducks and rabbits he didn't know how it would feel to kill a human being. His stomach knotted with frustration and he couldn't make himself go into the house.

He stood on the stoop fighting back tears as Marjorie's dog came sniffing through the bush into the yard. Sandy trotted slowly past the house, on a path to veer back onto the road behind an old lame cow that was having difficulty keeping up with the rest of the herd.

Norman watched the little dog. For no reason except the desire to shoot something or someone at that moment, he lifted the gun, took aim and shot the little dog.

Sandy let out a startled yelp as the bullet pierced her heart. The impact sent her flying into the air, before she landed by the pump house. Instantly regretting what he'd done, Norman watched as the dog whimpered then died. The sound of the gunshot brought the twins and Eunice running from the barn and Caroline and Domko from inside the house.

"What are you shooting?" Caroline asked.

Norman stood staring at the ground with the gun at his side. It was then his mother noticed the dog lying just a few feet away.

"Norman!" she exclaimed. "What did you do that for?"

He shrugged his shoulders as Domko grabbed the gun and took it into the house.

"Why did you shoot Sandy ?" Caroline chastised.

"I dunno," he said angrily. "I just did."

"Well, now we're going to be in trouble with the Harwarts," she said angrily. "We don't need any more trouble with the neighbours." Grabbing him by the ear, she pulled him into the house and slammed the door.

Standing in the barnyard the twins could hear the muffled sounds of their mother yelling at Norman.

"Norman shot Sandy!" Dennis exclaimed. "Why'd he do that?"

"I dunno," David said.

"What's Marjie gonna say?"

"We gotta hide her so nobody finds out."

Dennis nodded. The boys walked slowly to where the dog was lying in the grass.

"Are you sure she's dead?" Dennis asked.

"Lemme see," David said. He picked up a small stick and gently poked the dog's side. The animal made no response. He then lifted a limp paw. "Yep, she's dead," he concluded.

"What are we gonna do with her?"

David looked around. "We'd better bury her before Marjie gets back."

Dennis agreed. They picked up the dead dog and carried it into the bush. They dug a shallow grave and covered the body with earth.

"Whadda you think Marjie's gonna do when she finds out Sandy's gone?" Dennis asked.

"I dunno," said David. "But I hope she don't cry too much."

That night David and Dennis covered their ears as they lay in bed. Occasionally David would remove his hands and listen, but the sound of Marjorie's voice calling her beloved dog caused him to cover his ears again. The guilt was overwhelming as they tried to block out the sound of their friend searching the bush for her dog.

During the next few days, the boys avoided Marjorie, especially when she came asking for help in finding the dog. Caroline and Domko had warned them to say nothing, so they made excuses that they could not help because they had to work.

Another school year began at the end of August. Because Norman was home, the twins didn't have to work as much and were able to start class with the other neighbourhood children.

Mrs. Collier stood at the front of the room and organized the grades on the first day. The older students chuckled, wondering if she would ever retire.

The twins had been promoted to grade four, while Eunice was in grade six and Rosie in grade three. Marjorie didn't attend classes at Bayton anymore since she was taking grade ten by correspondence. This was a relief to the twins who couldn't bear to face the girl after what had happened to her dog.

Norman's plan to enroll in grade eight was put on hold for a few weeks while he finished some farm work. His mother had promised that as soon as he finished hauling the last stacks of hay closer home and manure to the garden, he could begin school.

Norman still hadn't been paid, but decided to finish the work rather than give Domko an excuse not to pay him.

One Saturday morning in early October, Domko told Norman and the twins to haul manure to the far garden. The potatoes and carrots had been bagged and a heavy frost had blackened all the remaining greenery. Domko hoped to work the manure into the ground before snow fell.

The twins followed Norman out to the barn where the horses were hitched to a rickety flatbed wagon made of old planks. They shoveled manure onto the flatbed, then rode out to the far garden to spread it. The boys spent the day working and teasing each other, making numerous trips between the barn and the garden. Since Norman was the oldest, he was able to get away with doing the least amount of work under the guise of being supervisor. The twins soon caught on to this and began teasing their older brother by by calling him lazy and 'goot for nuthink'.

"Hey Schtink Schtank," David laughed. "While you're relaxin' there, don't take off your boots, o.k.?"

Norman laughed. "You think my feet stink? Smell this!" he said as he farted loudly.

The three laughed as they continued to work and soon the flatbed was empty again.

"This will be the last trip for today," Norman said. "It's gettin' late and I wanna go to town."

The twins jogged beside the flatbed as Norman drove towards the barn.

"Hey Norman, you drive pretty slow," David teased.

"Yeah," said Dennis. "We can run faster than you can drive."

Norman scowled at the two. "Oh yeah? Wanna bet?" he challenged.

The twins laughed as they ran beside him. They stuck out their tongues and made faces at him, knowing he couldn't chase and catch them as long as he was driving the team of horses.

"You think you're fast, eh?" Norman said. "Try grabbin' a hold of the back and runnin' behind. I bet you won't be talkin' so smart then."

The twins looked at each other and laughed.

"Sure!" David said cheerfully. He and Dennis were getting tall. They were also getting fast from running away from Domko. Sometimes they even out ran him, so holding onto the back of a slow-moving flatbed sounded easy.

"O.k., the rules are that you guys can't let go," Norman ordered. "If you do, then you lose."

"Alright," David yelled. "We'll start now."

The twins gripped the back boards and ran easily behind. Norman looked over his shoulder at the boys, then flicked the reins twice. The horses responded by quickening their pace. Norman glanced over his shoulder to see the boys still holding on. He snapped the reins again, this time harder and the horses began to gallop.

Norman looked back and began to laugh as the twins struggled to keep up. They were now bounding with huge strides through a freshly ploughed field.

"Ah, hah!" Norman laughed as he watched. He snapped the reins once more and the horses jolted the flatbed forward. The twins lost their balance and tumbled to the ground, knocking one of the loose boards forward. The board banged into the back of one horse's leg, causing the animal to panic. Without warning, the innocent game had turned serious as the horses pulled the flatbed through the rocky field at a frantic pace.

Norman stood up and pulled the reins back with all his strength, but to no avail. The horses continued to race through the field creating a huge cloud of dust behind them.

"Runaway!" David yelled as he watched the horses accelerate to top speed.

The twins watched as Norman fought to control the runaway team. He pulled the reins and suddenly the galloping animals turned to the right, running away from the farm towards the bush. Boards from the wagon began to shake loose and soon pieces were scattered across the field.

Suddenly Norman let go of the reins and began crawling toward the back of the hayrack as the loose boards vibrated loose beneath him. Some boards worked their way forward while others skittered back. Norman seemed to be planning to jump off the back of the flatbed.

Two boards beneath Norman's knees shifted forward then dug deep into the ground directly behind the horses feet. The back end shot up, catapulting Norman into the air. He flew over the front of the team, somersaulting in the air before landing on the ground in the path of the horses. The boys watched in horror as the team and wagon ran over their brother. The horses continued through the field and into the bush where they were forced to stop when they became hung up in the trees.

The twins stared at their brother who lay motionless on the ground. The dust settled around him and the twins could see him struggling to breathe.

"Norman, are you o.k.?" David asked as they ran to his side.

At first Norman couldn't speak, then slowly began to groan. The wind had been knocked out of his lungs and he gasped to catch his breath.

"Hey, Norman did the horses step on you?" Dennis asked.

Suddenly, the twins could hear Domko yelling. They looked towards the house and saw him storming through the field. He'd seen the horses running out of control and believed Norman had driven them that way intentionally.

"Norman, he's coming, get up!" David yelled, as he backed away. "C'mon! Denny let's go."

The twins turned and ran towards the bush. Domko yelled at them to stop but they kept running until they were a safe distance away. They stood at the edge of the field and watched as Domko stood over Norman and began yelling at him.Picking up a piece of board from the wrecked flatbed, he began beating Norman with it as he lay writhing on the ground.

The twins helped Norman home that night. It took him three days to recover from the accident and the beating. He awoke one morning determined to leave the farm, but kept the decision to himself. He avoided Domko's gaze and ignored his sarcastic comments about being 'lazy' as he slipped out the kitchen door. He was able to catch the twins before they went to school.

"Hey you guys, come here," he called as he hurried around the side of the house. "I need your help."

The twins followed, glancing over their shoulders as they went.

"What?" David said as Norman stopped near Domko's car, a 1952 Chev which their stepfather bought to replace the car destroyed in the accident.

"Here, hold this," he said, handing David a small rubber hose and a tobacco can.

"What's this for?"

"You'll see."

Norman uncapped the gas tank of the car. He took the hose from David and dropped one end in. He then began sucking on the hose.

"What are you doin'?" Dennis asked. "Drinkin' gas?"

"No, stupid," he said. "It's called syphonin'."

The twins watched as Norman sucked the gas up the hose then quickly put the tip in the tobacco can. It took about four tries and a mouthful of gas before Norman got the liquid flowing into the can.

"Hey, that's good!" David exclaimed. "But we better be careful Domko don't see us. Denny, you go watch."

Dennis nodded and went to stand at the corner of the house.

"Ole' Satan would call this stealin' you know," David warned.

"Yeah, well the way I see it he owes me anyway," Norman said. "The old bastard never did pay me."

David wasn't surprised. He watched as his brother filled the can, then slipped the hose back in his pocket. He capped the tank and the three of them sauntered towards the motorcycle.

Norman motioned for Dennis to watch while he and David filled the tank of his motorbike. When all the gas had been poured into the tank, Norman tossed the can in the grass.

"Gimme a push," he said to David.

Since the kick-start was broken, the twins had to run behind the bike to start it. When it sounded like it might start, Norman jumped on. David continued pushing Norman down the driveway as the bike backfired a number of times then finally started.

"O.k., let go!" Norman yelled over the roar of the engine.

David couldn't hear him and continued pushing the bike, making it difficult for Norman to steer. He reached back to punch David's shoulder, but accidentally hit him in the nose instead.

The force of the blow sent David sprawling on the ground. The pain radiated up his forehead, causing his eyes to water and blood to flow out of his nose. He stood up and staggered to the house, wiping blood from his face with his shirt. Norman turned the bike around and drove back in the driveway.

David walked into the kitchen. The sight of him covered in blood startled Caroline.

"What happened?" she said, rushing to her son with a rag. "Where's the blood coming from?"

"My nose," David mumbled. "I was helpin' Norman start his bike an' got hit."

"What?" she said angrily.

"Vat he's be doink?" Domko demanded.

Just then Norman walked in the door to check on David. The sight of him sent Domko into a rage. He grabbed Norman and pushed him against the wall. Both boys tried to explain what had happened, but Domko and Caroline were too angry to listen. Caroline slapped Norman hard in the face a number of times. David watched in shock as their mother joined Domko in beating Norman.

Later that morning, Norman snuck out of the kitchen and pushed his bike to the school where he asked a few of the older boys to give him a push. He drove to Jim's house and asked if he'd find him a place to live.

Norman had stayed with a number of different people over the past few years on a temporary basis, but now was looking for somewhere permanent to live. Although the Nachtigalls had been nice to him, they were from his mother's church. Norman feared that if he went there, it would be too easy for his mother to find him and force him back to the farm.

Norman told Jim that he would work hard and be a good kid as long as he was fed and not beaten. Jim decided not to call the police, but to contact people he knew in the Ashern area. Norman ended up in bare feet and with no jacket on the doorstep of Leonard and Emma Geisler. The Geislers were kind, generous people who treated their young workers like family members. They took the boy in and the first thing they did was buy him a pair of shoes.

Chapter 25

Divide and conquer

THE TWINS WERE FINDING it difficult now to lose themselves in their twin world of make-believe. The could no longer escape the cruel realities of life by daydreaming and wishing Domko would miraculously disappear.

Now they were almost teenagers and understood their circumstances. Still too young to fight back, the boy's lives were made more difficult by the knowledge that Domko wasn't going anywhere. They knew Norman wouldn't return, which made their workload overwhelming as Domko continued to starve, tease, beat and condemn.

The twins were under further pressure because their mother was beginning to act like Domko. David and Dennis even began quibbling amongst themselves which meant Domko's strategy was working.

The twins were constantly having to save themselves at the expense of the other. This caused a rift in their relationship. Because Dennis was the quietest, he was singled out and beaten more than the others. The twins would never be able to pull together to defend themselves against Domko as long as Dennis was continually beat up and downtrodden.

One afternoon Domko attacked Dennis in the kitchen. As Dennis fell to the ground, his leg kicked out and his foot caught Domko on the shin.

"He's be kickink me!" Domko screamed.

Caroline came into the room to see what had happened.

"He's be kickink me! That soneebeech be kickink me!"

Caroline turned to David. "Is that true?"

David looked at his brother huddled on the ground then at his mother' angry face. Domko was shaking his head in disgust, convinced that Dennis had kicked him. David knew it had been an accident, but how could he convince them?

Domko glared at David. Desperate for an excuse to beat either boy, he gave David a look which said that if it wasn't Dennis, it would be David the minute Caroline's back was turned.

David nodded then turned away.

Caroline lashed out at Dennis in the same way as she had turned on Norman just a month before. Dennis received a horrible beating from both Caroline and Domko. His face was left swollen and bloody.

Without emotion, David dragged his twin up the stairs. Dennis' face was beaten so badly that he was almost unrecognizable.

"Why didn't you tell her it was an accident?" Dennis asked. "You saw!"

David was ashamed and stared at the ceiling. "I dunno. I was scared."

Dennis started to cry. His mother and brother turning against him had been the final betrayal. "I'm scared all the time. I can't do it no more. I'm cold an' hungry an' stiff. I just wanna die."

David gazed at the ceiling. He was cold and hungry too, but knew there was a difference between how he felt and the despair engulfing Dennis. Domko was breaking the boy's spirit.

In the days that followed, David noticed how much more jumpy and irritable Dennis had become. His twin was totally inconsolable. The brothers barely spoke to each other and when Dennis did say something, it was usually about dying. Domko teased Dennis about his face, calling him ugly and deformed.

Friends from the church came to visit. Outwardly, these people supported Domko so they were allowed in the house.

Everyone sat at the table through the small talk, then the discussion turned to religion. While the church members were still concerned about the cleanliness of the house, they were pleased that Caroline and Domko seemed to be getting along better.

"Cleanliness is next to godliness, Caroline," the male Witness said. "And your husband would be much more comfortable if the house was kept clean and tidy."

Caroline nodded.

The visitors commended on the Domkos keeping the children under control. They hadn't heard any more reports about the children stealing or running away.

"What happened to Dennis' face?" the man asked.

"He's be fightink ant be losink it some," Domko said. "He's be some goot for sheet."

The boy looked at the floor and his bruised and swollen face turned scarlet.

Friends usually knew better than to initiate a conversation about the Pischke children because it always sent Domko into a tirade of insults that made it uncomfortable for everybody.

"Ant they's not be stealink no more," Domko said proudly. "I's be tellink her they's be stealink but she's not be hearink."

Caroline fidgeted through the lie as Domko continued to congratulate himself. Everyone but the visitors knew it was an effort to re-direct rumours about himself to the twins.

The boys sat quietly and listened, knowing better than to contradict Domko's interpretation of the truth. It was embarrassing being called thieves, but they accepted that far easier than a beating.

Dennis wondered why their friends from the church never said anything about Domko's own personal cleanliness. He stunk horribly and it was surprising that the neat, clean visitors could stand sitting beside him.

The Church members read aloud from the bible and left a Watchtower magazine. Dennis enjoyed reading the little magazine and snatched it up, running to the bedroom just before the end of the visit. David followed shortly afterwards to find Dennis engrossed in the magazine.

"What you readin' that for?" he asked.

Dennis didn't answer.

David reached down and grabbed the magazine from his brother's hands.

Dennis jumped up and shoved him. He took the magazine back and angrily flipped to the page he was reading.

"I don't like readin' the Watchtowers," David scoffed. "They're stupid."

"You're stupid," Dennis argued.

"Well, I ain't that stupid," he said pointing to the magazine.

Dennis turned his back on his brother and continued reading. David climbed in beside him and the two didn't speak for the rest of the night.

"Where's the ole' bastard?" David asked Eunice the following morning as they sat in the front room.

"Him an' mom went to town," she replied.

"How 'bout Dennis?"

"I dunno," she said. "I made fun of his face an' he got all mad an' ran out."

David cringed. He knew he should go look for his brother but didn't want to go outside in the cold. It had snowed a little bit and he didn't have anything warm to wear on his feet.

Just then the door opened and Dennis walked in. David looked at him and immediately knew things weren't right with his brother. Dennis walked stiffly into the front room, eyes glazed with determination. He carried their father's old rifle in one hand and a handful of shells in the other. David could see his twin's arms were shaking with either anger or fear - or both.

"What are you doin'," David asked casually.

"Nothin'," Dennis said as he walked from one end of the room to the other. "Nobody cares anyhow." His chin began to waver as he shook his head.

"Nobody cares, not you, not mom and nobody from the church. We don't got no friends an' mom's family don't like us. Ruby don't care 'cause she left an' we can't go to Emma's no more."

Dennis began to sob. "Momma always says we're gonna die 'cause of Domko an' I keep hopin' he kills me but he never does. He just smashes me so that I feel dead."

David's heart began to pound as he watched his shaking brother. Eunice stood speechless in the center of the floor.

"It's o.k., Denny," David cooed. "Things will get better."

"No they won't!" Dennis yelled, stamping his foot on the ground. He shook his head violently as he screamed at his siblings. "They won't an' you know it, too! He's gonna kill us someday, I know it."

Dennis looked at the gun and his voice softened. "We can't live like this no more. I'm gonna kill you guys then kill myself. That way Domko won't have nobody here to do the work. Then we'll see how long ole' Satan lasts without us. That'll teach him a lesson."

David had never seen Dennis so defeated. His mind raced to find the words to console his brother.

"No, Dennis, don't do it," David pleaded softly. "We can get away. Just you an' me. We can go over the beaver dam, you'll see. As soon as winter comes, we'll walk across the ice an' never come back. We work good, you an' me. We'll find some place to live."

Dennis stared angrily at his twin. For the first time since he'd come into the room, he looked directly into his brother's eyes. It was like seeing his own reflection and the fear he saw there was unsettling.

Dennis didn't really want to kill everyone and die too, but he didn't want to live either. He was tired of being Domko's victim.

David sensed his twin's uncertainty and used the moment to his advantage. "We can start out today," he said. "I promise."

Dennis hesitated. Never before had he done something to frighten David. He realized that bringing the gun into the house had taken a lot of nerve. For the first time, he understood that he did have some control over what happened in his life.

He stood quietly facing his brother who took a few steps forward and took the shells out of Dennis' hand.

"C'mon," David said. "Let's go."

The boys trudged through the snow in the bush for the rest of the day. David made a makeshift shelter, but as evening approached, it became too cold to sleep outside.

They continued walking and circled back, finding themselves in the church yard. They climbed in through the back window and lit the tall white candles as they had on so many other nights.

Too afraid of what awaited them across the beaver dam, they returned home two days later, hungry and tired but determined to stay away from Domko. They made a pact to resist Domko's attempts to intimidate them. They would stick together no matter what.

The following night Caroline poured herself and Domko a small glasses of moonshine from the still they had hidden under the kitchen counter. The boys watched fearfully as their mother and Domko drank and talked happily, then poured themselves another drink. The couple gossiped about the neighbours, relatives and friends from church.

David remembered Jim had told him to be wary of people who couldn't handle their liquor. He motioned to Dennis that they should run.

Dennis nodded and the boys crept around the table towards the door. Just as David reached for the knob, Domko let out a roar.

"David! Dennis!" he called. "Coom here."

The boys froze. Dennis grabbed David's arm.

"Don't leave me," he begged. "you promised."

David nodded as the boys turned around.

"Come here boys," Caroline called, her voice thick with drunkenness. "We want to talk to you."

Reluctantly the twins went to stand beside their mother. Domko stood up and staggered over. He bent down and put his big face a few inches from them.

"You's not be runnink away no more," he said, raising his finger and pointing it at them. Then his gold tooth shone as he flashed them a wide, sincere smile.

"Now, go on up to bed," Caroline snickered, tapping each boy lightly on the rear end.

Still holding Dennis' arm, David took off. He ran through the front room then up the stairs, pulling his brother behind him.

Astonished, the boys jumped onto the bed.

"Did you see that?" Dennis asked in amazement.

"Yeah! I hope he drinks moonshine more often!" David exclaimed.

Domko recovered from his hangover and resumed being his usual, miserable self. The children avoided him and spent as much time in school as he allowed. One December afternoon, the boys were helping him bring home a load of hay from the field when David slipped and fell head first, wedging himself between the hay rack and stack. As Domko drove off, David's neck was wrenched and he screamed in pain. Domko heard him fall, but continued to drive expecting the boy to catch up later.

The moment David hit the ground, he was unconscious. When he awoke hours later, it was dark outside. He didn't know how long he'd been knocked out. He struggled to stand up, but his arms and legs were stiff from the cold. His neck was so sore that it could no longer support the weight of his head. David cried out each time he took a step an unbearable pain shot through his neck. Clasping each side of his head with his hands, he stumbled home and went straight to bed.

David stayed there for nearly a week. His neck was swollen to double its usual size and he was plagued with an excruciating headache that throbbed so hard he couldn't stand to have the light on. He turned away from the light that shone through the bedroom window, praying that Domko wouldn't become irritated because he wasn't working. His mother seemed sympathetic and this helped David relax.

Caroline came upstairs to check on him and brought some soup.

"Ma, I gotta go to the doctor," he said, voice quivering. "My neck don't feel too good. I think it's broken."

Caroline tried to assess her son's condition. "It's not broken, otherwise you wouldn't be able to walk," she said. "I'll talk to Domko and see if he'll let you go."

David overhead them arguing in the kitchen later that day. Caroline argued that her son needed to see the doctor while Domko scoffed at the suggestion.

Caroline watched her husband carefully as his eyes narrowed and he scowled in a familiar way. Not wanting to make him more jealous than he already was, she changed the subject. When she had a spare moment, she snuck upstairs to talk to David.

"You can't go but don't worry, it'll be better soon," she said. "Can you lift your head yet?"

David had been trying to sit up all day but the pain was too intense.

"No, it hurts too much."

"We'll see how you're doin' tomorrow," she said. "Just be quiet until then and if it doesn't get better, I'll take you to see Dr. Steenson when Domko's not around."

After staying in bed for a few more days, David was gradually able to sit up and walk around, as long as he held his head in his hands. He came downstairs and noticed how suspiciously Domko was watching him. David decided it would be best to go to school. Dennis helped him put on his boots and coat, and David followed his siblings down the road. He walked delicately, trying not to pound his feet on the ground. This was a very difficult task for an 11 year old boy.

"How come you're walkin' so stupid?" Rosie asked.

"Yeah," Eunice giggled. "You're walkin' like Dennis."

"Shuddup!" Dennis said as punched his sister playfully on the arm.

"I gotta walk like this, 'cause my neck hurts so much," David winced. "I gotta carry my head."

"If we put a metal box on your head it would look like you're carryin' your lunch," Rosie quipped.

The rest of the children laughed, including David who grimaced from the pain. "Yeah, well ole Satan never let us have a lunch this heavy."

* * * * *

David continued to support his head with his hands, until the middle of March. Finally, Domko agreed that since the boy was incapable of working, he should be taken to a doctor, but he would not drive them.

Caroline did not want the neighbours to know about the accident for fear they would tell the social worker, so she contacted her former brother-in-law, Herman Pischke. Herman drove Caroline and David to Grahamdale.

Dr. Steenson examined David then recommended he see a chiropractor.

"A what?" David asked. "He's not gonna give me a needle is he?"

Dr. Steenson chuckled. "No, he'll just adjust your neck back in place.

It won't hurt too much. Do you know what I mean?"

Steenson opened the door and called Caroline in. She looked worried when she sat down with the closed the door behind her.

"If you don't do something soon, this boy could end up crippled for life if he gets another jolt," the doctor said. "David needs to see a chiropractor, do you know what that is? He's hurt his neck severely and I believe it's the only way it can be fixed. The procedure is relatively new out here, but quite common in the cities. He'll have to be taken to Winnipeg."

Caroline nodded. Dr. Steenson led them out of the office then instructed his receptionist to make an appointment with the chiropractor.

Caroline told Herman what the doctor had said and he offered to take them to Winnipeg the following week. David was looking forward to his first trip to the city.

The chiropractor was astonished by the condition of David's neck. He massaged the gnarled lump that had formed at the base of the boy's head.

"It's a miracle that you're still walking," he said as he explained why David's neck had been so swollen.

"T-that's what Doc S-steenson told me," David stammered.

"You've fractured your neck. Most injuries this serious leave young men like yourself crippled. You're very fortunate."

David nodded then sat absolutely still as the chiropractor manipulated the boy's spine then once again massaged his neck. It was an odd sensation since it hurt but felt good at the same time.

The chiropractor called Caroline into the room and chastised her for not bringing her son in sooner.

She nodded but said nothing.

The well-dressed man looked at the mother and son and shook his head. It was obvious that a lack of money was the reason the boy hadn't been brought in sooner. The chiropractor wrote a quick note on David's chart and passed it on to the receptionist.

As they left the small office, the man gave David a brief pat on the shoulder. "I expect to see you back in a week," he said.

Caroline paid the fee and was relieved to discover that they had been charged a nominal amount. They left the office and David was disappointed that his neck was still sore. He walked behind his mother and Herman along Winnipeg's busy Portage Avenue, still supporting his head with his hands. Amazed, he looked at all the tall buildings and was surprised by the number of cars on the street. He was anxious to tell Dennis all about Winnipeg. He liked the chiropractor and looked forward to returning the following week.

Within a few days, his neck began to feel better and soon he was able to do light chores. The headaches began to subside so Domko would not allow him to go to the second appointment. David still 'carried his head' on occasion, especially if he had to run or do anything that jolted his spine.

The older Raymond got, the more of a pest he became. The chubby, dark skinned, whining three year-old was the image of his father. The twins, now 12 years old, had a difficult time being nice to a youngster who enjoyed getting them into trouble.

In his father's eyes, little 'Raymie' could do no wrong. The child sensed how favoured he was and had become quite spoiled as a result.

He followed the twins and spied on them at every opportunity. The older boys soon discovered that they were being watched and that Raymond was reporting their activities to his father. After a few beatings for eating when they weren't supposed to, the twins began avoiding their half-brother.

"Do you see how he watches us?" Dennis said one day.

"Yeah, I wish he'd leave us alone," David answered.

Disgusted, Dennis looked at the little boy and made a face. "Shoo!"

"Nooooo," Raymond whined. "Raymie wants to coomme."

The twins walked to the barn carrying milk pails with Raymond close behind.

"He even talks like him," Dennis whispered. "An' do you see how black his teeth are?"

"Too much candy," David chuckled as he looked at Raymond who was covered in filth. Dirt stuck to his face and his hair was grimy and matted.

"He smells like the ole bastard, too!" Dennis laughed as he ran ahead and opened the barn door. David walked in and Dennis closed the door behind him.

"Not you poker, go away!" he said before the little boy had a chance to slip in.

Raymond let out a howl and ran to the house. Dennis was pleased that the name-calling had worked so well.

Since the incident with the gun, Dennis had been in better spirits. It was as if he'd come to terms with his situation. He was determined to find ways to outsmart Domko rather than giving in to him. Thinking of ways to thwart Raymond helped him focus on something other than the bleakness of their predicament.

Later that evening, Dennis called Raymond 'poker' again, but this time Domko overheard. He roared from the front room into the kitchen and smashed Dennis over the head with a broom handle.

"You's not be callink him poker!" Domko yelled. He then picked up his crying son and carried him into his bedroom. Raymond emerged a few moments later carrying a chocolate bar, which he waved at the twins.

Dennis stuck out his tongue. David nudged him in the ribs, a signal for him to stop before Raymond cried out to his father again.

One cold, snowy early April night just as everyone was preparing for bed, David warmed himself a cup of milk on the stove. He had a head cold and was suffering from the chills that accompanied a fever. Domko was in the front room and he called Raymond to him.

"You's be goink to see vat he's be doink," he whispered to Raymond.

The youngster nodded and eagerly went to the kitchen to spy on David, who had just finished pouring milk from a pot on the stove into a mug which sat on the table.

David had just turned his back when suddenly Raymond let out a horrendous scream. David spun around to see Raymond standing stiffly by the table, his face, chest and arms wet. The small boy had reached up to peer into the cup and had spilled the scalding milk on himself.

His screams sent the children running towards the door. Eunice and Rosie bolted outside, followed by Dennis. Caroline and Domko ran to the kitchen to find Raymond standing in the middle of the floor pointing at David.

David tried briefly to explain what had happened, but ran outside when he saw Domko was wild with anger. His siblings were standing in bare feet about 10 yards away.

"Where should we go?" Eunice asked.

They heard Domko screaming as he ran through the house.

"I's be shootink you soneebeech bastards!" he yelled. The children suspected he was getting the rifle from the bedroom so they turned and ran towards the bush. They slowed to a stop as they reached a waist-high snowbank. Suddenly, a bullet whizzed overhead and the clap of a rifle shot echoed in the crisp, clear air. Screaming, the children dove over the snow, then crawled into the bush. Their stepfather continued to curse as another bullet whirled by. The children ran in blind panic as far as they could in the darkness. A third bullet came through the trees, as they slid together in a heap on the ground.

"Is he coming?" David whispered.

"Ssshh!" Eunice said. They listened carefully, but all they could hear was their own heavy breathing and pounding of their hearts. Each of them expected Domko to sneak into the bush. Every little sound caused them to twitch in fear.

"He almost got me that time," Dennis whispered.

"Me too," Eunice said, sobbing as she gripped her feet. "My feet are freezing!"

"Mine too," David said.

"Yeah, but not like mine," Eunice argued. "Ever since I froze 'em that time, they've been gettin' cold real easy."

David remembered a very cold January day the year before when, he and Eunice had been roughhousing in the bedroom and Domko had flown up the stairs. They had jumped out the window, and frozen their feet. Eunice was in great pain and they had begged their mother to protect them if they came back inside. Eunice had screamed all night as the pains shot through her feet slowly warming feet. The ugliest part came when all the skin peeled off, leaving them tender and raw. Of course, Domko had forced her to keep working so it took the feet months to heal. David didn't want to repeat the frozen feet episode.

"Yeah," he said softly. "We better get to the barn."

"What if he shoots us when we go by?" Eunice asked.

"He won't," David said.

"He might," Dennis added. "Momma says he's gonna kill us someday, an' her too . . ."

David interrupted. "How are we gonna get away if you keep talkin' about dyin' all the time?"

Embarrassed, Dennis looked at Eunice's feet. He couldn't help but talk stupid when he was nervous.

"Shh!" Eunice said again.

They listened carefully to the sound of the house door slamming. A few moments later, Domko's car started and bumped out of the driveway. It turned south on the road, its lights shining into the bush. The children hid low so they wouldn't be seen, then stood up once the car sped by.

"Where do you think they went?" David asked.

"Probably to the doctor," Eunice said. "I think Raymond was burned pretty bad."

"Did momma go too?" Dennis asked.

"I think so. I could hear her voice," Eunice replied.

The children ran to the barn and found themselves a place to sleep in the loft. They expected that when Domko returned, he would be calmer. They gambled that he wouldn't check the barn, and they prayed that if he did, they wouldn't be the one he caught.

Domko and Caroline arrived home with Raymond later that night. The doctor had advised them that the youngster would have no permanent scarring. For the next few days, the children avoided Domko, hoping he'd forget the incident. Within a week, Raymond was back to his usual annoying self.

* * * * *

Domko and the twins went to an auction sale in Moosehorn later that spring. While the boys were shy about being seen in public, they were curious about the world outside the farm. They didn't want to run away from strangers anymore and Norman's comment that they were 'bushed' made them to want to prove otherwise.

Unfortunately, their reputation had proceeded them.

"You have to watch those Pischke twins because they're thieves," a man said as he looked at the items for sale. His companion nodded, not realizing that David could overhear the conversation. The comment humiliated David who turned away, hoping they couldn't see his hot and flushed face.

Later that afternoon when they were back shoveling manure out of the barn, David told Dennis what he'd heard.

"Bein' called a thief is worse than bein' called bushed," David said.

"Yeah," Dennis agreed. "If we was such thieves then how come nobody sent us to jail yet?"

David thought for a moment. His brother had raised an interesting point. Thieves did go to jail. So did people who robbed banks and burned down buildings. The thought of going to jail didn't seem too bad compared to living with Domko another summer.

The following morning the boys ran down their usual path to school. The snow was all gone and leaves were beginning to bud on the trees. David pushed his wheelbarrow wheel, affectionately named the 'wee-wee', as Dennis ran behind. Suddenly David was knocked slightly off balance when the wheel passed over a bump that he hadn't remembered on the path. Then Dennis let out a scream.

David turned to see Dennis holding his right foot.

"I stepped on somethin'!" Dennis winced. "It was real sharp an' poked through my foot."

David looked at his brother then at a small mound on the path. He thought it must be a rock that had worked its way to the surface as the frost came out of the ground. David examined it closely.

"Hey Dennis, look," he said pointing to the ground. "There's something here."

The boys knelt beside the small mound and brushed back the leaves and dirt. What at first looked like a stick turned out to be a spike poking straight out of the ground. They scraped back the mud to find a board concealed in the dirt.

It took a few moments for them to realize what they had found. Domko had sabotaged their path! David jumped up and grabbing his wee-wee ran towards the church. Dennis ran as fast as he could behind. Their minds whirled, expecting their adversary to jump out from behind every log and tree along the way. They made it safely to the church, then stopped to catch their breath.

"He did it I just know it!" Dennis said as he massaged his bleeding foot.

"Yeah, 'cause we've walked on that path a thousand times an' it wasn't there before."

"We better go on the road, the rest of the way 'case he's put some more boards on the path," David said, leading the way through the church yard. "An' don't you limp or nothin' when we get home, 'cause we don't want him to know you stepped on it."

Dennis nodded. It was best to give the impression that Domko's plans had been thwarted since that always seemed to leave him discouraged.

Mrs. Collier reviewed homework with pupils in each grade. The twins had worked late in the barn the night before and hadn't had time to complete their assignments. A few of the older students giggled while the boys stammered and stuttered as they tried to explain.

"W-we didn't do it," David finally blurted out.

Mrs. Collier looked at them with exasperation, for what must have been the one hundredth time. She was tired of the problems with these boys who were either absent, late, or otherwise ill-prepared for class.

"Sit down," she said quietly, then called on the next grade.

David's face flushed. He was tired of having to apologize or explain situations he and Dennis were forced into by Domko. For a split second, he felt as if he were in Norman's body. He now understood his older brother's feelings and felt an urgency building in his gut. He was tired of being pushed around and humiliated.

That weekend the twins went on a rampage as only two 12 year-olds can. They hid in the ditch and threw rocks at passing cars. They took their dad's rifle and shot at planes passing overhead. David climbed in the church window, followed closely by Dennis, then they vandalized the interior, knocking down objects and ripping pages out of the bible. They broke a few windows then left, chuckling about the damage they'd done.

The boys finished their weekend spree by breaking into the school.

"Hey Davey, it feels funny bein' in here on a Sunday, don't it?"

David nodded. "Yeah, it's different when there's nobody around."

Dennis picked up a piece of chalk and began drawing insulting pictures on the blackboard. David knocked all the items off the teacher's desk and emptied drawers on the floor. Together, they knocked all the books from the library shelves, then kicked them across the floor.

They turned over the desks of kids who teased them. Kicking a few books into a pile, David told Dennis to go wait outside. Dennis laughed as he pushed over another desk, then went to the cloakroom.

Reaching up to the shelf above the wood stove, David took down a box of matches. He examined one long wooden stick for a minute, then struck it on the edge of the box. A small voice inside his head told him to drop it on the books on the floor.

He watched as the match burned slowly towards his thumb and forefinger. Resisting the temptation, he then blew it out. Throwing the box against the wall, he turned and ran out the door.

He grinned at Dennis then the boys strutted down the road, defiantly hoping that someone would come along. They didn't care if they were caught, not by the teacher, the neighbours or the police. Everyone thought they were bad anyway - so what difference did it make?

They were slightly disappointed when they arrived home. Nobody seemed to care or even know about the things they'd done. As they went upstairs to their bedroom, Dennis tried to create excitement about the willful damaged they'd caused. David played along, daring anyone to try and prove them guilty.

David quietly hoped that the police would come the next day and take them both away to jail. He was a little bit afraid, but knew it was their only opportunity to escape the farm.

He thought about the odd looks people had given them that day as they threw rocks. Guilt washed over him as he remembered emptying the teacher's desk onto the floor. He thought of the broken windows in the old church and how that building had never been anything but a friend to the twins. He knew what they had done that day was wrong. He also knew that the hollow, empty feeling in the pit of his stomach meant it was something he'd never do again.

Half-heartedly hoping the police would be waiting for them, the twins went to school the next day. The entire school room was unusually quiet as Mrs. Collier and the older students cleaned up the mess. Nobody knew for sure who had committed the crime, but more than a few glances were directed at David and Dennis.

When classes finally began an hour later, Mrs. Collier stood at the front of the room and stared at the twins.

I'm getting too old for this, she thought to herself. No doubt the brothers were also the culprits who had dug a deep hole in front of the teacher's cottage outhouse in January. It was the same hole she'd fallen into in the middle of the night. Too short to climb out, she was fortunate that a neighbour had heard her yelling for help. Otherwise she might have frozen to death.

The twins avoided her gaze and their guilt-ridden expressions told her all she needed to know.

The little beggars just don't know any better, she thought as she looked at their manure covered clothing and dirty bare feet. *In all the years I've taught, I've never seen anything like this. These poor disadvantaged souls have given me more stories than I care to repeat.*

Chapter 26

A trip to Winnipeg

TWICE A YEAR THE TWINS WERE GIVEN a haircut. This was a frightening experience as Domko ordered them, one at a time, to sit on a chair outside. With a long pair of shears, he snipped their overgrown locks.

The boys sat very still as the large scissors clipped close to their ears and throat. Domko seemed to like the job and especially enjoyed the fact that he wasn't particularly good at it.

One afternoon in May, he finished cutting Dennis' hair, then stood back and laughed at the sight of him. The twin was then ushered off the chair and it was David's turn. David dared not say a word for fear that Domko might get angry and purposely slice his neck. He watched as chunks of wavy blonde hair fell to the ground.

"No more hobos," Domko said proudly when he was finished.

The twins waited until their barber went back in the house before examining each other's hair cut.

"What do you think we look like?" Dennis asked.

"I dunno," David said running his fingers through the short, stubbly cut. "But I sure hope I don't look like you do."

Domko had promised Caroline that this would be the year he would take her and the children to an annual gathering of Jehovah's Witnesses. This year it was to be held in the Winnipeg Arena. Caroline had wanted to attend for years. When the appointed July weekend arrived, she was mildly surprised and delighted that her husband kept his word.

The car was loaded with food and bedding the night before they left for Winnipeg. Early the next morning, everyone in the family except Eunice piled in the vehicle for the trip. Eunice preferred to stay home and do chores, which worked out since the cows had to be milked twice a day.

The twins were excited about going to the city and Dennis listened wide-eyed as David told him what an interesting place it was.

"There's cars everywhere," he whispered, as Domko sped along the gravel highway. "An' there's lights all over the place. The road gets smooth and it makes the car go faster."

Dennis was anxious to get there and was disappointed when they had to stop for awhile in Lundar, a large town about 50 miles south of Moosehorn on Highway No. 6.

They were back on the road by late afternoon and the children listened to their mother complain about Domko's driving.

She told him to slow down and drive straight, but he continued to waver over the center line and then drive too far onto the shoulder. He appeared to become more agitated the further south he drove. This attracted the RCMP who pulled up behind them and motioned for Domko to pull over to the side of the road.

He swore and began to sweat profusely as an officer approached. The policeman asked where they were going and wanted to see a driver's license. Domko pulled the paper out of his wallet and handed it to the officer who examined it as he walked around the car on a quick inspection. He returned, handed Domko his license and warned him about travelling too fast.

Domko nodded sheepishly.

"Oh, and a stone has knocked out one of your headlights," the policeman said. "You'd better get that fixed since it's getting late. It will be dark before you get to Winnipeg."

Domko cursed under his breath as the officer left. He waited on the side of the road until the cruiser was out of sight before continuing. He didn't want another encounter with the police, so he stopped at the next town, which was called St. Laurent, to have the headlight fixed.

The twins covered their faces with embarrassment as he argued with the garage owner about the bill. Domko complained that it cost too much to fix the light, but the mechanic stood firm. Domko grudgingly paid the bill then stomped towards the car.

He gave the mechanic a single finger salute as he sped away. Caroline grabbed the dashboard and yelled at him to slow down. Suddenly, the car hit a small bump and the ride became incredibly smooth. No stones flew underneath the vehicle and the wind coming through the windows was clear of dust.

Domko slammed on the brakes and came to an almost complete halt.

"What's wrong?" Caroline asked.

He was now sweating profusely as his hands gripped the steering wheel. He watched the odometer as he gradually accelerated to 20 miles an hour.

"First you're driving too fast, now too slow. What's wrong?" Caroline asked again.

"I's not be knowink but a some road!" he exclaimed. He'd never driven on pavement before and complained that he felt as if the car was going to slip into the ditch.

"But you can go faster than this," she countered.

He shook his head in disagreement. "I's be drivink ant you's be seetink," he said angrily.

She looked over her shoulder at the traffic nearing from the north. "You're going to hold things up. The other drivers will smash into the back of us at this speed!"

He growled at her as he kept his eyes fixed on the road. The twins looked out the back window in time to see a car come up behind fast, slow down, then pull out to pass.

"Where'd you learn to drive?" the man shouted shaking his head as he drove past.

"Fraa!" Domko yelled.

The same thing happened with countless more vehicles and the boys skulked down in the seat as Domko swore and made obscene gestures at the other drivers.

His wavering back and forth increased on the pavement. He momentarily lost control of the car each time one wheel would slip onto the shoulder. He'd swear and then spit out the window. Eventually David had to roll up his window so that the stream wouldn't blow back and hit him in the face.

At one point, a Ford tractor pulled out to pass Domko who still refused to drive faster than 20 miles an hour. Caroline shook her head as the boys snickered, resigning themselves to a very long ride.

"Look at Domko's window," Dennis whispered.

David peered over his stepfather's shoulder to see the half open window dripping with slime from poorly aimed nose-blowings.

"Blech!" David said then began giggling.

"Vat? You's be seetink and sayink nuthink!" Domko roared as he looked in the mirror. He was too nervous to take his hands off the steering wheel to slap either of them, and that made them giggle even harder.

It was late at night before they arrived in Winnipeg. The boys estimated it took them more than six hours to travel the 90 minute trip from St. Laurent to the city. Caroline was vibrating from a bad case of nerves by the time they arrived, knowing they still had to travel down town. They had plans to stay at her father's house.

Domko turned onto Oak Point road which led him into the city. As he drove slowly along, more houses and businesses appeared and the street became congested. Fortunately it was late and there wasn't a lot of traffic on the road, but even a little was too much for Domko.

"Look at all the lights, see how beautiful they are?" David whispered as he and Dennis craned their necks out Dennis' open window. "See Denny, I told you. An' see all the cars an' houses. They got lots of great stuff here in Winnipeg."

Dennis nodded as he absorbed the activity around him, his stomach churning with excitement.

Domko made a left hand turn from a right hand lane as he neared the city's downtown area. He cut off more than one vehicle and continued to drive so slow that honking from the other motorists sent him into a rage. He suddenly turned and found himself alone on a street. He drove for two blocks when suddenly a steady stream of cars came straight towards him. The cars veered around Domko's vehicle and one car slowed long enough for the driver to yell: “You’re on a one way street!”

Domko looked surprised. “But she’s be goink but a some way!” he yelled back.

The man shook his head and kept driving.

“I’s be goink but they’s crazy bastards be comink!” he said to Caroline.

She explained what the man had meant by ‘one way street’ and Domko began to swear. He cursed the man who’d designed Winnipeg streets. Suddenly, he turned abruptly to the left and drove over the boulevard and into the traffic going in the opposite direction.

“Stop here!” Caroline exclaimed, pointing to a service station. Domko cut off another car, then drove over the sidewalk into the station parking lot. They sat quietly for a moment then Caroline decided it would be best if her husband didn’t drive in Winnipeg any more. She got out of the car and went to the public telephone. She returned to say that her son Walter would be there soon to pick them up.

The twins were so excited that they had a difficult time falling asleep on the makeshift beds on the floor of grandpa Kolodka’s front room. The street lights and traffic noise kept them awake most of the night.

The next morning they rose early and Walter arrived to take them to the meeting. At first the boys were quite excited until they noticed the throngs of well-dressed people in the crowded arena.

David felt badly when people glanced at them then veered away from the impoverished family wearing threadbare clothes. Dennis became suddenly aware of his gangly limbs and shirt and pants that were two sizes too small.

He cringed with adolescent embarrassment at the sight of his unsophisticated mother and crude stepfather. Domko carried a flour sack of food over his shoulder while Caroline carried Raymond who shrieked continually, his voice echoing loudly through the vast corridor. His siblings were no better - timid Rosie shrunk from the crowds while blind Kathy marched along, chatting loudly.

David was the only family member who was not an embarrassment to Dennis, even though he was still recovering from the bad haircut. Dennis looked at the ground in shame as he avoided the gaze of people around him. Their expressions weren’t of sympathy nor concern for the bedraggled family. He wondered what had happened to the kind, gentle, loving people that the bible and Watchtower publication spoke of so often? These people looked at them with disdain, not love.

Caroline led the family to a corner near a concession stand where the family set up a makeshift camp while most other people at the gathering filed into the arena auditorium. The family listened to lessons that were broadcast over the loudspeaker system. Mostly, the speaker talked about how to go ‘door to door’, saying that Witnesses should be meek when approaching difficult people. They listened to sermons on how husbands and wives should love each other. They were all encouraged to send money for missionary work.

Caroline and Domko went into the arena to listen for a while, taking Raymond and Kathy along. Occasionally, loud applause and cheers would boom through the building, causing the boys to cover their ears. The twins and Rosie wandered along the cement corridors, returning during the lunch break when the corridors filled with people. While most of the meeting delegates purchased food at the concessions, left to go to restaurants or opened neatly packed lunches, Caroline knelt on the ground and cut slices from a cooked pork hock. The slices were slapped between crookedly sliced bread. Domko scowled as he watched the twins each take a sandwich and disappear silently behind a post to eat.

"Do you see them kids?" Dennis asked, his voice thick with envy. "They got store-boughten hot dogs an' pop.

"Shhh!" his brother warned as he looked over his shoulder. "He'll hear you an' then you'll get it. Don't say nothin' 'bout them kids 'cause he'll think you're jealous. An' remember he hasn't beat anybody for a few days an' will be lookin' for an excuse."

Dennis looked at his stepfather who watched them with distrust. He shuddered then turned back to silently watch the people stroll by. The boys sat quietly for a short time until the meeting resumed and most delegates filtered back inside. Domko took Raymond for a short walk outside.

The twins relaxed when they knew he was gone. They edged their way over to a concession stand. A bright, bubbling soft drink fountain machine caught Dennis' attention.

"Look!" he said.

David looked at the interesting machine. It was divided into two glass sections with a dark pink liquid bubbling on one side and orange on the other. The drinks looked cold and delicious. The boys stood at the counter and stared longingly at the machine.

"I want to taste that," Dennis said.

David agreed. "Me too. It looks good."

The twins watched as people approached and bought drinks for themselves and their children from the machine. They watched hoping that one of the drinks would be abandoned but none were. They walked around the corridor for a while then back to their mother who was cleaning up from lunch.

"Go get some milk for Raymie," she said, handing them twenty cents and pointing to the concession stand at the end of the hall.

The boys approached the young man serving in the concession and after a few moments of stammering and stuttering were told that sales weren't allowed during the meeting sessions. He advised]them to return at 2 p.m.

"Oh, no," David said as they walked back towards their mother.

"Ma, they won't sell us nothin' until 2 o'clock. He said it's closed," David explained.

"What? Raymie needs milk now. Are you sure?" she asked.

"Yeah, we asked but he won't sell it to us."

Caroline frowned, just as Domko came around the corner. The twins backed up as she relayed the information. Domko angrily looked at the boys then strode past them towards the concession stand.

"I's be gettink it some!" he yelled.

"What time is it?" Dennis asked.

"I dunno, but I hope it ain't two yet. What if he sells it to him?"

"Then he'll think we're playin' a trick."

The boys shuddered then followed Domko to the concession stand. They hid behind a pole to watch. Just then a loud roar of applause rang over the loudspeaker.

"And there is so much love in the air this afternoon . . ." the male voice boomed.

The boys watched as Domko began talking to the vendor. The young man shook his head no, then pointed to the clock.

"Stand up and greet the neighbours around you . . ."

The twins could see Domko's head shaking and his lips moving. The vendor shook his head again, since it was against the convention rules to sell food during the presentations. Domko stamped his foot, then strode out of sight for a moment before re-appearing in the concession. The young man retreated as Domko backed him against the wall. He grabbed the fellow by the front of his shirt and lifted him off the ground.

"With all the love that radiates through the room today, I say to you what an uplifting experience this is!" the voice boomed from the arena, followed by another chorus of applause.

Domko dropped the vendor, then strode to the cooler, opened it and took out a carton of milk. The vendor stood helplessly and watched as Domko screamed a few insults then strode back down the hall.

The boys snickered to themselves. It was a relief to see Domko being nasty to someone other than them.

"That was some uplifting experience, eh Davey?" Dennis laughed.

The boys turned and ran in the opposite direction. They found themselves outside in the parking lot. They walked between the many cars, trying to guess what jobs people had to have to afford such luxurious vehicles.

"Look at this one!" David called. "It's bran' new."

The boys walked through the parking lot, stepping out of the way as vehicles entered and went. Bored, they began running after cars that drove by. More than a few drivers looked in their rear view mirrors to see the boys chasing them. Curious pedestrians watched as the boys edged up to the cars and chased them in the same way a dog would. The twins did this for a few hours until somebody reported them to security personnel. They were told to stop, so they went back inside and their mother sent them into the arena to listen to the lessons.

That night the twins were billeted by the conference committee at a stranger's house, only to find themselves objects of scorn. The people were expecting more affluent visitors and were openly offended that they had to serve their elegantly prepared meal to the twins. While the boys ate happily, the phone rang.

"All of our plans are ruined now," the woman said to her caller as she stood along the kitchen wall with her back to the twins. She didn't even try to hide the disappointment in her voice. "We've got two boys here from some place in the sticks called Moosehorn. so we can't come now." She listened for a moment, then continued:

"Yes, I thought of that but we just can't." Pause. "Yes, I'm sure." Pause. "Trust me about this," she whispered, winding the cord around her waist as she turned the corner. "You'd have to see it to believe it."

The boys sat pretending they couldn't overhear the woman. They ate the last of the supper as their faces burned hot with humiliation. The husband sat coolly at the end of the table asking a few questions and waiting impatiently as David stammered his reply. Of course the man made him terribly nervous which didn't help matters.

The woman hung up the phone. She rolled her eyes.

"Well, we're staying home," she said resentfully. "And I really wanted to go, too."

David sat for a moment, then summoned the courage to speak.

"D-don't stay o-on a-a-acounta us," he said. "Me an' Denny are g-good at bein' by oursel-lves."

The adults looked at them.

"No, it's alright," the woman said as she stood to clear the table. Then under her breath - "We want things to be here when we get back."

The next morning the boys went outside to wait for their ride. Their brother Walter drove up just before 10 a.m. and gave them a vigorous wave. The boys climbed in the front seat beside him. This was their first opportunity to speak to him without their mother or Domko around.

Walter lived in Winnipeg and worked as a pressman at Union Carbide. He had only visited the farm a few times since moving to the city. Mostly, he came when their mother needed help or if Domko wanted to borrow money. Domko still owed him $150 for a bull he bought the spring before.

Walter thanked the people for keeping the boys then drove along the narrow streets towards one of the city's largest streets, Portage Ave.

"G-guess where we're goin?" Walter smiled.

"I dunno, where?" David asked.

"To the zoo."

The twins cheered since they'd never been to a zoo before.

"Yeah, we're meetin' mom and Domko there," he said.

The boys stopped cheering. "Can't we just go with you?" David asked.

Walter could sense that they boys weren't getting along any better than he had.

"How is it on the farm, anyway? Is he treatin' you guys good?" he asked.

"No, he works us all the time," David said.

"An' he starves us," Dennis added.

Walter looked at the twins. They'd grown a lot since the last time he saw them.

"Well, I see you boys talk good now," he said. "Nobody ever understood what you guys said before. What was that strange language anyway? "

David blurted out a few of their words, and Dennis answered back.

Walter shook his head.

"So, whadda you think?" David asked.

"What?"

"What we just said."

"I dunno. I can't understand you guys."

"Just say yes."

"No, I'm not gonna say yes to somethin' that I can't understand."

"Please!" David begged.

"O.k., then, yes."

The boys cheered.

"What did I agree to, anyway?"

"You'll see."

Domko, Caroline and the kids were waiting in the zoo parking lot. Domko was pleased to discover that admission to the zoo was free and herded the family in. Excited, the children scattered in all directions. The twins pointed and yelled loudly as they ran between animal exhibits, enthralled with the monkeys, bears and exotic animals. The twins sat for a long time in front of the rocky pit where the polar bears lived.

They also watched the monkeys playing in their cages and after examining the monkeys for quite some time, they both came to the same conclusion.

"Eunice don't look like no monkey," Dennis said. "Why does he call her that?"

David shook his head. "I dunno. Maybe 'cause she runs kinda slippery."

Walter bought each of them a pop and ice cream cone near the end of the day. As the boys licked the creamy, thick ice cream, they agreed that this was definitely the best day they'd ever experienced.

As the family congregated near the exit, David and Dennis began speaking in the secret language so that Domko couldn't understand them.

"You ask him." Dennis said.

"No, you ask him."

"I can't. You do it 'cause I'm too scared."

David nodded. "As soon as ole Squeezer ain't lookin'."

Domko told everyone to wait while he went to the rest room. Caroline also took the three youngest children also, because it was time to begin the drive back to Moosehorn.

The boys stood on either side of Walter, looking up at their big brother.

"Hey Walter," David began. "So are we ready to go?"

"Yep, I'm ready."

"Us too," he said hesitating. Then he grabbed Walter's arm. "Can we come home with you?"

"What?"

"We don't wanna go back to the farm," David said, looking over his shoulder towards the men's rest room then back again. "We wanna live with you Walter, here in Winnipeg." David equated Winnipeg with heaven and his tongue wrapped lovingly around the word as he said it.

Walter was stunned. "You guys can't live with me, you're too little. Besides, I only have one room. Where would you sleep?"

"It don't matter," Dennis interjected. "We'll sleep anywhere. On the floor or in the porch."

"Yeah, or we can sleep in your car!" David pleaded. "That'd be o.k. - do you got a garage? We could stay in there an' make up a good spot to live. We've been thinkin' 'bout this, we could get jobs an' everything so we won't even cost you no money."

Overwhelmed by the boys' begging, Walter took a few steps back and held up his hands.

"Hold on!" he exclaimed. "I don't got room for you guys an' besides, Mom an' Domko would never let you guys live with me. They need you on the farm."

David looked at the rest room. "We could go now, before they get back," he said, the urgency building in his voice as he grabbed his brother's arm. "C'mon, Walter!"

"They'd just come get you right away and then beat the hell out of all of us," Walter said.

"Yeah, but you know what it's like. You ran away too! Only you're lucky, 'cause we don't got no place to go."

Walter began to soften, just as Domko came out of the rest room. Instinctively, the twins started talking in the secret language, but of course their brother couldn't understand what was being said. They could tell by the look on Walter's face that he felt sorry for them and wanted to help. The sight of Domko approaching with their mother just a few feet behind, caused the three of them to begin trembling. If he guessed what they'd been talking about, he'd beat them on the spot.

The family filed through the exit and as the twins walked towards the car. Everyone climbed into Walter's car since he was going to drive them out of the city to the edge of the highway, where a friend of Walter's would be waiting with Domko's car. The boys sat in the back and watched Walter carefully. The could tell he was thinking about what they'd asked.

When they reached the highway, they all got out of Walter's car. He glanced at the twins, then looked away.

Walter wanted to confront Domko about his treatment of the children and also to ask for his $150, but was afraid of Domko's reaction. He said goodbye to everyone as his friend climbed in beside him, then waved and drove off.

The twins felt as if they'd stepped from paradise into hell. The stark reality that they'd have to leave the enjoyment of Winnipeg and return to the confines of the farm caused the boys to begin weeping quietly. They sat in the back seat and daydreamed about how wonderful it would be to live in Winnipeg. They were not looking forward to the long, slow drive home.

The family arrived back at the farm as the sun was rising the following morning. They found that Eunice had done a good job keeping up with the chores. Within a few hours, they were back to their usual schedule.

* * * * *

In mid-July, the health nurse visited the family to discuss education options for Kathy. At six years old she was ready to start school in the fall. Mrs. Burnett brought information about a school in Brantford, Ontario, specially programmed for blind people.

The twins returned home from school to find Domko and their mother in deep conversation with Mrs. Burnett.

"If she's going to manage in the world, she'll need a proper education," Mrs. Burnett said. "They will teach her how to take care of herself and to read braille."

"But she's so young," Caroline protested.

"I know but the sooner she learns, the better it will be. If you wait too long, she may become stubborn and not want to learn. Children her age are like sponges - they are eager to try new things."

Caroline glanced at her daughter who sat on the chair listening. Kathy wasn't able to fully comprehend what attending school in Brantford would mean.

"And there would be a cost associated with this," Margaret Burnett warned. "This type of schooling is not cheap, but you have to remember that her future depends on it. Being blind means her life will be different from all the other children. It will be difficult for her to marry and she will likely never have a job or be able to travel on her own. At least if she learns to read with her hands, it will give her some enjoyment in life."

Caroline nodded. "We'll think about it, and let you know."

"If you decide you want to do this, I can help make the arrangements."

"Thank you."

Domko nodded. He always wanted the best for his children and didn't want to deny Kathy any opportunities. He also felt very guilt about injuring the girl when she was a baby. He told Caroline this many times, but never admitted what he'd done to others.

Margaret quickly assessed the family's situation before she left. It appeared that Caroline and Domko were no longer fighting and that the children were adequately cared for. While they were still awful thin, there had been no more reports to the police about Domko.

Stepping outside, she asked Dennis if everything was alright.

"Yes, ma'am," he said, his eyes brightening. "We was in Winnipeg an' we went to the zoo an' saw the animals an' Walter bought us pop an' ice cream."

Margaret smiled. It was nice to see these children happy about something. She was satisfied that things had improved and while she didn't believe that people like Domko changed, she wanted to give him the benefit of the doubt.

She made a mental note to review the family's file with the new social worker who had recently been hired to cover the area. She would be unfamiliar with the family and would need some background information in case the situation took a turn for the worse.

Caroline was outside one afternoon when she had an unexpected visitor. Jim Deighton had been checking the hay in one of his fields when he saw Caroline. He decided to stop by for a chat. It was the first time they'd had the chance to discuss Ruby's departure. Jim was embarrassed about the rumours that were circulating and he told Caroline his side of the story while they stood in the front yard.

"How's Domko doin' anyway?" Jim asked.

"He's alright," she said brightly. "Things have gotten better since the kids stopped running away."

Jim flinched. He knew this was a sore spot with Carrie.

"Well, I'm glad to hear things are good," he said, although the words didn't come out as sincerely as he'd hoped.

They smiled at one another and Jim got back on his tractor and drove home. Caroline went into the house, slightly buoyed by the visit. Jim always had a way of making her feel like she was worthy.

Caroline opened the door to find her husband standing by the window. His eyes were bright with anger as they followed her into the kitchen.

"You's be beechin' around again!" he seethed.

"What?" she asked in surprise. She was momentarily flattered by his jealousy, but that quickly dissipated when she saw the look of utter hatred that accompanied the comment.

"Me and Jim? What are you talking about? I haven't seen Jim for a year. We were just talking about Ruby and doing a little gossiping."

"Talkink!" he roared. "You's be lazy beech talkink all day! I's be but a some seek from work and you's be runnink arount."

"What do you mean you're sick?" She knew he'd been complaining of bad headaches since returning home from Winnipeg, but he complained so much about even tiny ailments that she no longer took him seriously.

He turned and went to the table. "I's be readink it," he said lifting her Bible up from the table. "You's be goink to heaven? Fraaaaa! Murdering beech. She's be goink to heaven?"

"What?" she exclaimed.

He strode towards the cookstove, still carrying the Bible.

"No!" she screamed, grabbing his arm. Holding her back with one arm as she reached across him to rescue the book, he flipped open the firebox door and tossed the Bible on top of a burning log.

"Dat's vere you's be goink!"

"Boleslaw, you've got no right!" she screamed. "Burning the Bible is a sin - you can go to hell for that!"

"I's not be goingk to hell, you's be!"

"Well, anything is better than bein' here with you!"

"You's be tryink to kill me like some Beel," he screamed.

She pushed past him and pulled the Bible out of the stove. The cover and a few of the inside pages were on fire. She pounded the book until she was able to put the fire out.

Domko strode out of the house in anger.

That night friends came to visit and during the middle of the conversation, Domko suddenly passed out, his head landing on the table with a thud. The children jumped down from their chairs and ran into the front room. They watched as the visitors and their mother tried desperately to revive Domko. A few minutes later, he woke up as if nothing had happened.

The friends and Caroline insisted that he must be taken to see the doctor. As he tried to stand, he discovered that he'd lost all feeling on his right hand side. They loaded him into the car and Caroline sped towards the hospital in Ashern.

As they drove down the highway, Domko complained in a child-like voice about the pain in his head. His erratic behaviour was beginning to frighten Caroline who visualized having to care for not only six children, but an invalid husband as well.

They arrived at the hospital and two nurses rushed to help Domko inside. Doctor Steenson was summoned and within a few minutes the patient was being examined. Domko complained incessantly that it was Caroline's fault that he was not well. She stood quietly listening as her eyes filled with tears. The doctor calmed Domko, then recommended to Caroline that he be sent by ambulance to a Winnipeg hospital. She nodded in agreement and within the hour they were on their way south.

Caroline arrived home late the next day to report that Domko had been taken to Winnipeg for x-rays and observation, and was now resting in the

Ashern hospital. The x-rays revealed a blood clot in his head had become dislodged. It was not a stroke as they had originally thought but he needed to stay in the hospital for a few more days.

Chapter 27

Kathy goes to Brantford

DOMKO MADE A FULL RECOVERY and returned home a few days later. He believed that the blood clot had has been caused by anger and was frightened that he might have another seizure. He made an effort to control his temper, but claimed that Caroline and children were trying to make him angry on purpose.

"You's be keelink me like but a some Beel!" he said sarcastically.

Caroline tried to explain that she hadn't killed Bill and that they weren't plotting against him, but her words fell on deaf ears. Eventually, she began to ignore him.

August came and the twins spent long hours in the hayfield cutting and raking hay. Eunice and Rosie helped on stacking and hauling days. One morning while David was cutting and Dennis was raking, Eunice stayed in the house to help her mother.

Domko had been belittling Caroline so much lately that she refused to get up that morning. Eunice decided to wash the floor to make her mother feel better. The children needed her to be strong, since she was their only defense against Domko's erratic behaviour.

A dirty floor makes the whole house look bad, Eunice reasoned. *I'll wash this up and surprise mom with how much better it will look.*

"Kathy, you, Rosie and Raymond go outside to play," Eunice ordered, guiding the children out the door. She could hear Domko cutting tall grass near the house, so she wasn't concerned about Kathy and Raymond wandering too far since their father was nearby.

Eunice hummed softly as she filled a pail with soap and warm water from the cook stove. She swept the floor then began scrubbing the worn linoleum on hands and knees. She started near the kitchen cupboards, working her way towards the table. The area around Domko's chair was by far the dirtiest because he never removed his manure-covered boots when he came inside. She decided to do that spot last.

This isn't so bad, she thought. Eunice was happy to be working inside instead of out in the hot sun.

When she had almost finished the floor and was thinking about the next cleaning job to tackle, she heard a scream outside. She ran to the window and saw Kathy crying just outside the door crying. She was holding her finger out to her father who had come around the edge of the house to see what had happened.

Eunice immediately crouched down and began scrubbing the floor hard. Her mind whirled as she wondered what Domko's reaction would be to his daughter's tears. The door swung open and he strode inside. As always he was looking for somebody to blame and this time it appeared to be Eunice. As he towered over her he shouted that she never should have sent Kathy outside in the first place. He still carried a scythe in one hand. Its sharp metal blade curved heavily towards the floor. The sight of it in the hands of her shaking stepfather caused blood to drain from Eunice's face. She said nothing as she looked helplessly at the rag she grasped tightly in her hand.

Domko took a few steps forward and now stood directly over her.

This is how it feels to die, she thought, imagining the heavy metal knife slicing through her body. She knew at that moment the utter terror people felt when they knew they were soon to be murdered. A calm came over her as she turned her eyes up and stared at her stepfather. His arms shook with anger and his eyes were pained with confusion. She faced him, hoping that if he did strike her with the blade, she would die instantly and not suffer.

Everything in his stance indicated that he might lunge at any minute. The scythe was positioned to kill. Her body tensed and she held her breath, waiting for the fatal blow. Instead of lashing out at her, though, he slowly lowered his arm. Eunice could sense as he stood above her that he understood the way he treated the children was wrong and most of the time could not help himself. She was thankful that, this time he had.

He grunted at her and strode across the kitchen. Then he stormed back outside.

It was then that Eunice started to breathe again. Her heart raced and in a delayed reaction to fear, she felt adrenalin pump through her neck into her throbbing head. Eunice felt an overwhelming sense that her head was going to burst as she gasped for breath. Leaning against a wall, she closed her eyes and listened to the sound of her heart pounding.

She was still alive! But at what price? All she had to look forward to was more fear, uncertainty and no doubt, lewd glances and beatings. In that instant, she knew she could no longer tolerate life on the farm unless the situation improved. Her stepfather's behaviour was so erratic and predictably violent that she believed that he might some day kill one of them. Eunice vowed to make her mother understand before it was too late.

* * * * *

As the remainder of summer went by, something traumatic happened to the children almost daily. Suffering from sunstroke because he'd been working too long, for too many days in a row, David fell off the mower seat and almost caught his legs in the blades. Afraid he'd faint again, he tried to drive the team home, but was intercepted by Domko. Jumping off the tractor, he accused David of being lazy and hit him over the head with the large knot in the horses reins.

This sent David sprawling unconscious on the ground. He awoke hours later under the shade of an old oak tree, some distance from where he'd fallen. He must have crawled there in delirium. The shade from the tree helped soothe his sunburned body. It was also some comfort to the itchy sores he had all over his arms and legs from poison ivy.

Domko pressured the children to complete as many chores as they could before school started. Of course, the harder they tried, the more likely they were to make mistakes. Trying to please Domko had by now become impossible - no matter how hard they tried or how much work they did, it was never enough.

One afternoon the children went running into the bush to look for a fencing hammer that had been lost earlier that spring. Eunice and the twins searched for hours near the place where they had repaired an old strip of barbed wire.

"Do you 'spose he's gettin' worse?" David asked as they shuffled along, heads bowed and bare feet in the underbrush.

"Worse? I can't 'magine it," Dennis said.

"Yeah, he's gettin' worse all right," Eunice said. "I hear him talkin' to mom at night. He's complain' that if Kathy goes to the blind school, he'll only have one kid here matched up against us four. He says it's not fair an' we'll get the farm instead of Raymie."

The twins were stunned. They weren't thinking about stealing the farm from anybody.

"Well, that's stupid, 'cause I ain't stayin' around here," Dennis said. "How 'bout you Davey?"

"No way! I'm gettin' outta here as soon as I can save up enough an' buy a motorcycle like Norman. "Only I'm gonna get one that I can start without runnin' behind it."

The children laughed.

"Well, I know I'm gonna get outta here too," Eunice said. "Momma's not helpin' us any when she's lyin' in bed all the time. Me an' her have been fightin' a lot lately."

Then she thought for a moment. "Who's her favourite kid?"

Dennis was the first to speak. "Steven."

"Nope, I say Raymond," David said.

"I say you!" Eunice said pointing at David. "She never gives you heck."

"What about Norman?" David asked.

"Well, I know it ain't me," Dennis said sadly.

"Me neither," Eunice added.

David thought about his mother and how she seemed to favour a few of the children. He did get along with her better than Eunice and Dennis, but he never thought of himself as her favourite child.

"Me an' momma get along o.k.," he said. "She's just stuck that's all. She can't help it 'cause the church says she has to listen to flatfoot 'cause he's the head of the house. I'm glad I ain't no girl, 'cause I'm tellin' you right now when I grow up nobody's gonna boss me around."

"Me neither," Dennis added cheerfully.

"Yeah, well me neither," Eunice said emphatically. "Even if I am a girl."

They continued to search the grass.

"If we're gonna find that thing before he comes lookin' for us, we'd better split up," Eunice said. "Me an' David will stay here, Dennis you go look up ahead."

Dennis nodded. "If I find it, I'll yell back."

The children continued to look in the grass, then Eunice and David sat down for a rest.

"How come you haven't left the farm yet?" David asked. "You're 14 an' lots of kids leave home when they're 14."

"They won't let me go," she said sadly.

"I hope I'm not still here when I'm 14," he said.

"You will be."

"Whadda you mean?"

"Well, when I go do you think he's gonna let you go? Who's gonna do the work?"

"I dunno."

"Not Kathy and Raymond, that's for sure," she said. "How's Dennis doin' anyway?"

"You saw him, whadda you think?" he asked.

"He still seems kinda sad to me," she said. "But he seems tougher than before."

"Yeah," David said. "Sometimes it bugs me when he talks about dyin' an' stuff but he's better."

"He can't help it you know," she said. "It's worse for him than us 'cause Domko hates him the most. You gotta keep helpin' him."

David agreed with his sister.

Suddenly the children sensed something was wrong. They stood up and looked around them. Out of the corner of his left eye, David saw movement beside the bush where they had been sitting. Turning his head slowly, he saw Domko crouched low, hiding from them. David slapped Eunice's shoulder and then pointed towards the bush. Her eyes widened and both took off running down the path along side the fence. Suddenly, a large hammer flew through the air, just inches over their heads. It landed in front of them.

"Fraaa! You lazy soneebeech bastards be not workink!"

He'd come looking for them and caught the children resting. He had overheard parts of their conversation. This was the conspiring against him that he hated so much.

David and Eunice caught up to Dennis who had started walking back towards them.

"Run!" Eunice yelled. Dennis stood frozen for a moment, then turned and ran like a rabbit into the bush. The children kept going until they were certain they weren't being followed.

"That was a close one!" Eunice exclaimed.

"What did Satan do?" Dennis asked.

"He threw a hammer at us," his sister said. "It almost took our heads off."

Dennis shuddered. He was thankful Domko hadn't snuck up on him.

The children stayed in the bush overnight. They returned the next morning hoping that Domko had cooled off. Eunice tried not to think about Rosie being left alone with their stepfather. She hoped that their mother would have the good sense to protect her.

*****

One day in late August, Kathy kissed her mother goodbye. Clutching a suitcase of brand new clothing, she climbed into the car with Domko. She and her father were leaving for Winnipeg with friends from the church who had agreed to drive them to the train station so that Kathy could go to the school in Brantford, Ontario. This had been a very difficult decision for Caroline and for Domko who lamented that he had caused his own daughter's injury. In the end they had agreed that this would be the best thing for their daughter.

It was difficult for Domko to part with Kathy at the station and he arrived home later that night in a somber mood. He was also angry that the people who had driven them to the city had asked him for $15 to cover the cost of gas.

As he went to his room for the night, he complained to Caroline that her friends were 'mooney hungry'. He fell into a fitful sleep and began behaving very strangely the next day when he awoke. He was more suspicious and angrier than he'd ever been. Caroline and the children avoided him as he paced back and forth, worried about Kathy and the farm. He held Raymond tightly and even mistrusted Caroline where his son was concerned.

Over the next few weeks, he refused to shave and seemed to almost enjoy the stench of his unclean body. Caroline became very quiet as she wondered what was happening to her husband. She knew that he became depressed during fall and winter, but this was only early September.

She prayed that he would get better, but nagging thoughts kept entering her mind. She remembered something that Doctor Steenson had told her and how mad it had made her at the time. Steenson thought there was something seriously wrong with Domko's mind, but Caroline had refused to believe it. He had told her it would get worse if left untreated, but she believed that if she prayed long enough, things would get better.

Since the blood clot, something had changed in his head. All of the oddities he once displayed were suddenly magnified. He seemed to be unravelling and she didn't know what to do.

Caroline knew she couldn't go to the church for advice, since the blame was always shifted from him to her. She felt trapped by his sudden possessiveness and hoped his mood swings would abate. She hated admitting she was wrong and didn't want to face Doctor Steenson again.

The new school year began and the children were curious to meet their new teacher.

Mrs. Collier had retired from teaching in June. Although the twins knew she was long past retirement age at 69 years of age, they still felt partly responsible. It was their prank the winter before that had sent her into a snow-filled hole wearing not much more than a nightgown. They promised themselves that they wouldn't do anything like that to her replacement.

The new teacher, Mrs. Marion Gering, was a tall, dark-haired woman with glasses. At thirty years of age she had three children and farmed with her husband Roy west of Grahamdale. She was familiar with most people in the area, including the Pischke and Kolodka families.

She had heard rumours that the Pischke children couldn't be controlled and was initially apprehensive about accepting the job at Bayton School. She was pleasantly surprised to find the children polite, helpful and well-behaved.

Eunice was now in grade seven. She and her friend Larry Meisner were two of the oldest children at the school. The younger ones liked to call them "Mom & Pop".

Because the twins had been attending regularly, they were promoted to grade five and Rosie, who was very smart and also seldom absent, was now in grade three.

A couple of months went by and in late fall Mrs. Gering had the opportunity to meet Domko. He was waiting for the children at the end of lane when school finished for the day. She introduced herself, pretending she hadn't heard many rumours about him. His crude way of speaking and piercing eyes made her feel uncomfortable. That night while she prepared supper, she told her husband about the encounter.

"Well I spoke to Bob Domko today," she began. "I don't know what you think of him Roy, but I sure don't like him. I think there's something wrong with that man. He's got absolutely no social skills at all."

"Why do you say that?" Roy asked.

"I don't know. There's just something about him, I guess. He grunted at me in a way that made my skin crawl. Now, I know the community is divided over what to think about that family, but I'm siding with those children. You know, I've spent nearly eight weeks with them now, and those twins are just fine. Except for the fact they miss too much school."

"But you know, Roy, I think Domko makes them stay home to work. The only one with perfect attendance is Rosie and she attended regularly last year too. She's the youngest one."

"So what do you think?" he said.

"Well, I'm not sure. It's hard to tell because they are such happy-go-lucky kids. They're pretty poor, but so are lots of families in the area. I'm sure the Pischke kids aren't as bad as people think."

Late one afternoon, a family from the church stopped by the house for a short visit. This was the same family that had taken Domko and Kathy to Winnipeg, but they hadn't been by since.

Caroline was pleased when they stopped to visit because they were always kind to her. They didn't mind the state of the house or how the children behaved. She invited them in, happy for the company and called to Domko who was resting in his bedroom. The couple sat down at the table and began making small talk with Caroline. She laughed at a joke the husband told, just as Domko came into the kitchen.

She knew immediately by the look on his face that something was wrong.

"You's!" he exclaimed pointing to the man.

He turned to Domko and smiled widely. "Hi Bob, how are you doing?"

"Huh! You's be chargink me fifteen dollar! I's be chargink you fifteen dollar for but a some coop!"

"Pardon?" the man said, truly bewildered by Domko's comments.

"You's not be comink here no more!" he shouted as he went back into his bedroom.

Caroline jumped up. "Boleslaw, what are you talking about?" She could see him pick up his rifle from the top of the bureau and begin searching for bullets.

"You'd better go right now!" Caroline said to the couple. "He's got the gun and he's going to shoot you."

The man and his wife jumped up. "Why? What did we do?"

"Just go!" she said waving her hand.

"Are you going to be alright?" the husband asked, but didn't wait for the answer as he ran out the door. Caroline's children followed closely behind then scattered in the bushes.

Domko came roaring out of the bedroom carrying the gun. Caroline tried to stop him, but he pushed his way out the door. He stood cursing in the yard as the visitor's car sped away.

After that, Domko wouldn't drive Caroline to church at Grahamdale or Ashern. Anyone from the church who came to visit was watched with suspicion. There were few who would come, since Domko had found fault with nearly every single person in the area. He had thrown many of them off the farm, telling them never to return.

Caroline was so angry with him that she moved permanently out of the bedroom and slept upstairs with the children.

* * * * *

The temperatures became frigid and the snow began to fall as another winter set in. The only respite for the children was school, which they gladly attended now because they were doing better. They noticed that Mrs. Gering took a special interest in their well-being.

While Eunice enjoyed the reading period, David and Dennis shone during art class. One afternoon after the lunch recess, Mrs. Gering announced that the each student was to draw a picture as an entry in a school art contest. The contest was sponsored by Brooke Bond, a New Brunswick company that made Blue Ribbon tea. She showed the students the location of New Brunswick on the large map that hung on the wall.

Since Mrs. Gering didn't want anyone to be disappointed, she emphasized the fun of entering the contest rather than winning.

David and Dennis looked at each other and smiled. Both boys were anxious to begin and worked hard on their drawings. Over the next few days, pieces of finished artwork gradually appeared on Mrs. Gering's desk. She thanked the students and carefully studied the work, giving each child a fair share of praise.

Some of these children are good little artists, she thought, as she piled the work in a neat stack at the end of her desk. That afternoon during the recess break, Mrs. Gering noticed that two more pictures had been discreetly added to the pile. She picked them up and saw to her astonishment, that the drawings were excellent. The small signatures on the bottom belonged to Dennis and David. It was apparent that the twins were both very artistic.

Studying each one, she couldn't decide which drawing was better. Their work was so much more detailed compared to their peers that she felt slightly embarrassed for the other students. Dennis had drawn an exquisite farm scene that showed detailed farm equipment and animals along with a farmer. The farmer sat high on a tractor while four people worked on the ground below.

David had drawn a picture of a young man sitting at the edge of the bush, by a lake. It appeared that the young man lived near the lake since he had a little camp set up with a shanty and campfire.

As Mrs. Gering placed all the drawings inside an envelope and carefully sealed the package, she thought it was a shame that the boys would be competing against each other.

Their work is so good I'm certain that one of them will win a prize, she thought.

Chapter 28

The birthday party

AT THE END OF JANUARY, THE BEATINGS intensified and Dennis became so afraid that he couldn't sleep or eat. Everywhere he turned, Domko was there, stalking and waiting for him. David helped his brother as much as he could, but mostly sat in numb shock as his brother received yet another beating.

It appeared that their mother had given up all hope. The days were short and she spent a lot of time in the upstairs bed. One evening after working late into the night hauling hay, the twins came inside. Dennis was still recovering from a beating two nights before. The felt tops of their boots were soaked from freezing rain that had pelted them all afternoon. Drenched and shivering uncontrollably, the boys didn't dare stop by the furnace to warm up.

Domko was waiting in the front room, his chair positioned so that the children had to walk past him to seek refuge upstairs. Their hearts were beating loudly in their chests as they skulked along the wall, trying to make themselves as small and inconspicuous as possible.

They kept their boots on instead of putting them by the stove to dry. They went straight to bed with nothing to eat.

Upstairs, the twins slipped off their boots and wet clothing and left them on the floor to dry. Climbing into the warm bed beside their mother, Dennis snuggled close to her back. It felt good to have her near and for the moment the twins felt safe.

The next morning they awoke to Domko's yelling. He was calling the twins to come and do the milking, since they'd slept late and were behind schedule. The boys jumped out of bed, dizzy from starvation. They lifted their clothes and found that their socks and pants were frozen stiff. The clothes scratched coldly against their skin as they pulled them over their skinny legs. The boys hurried downstairs, carrying the felt rubbers which they knew from experience were going to be painfully difficult to put on. They struggled with the frozen felts, pulling them over their socks before they ran out the door.

The boys worked in the cold all day, still with empty stomachs. Their hunger had become unbearable, as their stomachs cramped and intestines turned into knots. Their body functions had slowed almost to a halt, as the boys hadn't had a bowel movement in more than a week and urinated only twice, once in the morning and once at night.

That evening they sat anxiously waiting for an opportunity to find something to eat without being caught. Suddenly, they saw Raymond emerge from his father's bedroom with a banana. They watched in envy as the youngster peeled back the skin and began eating the soft, hearty fruit. Raymond paraded back and forth as he ate the banana, then tossed the peel on the floor by the wood stove. He laughed and went into the front room.

The moment he was gone, the twins lunged for the discarded banana peel. Dennis got there first, but David wrenched it out of his hands. Pulling the peel back as far as it would go, he picked the remaining grey little knob of the banana off and popped it in his mouth. Dennis watched and nearly burst into tears.

The sight of the boys fighting over the peel caused Eunice to start giggling. It wasn't so much the struggle over the banana that elicited her laughter as much as it was embarrassment, pity and nervousness. She was able to sneak food because Domko didn't watch her as closely, but her brothers? They were doomed to die some day of starvation.

The twins began fighting over the banana peel and that combined with Eunice's giggling, sent Domko into a rage.

"I's be shootink you some!" he screamed.

Eunice, who saw him go into the bedroom and pick up his gun, jumped up and ran outside with Rosie close behind. The twins grabbed their felt rubbers by the door and sped into the deep snow in the yard. Behind them they heard Domko roar, then a bullet passed overhead.

"C'mon!" David yelled as he ran into the bush with Dennis so close behind he stepped on his heels. They heard another shot and the girls screaming, the wind whipping their faces as they ran.

"He got Rosie," David panted as he continued running down the snow-covered path. The boys kept running, sometimes through knee deep snow, instinctively towards the beaver dam. The freezing rain the day before had melted the top layer of snow, and the trees dripped on them as they pushed the branches aside. They were cold and exhausted by the time they reached the bank of the frozen lake.

"I can't go no further," Dennis said. "Let's make a fire here."

David looked around. "With what? We can't make no fire here Dennis, 'cause everything's all wet. Reaching into his pocket, he pulled out a small book of paper matches. They were too wet to strike.

"Maybe we can dry 'em out," Dennis suggested.

David looked up at the sky. "They'll never dry," he said. "It's gonna rain again an' we'll freeze before they dry out."

Looking out over the dark lake, David could see a series of lights in the distance. He estimated they were about three miles away. He looked behind him and saw nothing but darkness. Raising his eyes to the sky, he could see the silhouette of a full moon shining through heavy cloud cover. There was a chance it would begin to storm, he thought, clasping his hands together. Looking again at the lights, he made a decision for them both.

"C'mon Dennis, we're gonna walk across the beaver dam."

"I can't," Dennis moaned. "I'm too tired an' cold. Let's just stay here a little longer."

"If we stay here any longer we're gonna freeze to death."

"I don't care no more," Dennis said, sitting on the bank. "It's over for us anyhow. Nobody cares 'bout us and nobody does nothin' 'bout Domko."

"C'mon," David coaxed. "There's new people over the beaver dam and they will help us."

"What if they don't?"

"Well you can die then, but we're sure not gonna die here, not after we got this far and not as long as I can see those lights," he said pointing.

David's voice sounded so full of strength that it gave Dennis hope. He stood up and grabbed his brother's arm. Together, they walked down the lake bank and onto the frozen shore. The top of the ice was covered with slush from the freezing rain. Dennis shuddered when he remembered the swirling water that flowed underneath. Gingerly, they stepped onto the lake, then began walking towards the center. About fifty feet from shore, they came to reeds that grew on the lake bottom and stretched up to 12 feet above the water.

Dennis looked at the sky, but the reeds moving with the wind mesmerized him, making him feel disoriented. "Do you know where to go?" he asked.

"Yeah, I'm followin' that light," David said.

Dennis held onto David's arm and stared at the back of his brother's coat as David pushed his way through the reeds. Because the snow was too deep in places, they had to go left and then to the right, soon finding themselves surrounded by reeds like fleas on a dog's back.

"I can't see nothin," Dennis said, his voice panicking slightly.

"Me neither," David said as he tried to sound brave. The boys stopped for a moment and watched the tops waver in the cold, wet wind as it whistled through the reeds.

"Which way do we go?" Dennis asked.

David strained his senses hoping for a signal. He could no longer tell which way the wind was blowing and had become disoriented like Dennis. He looked into the reeds, and miraculously the tall grass parted for him, allowing him to suddenly see a glimmer of a light straight ahead. It disappeared again, but reappeared when a huge gust bent the reeds to the north.

"I see the light," he said and began trudging forward.

It felt like the boys had been walking for hours. By now their feet, hands and ears had no feeling, and the same stiffness was beginning to creep into their arms and legs. Their cheeks smarted as the reeds whipped their faces while they pushed their way through.

"How much further?" Dennis asked.

"We're almost there," David said confidently. "Once we get outta these reeds, the house is right there and the people will let us in. Just think about them givin' us something good to eat an' how nice an' warm it will be."

Dennis nodded. His mind wandered back to some of the good days they'd had. Days at Emma's and Ruby's, and the wonderful day at the zoo. Dennis remembered stretching out on the pavement in the arena parking lot in Winnipeg, and how hot and wonderful it had felt on his arms and legs. How he longed for that feeling now!

"Just a little bit further, we're almost there," David said, his spirits brightening. He could no longer feel his limbs, as he dragged his frozen feet across the ground. "I can see the light really good now, we're almost there."

Gradually the wall of grass became shorter and sparser. Soon they were on the lake shore bank. It began to snow lightly as they climbed the steep edge. They emerged from a small clump of trees to find themselves in a huge hayfield. Beyond that was a thick spruce bluff and beyond that the light.

Disappointed, David stared ahead. His limbs were screaming from the cold and utter exhaustion that was the end result of too much work, beatings and starvation over the past few months. They had been walking for a long time and the light didn't appear any closer!

"Where's the farm?" Dennis asked in a dazed voice as he looked around.

"It's over there," David pointed with a shaky hand.

"There? That's too far! I'm frozen and hungry, I can't go no further."

David stared at the light then resigned himself to the bleakness of their situation. They'd never make it through the deep snow in unfamiliar territory to a light that could end up being nothing at all.

"Me neither."

The boys fell to the ground in exhaustion. Dennis closed his eyes and relaxed on the frozen ground. He noticed that it suddenly didn't feel so cold anymore. It only felt bad when he was moving. Now his body felt like it was on the hot pavement again, and he began to float in and out of sleep.

When David hit the ground, he'd landed on a sharp rock which now poked into his back like an old spring he remembered on the bed at home. He closed his eyes and tried to relax, but the annoying rock kept him from falling asleep. The snowflakes landed softly on his cheeks, burning as they melted.

In the distance David could hear the sound of a coyote howling at the moon. Then call was suddenly answered by series of howls from a nearby den. The closeness of the animals sharpened David's senses. Soon his eyes were open and he was sitting erect.

Where are the coyotes? he thought as he looked around. He could hear them calling from all directions and the eerie sounds made him want to run. The surge of adrenalin that pumped through his veins was all he needed to get him going again.

"C'mon Dennis!" he yelled, staggering to his feet and grabbing his brother by the arm. "We gotta go. There's coyotes all around us."

"I don't care," Dennis mumbled.

"Yes you do," he said. "C'mon, get up."

"No!" Dennis whined, pulling his arms close to his chest. "You go if you want 'an bring back someone to get me, but I'm gonna stay here."

Frustrated, David kicked the snow with a frozen foot. In the many times they had slept in the bush, they'd always tried to make each other feel safe. David always told Dennis that there was no danger nearby and vice-versa. They always comforted each other when scared.

For some reason, David knew deep in his gut that if he left Dennis now, his brother was going to slip into a deep sleep and die.

"The coyotes are comin'!" he yelled, playing on his brother's worst fear. "I can see them runnin' through the field towards us. They're hungry and they're gonna eat you Dennis - get up!"

The desire to survive is a strong instinct that gives even the defeated enough strength to go on. Dennis wanted to live, just as much as his brother, and the image of a pack of frenzied dogs eating his limbs caused him to roll over and stagger to his feet.

"Where?" he cried.

"Over there!" David said, pointing in the opposite direction to the the light. "C'mon, as long as we keep moving they won't get us.!"

With a slight feeling of renewed energy, the boys began running across the field. Within a few minutes, Dennis realized that no coyotes were chasing them, but he was glad for the rush of adrenalin which had boosted him to his feet and awakened him from the fuzzy sleep.

"How much further?" Dennis asked.

"Not much. We just gotta get through the field and the spruces and then we'll be there." David hoped that the light was shining from somebody's yard. He jammed his fists deep in his pockets, squeezing the damp matches with his left hand.

"They got electricity, but we don't got electricity," Dennis mumbled.

"Yeah, but we got matches. If they weren't wet, we could make a fire right here," David said, his mind beginning to numb from the cold. He felt his wits softening and shook his head in an effort to keep awake.

They stumbled through the field to the edge of the spruce bluff.

"Should we stop here then?" Dennis asked, confused.

"To make a fire? We can't 'cause we need to get some matches first. We gotta keep goin'. It won't be much further now."

David knew that if Dennis succumbed to the cold this time, he'd never get him up. Grabbing his brother's arm, he pulled him into the dense forest. "This is a good spot, see? We'll come back here once we get some matches an' we can hide from everybody."

Dennis nodded. "Guess what Davey? We're over the beaver dam! We're in those trees we've always looked at. It's gonna be good here, just like we thought. We never have to go back."

The boys continued walking but their movements became sluggish and their minds foggy. All David could think about was getting matches, while Dennis kept raving about how much better it was in the forest over the beaver dam than in the bushes near home.

Finally the boys stumbled out of the spruce bluff and found themselves at the edge of another field. David had tried to follow the light, but sometimes it appeared ahead, while at other times it seemed to be to the right or the left. He shook his head and kept going.

"We're almost there," he said as he dragged his frozen feet, stumbling over hard chunks of snow.

Too numb to argue, Dennis trudged behind him. They walked through a small line of trees, then suddenly found themselves only 20 feet from a snowbank. They stopped and looked, not sure of what was ahead.

"What's that?" David asked trying hard to focus his eyes. The harder he tried, the more abstract it looked. He rubbed his eyes and looked again. It was a huge, lumpy pile of snow. The light from the moon cast uneven shadows across it.

"Look at that big snow! We'll never get over that!" David said, his heart sinking.

Dennis looked back towards the bush. "Let's go back and go to sleep where it's warm."

David focused on the huge mound ahead. He'd seen snow like this before, but was disoriented from the cold. He tried to remember, then suddenly a thought fogged his memory.

"A road!" he blurted out. "Denny, it's a road on the other side of the snow. We gotta get over it an' walk 'til we find a house."

"Where?" Dennis asked as he looked around in confusion.

"Over there, over the snow. C'mon, lets go."

"No, I'm not gonna go. I'll wait here."

"No! You gotta come 'cause I won't be able to find you again."

Dennis relented and the pair helped each other climb over the snowbank. They slid down and found themselves on the other side. Directly ahead of them was a small farmhouse, with a light shining through the window and a soft puff of smoke rising from the chimney.

"We're here," Dennis said beginning to cry softly.

"C'mon, let's go!" David said as he began walking towards the driveway.

"No, I can't," Dennis said. "I'm too scared. What if they're not nice people? Or if they call ole Squeezer an' tell him where we are."

David thought for a moment and looked at his brother then at the house.

He remembered what Jim had said about being careful where they went in the middle of the night. His mind was foggy and he tried to think straight, but everything seemed to be in slow motion.

"You're right," he said. "I'll go an' knock an' get matches so we can make a fire. We won't freeze if we got a fire. You wait here and if I yell, you go runnin' that way," David said pointing to the north.

Dennis nodded solemnly.

Slowly David walked towards the house.

Just then the light in the window went out!

David looked back at his brother. Whoever lived there must be going to bed. He stopped for a moment then continued shuffling down the snow packed driveway. The sound of his boots alerted a dog who came barking from a doghouse. It was a medium-sized dog with a friendly bark. David extended his hand as he walked by and the dog stopped barking to sniff him.

David approached the door and stood for a moment before knocking. He was hoping to hear a noise from inside. All was quiet. He rapped on the door and waited. Through the window, he saw a light come on and then heard the muffled sounds of people talking. He looked back at Dennis, and tried to think of what he would do if the people grabbed him. He formulated a plan in his mind, then unzipped his coat. He knew from experience that when adults grabbed kids, it was almost impossible for them to hold on to if the kid's coat was not done up. He'd wiggled free from his stepfather more than once using this technique. He took a deep breath then rapped on the door again.

The voices inside stopped. David could hear footsteps coming across the floor before the door opened. David was relieved to see a woman in her night dress in the doorway, but became fearful when her husband appeared over her shoulder. David stood and said nothing for a moment while he looked at the pair.

"Oh my goodness!" the woman said in surprise.

"C-c-can we have s-some matches? Ours are all wet," David stammered timidly as he opened his hand to reveal the wet, faded matchbook.

"Matches? What for?" she asked.

"T-to m-make a fire."

The people stared at him in disbelief.

"What are you doing outside in the cold?" the man asked.

"H-he kicked u-us out again."

The woman let out a tiny gasp as she stared at the boy. This was one of the Pischke twins standing before her. He'd grown since she'd seen him last. They had been neighbours in Ashern and she hadn't seen Caroline much after she moved back to the farm.

The woman looked at the boy and couldn't believe how he was dressed for the frigid weather. He had no toque or mitts and wore a thin, spring jacket over what looked like a torn, short-sleeved shirt. His pants were obviously too small and made for summer wear. He wore a pair of worn felt rubbers which in her opinion, were not warm enough for a child in the winter.

The boy's clothes had somehow become wet and were now frozen stiff. There were dark circles under his eyes and his skin was a ghastly grey colour. His eyes had lost the bright inquisitiveness that she remembered and if it hadn't been for the crazy stutter, she might not have recognized him at all.

"You said 'we'. Is there somebody with you?"

David looked towards the road. "D-dennis."

The woman stuck her head outside and looked down the driveway. She could see a shadowy figure standing near the road.

"You boys have to come inside before you freeze," she said. "Tell your brother it's o.k. to come."

David looked at the woman. She was tall and pretty with curly dark hair and soft brown eyes. He felt comfortable as she spoke, her soft German accent twirling around the words in a way he longed for. Her husband was tall with dark hair and he looked to be a gentle person as well. In his soft voice, he agreed with his wife that that boys should come inside. Just then, two young heads appeared from behind their father. One was a boy who looked to be a few years older than David while the other was a much younger boy with a bright smile. These people looked vaguely familiar, but David's mind was still too foggy to think straight. The heat that escaped from the house through the open door felt good.

"Go call him," the woman coaxed.

David put the soggy matches back in his pocket and stepped off the stoop. He motioned for Dennis and called for him to come. Dennis responded by walking slowly toward the house. David stepped closer to the stoop, but waited for his brother before going inside.

"It's alright Denny," he said in their language. "These people are good."

Dennis stood timidly behind his brother as they stepped inside. The man came forward and closed the door behind them. The boys' cheeks burned from the sudden heat of the wood stove that crackled warmly nearby.

"I'll get you some dry clothes," the woman said as she disappeared into the other room. The husband and boys stood looking at the twins, who stared at the ground as they took off their rubber boots.

"I'm Kenny," the older boy said.

"An' I'm Alvin," the little boy said. "Who are you?"

"Shhh, " their mother chided when she returned, carrying an armful of fresh clothes. "Give them a chance to settle in before you start asking a whole mess of questions."

The woman divided up the clothes, fussing as she wondered if they would fit properly. She looked down at their swollen, red feet.

"Where are your socks?"

"W-we don't got n-none."

The boys climbed out of their stiff clothes and the woman winced at the sight of them. The boys were covered in bruises, especially Dennis. She turned away out of politeness, as the boys pulled on the warm, heavy underwear, thick pants and flannel shirts. The clothes were too big, but were a noticeable improvement over what they'd arrived in.

"Are you boys hungry?"

Dennis looked at David. "Yes, ma'am."

"Well come sit down, I've got some left overs from supper that you can have."

The boys walked timidly to the table and looked out of the corner of their eyes as Kenny and Alvin watched them closely. Their hosts were anxious to hear what had happened.

"So, how did you boys get here?" the man asked.

The twins ate for a moment, then once his mouth was clear, David answered: "We walked across the beaver dam."

"The beaver dam? Do you mean Pischke lake?"

"Yeah."

"You walked all that way, in the dark, by yourselves?"

"Yeah. I kept followin' the light an' a few times Dennis wanted to go to sleep but I wouldn't let him."

"How come you ran away?"

"Ole Satan got mad an' was shootin' at us."

"Domko?"

"Yeah."

"Shooting?"

"Yeah. W-we ran in the bush an' the bullets went by our h-head."

Kenny and Alvin listened in awe as the twins described what had happened that evening. As they warmed up and began to trust the family, the two visitors began telling this family some of the other things that Domko had done.

The adults listened in stunned silence, as the twins alternated telling the family about Domko's rages and how he threatened to kill people.

"An' he always comes to get us or makes mom come. Emma had to hide us, 'cause he came with the gun an' he said he'd shoot Gus if we went there any more so we stopped goin'. "

When the boys had finished eating, Kenny and Alvin were told to take the twins into the front room.

"What should we do?" the woman asked her husband.

He shook his head in disbelief. He'd heard many stories about Domko but until that day had thought they must be exaggerated rumours coming from overactive imaginations.

"We could call Margaret."

His wife thought for a moment and glanced at her watch. It was close to 11 p.m.

"Should I call her tonight?"

"You'd better. Someone had better get over to that farm to check on Caroline and the rest of those kids. Who knows how many of them are wandering around in the snow?"

His wife agreed. She went to the telephone and dialed the health nurse's home phone number.

"This is Anna Koch," she said when Margaret groggily answered the phone. "It looks as if Domko is up to his old tricks again. We've got the Pischke twins here at our place." Pause. "They got here less than an hour ago." Pause. "Half froze! One boy was half out of his mind standing at the door, asking for matches. They must have walked four miles to get here across that lake. Leo says it is a miracle that they didn't get lost in the reeds. If there had been only one of them, he likely wouldn't have made it at all." Pause. "He tried to shoot them." Pause. "O.k., we'll wait up."

Anna gave her husband a confident nod. Margaret would be there soon and she'd know what to do.

Trying to put Alvin back to bed that night was next to impossible. The youngster had been asleep for almost two hours when the boys arrived, enough of a rest to keep him going for the rest of the night. His parents knew he'd never sleep with all the excitement of the twins arrival, so they let him stay up longer.

The boys sat and talked while Alvin brought out his toys. This pleased the twins who pushed the cars along the floor and across the chesterfield. Both had shooting pains in their feet as they warmed up, but barely complained as they rubbed their toes and played. Leo and Anna sat and watched as the twins began to relax and feel comfortable in their surroundings.

Soon afterwards, a set of lights shone through the front room window as a car slowly turned in the driveway. Leo stood and looked out.

"Who is it?" Anna whispered. "Is it Margaret?"

"I can't tell," he said. "What kind of car does Domko drive?"

"It's not him is it? Would he come looking for the boys at this hour?"

A look of utter terror came over the twins' faces. The family watched in disbelief as the boys ran from the front room into the bedroom, in one motion hit the floor and slid stomach first under the bed. The edge of the quilt swayed for a moment, then stopped. Not another movement or sound came from the bedroom.

"Is it him?" Kenny asked.

His father cautiously went to the kitchen window. He knew by his parents' expressions that they were concerned it might be Domko. He envisioned Domko bursting into the house carrying a gun and shooting his parents.

Kenny's heart throbbed and his throat became thick as he wondered what to do. He wanted to get his father's gun, but didn't want to overreact. He thought of the boys' fear and then wondered if overreacting was possible when it came to Domko.

Although nobody said anything, little Alvin could sense that something was wrong. His playmates had suddenly disappeared under the bed with such urgency that he'd been frightened by it. He didn't know who this horrible Domko was but he knew he never, ever wanted to see him face to face. He stood behind Kenny as his parents went to the kitchen door.

Kenny prepared himself for the worst. If it was Domko, he'd sneak around and pick up the gun and load it. He vowed to protect his family although the thought of a violent confrontation caused his body to quake with fear. He listened as his father opened the door and began talking to whomever had come. A few moments later Kenny could tell the voices were friendly. He peered around the front room wall to see the health nurse and her driver standing in kitchen.

"They're in here," Anna said as she led Margaret to the front room. Pointing to the bedroom doorway and the double bed. "Under there."

Margaret looked at her and tsked: "The poor little guys."

"You should have seen them, Margaret, it was awful. We didn't mean to scare them," Anna said looking at her husband. "We though you might be Domko and the boys overheard. Well, they shot off the chesterfield like a pair of scared jack rabbits and slid under that bed so fast - I've just never seen anything like it in my entire life. I've never seen anybody so scared before."

Leo nodded in approval. Anna was relaying the story well, so he stood back and let her do most of the talking.

Margaret walked slowly into the bedroom. Kneeling down, she slowly lifted the quilt.

"Boys, it's me, Mrs. Burnett," she said gently in her lilting accent. "You can come out now."

There was still no sound or movement from under the bed.

"It's alright, I'm alone. Domko's not here and he won't be coming neither," she said. "I'm here to help you, not take you back to the farm, but I need you to come out and talk to me first."

A few seconds passed, and she heard some whispering from under the bed. The boys were deciding in their language if this was one of Domko's tricks. They recognized the English accent and knew that Mrs. Burnett always tried to help them. Slowly, they slid out from under the bed.

Margaret's harsh voice softened as she sat down. She reached out as the twins inched towards her, each starting to cry softly.

The deplorable circumstances these boys were living with caused a lump to rise in Anna's throat.

The twins were uncomfortable at first, but once they began talking to Margaret, the flood gates opened and they told her everything that had happened. Anna glanced towards the door which sat ajar, and saw Dennis lift up his shirt. Margaret gently reached out and carefully turned him around. Anna looked away, feeling the boys' shame as they revealed private, degrading truths.

The Kochs busied themselves with other things. Everyone except Alvin who stood curiously by the door.

"Come away from there," Anna said as she picked him up. "Enough excitement for you for one evening. It's time to go to bed."

"Aw, Momma, I wanna stay up an' play with Dennis an' David."

She carried him into the boys' small bedroom. She consoled him by saying that if the boys were still there in the morning, he could play with them all day if he liked. The little boy continued to protest, but suddenly was worn out from the evening's excitement and fell into a deep sleep.

The interview took about fifteen minutes. Margaret appeared from inside the room, with the boys following closely behind her.

"You boys sit down while I make a phone call," she said. With steely resolve, she walked towards the phone. She took a deep breath, then picked up the receiver.

"Yes, this is an emergency," she said. "Put me through to the RCMP."

The family watched as Margaret's call coaxed a tired officer out of bed. She turned away from the Koch family in the interest of confidentiality and began explaining the situation to the officer. She listened for a moment, then told him more. She listened and then in an exasperated tone, made the situation and her feelings quite clear.

"I don't care what time it is," she said between clenched teeth. "Something has to be done tonight!" Pause. "Yes." Pause. "Yes, jail. It's the only way." Pause. "I won't tolerate anything less and if need be, I'll be on the phone all day tomorrow." Pause. "Who knows what's happening in that house this very moment. That whole family could be dead!" Pause. "On the grounds that he needs a psychiatric evaluation." Pause. "Thank you and good-bye."

Margaret hung up the phone, her hand shaking. "It took some prodding but the RCMP are coming tonight." she said. "I'm going to meet them and we're going to the farm. Would you mind keeping the boys here until we have everything settled?"

Anna looked at her husband.

"Not at all," he said with a strong smile. "We'll keep those boys as long as needed."

Margaret smiled. She didn't have to tell the Kochs how pleased she was to hear this.

The twins slept on the Koch's chesterfield which folded out into a bed. They awoke the following morning to the smell of breakfast. Anna insisted they eat their fill and the boys happily complied. The twins offered to help with chores to earn their keep.

The Kochs brushed off the suggestion, encouraging the boys to relax and play with Alvin who stuck to the boys like chewing gum on a shoe.

He asked the boys question upon question about how they escaped from Domko and where they had hidden. It got to the point where Anna had to ask the boys to ignore Alvin's questions, since the five year old was beginning to scare himself.

The phone rang early that afternoon. Anna answered and had a long discussion with the caller. When she hung up, she called the boys and told them that their mother, Eunice and Raymond were fine but they hadn't found Rosie yet. The police had taken Domko to jail, and that's all the caller knew. Anna had made the person promise to call her back as soon as she heard anything else. The boys seemed pleased that Domko had been taken to jail, but reserved since they'd lived with fear so long they'd grown accustomed to it.

Early the next morning, the phone rang and Anna was relieved to hear that Rosie had been located unharmed, burrowed in a haystack somewhere on the farm. She'd been so traumatized by the events of the past few weeks, that the shooting had sent her into hiding. She'd been too frightened to come out. Domko was now at the hospital and the boys were to stay at Kochs until it was safe for them to go home.

That afternoon the twins looked at the calendar and realized that the following day was their 13th birthdays. Alvin immediately told their mother who, with a twinkle in her eye, began secret preparations.

The next day the twins were unaware of the whispers and quiet plans that were being made on their behalf. Everyone was excited, and Alvin looked as if he was going to burst at the seams with the secret. Anna and Kenny kept hushing him whenever it appeared he would spoil the plans.

Everyone rushed to finish the evening chores, and Dennis and David eagerly helped, not understanding why. After supper while everyone sat at the table, the lights were dimmed and Anna produced a birthday cake. She and Alvin broke into a chorus of 'Happy Birthday' while Leo and Kenny, not wanting to draw attention to their singing voices, mumbled softly along.

Anna put the cake on the table in front of the twins as they looked in wonder at the thick icing and beautifully lit candles.

"Make a wish and blow out the candles," she said, sitting down. She watched the boy's faces in the glint of the candle light as each thoughtfully closed his eyes tight and whispered a silent wish. She felt her eyes fill with tears, knowing what they'd wished for.

Then they opened their eyes and looking around, took in a deep breath.

"Wait fer me!" Alvin exclaimed as he stood on his chair. Kenny tried to hold him back but let out a spit-filled blow at the same time as the twins, causing the candles to go out and everyone to laugh.

"You're not supposed to," Kenny scolded quietly.

"You always let me!" he said jumping off the chair. "Can I bring 'em now Momma?"

"Yes, but don't open them."

"I won't," he said indignantly as he disappeared to where he'd hid the gifts. The twins were surprised when Alvin appeared and plopped a present on each boy's lap. Leo got up and switched on the kitchen light. His eyes glinted softly as he watched the boy's expression as they fumbled with the gift wrap.

Anna wrung her hands as she watched.

"It's not much and maybe you boys would like somethin' else . . ." she said, her voice trailing off just as each boy unwrapped a pair of socks.

"Davey, look," Dennis whispered in wonder. "New socks."

"Yeah," David said examining them closely. "Look, Denny - store boughten ones. They still got the tags on."

The boys carefully set the new socks down on the table, as Anna reached across to hand them the knife.

"Now, wait," she said mockingly. "Twins - hmmm, I wonder who gets to cut first."

"I do!" David said almost jumping off his chair.

"No, I do!" Dennis argued.

Pulling back the knife, she needed a fair answer to this serious birthday question.

"Which one of you was born first?" she asked.

"I was!" David said again.

"No, I was an' you know it!" Dennis said. "Momma said so, 'member? She said you was in such a big hurry to get out an' I was in the way so you kicked me out first."

Everyone laughed at Dennis' story and David pretended to pout.

"Well, it's decided Dennis cuts first," Anna said handing him the knife.

Dennis stood and cut himself a big, thick piece of chocolate cake then handed the knife to his twin. David looked at how much Dennis took. Never one to be outdone, he took an even bigger piece. The boys sat and began eating the cake as Anna served the remainder.

That night, as the twins climbed into bed holding their socks, they discussed the day. They agreed this was the happiest day they'd ever had, comparing it to going to the zoo and having Christmas at with Deightons.

Dennis took his socks and put them under his pillow while David stroked them gently across his cheek. The socks smelled so fresh and new. He laid them on top of his pillow then fell asleep.

The boys stayed at the Kochs farm for nearly ten days. Anna received a phone call but kept the conversation to herself, telling Leo but not the boys.

The twins began to notice a change in her, that she seemed distant and they tried to think of what had made her unhappy.

"We musta done somethin'," Dennis said as they relaxed in bed that night. "Whadda you think?"

David thought back to each day, trying to remember something that might have made her angry or upset. Then it came to him, and his face flushed with embarrassment as he remembered.

"I know what it was," he said, a lump rising in his throat. "I took too much cake."

Dennis remembered. He'd take a lot too. Even Kenny, who was three years older, hadn't taken a piece that big.

The boys eventually fell asleep and spent most of the next day embarrassed by their gluttonous ways. They told Anna that they hadn't had cake since they lived in Ashern and that sometimes, well, they just couldn't control themselves. The boys skirted around the subject and watched her expression, which never seemed to change. Anna still looked sad.

That afternoon Caroline arrived with Herman Gall. The boys tried to hide, begging the Koch's not to tell her where they were.

Caroline was invited in and the boys were coaxed out of the bedroom into the kitchen. They'd missed their mother, but the thought of going back into the same wretched circumstances was more than either child could bear. Dennis and David began crying as they begged her to leave them there.

"Hush now!" Caroline said, a hint of sadness in her voice. "You boys don't have to worry no more. Domko's gone. He's gone to the hospital in Selkirk."

"Gone?" Dennis asked sobbing, his voice rising in hope.

"Yes," she said her voice wavering. ". . . and he won't be coming back."

Chapter 29

Life without Domko

DOMKO WAS ADMITTED TO the Selkirk Mental Health Centre on February 6, 1961 after the Justice of the Peace at Ashern signed an order of committal supported by a medical certificate from Doctor Steenson. Caroline accompanied her husband to the hospital and stayed until he adjusted to his new surroundings.

After returning home, she contacted the hospital on a regular basis, discovering that Domko's discharge date was set for December 20. In the meantime, she would have to manage financially and supervise the operation of the farm without him. The children were overjoyed and life was better than it had ever been.

Life for the children had gone from unbearable to unbelievably good. While they still had to work before and after school, they did so with enthusiasm. A new attitude prevailed - they wanted to prove to everyone that they didn't need Domko in their lives. They could do the farm work themselves.

Margaret Burnett visited the family a few times over the next few weeks, bringing a basket full of food on one occasion. Because Domko controlled the family bank account the only money Caroline had was from the sale of the cream each week. She thanked Margaret for the food and said that once they got on their feet, things would be much better.

The twins had never been happier. They ate regularly and while the food was not fancy, they were never begrudged a meal by their mother. She complained that there wasn't enough money, but this was of no concern to the children who worked, played and went to school.

Caroline had a telephone installed, which the children thought was an excellent idea. Later they overheard frugal women in the community complain that Caroline was wasteful with her money, that she made frivolous purchases instead of paying bills. The children didn't care about this though. To them all that mattered was that their stepfather was gone.

The months flew by. Kathy returned home from Brantford and the family was happy to see her. She was anxious to sit with her father so Caroline explained that he was in the hospital and would be back soon. This seemed to satisfy the little girl who had learned some manners and now spoke clearer than she had when she left.

There were visits from Caroline's church friends who had mixed reactions to her husband's hospitalization. Those who were afraid of Domko agreed that he needed psychiatric help while those who sided with him believed that Caroline and the children were the ones responsible for putting him in the mental hospital. This group argued that seeking psychiatric help was 'evil' and that more obedience and patience from Caroline and the children would remedy Domko's condition.

One afternoon a man from the Ashern congregation visited Caroline and the children. He was new to the area and came by to introduce himself. He was of medium height, he had blonde hair and a smooth, convincing voice, but the children sensed there was something insincere about him. When he looked at them, he curled his lip as if he was seeing something distasteful.

Caroline politely invited him inside and they made small talk. He asked her a lot of questions, about the farm, Domko, the children and her studies. She soon became uncomfortable, believing he had been sent to spy on her. She felt he would report to the others how 'unworthy' she was.

This angered Caroline who desperately wanted to fit in and be accepted by the Witnesses. But they seemed to belong to a secret club with a set of unspoken rules. Rules that she didn't instinctively know how to follow. She always felt she was on the brink of being thrown out of the religion. Since only the best would be rewarded, it seemed to her that she fit nowhere.

Because of her religion, she had no friends on the 'outside' and an unsympathetic family as well. If shunned by the congregation, she would suddenly be all alone.

To be kicked out of the church would be an awful disgrace for herself and her family. She'd been conditioned to rely on the church members who had convinced that all other religions and beliefs were evil. She desperately needed to cling to a religious dogma and considered herself a devout Jehovah's Witness, even if nobody else did.

One morning in early June, Caroline took Raymond with her when she arranged a ride to Moosehorn. Word was sent back that the twins were to start the tractor, drive it to town and pick up their mother and brother. Seldom allowed to touch the tractor, the boys had a difficult time getting it started.

"I think it's the battery, whadda you think?" David said.

"Maybe. It hasn't been started for so long. Maybe it needs to be warmed up?" Dennis suggested.

Bending over, David unscrewed a little knob on top of the battery and peered in. "I think I know what the problem is," he said confidently as he loosened the clasp that held the battery to the mount near the engine. "I think it needs more water. I can see some in there, but it stinks pretty bad. I figure that if we put some fresh water, in it will work."

He lifted the battery off the mount and turned it upside down to drain it. A stream of stinky liquid spilled all over the front of his shirt and pants.

"Yuk!" he said as he shook the battery.

Carrying it to the outdoor pump, the boys re-filled the battery with water. They attached it back to the mount, but were still unable to get the tractor started.

"I hope mom ain't waitin' for us," Dennis said.

"Somebody will give her a ride if she is," David said. "I just don't know what's wrong with this tractor."

Finally, the boys gave up and went outside to play 'kick the can'. They played for a while then stopped to watch as a car pulled slowly in the driveway.

The twins couldn't believe what they were seeing. Domko was sitting on the passenger side of the car.

"Oh no, he's back!" Dennis exclaimed.

They watched as their mother and Raymond got out of the back seat and she thanked a neighbour for the ride. Domko stepped out of the car, opened the back passenger door and lifted out his duffel bag.

The boys hearts sank. Now it all made sense! Their mother had been making a lot of phone calls lately. She must have been arranging for Domko's return without telling them!

The twins were angry at her and decided they would never speak to her again because of this betrayal. After all the hard work they'd done, it was very insulting to have Domko suddenly re-appear.

The twins watched from a distance as their mother led Domko into the house. He glanced towards them as he passed, but there was no expression on his face.

"She looks happy! How can she be happy?" Dennis asked. "He smashes her and tries to kill us and then she goes an' picks him up!"

"I'm gonna talk to mom as soon as she's alone," David said trying to sound authoritative. "She just can't do this to us."

The twins went to the door and waited. They opened it slightly and peered in, listening to their mother and stepfather talking in quiet tones. David waited until Domko went to the bedroom for a nap, then went into the kitchen.

"I'm waitin' out here," Dennis said indignantly as he sat on the ground and folded his arms.

Caroline stood humming softly by the stove as she prepared supper.

"Ma," David said. "How come he's home?"

Caroline turned to her son. "Because this is his farm too."

"But Ma, we thought he was stayin' in the hospital 'til December. How come they let him out?"

"He's improved so much that they let him come home on what's called 'probation.' He's really a lot better now. You'll see, David. He's got some medicine that makes his head feel better and the doctor said that as long as he takes it, he'll be o.k."

"Was he mad that me an' Denny didn't pick you guys up with the tractor?" David prodded. "We couldn't get it started, you know. We didn't do it on purpose."

Caroline looked as if she didn't believe him.

David awoke the next morning and all was quiet in the house. For a moment, he had to think hard to remember if it had been a nightmare or was Domko really back? He sat up in bed to discover that the clothes he had on when he fell asleep were mostly gone. The buttons from his shirt tinkled from his chest onto the bed, attached to tiny scraps of what had been his shirt. He felt around and discovered he still had on the collar and one sleeve. The back of the shirt dangled from the collar. Little bits of shirt were scattered throughout the bed. Looking down, he discovered the front of his pants were also gone almost up to the knees.

"Dennis! Wake up!" he said. "Look, my clothes are gone."

Dennis rolled over and woke with a start, also remembering that Domko was home. He looked around sleepily for a moment, but closed his eyes again after realizing they were in no immediate danger.

"Look!" David exclaimed. "Where'd my clothes go?"

Dennis looked at him and laughed. David looked very silly with just a collar and one arm covered.

"I gotta get some clothes on before Squeezer sees me," he said. "You run down an' look through the box."

Dennis nodded and climbed out of bed. He went quietly downstairs to the box of second hand clothes that lay at the bottom of the stairs. He searched through the box, throwing dirty items on the floor in search of something clean underneath. This was the box that Domko exchanged twice a year except that spring. Now the selection was minimal. The children wore the clothes until they were either too dirty or too ragged to put on again. Caroline instructed them to pile the dirty clothes beside the box for washing, but it seemed she never got around to washing it.

Dennis found a pair of blue plaid polyester pants and a beige and brown checked shirt then ran back upstairs.

"They were good pants too," David mumbled as he removed what was left of his clothes. Dennis threw the clean ones on the bed.

"What the hell?" David said picking up the pants which had big holes in the knees. "I already put these at the bottom of the box a few times. I don't wanna wear these!"

"It's all there was," Dennis said, chuckling at his brother's indignation. David gave him a dirty look then pulled on the pants. "I gotta go to school like this? An' the worst goddamned part is that flatfoot is gonna say I broke them. Are you sure there's nothin' else?"

The commotion awoke the girls who had been sleeping on the floor mattress.

"Hey, Beanie, look at David's pants," Dennis chuckled.

Eunice looked at her brother standing in the middle of the floor and rolled her eyes. "We're poor enough without you wearin' them to school. Where'd your other pants go?"

"I dunno - they just fell off! I think some moths must have ate them in the night," he said. Eunice didn't look like she believed him, so he grabbed the collar and remainder of his pants.

"See!" he said, following her down the stairs.

She glanced at the rags he carried but since he offered no decent explanation, she refused to believe him.

Exasperated, he ran back upstairs and into their hiding place behind the wall. He stuffed the rags under the eaves, hoping Domko would never find them. Then he hurried to school before Domko woke up.

That afternoon the classroom was warm and bright and smelled of little children's sweat. In June it was always difficult keeping the children focused on the lesson, since they thought only of playing outside in the sunshine.

The students were anxious for afternoon recess and whispered back and forth about who was still on second base in their baseball game which continued for many days.

As Mrs. Gering sent the children outside for the last break of the day, she said she had an important announcement to make when they came back. This piqued the children's interest as they ran outdoors. When the teacher rang the bell, they returned promptly and chattered loudly as they sat in their seats.

Mrs. Gering waited patiently at her desk, but said nothing until everybody was quiet. A chorus of 'ssshhh!' drifted through the room until there was silence.

"Do you remember the drawings that you all sent in for the art contest?" she began.

The children nodded that they did.

"Well, I have some very good news," she said bending over her desk and picking up a big, brown envelope. "One of you has won second place in the contest."

The children gasped and looked around. They all hoped that they were the lucky artist. They watched as Mrs. Gering opened the envelope.

"The winner has won a certificate, a set of encyclopedias and a $50 bond that will be held in trust until he or she finishes grade eight."

The children cheered as the tension built in the room.

"Do you want to know who the winner is?"

"Yes!" they cheered.

"Alright," she said pulling out the certificate. "It says here, that the winner is . . . David Pischke!"

All eyes turned to David who beamed with pride. Some of the children sighed in disappointment, but most cheered and clapped in congratulations.

"Come on up here David to see your new books," Mrs. Gering said.

David stood up and proudly walked to the front of the room. He'd forgotten about the huge holes in his pants. Normally he would have been teased about these pants but none of the students dared say a word. David was by all accounts a local hero.

Mrs. Gering stood and presented him with the certificate. She told him that when a person receives such an honor, it is customary to shake hands with the presenter. He blushed as he shook her hand and took the certificate.

"Now, I have the set of encyclopedias here and if it's alright with David, I'd like to suggest that he open up the boxes and give everyone a chance to see the books before he takes them home. Is that alright with you?"

"S-sure," he smiled.

"Well, here you go," she said, handing him the first box. He took the carton to the side shelf and broke open the top. He pulled out the books as the children gathered around him. He opened one and was fascinated by all the beautiful pictures and wonderfully clean, shiny pages.

Mrs. Gering watched closely, checking everyone's hands before allowing them to touch the new books. David noticed this and wiped his hands on his shirt, before picking up another book.

The students spent the rest of the afternoon looking through David's new books. When it was time to go home, everyone had to take the books back to him.

Mrs. Gering dismissed the class then took David aside. She told him to bring the wheelbarrow the next day or have his mother come in the car after school to take the books home. Then she reached out and gave his shoulder an affectionate squeeze.

As David skipped home that afternoon, he recalled how this day had started poorly, but had turned out excellently in the afternoon. Drawing had always been his favourite pastime and now he had been rewarded for his efforts.

He wondered if there were people in Winnipeg who had jobs drawing. At that moment, he decided that if this was the case, it was the job he wanted to do when he grew up. He thought of everything that looked as if it had been drawn - comic books, pictures in the Eatons catalogue, food labels and even the encyclopedias had drawings in them!

That's what I'm gonna do, he thought as he sauntered into the kitchen, his heart bursting with pride. He felt Domko didn't deserve to share in the good news and was pleased to find him napping.

"Ma, guess what?" he beamed.

"What?" she answered in a distracted tone.

"I found out that I won second place in Manitoba for my art," he said.

"What?" she asked.

"A contest, I got second place in a contest an' guess what I got? Look here, a certificate with my name on it an' I got a set of encyclopedia books an' fifty dollars that they're gonna give me when I finish grade eight."

"All that for drawin' a picture?" she asked.

"Yeah, isn't that good?"

She turned to face him and placed her hands on her hips. Her eyes filled with anger and then she exploded.

"What? Is that what I'm sending you to school for? To draw?"

"No, Ma, it's not like that . ." he interrupted.

"Yes it is if you're enterin' contests when you should be reading and learning arithmetic. What kind of a school is this anyway? And this new teacher of yours, what what is she doing, wasting time teaching art?"

"But Ma, I won all this good stuff," he said, shocked by his mother's reaction.

"I don't care about none of that. You'd better not let Domko hear about no art contests and encyclopedia books. Drawin' pictures will never get you anywhere in life an' I don't want to talk about it no more. Remember what the Bible says: 'Bad associations spoil useful habits.'"

Crushed, David slowly walked to the barn. His ego had been deflated and he finished the chores without a word to his siblings. When he came in the house, Domko watched him carefully as he went quietly upstairs and took the folded certificate out of the breast pocket of his shirt. He pressed it flat on the bed and admired it for a while. Then he folded it again and crawled behind the wall, concealing it in the sawdust insulation of the eaves.

The next morning when he went downstairs, his mother let all the other children go to school but kept David home. She made him go outside to work, assigning him extra chores and saying that he wasn't learning anything at school anyway. Domko sat and chuckled as David stormed outside.

Caroline hoped to make an example of David to the other children. She refused to let him go to school for the remainder of the week. She reasoned that he'd been much too 'full of himself' when he'd won the contest. She felt that his accomplishments should be less selfish so that he could do a better job of serving God.

The following Monday, David went to school and Mrs. Gering casually asked him when he wanted to take the books home. He said he would take them by the end of the week, but too embarrassed to face her again, he skipped Friday classes and left the books at school.

To the children's surprise, it appeared that Domko really had improved.

While still leery of him, they didn't live in constant fear like they did before. He was much more subdued, almost childlike as he demanded that Caroline look after his every need. She did so, but the older children could see that after a few weeks, she was beginning to tire of this. She made a few sarcastic comments about him being 'just like Raymie', and the children chuckled quietly to themselves.

Domko now kept himself clean, shaving and washing himself at the basin every day. He was calm, and almost pleasant, but still regarded the children, especially the twins, with suspicion. He didn't swear as much, and actually said hardly anything at all. What surprised them most was that he wouldn't allow Caroline into his bed. He explained that he'd grown accustomed to sleeping by himself at the hospital and now enjoyed it very much. She slept upstairs and within two weeks of his return, she was becoming increasingly resentful. To escape her sarcasm he would go outside and putter around the yard.

The children did the haying that year without Domko watching them for the first time . He complained of being too tired and having headaches that made him unable to work. He seemed to only enjoy two things - spoiling Raymond and his hobby of raising pigeons. He spent hours building roosts and caring for the birds. The twins discovered that he was still an excellent marksman, shooting hawks out of the air as they swooped down on his pet birds.

Caroline and the children went to the Jehovah's Witness gathering in Winnipeg again this summer. They rode with a family from the church. This time, Eunice went along because Domko refused to go. He kept Raymond and Kathy at home also, because he wanted to raise his children Roman Catholic.

Caroline and the children arrived home two days later. Domko was walking from the barn carrying pails of milk, when he noticed them standing in the driveway. He flew into a rage, dropped the milk and ran to get his gun. The friends from the church quickly drove away while Caroline yelled for the children to run in the bush. This time she followed and they walked cross-country to her brother's farm near Faulkner. They slept in his barn for nearly a week, before her brother persuaded her to go home.

Domko was back to his old self.

In early August, he became ill and begged Caroline to take him to the hospital. Domko was admitted with a severe case of bronchitis. While there, he became very suspicious of people he was not familiar with. He was friendly to the nurses but forced Caroline to tell him each nurse's last name.

If it was a German name, he would not listen to the nurse and refuse his medication, fearing she was trying to poison him.

He began demanding more of the children and complained that if Caroline didn't stop working him so hard, she was going to kill him. This nonsense caused her to stop talking to him, which made him even more belligerent.

One afternoon late in the month, the Witness from Ashern came to visit.

Caroline wasn't pleased to see this man again, realizing that he'd been 'assigned' to her home. Reluctantly she let him inside and discovered that he and Domko got along quite well to her dismay. They joined in criticizing Caroline who still kept a dirty house.

"How can I keep a clean house when I have so much to do around the farm?" she argued.

"You? Vat you's be doink? Nuthink! You ant them lazy keets be doink nuthink. I's be seek ant be doink it all!"

Caroline tried to argue but there was no point. It was obvious that the visitor sided with her husband. She left the pair to talk and kept her opinions to herself.

Eunice and the twins didn't start school in September. Instead, David was kept home to do chores while Eunice and Dennis were sent to a neighbouring farm owned by the Gall family to help with threshing. This was hard work but they didn't mind since they were treated like young adults instead of children. They enjoyed listening to the men tell jokes and grown-up stories during the lunch and coffee breaks.

They brought along Domko's equipment which, by the neighbours' standards, was quite antiquated. They worked for three weeks under the supervision of Arnold Gall who was Robert Gall's oldest son. Arnold was a short heavy man about 30 years of age with a big face, bushy black hair and jack-o-lantern teeth.

Neighbourhood children called him a retard because his thinkin processes were a little slower than everybody else. As a youngster, Arnold was injured by an enraged bull that left him fighting for his life and not quite the same when he eventually recovered.

It didn't take Eunice and Dennis long to discover Arnold's weakness. They were soon harassing him and he was equally nasty back. To annoy him, they'd throw dried cow manure at him when he turned his back. This infuriated Arnold who would chase them, but never caught the quick teenagers because of his size. After three weeks of working together, a friendly hate had been built up between Arnold and his two helpers.

Near the end of September, Caroline felt that Domko's moods were worsening, and she attributed it to the onset of fall. An empty pill bottle on his bureau revealed that he had finished all his medication.

"How long have you been off your pills?" she asked one morning.

"I's not be know," he said. "Two, maybe tree weeks."

"Well, we have to get you some more," she said. Caroline knew how disruptive it was for the body to be suddenly taken off regular medication. "You're still on probation and you have to take your medication the entire time."

"You's not be tellink me!" he said as he strode out of the house.

Caroline contacted Margaret Burnett soon afterwards and explained the situation. Domko was beginning to lose his temper with the children again. While she didn't tell this to Margaret, he had beaten one of them the night before, the first time since his return.

He'd bought himself another gun, since the police had confiscated the others, and kept it by his bed. Caroline could not afford to buy gas to take him to the doctor and she was reluctant to ask a neighbour since then they'd gossiped so much lately about her. Margaret told her not to worry and arrived the next day with the police. They persuaded him to go back to Selkirk for a check-up. He handed them his gun and went willingly with the police.

With Domko gone, Eunice and the twins decided they wanted to go to town. They'd never been to Moosehorn by themselves and thought this would be an exciting adventure. They asked their mother for permission to go and she agreed, saying that if they found a ride, she would give them each of them enough money for a hamburger and coke.

Elated, Eunice ran to get Marjorie and dragged her back to the house. They needed her wisdom to arrange the details of their outing.

After quite a long discussion at the kitchen table, they decided to persuade Arnold Gall to give them a ride.

Marjorie was skeptical. "Why would he want to take you guys to town?" she asked.

"He's the only one we can think of who can drive an' isn't working," Dennis said.

"Yeah, but because he's so slow it's like he's our age," Eunice said.

"I don't know," Marjorie said. "What will you say to him?"

"Maybe if we just ask him nice to take us, he will," David said.

"Not a chance!" Eunice and Dennis chorused. "We teased him too much. He hates us!"

Then they all looked at Marjorie.

"If you came along, he'd take us for sure," Eunice said.

"ME? No way! I'm not going to pretend to be his girlfriend," she exclaimed.

"Oh, come on Marjie it'll be fun!" Eunice coaxed.

"Fun? For who? Sorry, but you will have to find somebody else."

Realizing the bait had refused the hook, the teenagers started to think about another girl.

"Alright, what about Eunice?" David suggested. "She's a girl, sorta. He might like her."

"Me? An' Arnold Gall? You can go lay an egg!" Eunice laughed.

"C'mon Eunice, he likes girls, you heard the men teasin' him that he's never had no girlfriend," Dennis said. "If you call him, he'll take us."

"Yeah, an' you're beautiful, too." David said trying not to laugh.

"Shuddup!" Eunice said, punching him in the arm.

"C'mon Eunice he won't take us without you," Dennis said.

"I'll go but I'm not sittin' with him," she said.

"Hmm. Eunice an' Marjie won't be his girlfriend, so who can we get?" Dennis wondered.

"Too bad we don't have some unsuspectin' cousin that we could bring along," David laughed.

The teens sat quietly for a moment, then Marjorie, David and Eunice looked at Dennis who was thinking very hard about who could be Arnold's girlfriend. They looked at each other and laughed.

"Dennnnnis," David sang. "I've got an ideeeeea!"

Dennis suddenly felt all eyes upon him. He realized what they were thinking and jumped back.

"No!" he screamed. "Not me! I'm not gonna go nowhere as Arnold's girlfriend!"

"C'mon Dennis, you can do it," Eunice coaxed.

"How about David? Make him do it!"

"I can't 'cause I got a deeper voice than you, he'll know it's me. Besides, you're taller. You can be our older cousin from Winnipeg who's visiting," David said. "C'mon, it'll be fun."

Eunice and Marjorie laughed as they looked Dennis over.

"Hey, stop that!" he said trying to cover his face. Eunice reached out and pulled his hands away. He blushed and started to laugh.

"Come on Dennis, you'll make a great girl. We can dress you up real good and he'll never know."

"Never know? Of course he'll know! I don't look like no girl."

"You will when we finish with you," Eunice said. "An' besides ole Arnold is as dumb as a post. He'll never know the difference."

"C'mon Dennis, just think how good the hamburger and pop will be," David coaxed. "We won't be able to go if you won't do it."

It took some persuading, but Dennis finally agreed.

Caroline, who was listening to the bantering from the front room, let out a howl of delight. The girls jumped up from the table and ran into Domko's bedroom, where Caroline still kept her clothes. She joined in and they returned to the kitchen carrying an armload of things.

The kids were pleased that Caroline was joining in, and Dennis noticed it was the first time in months that he'd seen his mother smile.

"O.k., but first before I put all that girl stuff on, make sure he'll come," Dennis said enjoying being the center of attention.

The children looked at Caroline.

"Ma, you gotta make the call for us," David said. "None of us can do it, 'cause we'll laugh."

"Yeah, Ma, please," Eunice begged. "It'll sound better if it comes from you."

Caroline was pleased to be included in the fun.

"Alright, but you's be quiet," she said.

The kids nodded as Caroline summoned her courage, tried not to laugh, and dialed one long and three short rings to the Gall house.

"Could I talk to Arnold, please" she said into the phone then waited.

"Hello Arnold, it's Caroline Domko." Pause. "I'm fine. I am calling to see if you would be interested in coming to the farm to meet my niece." Pause. "Her name? Ummmm, it's *Mary Maxwell*." Pause "Yes, and if the two of you like you can go to town for a while." Pause. "The cafe would be nice." Pause. "How about two o'clock?" Pause. "Yes? Alright we'll see you then."

The teens held back their laughter until Caroline hung up the phone, then they cheered loudly.

"Well, we'd better hurry, then," Caroline said as she hurried into the kitchen. "We've got less than an hour to make Dennis look like a girl."

"Hey, Ma how did you get the name Mary Maxwell?" David asked.

Caroline laughed as she held up a small catalogue. "It's the name of a pattern company!"

"O.k. Dennis, take off your clothes," Eunice said

"Take off my clothes?"

"Yes, you've got to put these on," she said lifting up a pair of stockings.

"Do I have to take everything off?"

"No, you can leave on your underwear," she said as she lifted up one of her mother's brassieres. "An' you gotta wear this too!"

Dennis and David blushed and turned away from the sight. Eunice took the wide elastic, ample cupped apparatus and giggled at Marjorie as Dennis began stripping off his shirt and pants.

"Lift up your arms," Eunice said cheerfully.

"I'm not puttin' that on!" he yelled and ran to the other end of the kitchen.

"C'mon, we can't have a cousin Mary with a flat chest," Eunice coaxed as she ran behind him. "Otherwise poor old Arnold will be disappointed."

Dennis shrunk from his sister and David fell off his chair and onto the floor. He and Marjorie laughed so hard at the sight of Dennis' discomfort that they could barely catch their breath.

"Dennis," Eunice said in exasperation. "If you're gonna do this, hurry up, we're runnin' outta time."

Dennis rolled his eyes and relaxed. Squeezing his eyes shut, he stuck his arms straight out.

"Good," Eunice said slipping the bra over his arms and fastening it in the back.

She stood back and giggled at the sight of the large bra over his thin white chest.

"Marjie, bring the stockings while David finds something to stuff in here," she said. Dennis grunted as Eunice patted him hard on the chest.

The girls pulled the stockings over his skinny legs just as David returned with an armful of potatoes.

"How 'bout these?" he asked.

The girls took the potatoes and stuffed them inside the bra. Stepping back to observe, the girls adjusted each side to make sure they looked even. Then they helped Dennis pull on a full slip followed by Caroline's favourite dress. They slipped her high heels on his feet, which were about the right size.

"Finally, a use for this," Caroline laughed, as she lifted up an old blonde wig that had showed up one time in the clothes box. She pulled the wig onto Dennis's head and adjusted it.

While the girls covered his face with Caroline's make-up, which she had bought while Domko was in Selkirk, Caroline combed the blonde wig into a 'bouffant' style. Marjorie strung pearls around the twins' neck.

"This don't fit so good," Dennis complained as he adjusted the wig. "It'll fall off if I bend over."

Caroline went to the bedroom and returned with a scarf. She folded it and put it on top of Dennis's head, tying it tightly under his chin.

"Ma, it's too tight now," he complained, his cheeks puffing out from under the scarf. "It's makin' my lips stick out."

"Here, I'll fix that," Eunice said, slathering thick red lipstick across his puckered lips.

Then they all stood back to admire their new cousin, Mary Maxwell.

Everyone bent in laugher except Dennis who hadn't yet seen himself in the mirror.

"What's so funny?" he asked innocently.

By two o'clock, Dennis looked very much like a girl as he practised walking across the floor in his mother's shoes. It took some coaxing, but he agreed to carry a purse and even tried to wiggle his hips as he walked.

Eunice and David were ready to go and the three of them waited anxiously by the door. Dennis wasn't as scared as he thought he'd be. He felt quite unrecognizable in the dress and make-up. For once, he enjoyed being on the other end of a joke.

Caroline gave each of them fifty cents to spend. Arnold drove into the yard at five minutes past two. He got out of the car, dressed in clean clothes and slapped a hand over his freshly Brylcreemed hair.

The children whispered frantically as Caroline opened the door. She invited Arnold in and introduced him to 'Mary', who stood shyly between David and Eunice.

Arnold's eyebrows shot straight up into the air then he smiled. Caroline choked back a giggle and hurried them out the door.

Eunice and David followed close behind their cousin, giving 'her' little nudges since it appeared 'she' was changing her mind about going. When they got to the car, Arnold grunted at Eunice and David.

"We have to come too," Eunice said. "Mary barely knows you."

He smiled at Mary and opened the passenger side door. Mary got in and

Arnold glared at Eunice and David.

"Get in the back!" he said.

David and Eunice climbed in as Arnold started the car. He put his arm across the back of the seat as he backed up, leaving it there as he chatted quietly with Mary.

David pointed to his arm and began to giggle. Eunice slapped her hand over her mouth as she looked out the window.

Arnold shot them an angry glance in the mirror then continued to sweetly tell Mary about 'his' farm and how many cattle he had.

"Yes, uh-huh," Mary said in a sweet voice. She stared straight ahead to avoid looking Arnold directly in the eyes.

The car bumped along and Eunice and David began giggling when the back of Mary's big, babushka-covered head started bobbing up and down.

"What you laughin' at?" Arnold demanded, looking over his shoulder at the two in the back seat. Then shaking his head, he looked back at Mary.

"There's two of them little bastards somewhere," he said pointing at David. "But I don't know where the other one is."

David and Eunice broke into fits of stifled laughter. The sight of Mary holding back a giggle caused them to laugh even harder.

They were thankful to finally arrive in Moosehorn without Arnold any the wiser.

"Where do you want to go?" he asked Mary.

"The cafe," Eunice piped up.

Arnold drove into town and pulled up beside the cafe.

"Get out!" he yelled into the back seat. David and Eunice scrambled out of the car.

Mary reached for the door handle, but Arnold told her that they had another stop to make. He yelled out the window to David and Eunice that he'd be back in a while.

They watched from the sidewalk as Arnold and Mary drove away.

"Where's he goin'?" David asked.

Eunice shook her head. They watched until the car was out of sight then went into the cafe. They sat down, ordered a hamburger and coke, expecting Arnold and Mary to be back in a few minutes. Both agreed that they'd never laughed so hard in all their lives.

"I'm hungry," Mary said bashfully as Arnold drove down the street. He turned then parked in front of the hotel.

"I'll be back in a minute," he said. "You wait here then we'll go back to the cafe."

Mary nodded. Once Arnold had gone inside, she relaxed and adjusted her clothing, hair and bosom. About ten minutes later, a group of men came out of the bar and approached the car. They wanted to see if Arnold really did have a girl waiting in the car. They bent down and looked inside at Mary, who stared straight ahead. Some peered in the front window, then all of them shook their heads and laughed as they left.

Arnold appeared about ten minutes later. He smelled of alcohol and carried a small case of beer. He apologized for keeping her waiting so long, then drove back to the cafe.

Eunice and David were waiting impatiently outside. Afraid that Arnold had discovered who his date really was, they were relieved to see that Mary was still intact and unharmed. Stomachs full, and with no more money left to spend, the pair were anxious to end the charade.

Mary made a faint indication that she was hungry but David and Eunice vetoed the idea of going into the cafe. While waiting on the sidewalk they had agreed that Mary wouldn't blend in very well with the cafe crowd. She looked far more convincing at home than she did in town! To think of their made-up brother trying to eat a hamburger, with a chest full of potatoes! It was a little too embarrassing.

Arnold shrugged in agreement. He'd had a few beer and had long since forgotten that he'd promised to buy Mary a meal. She didn't dare protest because that would mean saying more than two words in a row, so she kept quiet. They left for home a few minutes later.

"We made it," Eunice giggled quietly to David as they arrived back at the farm.

Arnold stopped the car and turned to the teens in the back seat. "Get out!" he yelled.

David and Eunice scrambled out of the car.

Mary, not famous for her quick reaction time, fumbled with the door handle a little too long. In an instant Arnold had backed out of the driveway and turned north on the road. To him, their date had just begun.

Eunice ran into the house. "Ma! Arnold took Dennis!"

Caroline ran outside in time to see nothing but dust as he sped away.

"Oh no!" David exclaimed. "If he finds out, he's gonna kill him."

'Mary' tried to stay calm as Arnold drove to a nice quiet spot where he said they could 'talk'. She looked around, realizing he'd taken her about three miles from home. Her suitor pulled off the road and into the bushes.

"So, Mary how long have you been living in Winnipeg?" he said handing her a bottle of beer.

"All my life," she said refusing the bottle.

"You don't drink?"

"No."

"So, what do you do in Winnipeg?"

"Go to school."

"What kind of school?"

"A big one."

Arnold looked at her and thought for a moment. "You're very shy, aren't you Mary?"

"Y-yes," she stammered, shaking her head.

He put his arm around the back of the seat and moved closer. The weight of his heavy forearm caught Mary's hair and gently tugged the wig backwards.

Giggling softly, she adjusted the wig and tried to move closer to the door. She was thinking about bolting.

Arnold made small talk for a little longer then reached across her chest. Mary closed her eyes and tried to slouch on the seat as Arnold pressed his body against her. Then Arnold puckered his lips and gave Mary a big kiss on the lips. His hand reached gently for her knee and began massaging her thigh.

"Ooohh Noooo," she said trying to sound prudish. "Not on the first date. I'm tooo shy."

Reluctantly, Arnold backed away. They sat and chatted for a few more minutes while Arnold finished his beer. Then he drove her slowly back to the farm.

David and Eunice were waiting by the door when Arnold's car slowly pulled in the yard and came to a stop. This time, Mary jumped out quickly. Arnold grabbed her arm insisting that he walk her to the door. A potato dropped to the ground, which Mary casually kicked aside.

Caroline opened the door. She tried not to laugh at the sight of Mary, obviously frightened and slightly dishevelled. Caroline knew better than to invite Arnold inside.

"Well, I'll see you tomorrow Mary," he said, planting another gigantic kiss on her lips.

Mary squealed slightly until the kiss was finished.

Arnold left and Caroline shut the door. They all gathered around Dennis and the sight of his lopsided bosom and lipstick-smeared face caused them to burst into laughter.

"What happened?" Eunice asked. "Where did he take you?"

"D-down the road into the b-bushes," Dennis stammered. "Oh, I was never so scared in all my life! Arnold kissed me an' - he grabbed my potatoes!"

Dennis' re-enactment of the afternoon sent waves of laughter through the house that lasted well into the night. It had been a truly fun time for all, including Arnold who was never the wiser.

"Well, Dennis," Caroline said, remembering her own teen years, "you're very lucky that Arnold is a gentleman."

Chapter 30

The lame leading the blind

THE PLEASANT ATMOSPHERE at the house was short lived once Domko arrived back on the farm for a second time. He took his pills long enough to convince the hospital to discharge him, then quit immediately after arriving home. His moods got progressively worse as each week passed.

Margaret Burnett left her job as health nurse and she and her family moved out of the area. Caroline was sorry to see her go because she understood Domko and the family's problems. Caroline found it difficult to confide in people, but knew she could always count on Dr. Steenson.

The social worker who replaced Martha had left and been replaced twice since then. These workers had no first hand experience with the family. Since the main problem had been pinpointed as Domko's mental condition, it was now the responsibility of the police to take him into custody when he became violent.

At almost 14 years old, the twins were beginning a growth spurt and starting to mature. They now knew that there was a difference between boys and girls and no longer worried about Eunice losing a valuable appendage. They were curious about girls and looked at the brassiere and underwear pictures in catalogues until they blushed.

One day while David was daydreaming during class, he began sketching a picture from his imagination of what a woman must look like without her clothes. He worked on the picture for a long time while Mrs. Gering gave a history lesson. She noticed his preoccupation with his art book and slowly inched her way over to see what he was doing. David continued drawing until he could sense someone standing beside him. He looked up to see Mrs. Gering's shocked expression. Fumbling, he tried to cover his work.

"We're doing history, Mr. Pischke," she said quietly. "And next time, could you put some clothes on me?"

David looked at the drawing and flushed. While daydreaming, he hadn't realized that he'd drawn Mrs. Gering's face on the woman! He quickly lifted up his desk top, and put the book inside.

Later that week, the school inspector visited the classroom. He spoke with the teacher, talked to the students, examined the register book, and wrote things down on a small notepad he carried in his breast pocket. Before he left, Mrs. Gering called him aside and talked to him for a long time. Soon the superintendent was standing in front of David's desk.

"David, could I have your art book please?" he asked.

Embarrassed, David reluctantly reached in his desk and took out the book. It was thick with the many drawings and caricatures he'd drawn since the beginning of the school year.

For the next few days, he expected to be punished for drawing the picture of Mrs. Gering, but nothing came of it. Soon he and everyone else forgot the incident.

Just when the boys thought that Domko had tormented them in every conceivable way, he thought of something new. That winter he bought a television.

This was the most fascinating, world expanding invention they'd ever seen. They desperately wanted to watch it - but weren't allowed.

The magical box was bought with money given to the family by Grandpa Kolodka. It sat in the corner of the front room and was only turned on in the evening while Domko watched the news. The children weren't even allowed to watch that and were sent to the kitchen or upstairs. They listened through the thin walls as a stranger's voice blared out information about world events like the Cuban Missile Crisis. The twins tried hard to grasp what the world outside the farm must be like.

Domko sat on the chesterfield and muttered to himself, calling anyone he disagreed with a 'Communist'. He seemed to like watching the news, but it always made him angry afterwards.

The boys would sneak a peek at the television by turning it on when Domko was away but Raymond reported them the moment his father returned.

The five year old even snitched when he overheard Dennis bragging that he was going to be just like "Little Joe" on the television program 'Bonanza' when he grew up. The twins had been sneaking into the teacher's cottage to watch Bonanza on Sunday nights just before 9 p.m. They received a beating for that - not for being in the teacher's cottage without permission, but for enjoying themselves.

Raymond was making their lives miserable with his tattling.

One night in March while the twins sat on the floor after receiving a beating, Raymond came into the kitchen carrying a bag of treats. The boys had heard Domko tell him not to give them any. By now, Raymond knew it was fun to tease his half-brothers.

Taking a candy bar out of the bag, he pulled back the wrapper. He began walking back and forth holding, holding the bag in his dirty fist, taunting the twins. He had a spoiled, mean look on his face that the twins had grown to loathe.

"We gotta think of new words so poker can't understand us," Dennis said in their language.

"Yeah," David answered. "Satan's always makin' him spy on us. I hear him askin' the little bugger where we go and what we do. He's tryin' really hard to understand what we're sayin'."

"We'll just have to trick him," Dennis said slyly.

"Yeah. That'll teach him a lesson."

From that day on, the twins baited Raymond. They discussed where they would be hiding in front of their younger brother, but then would go and watch from a different hiding place. Raymond would tell his father where the twins were supposed to be going, and Domko would stalk off in the wrong direction.

The twins pretended they were going to sneak out to watch television but hid in the church instead. They'd watch through the windows as Domko crept up to the teacher's cottage and burst in, only to walk home confused and disappointed a few minutes later. They changed their words so often that both Raymond and Domko had no idea what they were saying.

By April, spring had arrived. Except for the occasional cold day, winter was virtually over.

Domko was watching the twins continually now. He never accomplished anything on his own as he spent his entire day stalking and spying on them. The boys were nervous and irritable, never knowing what to expect next.

Caroline had spent most of her days in bed during the past two months. This was something the twins didn't understand, except that she was no help when they tried to please their stepfather. David and Dennis agreed that this was, by far, the lowest point of their lives.

One cool, misty morning after a meagre breakfast of plain, stale bread, the twins were sent out to shovel manure. Domko told them to take pitchforks and clean out the small lean-to attached to the east side of the barn.

The twins nodded and hurried out the door.

"He can't think of nothin' else for us to do so he makes us shovel shit," David said. "I'm sick of all this work an' I wanna get outta here."

"Yeah, me too."

"He's nuts you know," David explained. That's what the kids say 'bout goin' to Selkirk. That's where the police send all the crazy people. They told me that it's just full of crazy people there."

Dennis shuddered. "I ain't never goin' there then."

"Me neither."

The twins opened the barn door and picked up forks. They walked around the side of the barn to the lean-to. Opening the small door they stepped into the dank room. Their eyes quickly adjusted to the darkness. The only light came from thin rays shining through cracks on the far wall.

They'd shoveled enough manure to know that this was going to be a long, hard job.

Tapping his pitchfork on the hard earth, David's shoulders slumped. It had been a cold night so the eight inches of manure that had accumulated since the last shoveling, was frozen to the earthen floor.

"Hey Denny, we'll start here'cause it'll be softer," David said banging his fork again and pointing to the southeast corner, banging his fork again. Together they pried their pitchforks underneath the manure.

"Lift when I say," David said as Dennis nodded. "O.k., lift now."

The boys grunted as they lifted a big chunk of manure and tossed it in the corner. Steam rose from underneath where the ground had thawed the afternoon before.

"O.k., that looks alright," David said, heartened by the warmth underneath. "This won't be so bad." He stuck his pitchfork under the pile and as he lifted, two prongs suddenly broke off and the manure fell to the ground. Both he and Dennis gasped.

"Oh no!" he said. "Where's the third pitchfork?"

"I don't know."

Just then, the light shining through the door suddenly dimmed. The boys knew why and cringed, not wanting to turn around.

"Vat? You's be playink again?" Domko said as he strode in to the lean-to. It was then he noticed the broken pitchfork in David's hand. "You's be breakink it some!"

The boys braced themselves as Domko spun around and threw his right leg in the air in a karate-style kick. He landed a blow directly on David's face. The impact of his heavy work boot knocked David's feet out from under him and sent the pitchfork flying through the air. Instinctively, David curled his legs and rolled onto his side as he tried to cover his head. His face was in such excruciating pain that he barely noticed the heavy work boots kicking his arms and the front of his legs.

"I's be givink you some!" Domko grunted each time he kicked the screaming boy.

Dennis tried to run but Domko blocked the doorway. He reached out and slammed his fist into Dennis' face, sending him crashing into the lean-to wall. Too frightened to fight back, the twins curled up as he alternated between kicking David in the arms and knees and kicking Dennis in the legs and back. Eventually he began to tire and with one final, hard blow to Dennis' spine, he left the boys groaning and weeping on the cold ground.

David was the first to struggle to his feet. He wiped the manure from his face with his hands and tried to open his eyes but could see nothing. He staggered towards the light of the open door and peered out. All he could see was a faint glimmer as he felt the cool, spring wind on his face.

"Dennis, c'mon we gotta get out of here," he choked, as he tried to clear his mouth of the blood that trickled down his throat. He was beginning to panic because he was still unable to see anything but darkness. "Get up, I need you to come look an' see if he's out there."

Dennis tried to stand up, but couldn't. He crawled to where David stood, then pulled himself up and looked out the door.

"I don't see him nowhere," he panted. "I think my legs are broke, this time for sure. Where are we gonna go? I can't run."

"I can't see," David rasped his voice rising in panic. "Denny, I can't see no more. I think he poked out my eyes!"

Dennis looked at his brother's face which was covered in manure. Blood was flowing from a gaping wound just over an eyebrow. His eyes were puffed out so far that all that remained of his eyes were tiny slits.

"I can't tell," Dennis said, thinking of Kathy's injury with a shudder. "You're face is so beat up I can't see you're eyes."

"I think I'm blind, Dennis!" David cried. "Get me outta here before he comes back!"

Dennis poked his head out the door. Domko was gone.

"Let's go!"

Grabbing David by the arm, Dennis stumbled out the door. He lost his balance and landed on the ground with a heavy thud.

"Get, up!" David whispered. "We gotta go."

Dennis struggled up and hobbled along the side of the lean-to.

"Where are you?" David asked, the cuts on his face stinging from the ammonia of the manure.

"I'm behind you," Dennis panted. "I can't go no faster."

"But we gotta run!"

"I can't"

"Give me your hand, an' you tell me where to walk."

Dennis grabbed David's hand, but every labourious step he took numbed his senses and caused pains to shoot through his spine.

"I can't," Dennis cried.

Aside from the horrible stinging on his face, David was otherwise fine physically.

"Climb on my back, an' I'll carry you." David said. "But I can't see nothin' so you gotta tell me where to go."

Dennis climbed on his brother's back, wrapping his legs around David's waist while his arms went around the neck. David leaned slightly forward and grabbed Dennis's arms.

Dennis looked over his brother's shoulder. "O.k., keep goin," he said.

David trudged towards the bush behind the barn, visualizing the cattle trail that would take them east to the beaver dam.

"There's a big rock so you gotta go to the left," Dennis said. "O.k., now keep goin'. We're almost at the fence, so in a minute you're gonna have to turn to the right."

"He's not comin' is he?" David asked.

Dennis looked over his shoulder, then fearfully in all directions. He hadn't thought of that. What if Domko had gone to the bush instead of the house so he could stalk them again? He thought of the many times he'd received a beating from Domko. When his stepfather stopped, he always sat on his chair then lit a cigarette. Then the sound of his ominous chuckle would permeate the house.

"He's not comin' yet," Dennis said. "He's probably restin' in the kitchen."

David continued to plod along, as Dennis guided him back on the trail when he veered off.

"How far we gonna go?" Dennis asked.

"We gotta go to the beaver dam, 'cause he'll never walk that far," David answered. Feeling vulnerable from his lack of sight, he was relying on his brother to keep them safe. "You gotta keep lookin' around in case he does come. You just never know about ole Squeezer."

Dennis nodded, looking first to his left then to his right.

Eventually they arrived at the lake bank. Exhausted, David dropped to his knees and Dennis rolled off his back onto the ground. They both rested on the cold, wet ground as a cool wind chilled their undernourished bodies. The boys began to shiver uncontrollably, and Dennis rolled onto his side and began to weep.

David crawled over the small ridge towards the water's edge. The ice was still thick on the lake, but mushy from the previous week's warm weather. Tiny waves lapped at the water's edge where the ice had melted away. Cupping his hands, David splashed handfuls of water onto his aching face. He tried to rub the manure out of his eyes but the harder he tried the more it stung. He wiped his face and hands dry with his shirt, then stumbled back to his brother.

"Are you really blind?" Dennis asked.

"I dunno. Are you really crippled?"

"I think so. I still can't walk," Dennis said. "Can you see anything at all?"

"No, nothin'," David cried.

The boys sat on the cold lake bank for a long time without speaking.

Frustrated, hungry, beaten and now likely crippled, Dennis began to cry. "What are we gonna do, Davey? Where are we gonna go? We can't walk across the beaver dam 'cause the ice is too soft an' I can't go that far anyway. You'd get lost in the reeds for sure if you can't see. We're doomed! Domko's gonna find us an' if we're blind an' crippled, he'll shoot us an' throw us in the bush. Nobody will ever find us. He'll just say we ran away."

David listened to Dennis and for the very first time, he agreed wholeheartedly with his brother. They would be shot if they couldn't work. If they recovered, then Domko would never let them leave the farm. No matter how hard they tried, they'd never escape his grasp.

The words of the chiropractor rang loudly in his ears: "Most boys your age with this type of injury would end up in a wheelchair . . . "

How much longer could they be beaten and not die? he wondered. *Or worse, end up crippled and helpless?*

While David sat on the soggy ground, he wondered why he and his siblings had been chosen for such a horrendous life. He knew that not all children lived like this - only them. Life seemed so unfair and not worth living.

Tired of listening to Dennis, he got up and stumbled along the lake bank. A feeling of utter hopelessness washed over him as he tried hard to open his eyes. He groped his way along, grasping tree branches as he went. When David could no longer hear Dennis crying, he found a spot that was relatively dry and curled up on the ground. He decided that if he was going to die, this would be a good place.

David decided that he would no longer look for food or water. He would not go home, stay away from Dennis and hopefully die a peaceful death among the trees. His heart ached for all the things he'd longed to do and then he started to cry.

At first, he sobbed softly, then gradually large tears began to flow from his swollen eyelids. He cried long and hard as he remembered every incident from his childhood, every time he'd received a beating, and every disappointment and embarrassment. His stomach ached emptily as he thought about the few good days he'd had - remembering Ruby's bright smiling face and Mrs. Koch's sweet kindness. He thought of Emma fussing over him and remembered the trip to Winnipeg. Oh, how he wanted to live in Winnipeg and be a professional drawing person! He thought of the cars he'd never own and the friends he'd never meet.

He begged for an answer. Why him? Why Dennis? What could they do except die? The hours went by and his body, wracked with sobbing, began to ache. He drifted in and out of sleep, awakening suddenly, with a feeling that someone was standing near him. He reasoned it must be Dennis and mumbled softly for him to go away.

A hand reached out and gently squeezed his shoulder. David was too weak and dazed to move. He knew instinctively not to be afraid. This was a familiar hand, one that hadn't touched him in more than ten years. Then as if his mind was being read, a voice spoke softly.

"Tushie, you've got to stay strong," it echoed. "This is Tatoosh. You've got to look after my little Tush, Dennis. I will be back and remember - I'm always with you."

As quickly as it had materialized, the voice and pressure on his shoulder vanished. David sat in awe of the voice for a long time and then rolled onto his back.

Whether his father's presence had been real or imagined, David didn't care. He opened his eyes and through tiny slits he could see the fuzzy image of branches overhead. Sitting up, he looked at the ground and the faint sprouting of new grass around him. His tears must have washed the dirt from his eyes - he wasn't blind after all!

Ashamed that he had almost given up, he pounded the ground with his fist. He knew how silly and useless his ravings had been. Suddenly he felt older than his fourteen years. He stood up and with a renewed sense of energy, walked back to where Dennis was sitting.

He had cried for hours too. It seemed to clear his mind and ease his frustration.

The boys looked at each other and said nothing as a deep understanding flowed between them. Nobody else would ever truly understand the hell they lived with each day. Dennis gave his brother a timid smile.

"Can you see o.k.?"

David nodded. "Can you walk?"

Dennis smirked. "Well, unless I wanna sit here 'til I die, I'd better."

David grabbed his brother's arm and supported him as they walked towards the bush. He decided he wouldn't tell Dennis about his experience, for fear it might make him frightened or upset.

"C'mon, we gotta find us some place to sleep," David said. "There's a good spot in the bush over here. Remember when the ole bastard took our cooked rabbit? I bet that spot is still good an' clear."

Maybe there was no God, but David felt a renewed sense of hope, prompted by the thought that his father might be nearby.

And that's all the strength he needed.

The boys went home two days later. Domko sensed the change in David immediately. Normally, he would have taunted the boy about his swollen face and blackened eyes, but not this time. He stood back and said nothing as the twins came into the house. He didn't even ask them where they'd been as they picked up milk pails and went to the barn.

Raymond came strolling in behind them carrying a pail.

"What are you doin' here, poker?" Dennis teased.

"Don't call Raymie poker!" the child yelled, his temper flaring immediately.

"Well, what do you want?"

"I's be showink you how to milk but a some cow!" the spoiled Raymond said arrogantly. He strode up and down the aisle looking for the 'right' cow to milk.

The twins made fun of him in their language, which caused Raymond to screech again. He stuck out his tongue, then stopped in front of the biggest animal in the barn.

"Uh, Raymie . . ." David began.

"Shhh!" Dennis whispered. "Let him, since he thinks he's so smart."

The twins watched as Raymond stood directly behind Domko's big Brahma bull. He gave them a naughty glance, then put the milking stool on the ground. Sticking out his tongue again at the twins, he reached in behind the bull's tail.

Raymond grabbed something soft alright, but to his surprise, no milk was forthcoming. Shocked by the intrusion, the bull didn't like this one bit. He snorted and shot his leg out in one arc, sending Raymond, the stool and the milk pail five feet into the air. The pail and stool crashed against the wall and Raymond landed with a thud on the ground.

Howling with fear, he jumped to his feet and ran towards the door. He gave the twins an embarrassed look as he ran to the house for sympathy.

"Did you see that? The bull almost killed him!" Dennis laughed as he and his brother fell off their stools and onto the ground with laughter.

"Yeah, I's be showink you how to milk!" David mimicked. "That was a close one. It's a lucky thing for us he landed on his fat Pollack head!"

That evening the boys went quietly upstairs.

"Guess what I'm gonna do," Dennis whispered.

"What?"

"I'm gonna build a boat so that the next time he chases us out, we can float across the beaver dam. The water's too deep to walk across an' I don't think we can wait until winter again."

David agreed. Building a boat sounded like a good idea.

The following morning they finished chores then went to school. Afterwards Dennis disappeared into the bush beside the church. David went home and did chores with Eunice.

Dennis worked on the boat for the next two weeks and announced he was finished.

"You gotta help me get it to the beaver dam," he told David. "We can try it out an' then hide it in the bushes where Squeezer won't find it."

"When do you wanna do this?" David asked. "Tomorrow?"

"Yeah. It's Friday an' he always takes the cream to town. As soon as he goes, we can do it, alright?"

David agreed.

The next day the boys waited until Domko left. Excited, the boys ran to the churchyard. Dennis led his brother to the spot where he had hidden the boat. Pulling away the branches he'd used as a cover, he beamed as he stood back to admire his work.

"See? I told you I was gonna build a boat," he announced.

David looked at the odd shaped vessel. It was a flat, wide-bottomed boat with small sides. Dennis had made it from tin and wood, and while it didn't look like it could survive big waves, Dennis wasn't worried.

David admired his brother's work which was meticulous considering he had used old lumber and scraps of tin. He agreed that it was the best boat they'd ever had.

"It looks good to me," he said. "Let's test it out."

Each boy grabbed an end and lifted.

David groaned. "Denny, how'd you move this around by yourself?"

"I didn't, I just built it right here," he said.

The boys strained and groaned as the carried the heavy boat across the swampy field. They ignored the sharp edges which dug into their fingertips as they chatted happily about the boat. They laughed about how stupid Domko would feel chasing after them and then watching helplessly from the shore as they paddled across to Koch's farm.

Eventually they arrived at the lake. Dennis was anxious to set the boat adrift and dragged it to the water's edge. David stood back and admired the scenery.

How things had changed in only three weeks! The water was flowing freely now and the trees had tiny buds forming on their branches. Life seemed so much brighter on this day than it had the last time they were here.

"C'mon!" Dennis called impatiently.

David ran down the bank.

"O.k., we'll both push an' when I say, jump in," Dennis said handing his brother a long stick. "I'm gonna be in front an' you can be in the back."

"I guess you get to be the pilot," David said.

"Not pilot, that's for planes. I get to be the Captain."

"An' what do I get to be? The pirate?"

"Shuddup an' push," Dennis said laughing.

David stepped into the cold water and let out a howl as the small waves rolled in on his shins. Dennis followed and together they pushed the heavy boat .

"Is this far enough?" David asked.

"Yeah, give one more push an' then jump in."

The twins heaved and then jumped into the boat together. They floated for three seconds before water began flooding in at every joint.

"Eeeeaaahh!" David screamed as he jumped up and out of the boat in one motion.

Dennis, who was so shocked and dismayed that his boat wasn't going to float after all, stayed sitting long enough that technically he 'went down with the ship'. He jumped up as the water reached his waist. The twins scrambled out of the water and stood dripping on the shore.

"Oh no! What happened?" Dennis cried. "I built it so good, how come it didn't float?"

David started to laugh. "Good? You built it too good. Too many goddamned nails in the bottom. It didn't float 'cause it was too heavy."

"No!" Dennis argued. "It wasn't too heavy."

"Yes it was! It almost busted our arms off bringin' it here!" David said, teasing. "C'mon Denny, admit you put too many nails in."

"I'm not sayin' that," Dennis said.

"C'mon say it!"

"I had to put them nails in so the water wouldn't get in," he explained.

"Nails don't stop water, stupid," David said. "Only rubber stops water - an' whoever heard of a tin boat anyway?"

"Lots of boats are made of tin."

"No, they ain't."

"Yes, they is. I know 'cause I saw some in the encyclopedia books. One of 'em was called the TIT-anic."

"TIT-anic?" David asked. "Do you mean TI-tanic?"

"Yeah. It was made of tin."

"Denny, the Titanic sank all the way to the bottom of the lake," David laughed.

"No it didn't!" Dennis argued.

"Yes it did!"

Dennis thought. "Well, I don't care. I thought it would work an' it still might. Help me get it out."

"What for?"

"We gotta drag it home an' fix it."

David protested. He didn't want to go into the water again, but Dennis called him 'chicken'. Together they pulled the waterlogged boat up the bank of the lake.

"Well, if I drag the boat all the way back, I'm gonna help fix it so it's done good this time," David said.

"Whadda you think we should do?"

"Rubber," David said confidently. "Wrap rubber around it an' it'll float for sure."

The boys dragged the boat back to the bush by the church, then went home and began scrounging through a pile of Domko's junk near the grainary. They found an old tire which they rolled to the churchyard. Using a sharp kitchen knife, David cut the tire into pieces while Dennis happily nailed rubber on all the seams.

"Don't use too many nails," David warned.

The following morning they dragged the boat back to the beaver dam. They chatted again, but this time were not as optimistic. They took the boat to the shore once again.

"You go first, you're the captain." David said.

"I ain't the Captain no more," Dennis argued. "It's too cold a job."

The boys laughed. "Well, we'll push it an' watch. If it don't sink, we'll run an' jump in."

Dennis thought this was a good plan and together they gave the boat a little push since it was even heavier now, they had to struggle to get it off the pebbly shore. The boys waded in up to their knees and watched helplessly as the boat promptly sank once again. They dragged it back to shore and sat down in the sand.

"Are you gonna make me drag it back to the church again?" David asked.

"Well, we can't leave it here! We got to fix it. We'll take it back an' I'll take out some of the nails."

"No, I think we gotta make it out of just wood an' rubber - like a raft,"

David exclaimed.

"O.k., as long as we do somethin' with it," Dennis said hopefully. "It's gonna float, you'll see."

Groaning, the boys grabbed the boat and dragged it up the lake bank for a second time.

"Float," David mumbled. "That's what all them people on the Titanic said."

Chapter 31

Dennis escapes

ONE AFTERNOON IN EARLY MAY, the twins came in from outside to discover that Kathy was alone in the house. She stood in her usual spot between the kitchen and the front room, jogging on the spot and humming an unusual tune. She wrapped her knuckles on the wall the entire time, an annoying habit which the twins detested.

"Will you quit doin' that?" David said. "You're buggin' us."

Kathy ignored him and continued jogging and pounding the wall. The boys watched the strange activity she had started after returning from Brantford.

"How come she don't bug the ole weasel when she does that?" Dennis asked.

"I dunno," he said. "It sure bugs me."

"Hey Kathy, where's Ma?" Dennis called out.

"Walter came an' she went to Winnipeg with him," she said, not breaking her stride. "She's comin' back later."

"Later?" David asked. "When?"

"Don't know," she sang. "Maybe two or three weeks."

The twins looked at each other. When their mother was gone, Domko was always more brutal.

Dennis was being either kicked or punched almost daily now, and was convinced he couldn't take another full-blown beating.

"Oh no!" he said. "I'm not stayin' here with him alone no more! I'm leavin' as soon as I can get away."

They watched Kathy for a few more minutes then David pointed to the kitchen cupboard. Dennis knew he wanted to sneak some food, so he went to the door and looked out. Domko was not around so they both went to the cupboard. Dennis grabbed a raw potato and took a big bite.

"Where's Raymie?" David asked, trying to distract Kathy.

"He's with Ta-Ta," she answered. "They're outside."

Dennis finished chewing and swallowed. He coughed a little bit, then began talking to Kathy while David took a bite.

"Where did Eunice an' Rosie go?" he asked.

"To school."

They switched back and forth with questions to keep the girl distracted while they ate. Afterwards, they filled the front pockets of their pants with rolled oats. They hoped to run into the bush before Domko came back, but he arrived sooner than expected. Their pockets bulged and the red-faced boys hoped he didn't notice.

He stared at them menacingly, then told them to open their mouths. The boys did, but by this time, they had swallowed all they'd eaten. Worried that the boys would run away, he sent them upstairs for the rest of the evening.

Knowing that Caroline wouldn't be back for a few weeks, Domko became frustrated. As the next morning passed, he became increasingly irritable and the children knew he was looking for an excuse to beat somebody. They did the chores perfectly and stayed out of arm's reach.

Since he was mildly afraid of Eunice and David, Domko usually singled out Dennis who avoided him all morning.

As noon approached, Dennis decided to sneak into the house and try some of the soup Rosie was making. He walked through the yard and was almost at the door when he saw Domko coming. Dennis swerved back around the edge of the house and ran towards the barn. He climbed into the loft and found the oldest, deepest section of hay along the west wall. He was able to squeeze himself between the heavy hay and the wall by digging a small hole, then burrowing himself inside. He pulled hay on top of himself and waited fearfully, hoping his stepfather hadn't seen his escape.

The damp, mouldy hay that covered his head caused him to cough lightly. He tried to clear the hay away from his mouth. The air in his hiding place was becoming stale. He listened, then stiffened at every noise the old barn made.

Dennis been hiding for about fifteen minutes when he heard footsteps coming up the ladder. He knew it wasn't David because he'd heard him drive away on the tractor. Parting his lips, he tried to breath as shallowly as possible, hoping there was enough hay covering his body parts so that he wouldn't be visible. He could hear the footsteps on the barn floor as the old boards creaked under the weight.

Satan, he thought. *If he finds me, he'll kill me for sure.*

Dennis squeezed his eyes shut and prayed that he wouldn't be found. He could hear his stepfather poking the hay with something, first gently and then more vigorously so that the sounds became louder. Domko began grunting.

"Dennnnis," he cooed. "You's be comink out."

Dennis sat absolutely still. His mind raced as he tried to decide what to do. Knowing Domko, he would receive a mild beating if he came out right away after being called. If he waited and Domko found him instead, he would receive a much more severe beating for being defiant.

He could hear Domko inching his way closer, moving from east to west as he kicked and stabbed the piles of hay. Just when Dennis thought he'd be found for sure, Domko suddenly stopped looking. Somebody had driven into the driveway and Dennis could hear his stepfather walk to the loft opening. Then he climbed down the ladder and left the barn. Dennis didn't know what had distracted him, but was thankful for it.

The twin stayed in his hiding spot for more than an hour. Once it appeared that Domko wasn't coming back, he emerged slowly and cautiously. He walked with care to the ladder then shuddered at the sight of a pitchfork sitting menacingly in the hay. On his hands and knees, he poked his head through the loft opening in the floor, to see if Domko was nearby. Nobody was around, so he quietly climbed down the ladder. He peered through the crack in the barn door before swinging it open. He couldn't see anyone in the yard and recognized that this was his chance to escape.

Gathering his courage, Dennis swung open the door and ran as fast as he could through the barnyard, to the road. He was over the fence in an instant, then into the thick bush northwest of the house. Dennis couldn't bring himself to look over his shoulder so he kept running until he was certain that Domko wasn't in pursuit.

He'd done it! He'd used his wits to escape, just like he had told David he would! Dennis was overjoyed to be free.

Nobody's ever gonna hurt me again, he thought as he walked through the bush. *Not ole Satan an' not anybody else. If anyone tries, well, how bad can it be? Satan has almost killed me so many times, what can be worse than that?*

As Dennis walked through the bush, his confidence soared. He'd felt a slight change for the better in both himself and David since they were beaten in the lean-to.

David seemed different after they slept near the lake bank, stronger, somehow. He seemed to have more patience with his twin and Dennis sensed this. He decided that he too, would try to be strong. He'd run! He'd escape! His stepfather would never catch him again!

He walked for nearly two hours through bush and fields before stopping at the first farm house he came to. By now, it was early evening and he was becoming desperate to find a place to stay before it got dark. He didn't want to sleep outside alone, so he bravely went to the door.

I can do this, he thought as he reached out and knocked.

A tall woman answered and puzzled, looked at his feet.

"Yes?" she said.

"C-can I c-come in?" he stammered. "Mom is gone an' Domko chased me out." It was the best explanation he could come up with. Saying he ran away didn't sound good and he didn't want to make a bad impression.

The woman seemed to know who he was and opened the door wide. A man sat at the kitchen table reading a farm paper. He seemed surprised to see Dennis standing there.

"You're one of Bill Pischke's boys, aren't you?" the man said with a Scottish accent. "You're a heck of a long way from home."

His wife recounted what Dennis had said, knowing the shy child didn't want to repeat himself. Dennis was invited to sit at the table and have something to eat. He discovered his hosts were Mr. and Mrs. Stewart "Scotty" Brown. They had a nice, clean home and Dennis felt comfortable there. He stayed until it was dark, hoping for an overnight invitation.

"Would you like to stay here a few days until your mother comes back?" Mrs. Brown asked.

Dennis nodded yes without hesitating. That night while lying under crisp clean sheets and a thick quilt, he said a silent 'thank you' to whatever had guided him to the Brown house.

Dennis stayed for three days then Mr. Brown suggested that he'd better go to school or they might all get into trouble. Dennis reluctantly agreed and rode to school the next morning with the Brown's daughter Ruth.

Domko was waiting in front of the school that afternoon with his arms folded across his chest. Dennis came out of the school and his heart sank when he saw his stepfather standing there. Domko called him over and scowled at him. Dennis walked home sideways, refusing to turn his back on Domko who was watching him suspiciously.

Because the boys were older, Domko preferred to hit them from behind, waiting more often than not for that opportunity. Dennis wasn't giving him one that afternoon.

"How'd he find me?" he asked David that night.

"He was listenin' in on everyone's phone calls an' that's how he found out where you were. He's been watchin' the school ever since," his brother explained. "He's been makin' sure that me an' Beanie don't run away too. He got Rosie real bad the other night, so I guess you're safe for another day or so."

Dennis sat quietly for a moment. Aware that Domko would be harbouring resentment that he ran away, Dennis decided he wouldn't be around when his stepfather came to teach him a lesson.

"Next time I'm gonna go where he can't find me," he said before falling asleep.

Dennis woke the next morning and walked to school with the other children. He only stayed until the noon hour, then disappeared into the bush across the road. He walked to Jim's house where he spent the afternoon. He didn't feel comfortable without Ruby there, so he left before dark, staying in an abandoned building south of Jim's house overnight.

The next day he continued walking, arriving at a farm house near Grahamdale. He knocked on the door, and this time a tall, thin bachelor named Henry Sherbert answered. Dennis repeated the story he'd told the Browns and was invited in. Henry listened quietly as Dennis told him about Domko and lifted his shirt to show the kindly man his bruises.

Henry prepared supper and then at about six p.m. his brother Louis came inside from working in the field. Louis was a short, chubby man who initially seemed unfriendly and cool towards Dennis. Henry explained the situation and the brothers agreed that Dennis could stay overnight.

As Dennis rested on the chesterfield that night draped in a woolen blanket, he looked around the room with fascination. He could overhear Henry and Louis speaking softly nearby and wondered what they were saying. He glanced around at the many antiques and interesting things that the bachelors had collected over the years.

It was then that Dennis realized how many different types of people there must be in the world. He was glad that he and David had started venturing further from their farm to homes belonging to the Kochs, Browns and now the Sherberts.

For the next few days, Dennis shadowed Henry. He helped peel potatoes, wash dishes and cook. He enjoyed helping the man who listened to him patiently and when warranted, patted him on the back.

"Would you like to come to town with me today?" Henry asked.

Dennis said that he would and they drove together to Grahamdale to buy supplies. Henry took Dennis to the store where they stood for a while talking with a group of Henry's friends. They were invited to sit down and after the usual small talk about the weather and cattle prices, one of the men asked Henry who his young companion was.

"This is Dennis Pischke," Henry said. "One of Caroline's boys from across the lake."

The men nodded. Some of them recognized Dennis from auction sales.

"How come he's with you?"

Henry bought Dennis a chocolate bar and coke, then turned back to the men. He began explaining the situation and his voice became angrier the longer the spoke.

Dennis looked at the chocolate bar in wonder - it was an Oh Henry bar! Then he looked at Henry in awe. He knew his host was a nice man, but had no idea that somebody had named a chocolate bar after him!

Dennis felt all eyes on him as Henry acted out the scenes Dennis had told him.

"Stand up and show them," Henry coaxed.

Dennis looked at him, then glanced around the store. There were only a few people there and none of them seemed to be watching. Shyly, he stood up and lifted his shirt.

"Turn around, son," Henry said, voice softening.

Keeping his eyes on the floor Dennis slowly turned his back to the men.

"See what I'm saying?" Henry said.

Dennis dropped his shirt and sat down. He opened the chocolate bar package and noticed the men look at each other.

One man admitted he hadn't believed Gus's stories, but was convinced now that Domko really was crazy.

"Selkirk, that's where he belongs," another man said as he lit a homemade cigarette. "Jim has been saying that for years."

The others nodded in agreement.

Dennis finished his drink and he and Henry left soon afterwards. They drove back to the farm where Henry told Dennis to go inside. He said he had to go to Ashern for a while. Dennis offered to start supper. He did that, then puttered around the house until Henry's return.

"It's safe for you to go home now," Henry said the following morning. "Your mother is there and Domko has been taken by the police."

Dennis smiled, then went to gather up the things he'd brought with him. A pang of longing washed over him as he thought of David. He missed his brother, but had pushed the thoughts out of his mind. He had to! He'd been more determined to stay away from Domko than see David and now he was suddenly excited about the prospect of going home.

He refused Henry's offer for a ride, saying he didn't mind the walk

"Remember, son, you can come back here for a visit any time," Henry said as he stood waving at the door.

Dennis gave the man a wave then jogged towards the road. He arrived home two hours later to find the house quiet, except for Kathy who was jogging in her usual spot.

"Where's Ma?" he asked.

"She's upstairs Dennis," Kathy said.

"Ma," he called softly as he walked up the stairs. "Are you here?"

Caroline was sitting at the far end of the room on the bed. It took Dennis' eyes a few moments to adjust to the darkness and it was then he noticed a newborn baby at her breast.

Shocked by the sight, he recoiled. "What? Another baby?"

Instead of answering his question, she became angry with him.

"Why did you run away to the neighbours?" she asked. "Now the police have come and taken Domko away again."

"I couldn't stay here without you 'cause I was too scared," he cried.

"Well, what am I going to do now? I've got a newborn baby to take care of. I can't be working in the barn all day," she said.

"We'll do the work, me, Denny an' Eunice," Dennis promised. "Us kids can do all the work so that he don't got to come back."

The baby fussed and began to cry.

"Shh," Caroline scolded her son as she transferred her attention to the tiny, wiggling baby. She moved the infant from one breast to the other and soon it was content again.

"Ma, why'd you bring another baby home?" Dennis whispered.

"I had to because he was at the hospital waiting for me," she said as she stroked the bundle. "His name is Mark."

The simple explanation did not satisfy Dennis. He shook his head and went back down stairs. He couldn't understand why his mother kept bringing babies home! He knew that the storks brought them to the hospital and that mothers went to get them, but why couldn't another woman take her turn? The babies always grew up to be like the man in the house so now they were doomed to have another sibling like their stepfather.

Maybe he'll be gone for good this time, Dennis thought as he went outside to find his twin.

One afternoon in mid-June when Caroline was washing diapers, there was a rap on the door. She dried her hands on her apron and opened it to find Emma standing there.

"Emma!" she exclaimed. "How are you?"

"I'm fine," she said. "I thought I'd come for a little visit."

"You must come in," Caroline said stepping back. "Ignore the mess. The new baby has kept me up all night and there is just no way I can get everything done."

Emma smiled as she stepped into the kitchen carrying a big box. She and Caroline had barely spoken the past few years since their fight about the children. Emma pushed those bad memories aside. She planned to focus on the new start she hoped to forge that afternoon.

"Would you like to see my washing machine?" Caroline said nervously as she motioned for Emma to follow her into the laundry area between the front room and the stairway. "We thought this would be the best spot for it. It's the place where the kids throw all their clothes anyway."

Emma nodded as she looked at the shiny round white tub with ringers on top.

"Oh, it's nice, Caroline," she said. "Gus and I have been talking about getting some of these new appliances, but we just hate to go to the expense of putting hydro in the house. We're probably going to retire and move to town in a year or so."

"Hi Emma," Kathy called from the front room. The blind girl had a terribly good memory and a knack for recognizing voices.

"Hi Kathy, how are you?" Emma said in her kindest voice. "Did you like the school in Brantford?"

Kathy explained some of the things she learned while Emma listened. Raymond came bursting into the front room from the bedroom, awakening the baby who was sleeping in his crib nearby. Caroline sent Kathy and Raymond outside to play while she picked up little Mark.

"Things haven't changed much around here!" Emma laughed.

Caroline gave her an understanding grin. "That's for sure. One of these days I'm going to have to find out what's causing all these babies!"

Emma looked at her hands. She disliked the idea that Caroline still being in a relationship with Domko, but knew better than to bring up that subject. Instead, they made small talk for a few minutes, a conversation that was punctuated by the occasional awkward moment. Soon they fell into the friendly pattern each of them remembered so well. Caroline made coffee and they sat and chatted like old friends.

"I brought you some canning," Emma said casually. She had heard that

Caroline was having a difficult time financially, but had no desire to make her feel bad.

"Like I said, we'll be retiring soon and the kids keep telling me that I don't need to do so much canning, but you know me! I just can't help myself. I can't stand to see anything go to waste so I continue to put down enough fruit and vegetables to feed an army year after year. Honestly, Gus said to me, 'Emma, you have to stop doing all that canning' so I figured I'd bring it over here. Those boys must be eating a lot by now and all I can say is that I'm sure thankful I didn't have a whole mess of boys instead of girls."

Caroline laughed at the long speech. "The twins can eat their weight, I'm sure! And Raymond, well, he's growing too and I figure he's going to eat just as much if not more when he's their age."

"The children are fine?"

"Yes. We're all good. Walter has a good job in Winnipeg and Steven is working on a ranch in Alberta. He's coming home for a visit next week, which will be nice. Norman, well he's still at Geisler's farm and Domko's away right now on account of his episodes. I'm not sure when he's coming back."

Emma smiled weakly. She decided this was the time to change the subject.

"I've heard Marion won't be teaching school here next year," she said. "Sounds as if we'll have to find a new teacher."

Caroline was surprised. It was then she realized that her estrangement from Emma had isolated her from the community. Emma and Ruby had been her only friends in the district.

The women chatted until the children came rolling into the house after school. They were all surprised and pleased to see Emma. The twins each drank a glass of milk and had a piece of fresh bread, while peering into the box that Emma had brought. Eunice asked Caroline if she would make some corn starch pudding for dessert that night.

"Well, I can see you're busy, it's time for me to go" Emma announced. "I have to get home and get Gus' supper ready."

The two friends smiled at each other.

"Thanks for the canning," Caroline said. "I'll send the boys over with the jars when we're finished."

"Don't bother," Emma scoffed, waving her hand. "I have no more use for them, really."

Caroline spoke quietly on the telephone for the next few weeks and the children sensed something was wrong. They suspected their freedom would soon end and it was confirmed one afternoon when Caroline announced that Domko would be back July 3.

"I'll run away!" Dennis responded. "I'm not gonna stay here no more when Satan's around."

"Don't talk like that!" Caroline scolded.

"It's true. He smashes us an' if he does it again, I'm gonna tell some more people," the twin said.

Caroline watched her son's expression, his eyes set in steely resolve. She believed Dennis meant what he said, since he was the most stubborn of her ten children. She had been considering sending the twins to live elsewhere. Now seemed to be the time to pursue the idea.

"Alright then," she said. "I'll do what I can."

A few days later, she told the boys there was a farm family near Lundar willing to take them in. The boys would have to work in exchange for room and board. She asked the twins if they would agree to this.

Both nodded vigorously. "When can we go?" David asked.

"Steven's going to come for a visit and take us there tomorrow," Caroline said.

"Steven?" Dennis asked.

"Yes, he's coming to visit for a few days."

The boys packed their meagre belongings and were waiting patiently when Steven arrived. They were happy to see their older brother and after the usual chit chat, the twins were eager to go. They felt they would soon be as free and happy as their brothers.

David experienced a tremendous sense of relief as he climbed in the back of Steven's car. Dennis climbed in beside him and both boys sat near an open window listening to the radio as it loudly blared a song through the car. Their mother didn't seem to mind, as she talked and laughed with her son. They sped towards the highway, a huge cloud of dust rising behind them.

They arrived in Lundar in early afternoon and drove to a lovely farm just south of town. The house was modest but nicely painted and the yard was tidy. A stately barn stood behind and it appeared to Caroline that these were, wealthy farmers by the day's standards.

Caroline told the boys to wait outside while she went to talk to her acquaintances. These were Jehovah's Witnesses who Caroline had met on occasion. They had been friendly to her on the phone when she called about the twins earlier in the week. She explained that her husband and the boys from her first marriage 'just didn't get along'. They'd been sympathetic and said they needed help with the dairying.

The twins unloaded their belongings and stretched their long legs as they walked timidly up the driveway. They stood watching as their mother knocked on the door.

"Do you think these people are nice?" Dennis asked.

"Sure, they'll be good," David answered. "An' they can't be no worse than the ole black bastard anyway."

Dennis laughed.

They watched as a husband and wife came to the door and let their mother inside. She spoke to the couple for a few moments then returned to the car. They could tell by her expression that something was wrong.

"What is it Ma?" David asked.

"Just get in the car," she said. You're not staying here."

"What happened," David asked as he followed his mother. "We gotta stay here. We don't got no other place to go."

"Get in," she said firmly.

The twins got in the back seat, as Steven took his turn to ask what had happened. Caroline sat for a moment staring at the lovely house. They knew it would take her a little time to sort out her thoughts.

"They said they don't need help after all," she blurted out. "They tried calling this morning but we'd already left."

"What? How can they need help one day and not the next?" Steven asked. "Everyone will be haying soon. Do you think they're lying?"

Caroline rolled her eyes. She knew the truth was going to hurt the twins.

"They didn't admit to it, but I know what happened," she said shaking her head in anger. "They called people from our church to find out what our 'situation' was. They were told to keep away from us because we're nothing but trouble."

"What?" the boys jeered.

"They now think the twins are liars, and thieves and don't want to work," she said.

"Did he say that?" Steven asked, pointing to a man who stood watching from inside the door.

"He didn't have to. He admitted to changing his mind about taking the twins after talking to people from the church. What else could that mean?"

Steven backed out of the driveway, churning dust and stones as he sped away. The boys sat quietly in the back.

"What are we going to do?" Dennis whispered to David.

"I dunno. Lemme think a minute," his twin replied.

David was heartened by his mother's attempt to find them a place to live. He felt good that she'd defended them. Suddenly, he felt it might be alright to stay on the farm after all.

"We'll do somethin'," he said. "I just don't know what right now. We'll be alright for a few days 'cause ole Squeezer's good at first when he gets back. By the time that wears off maybe Ma will have found us some other place."

Two days later, Domko arrived in Moosehorn by bus, then rode the local taxi home. He said very little as he sat in his usual chair. He napped often and ate less, but continued to watch the twins with suspicion.

The boys had grown a lot in the past few months and it was as if their stepfather was seeing them for the first time. They were now lanky teenagers with hands and feet like adults. Adolescent muscles were beginning to develop on their arms and legs and while their strength and skills were still youthful, they wouldn't be for much longer.

Domko noticed the jars of preserves and vegetables that sat in a box beside the cupboard. Some of them were empty by this time. Domko was not pleased that Caroline had accepted food from Emma.

Caroline tried to reason with him but it was hopeless. He picked up the box and flung it out the door towards the barnyard. The jars shattered as they hit the ground. The twins darted outside and once Domko shut the door, they ran to see what could be salvaged.

"Now that ole Satan's back, we won't get nothin' to eat," Dennis said. "We better save some of this."

"Yeah, Ma shoulda known he'd be mad," David said as they stood over the broken jars. "I shoulda hid them."

David picked up the box and they tossed large pieces of glass inside. Some of the preserves couldn't be salvaged - the saskatoons and raspberries were too small to save, so the boys ate as many from the ground as they could. Two jars of jam could be saved, since the contents sat sweetly congealed in the broken jar. Dennis put these jars aside, then both boys made aprons of their shirts and began picking up the vegetables.

"You do the beets an' I'll do the beans an' carrots," Dennis said.

When the boys had saved all they could, and eaten all they couldn't, they ran to hide in the chicken coop. They waited until Domko went to the barn and then ran back to the house. They grabbed a bowl from the kitchen before going straight to their bedroom. They put the vegetables into the bowl and hid it with the two broken jam jars behind the wall.

Domko complained that he was too tired to work. He and Caroline decided they would have to bring in outside help. They were already weeks late with seeding, but decided it would be better to do it late than not at all. If the oats were too immature at harvest to sell at the elevator, they could be used as feed oats.

The children did not understand this logic since Domko never did any work, but they didn't argue against extra help.

Caroline called a bachelor friend of the family named Henry Harliss who lived near Grahamdale. Henry had known Caroline for many years and became friends with Domko. Henry also raised pigeons so this was something they had in common. Henry had always liked the family and agreed to work for them for a few weeks.

He arrived the following day to help seed the grain. Henry was a tall, quiet man who always saw the good in people. He refused to take sides between Caroline and Domko and for the most part, discouraged Domko's posturing. He preferred to talk about the weather, current events and community matters rather than how much Domko disliked the children.

While Henry and the children worked, Domko stood nearby and complained about his physical health. He said the medicine he took in hospital made him feel lethargic so he stopped taking it. Henry told him he didn't think that was a good idea. Domko argued that he was 'but a some goot man.' To that Henry said nothing, turning to the children to talk about their school work and friends.

This brightened the moods of the children who seldom found an adult taking an interest in them. They began looking forward to Henry's arrival each morning. They knew that as long as he was there, it would be difficult for Domko to torment them.

One afternoon in the field, Domko became increasingly irritated as he watched the children working normally. They were not slouching and fearful, and Henry allowed them to take lunch and water breaks. This upset Domko who hadn't beaten either twin in a week.

Since Henry had lunch and supper with the family, the children had been eating regular meals. As the week came to an end, the children were trying to think of ways to keep Henry on longer, while Domko was trying to hasten his departure. It bothered Domko that he had been the one who had suggested the hiring of extra help. He felt threatened and was beginning to unravel again.

While the children worked nearby, Domko lost his temper and began arguing with Henry.

"I's be shootink but a some keets ant killink Carlorka!" he seethed, as he patted the breast pocket where he kept his knife. "They's be goot for sheet. She's be killink me like but a some Beel."

Henry shook his head in anger.

"Domko! That's a terrible way to talk," he yelled back. "You should be ashamed of such thoughts! How can you say those things? If you want to have such evil and wicked ideas then fine, but don't ever tell them to me again. Since I have nothing against your wife and kids, I won't stand here and listen to you talk about them. It is disgusting, plain disgusting, and I am embarrassed that you might call me a friend."

Domko took a step backwards. He had never seen mild-mannered Henry so angry. He looked slightly afraid of the tall, imposing man. Henry's comments had been hard on his ego, and he strode to the house obviously deflated.

After Domko left, the children chuckled and stared at Henry with admiration. They were so surprised to hear such stern talk coming from the gentle man. They wished other people, especially those from the church, would stand up to Domko instead of running away.

Dennis thought of the Oh Henry chocolate bar. Now he wasn't sure which man it had been named after.

The following week the children began haying. Rather than beginning on their own land, Domko sent the boys to begin haying on a piece of leased land that belonged to Jim.

Domko told them that he had permission to hay it that year. When it appeared that they didn't believe him, he chased them with a shovel.

"Do you really think Jim said this is alright?" Dennis asked as they hitched the horses.

"No! Jim hates Domko, he'd let the hay rot before he'd give it to him."

The boys drove the haying equipment to the field and began cutting. The following morning Dennis began raking while David continued to cut. On the third day they pushed the hay into stacks.

Later that afternoon, Domko drove out to the field and told the boys to begin hauling the stacks home. Usually hauling waited until all the hay was put up. It made good sense to complete all the haying during good weather, but not this time.

"See?" David whispered. "He wants us to haul it home so he can hide it from Jim. Pretty tricky, eh?"

"Yeah, an' there's people who think he's got no control over himself," Dennis whispered back. "But he knows what he's doin'. Just like how he never hits Raymie or Kathy, just us."

David nodded. "Yeah, an' how he never lets us eat, but feeds them good."

They drove the horses home to hitch them to the hay wagon. They returned to the field and were able to haul one of three stacks home that night. The following morning, Domko told them to bring the other stacks home, before cutting again. The boys arrived at the field, loaded a stack and then drove the team home. Domko pointed to an area behind the barn, telling them to unload it there.

As they stood on top, forking the hay off the wagon, an unfamiliar vehicle entered the driveway. A man got out and began talking to Domko. The boys jumped off the the stack and walked around the barnyard fence so they could overhear what was being said.

"I's not be doink it, they's be," Domko said raising his hands helplessly in the air. "I's be seek ant tellink them to hay. Vat? They's be hayink in Jim's but a some fielt?"

The man nodded. The boys recognized him as a neighbour named Rudy Metner. It didn't appear that he believed Domko's explanation. During the conversation, it was decided that Domko would keep the stacks that had been hauled home, and Rudy would take all that was left in the field. Rudy shook his head in anger as he left. The twins ran back to continue unloading the stack.

"Now we gotta ask him what to do next," David said. "You do it."

"I'm not gonna ask him. You do it."

"Uh-uh. Not me. He's gonna be pissed off for sure an' he's gonna find some way of blamin' us for this."

The boys stood hiding at the back of the barn.

"Why don't we just go to the south quarter an' start?" Dennis suggested.

While they tried to decide what to do next, another vehicle drove in the driveway. They recognized the car as belonging to Domko's friend from the church. He was there for his weekly visit.

Domko approached the man and shook his hand.

"C'mon," David said.

Feeling safe that someone else was around, the boys walked boldly across the yard. David asked Domko where they should go next while the visitor gave them a distasteful look. Domko scowled. He knew the boys had overheard what had happened with Rudy and was embarrassed. He told them to go to the south field. The boys ran towards the horses.

"That was easy," David said.

"Yeah, I never thought I'd be glad to see that ole Devil visiting," Dennis laughed.

Chapter 32

Eunice's big chance

DOMKO'S CONDITION CONTINUED to deteriorate. As summer ended, he'd returned to his old habit of beating one of the children daily, then sitting back and chuckling. Later he would taunt the child and offer him or her a chocolate bar.

When they could, the children fled, staying at a neighbour's house until Caroline arrived to take them home. The children and neighbours did not realize that Domko was still on probation from the mental hospital and that police could pick him up if he violated the terms of his release.

School began but the older children were not allowed to attend. They had run away so often during July and August that haying was still to be completed. Bad weather also delayed the work so the children had to stay home from school to finishing putting up the hay.

Caroline had spent the early part of September depressed and bedridden once again. The children were receiving no parental guidance whatsoever. They were at Domko's mercy as Caroline worried only about herself. They came in one night to find their mother screaming and sobbing uncontrollably after yet another fight with Domko.

The following afternoon Eunice sat outside along the south side of the house. It was late September, but the sun was still warm on her face as she let her head fall gently back against the gritty wall. She watched the pale yellow and orange leaves, blow gently in the early autumn breeze. They were just starting to turn and looked beautiful.

It's not fair, she thought. *Life has been so unfair.*

She remembered being thirteen years old and her daily desire then to escape the confines of the God-forsaken place that people dared call her home. The days, months and years had crept by. Now at sixteen, she was still on the farm. She had lost all hope of leaving.

Eunice alternated between feeling sorry for her mother and despising her. They'd been fighting a lot lately and she remembered one of their first arguments. It had been the summer before, or was it the year before that? She remembered that Domko had wanted to knock her down a few notches so he forced her to sit on a chair while he cut her hair. He had grabbed her soft, long brown hair and cut a huge chunk from the back of her head right at the scalp.

He had stood back and laughed, calling her 'the Queen' - why 'the queen' Eunice never quite understood. She'd tried to hide the bald spot, but it had been impossible. Eunice had her mother cut her hair short soon afterwards. She left the front long and pushed it straight back to hide what was missing. The embarrassment! She'd been so hurt that she confronted her mother and demanded to know why she put up with Domko. How could she let him do this to her children day in and day out?

Eunice shook her head at the recollection. The fights escalated after that as Eunice tried to make her mother see what was happening to the family, but Caroline seemed lost in her own world and only concerned with herself.

Just a few weeks before, Eunice had said some hurtful things. She wanted to know if her mother cared about her children. If she did, then how could she let Domko get away with so much? Soon after their fight, her mother had taken a handful of pills in a half-hearted suicide attempt.

What if she does it again but dies next time? Eunice thought. Then I'd be here alone with him. She shuddered. There was nobody to talk to about this - the boys just wouldn't understand.They don't know what it's like for me an' Rosie.

She thought that her mother never did like her much because she was too much a 'Pischke'. Her mother told her so all the time. Eunice hated the way the word 'Pischke' rolled off her mother's tongue like a swear word.

The teenager sat leaning against the wall and began to weep. She sat like that for hours and listened without reaction as a car approached from the south. She was mildly surprised to see it slow and turn in the driveway. She wiped away her tears, embarrassed that the driver may have seen her crying.

He stepped out of the car and introduced himself as Henry Schedler. He told Eunice that his wife Irene was not well and that they needed a live-in housekeeper. He said they lived in Spearhill, a small hamlet near Moosehorn. The job paid $75 a month and he asked if she would be interested.

Although stunned, Eunice quickly accepted the position. Her employer told her he expected her to begin work after the weekend. Eunice agreed and ran to the house to tell her mother. Caroline did not seem surprised about the job offer and Eunice wondered if she had arranged it. She was too excited to ask and couldn't believe her good luck! This was the best day in Eunice's young life.

The following day they went to Moosehorn and Caroline bought Eunice a few new pairs of underwear. Eunice could sense that her mother was embarrassed by the condition of the clothes her daughter had packed, but Caroline didn't have enough money to buy her anything new. As it was, Domko would be mad when he discovered Eunice was gone.

Caroline took Eunice to the Schedler's home that afternoon. It was one day early but her new employers didn't seem to mind.

"I'll start workin' today an' you don't even have to pay me," the teenager said excitedly.

Caroline waved good-bye to her daughter then drove away.

Eunice's departure was difficult for the twins and Rosie. They missed their older sister's mothering plus the fact she'd been a very good worker. Without her on the farm, their workload almost doubled. The children slept in the bush the night Domko discovered Eunice was gone since he'd flown into such a rage that they feared for their lives.

The twins began school a few days later. The new teacher, 21 year-old Miss Leah D'Hoore, was surprised to see them. She instructed the other students to begin their lessons, then found a place for the boys at one of the larger desks at the back of the room.

"I thought you boys weren't coming this year," she said quietly as they settled in.

"We had to work," Dennis said.

"Where's your sister Eunice?"

"She's not comin'. She's got a good job at Schedlers, keepin' care of the house."

"Alright. Well, you boys can start at the beginning of the grade seven reader. You'll have to do some work at home to get caught up because you've already missed a whole month."

The twins nodded and watched Miss D'Hoore as she returned to the front of the room. Dennis stared at her in amazement. She was undoubtedly the most beautiful woman he'd ever seen! She had long red hair and lovely clear skin, with a spattering of freckles across her nose and cheeks. Her eyes were bright and she had a very womanly figure, which made Dennis blush when he thought about it. He and David agreed that attending school would be a lot less painful with Miss D'Hoore as their teacher.

For the next two weeks, the boys found themselves trying to catch up on their lessons. There was no time before or after school so they stayed in during recess to complete their assignments.

One afternoon during the lunch recess, Miss D'Hoore sat at the front of the room and watched the boys discussing a math problem. They seemed sincere in their attempt to learn and this surprised her. She'd heard that these boys were troublemakers she had initially been thankful that they hadn't started school. When they did, she was nervous that they would act up and that she wouldn't be able to control them. So far, they'd been well-behaved and helpful.

Suddenly, one of the children came running into the school.

"Miss D'Hoore, come quick," the boy yelled. "There's a big bull in the school yard."

Miss D'Hoore jumped from her chair and ran to the window. She could see a huge, black bull walking through the school yard. She ran to the door to find that the animal had strategically placed himself between the children and the school entrance. It was the biggest, ugliest bull she'd ever seen and it was obvious that she was afraid of him. She had heard horrible stories about people being killed by bulls and had no idea how to get him out of the school yard.

Just then David and Dennis pushed past her and stepped onto the porch.

"That's our bull, Miss D'Hoore," David said. "Sorry if he scared you."

The bull stood and watched solemnly as the twins split and walked slowly towards the animal. He let out a long, low bellow as the boys neared.

"We'll get him outta here for you," Dennis said.

"Be careful," she said weakly.

"It's o.k., we're not scared of him," they said grinning.

The boys waved their arms gently and coaxed the bull to turn around.

"Go on!" David yelled, once the animal started walking toward the road. "We'll be back as soon as we get rid of him."

Miss D'Hoore called the rest of the children inside and classes resumed. The twins returned fifteen minutes later and began working on their math problems as if nothing had happened. They smiled at Miss D'Hoore who at that moment decided that she liked these boys despite what others were saying.

Caroline sat in the kitchen and called David and Dennis from their bedroom.

"Go and see what those two Devils are talking about," she said pointing out the window. "Then come back and tell me what they're saying."

The boys could see their stepfather was with the man from the church who'd been coming weekly since Domko had arrived home from the hospital. The twins went outside in time to see the man reach out and pat Domko on the back.

"You're a good man, Bob," he said as they walked towards the barn.

The boys cringed. It was comments like that which gave Domko confidence. It seemed that after this man visited, Domko would be even more irrational than usual. It was either what the man said, or Domko's interpretation, but either way the children suffered afterwards.

Domko seemed to gain a strength from these visits. Even their mother had noticed and that's why she wanted the boys to spy on the pair.

"Why do they go behind the barn instead of coming in the house?" David asked.

"I dunno," Dennis said. "Maybe they're talkin' about us and Mom."

"I think so. Mom don't like the church man much. I think he gets her in trouble with the Witnesses 'cause of the stuff ole Satan says about us."

"I don't like him either. He looks at us in a mean way."

"Who's gonna go listen?" David asked. "I don't wanna go."

"But mom said to," Dennis warned.

"Yeah, but she was talkin' to you, not me," David said. "An' you understand the church talk better than me."

Dennis thought for a moment then agreed with this assessment. He wanted to help his mother and was very curious about what was discussed by the two men.

Creeping around the west side of the barn, Dennis climbed over a fence and moved stealthily through the tall grass. He hoped to hide at the back of the barn and listen. He rounded the corner, expecting the men to be on the far side, but they were sitting right there!

The men turned around and Domko glared at him. Dennis wheeled in a full circle and ran back in the direction he came. He hid until after the man's departure, and watched from inside the barn as David and Rosie went to get the cows. It was Dennis' turn to pump water by hand into the trough.

What should I do? he wondered. *If I don't go an' pump the water then it will give Domko an excuse to get me. If I do go, he might see me and get me for spying.*

Dennis reasoned that perhaps his stepfather was going to ignore his snooping on the 'secret' conversation. Looking out the door, Dennis could see nobody around so he ran to the pump house.

Once inside, he began pumping furiously. It usually took about 25 minutes to fill the trough and Dennis hoped to finish the job and then run back to the barn to hide. He worked for about ten minutes when, all of a sudden, Domko was there. Dennis looked up and Domko's boot slammed into his face. The inside of the pump house swirled in Dennis' mind as he was punched and kicked. He was slammed against the wall and floor over and over again. Then suddenly, everything went black.

Dennis awoke in agony some time later to the sound of himself choking. His mind was foggy as he tried to turn on to his side. Blood and vomit spurted from his mouth as he gagged and choked. He fought to breathe through his nose which had been smashed flat against his head.

Slowly he got up and staggered into the house. He cried out to his mother who was sitting at the table.

"What happened?" she said, running to his side.

"Domko hit me" he said, pointing at his stepfather who stood innocently between the kitchen and front room.

"Vat?" he said. "Vat I's be do?"

"What did you do?" she screamed. "You could have killed him. Look at his face!"

Dennis waited until Domko came into the kitchen, then he staggered past and upstairs to his room. He overheard his mother coming to his defense.

"What happened to Dennis?" she demanded.

"He's be fallink off some lean-to roof," Domko said.

"What?" she said angrily. "You don't expect me to believe that?"

"Yeah. He's be fallink,"

Caroline sensed the boy must have been caught spying and this made her angry. She began swearing at Domko and threatened to call the police. They fought well into the night, about Dennis, their relationship and everything else they could think of. It abruptly ended when Domko stormed out the kitchen door.

"Where's Dennis?" Miss D'Hoore asked the following morning.

David hesitated. "He's not feelin' too good this mornin'."

"Tell him I hope he's feeling better tomorrow."

David nodded.

The next morning Dennis looked at his face in the mirror. "How do I look? Can I go to school like this?"

David examined his blackened eyes and swollen lip. "Halloween's not for a few more days," he joked.

"Thanks a lot," Dennis said.

"I'm just kiddin'," he said. "If you go to school like that, everyone's gonna know."

"Everyone knows anyway."

"Yeah, but Miss D'Hoore don't know."

"Then we can tell her I fell off 'but a some lean-to roof' and landed on my face," Dennis said sarcastically.

David laughed as the pair quietly hurried down the stairs and outside. As they approached the school, Dennis kept his eyes cast downward most of the morning. At noon, the children ate their lunches then went running outside to play. Miss D'Hoore called the twins to her desk.

"How come you boys don't ever have lunch?" she asked.

"I dunno," David said.

"You don't know?" she challenged. "Do you forget to bring it?"

"No. We don't got none to bring," he said.

"You don't have one," she corrected.

Then she eyed them thoughtfully. "What happened to your face?" she said to the battered twin.

Dennis continued looking at the floor. "I h-had an accident."

"What kind of accident?"

He fidgeted and would not answer.

Leah could sense his discomfort and changed the subject.

"I have to go eat my lunch, how would you boys like to come with me?"

The twins looked at each other then nodded.

They went across the school yard to the school cottage. Leah opened the door and the boys followed her inside.

"Ever been in here before?" she asked casually.

The twins looked at each other and were left speechless for a moment.

"When Mrs.Gering was the teacher, she used to go home to Grahamdale so this was empty," David said looking around. "We used to come in here to get away from ole Squeezer, but then Raymie started tellin' on us so we had to stop."

"Who's Squeezer?"

"Oh. Our stepfather."

"Would that be Bob Domko?" she asked as she took a jar of peanut butter and bag of bread from the shelf.

"Yeah."

"I've heard a little bit about him. What's he like?"

The boys watched as she took ten slices of bread from the bag and put them evenly on the table. She opened the peanut butter and with a knife spread a thick layer on every other slice.

"He's nuts," David said.

"Nuts?"

"Yeah. He goes to the Selkirk hospital an' they give him pills an' mom lets him come home. After a couple weeks, we gotta run away again."

"Where do you children run?"

"Any place where he can't find us. We run in the bush an' to Gus and Jim's place. We go over the beaver dam. We just run 'til we can't run no more."

"What about the police? Do you go there?"

"No, ma'am. The police don't believe us."

"Are you sure?"

"Yeah, they just bring us home an' then it's worse."

Miss D'Hoore flipped the bare slices over and handed the boys two sandwiches each. She glanced at them then went to the refrigerator, took out a carton and poured each of them a glass of milk.

"I don't have anything but peanut butter," she apologized.

"That's o.k., we like peanut butter, don't we Davey?" Dennis said.

The boys bit into the bread and were astounded by the taste. Except for the ice cream they'd had at the zoo, this was the best thing they'd ever tasted. They quickly ate the sandwiches and drank the full glasses of milk.

Miss D'Hoore's conversation with the twins bothered her for the rest of the week. She went home to visit her parents for the Thanksgiving weekend and hoped that the twins would go to the teacher's cottage if they needed somewhere to hide. She left the door open just in case.

"Eileen, you're a more experienced teacher than me," she said to her older sister after supper. "I need to ask you a question. Have you ever had a family of kids that you've worried about?"

"Yes," Eileen answered. "A few times. Why?"

"You're never gonna believe what I heard earlier this week. I've got these students named David and Dennis Pischke, they're dirt poor and they've got a crazy stepfather, and when I say crazy, I mean he's been to *Selkirk,* anyway when he's home I'm certain he beats them. . . ."

Chapter 33

March 1963

THE COLD MARCH WIND WHIPPED through the bare trees near the beaver dam. The twins sat huddled around a small fire, nursing their injuries from another ferocious beating. It had been the worst winter yet.

Eunice was no longer there to share the workload and their mother and Domko were fighting constantly.

"How much longer can we keep livin' like this?" David asked.

He and Dennis had been outside since the day before. They planned to spend at least one more night in the cold before going home.

"I dunno," Dennis said. "Do you think he hopes we just freeze to death?"

David shrugged. "Maybe, but who'd do the farm work?"

"Not Raymie that's for sure!" Dennis said indignantly. "We can work like slaves, but not his son."

David tossed the small stick he'd been playing with into the fire and watched as flames slowly consumed it.

"Yeah, he always gets mad when we run away 'cause there's no one there to work," he said. "But he's just as mad when we go back an' he finds out we're not dead."

"I've never been able to understand the ole Bastard," Dennis said. "How 'bout you?"

"No! He don't make no sense," David said. "What does 'but a some' mean anyway?"

Dennis laughed, a quiet disgusted laugh. "I think he means 'the'."

"How can mom stand him?"

"I dunno," Dennis said as he stared into the embers. "I guess she can't smell him!"

Laughing about their tormentor was a survival tactic the twins learned at an early age and used often. It made talking about their situation bearable.

Dennis reached for another log then put it into the crackling fire. A small wisp of smoke rose and within a few minutes the log was burning. "Is he gonna kill us?" he asked solemnly.

David looked at his hands draped across his knees. He'd been thinking about their future a lot lately and wondered if they were going to get off the farm alive.

"He might," David answered. "He's gettin' worse an' if we don't go someplace soon, we're not gonna get away."

"Where should we go?"

"We'll go over the beaver dam again but his time we'll stay for good," David answered dreamily. "We'll find good jobs an' make lots of money."

Dennis nodded in approval. He knew that running away was the only answer. They would have to wait until the snow melted and the farmers needed hired hands. If they went too soon, they'd just be sent home.

David put his feet in front of the fire and unwrapped the rags he had tied around them. He had to wrap an old shirt around each foot after Domko took his felt boots away. David's feet had grown so much that the toes poked through the end and this had enraged Domko.

"Hey, Davey have you ever noticed how people look at us when we tell them about Satan?"

David laughed. "Yeah, some of them look like they don't believe us."

"When we get away from here, are you gonna tell people 'bout what he's done?"

"I dunno," David said. "Do you think people will believe us?"

Dennis stared at his brother in disbelief. "They'd have to! It's true! Why would they think we'd lie?"

David shrugged. "Who knows? People are stupid, you know. Squeezer's got friends an' they won't never believe us."

"Yeah, but everyone else will."

"I think I'm gonna just try to forget," David said as he shifted his weight and tried to get comfortable on the cold ground.

Dennis gasped. "You can't forget! We gotta tell people! If he don't kill us, we gotta tell people so they will know what happened."

David looked into the dark bush. "It don't matter if we do or not."

"Yes it does!" Dennis insisted. "You gotta promise that if he kills me first, you'll remember an' tell people."

David shrugged. A tiny lump rose in his throat. Both he and his brother had come to terms with the fact that Domko might kill them someday. David thought it was odd that telling people the truth seemed more important to Dennis than surviving.

The boys sat quietly watching the fire. David was lost in his thoughts when Dennis finally broke the silence.

"If we died, do you think anybody would miss us?" he asked.

David looked at his brother and his chin began to waver. He stared deeply into his twin's eyes and wished he could tell him that they were loved by many people. David tried hard to think of somebody who'd miss them. Ashamed, he looked at the ground and wiped away a tear.

"No," he whispered. "Nobody would."

The boys woke the next morning mildly surprised that they were still alive. It had been a cold night and while they had re-fuelled the fire many times, it was now reduced to ashes.

"Well, we ain't dead yet so we better go get somethin' to eat," David laughed, his spirits suddenly brightened by a new day and the prospect of a good meal in Emma's kitchen. He'd awakened with a new sense of purpose after being haunted all night by Dennis' request to tell people about their pain and suffering. Suddenly telling people what they'd lived through became paramount.

They began trudging through the deep snow.

"I've been thinkin," David said. "You're right, Denny. We gotta tell people if we live."

Dennis was pleased to hear that his brother agreed with him after all. "Yeah, if I live I'm gonna tell everybody how Domko treated us an' how some people helped us an' some didn't."

The boys vowed that they would not hide behind the shame.

"Someday when we're big," David said. "We'll find somebody who'll help us tell the whole world."

Emma invited the boys into her kitchen and fussed over them as she always did. Gus was outside working, so she welcomed the company. Her reconciliation with Caroline had been brief. Domko had arrived home from the Selkirk hospital soon after Emma's spring visit and he no longer allowed the women to socialize.

Emma fried three eggs for each of the boys and sliced fresh bread until it was piled high on the plate. The twins slathered thick gobs of jam on the bread and ate heartily.

"Have some more," Emma offered as she poured them another cup of cocoa.

They chatted for a while before the twins raised the serious subject on both their minds. It was, in fact, the real reason they'd come to see Emma.

"Auntie Emma," David asked. "If we freeze or drown goin' across the beaver dam to get away from Squeezer, then it's his fault, right?"

Emma looked at the boys. "I suppose so, why do you ask?"

"An' if he kills us some day even if it looks like an accident, will the police know?" Dennis asked. "'Cause he's tried but we just don't die. If we do sometime, will you make sure the police know it was him who killed us?"

Emma stopped sipping her coffee to stare at the teenager. She was left speechless by their matter-of-fact tones. David could sense they'd disturbed her, but finished what he was saying.

"'Cause mom always sticks up for him 'cause she's scared too," David said, lowering his voice. "If he kills Dennis, then I'm gonna tell everybody. But if he kills us both, then will you?"

Emma was flabbergasted. "Don't talk like that!" she blurted. "He's not going to kill you boys, I'm sure of it, especially since you've made it this far. You're almost grown now. Soon, you'll get off the farm and things will be better."

The twins stared at her, waiting for their answer.

"Well, will you?" Dennis asked.

Emma felt a pang of regret in her stomach. She wished that she and Gus had been more help to the family. Honestly though, she didn't know what more they could have done.

"Well, I know one thing for sure," she said. "I'll never forget you boys and I'll never forget what he's done to you. And I swear to God, if you boys turn up dead, I won't rest until people know the truth."

The twins smiled. That was the answer they both wanted to hear.

"But that doesn't mean I want you to give up, you hear?" she chided.

Emma got up and disappeared into the front room, her words trailing behind her. "And I want you to know I've been thinkin' about you boys."

She re-appeared a short time later carrying two white toques. "I'm ashamed I didn't give them to you sooner, but Domko chased me off when I brought them over. I thought he might take it out on you boys so I just put them away for a while.

She handed the toques to the boys. "I haven't seen you boys much this winter. Where have you been hiding?"

The boys pulled the identical toques over their heads and smiled at each other.

"We've been in the church an' the barn an' we've been in the bush," Dennis said. "Sometimes we stay in the school cottage on the weekends when Miss D'Hoore is gone. Please , don't tell nobody 'cause we don't want to get in trouble."

"I won't," Emma said waving off the idea.

"We're smarter now so we know how to trick the ole bast . . . I mean, ole Satan," David said. "We know how to sneak food when he's not lookin' an' Miss D'Hoore makes us samiches."

"That's SANDWiches," Dennis corrected.

"I know, that's what I said, samiches."

Emma laughed.

"Is it a school day?" Dennis asked. They hadn't attended for a few days and weren't sure.

"Hmmm," she said glancing at the calendar. "Yes, it's Wednesday. The 13th by the looks of it. Are you boys goin' to school today?"

They nodded yes and stood up to leave. The twins thanked Emma for the breakfast, pulled on their felt rubbers and waved good-bye.

"Puck puck Muchtork!" David yelled as he swung his legs out the bedroom window then let himself fall to the ground. He landed hard on his feet and rolled onto his side. He jumped up and ran to the edge of the house. He could hear Dennis' anguished screams as Domko whipped him with the belt. When he couldn't listen to the agonizing sounds any longer, he ran to hide in the chicken coop.

That's what he'd told Dennis in their language that he'd do - wait in the chicken coop, unless Domko came then he'd run to the beaver dam and wait there. David hoped that thoughts of going to the Koch's house would give Dennis strength.

David waited patiently behind the chicken coop door. He listened to the sound of the house door opening and shutting. He held his breath and listened to footsteps in the yard. The crisp sound of a gun bolt clicking in place caused him to stiffen. David could hear Domko's unmistakable grunting as he scoured the yard. Soon it was quiet, and David emerged from behind the door and peeked outside. He could see Domko walking slowly down the driveway, gun in hand as he looked from side to side.

He watched until Domko was on the road. Just then, there was movement at the window and Dennis leaped out. He landed hard on the ground, then in one motion got up and ran towards the chicken coop. David opened the door and stepped outside.

"Are you o.k.?" David asked as the boys ran towards the far bush.

"Yeah. I pretended I was dead an' when he left I jumped out the window," Dennis said.

"Lucky you didn't land on him," David said. "Let's get outta here, he's lookin' for me an' he's got the gun."

The boys ran into the bush and kept going until they found themselves on the lake bank once again. Every sound caused them to turn as they looked across the dark water. They shivered at the sight of tiny waves lapping on the shore. The other side seemed far away.

"How are we gonna get across?" Dennis asked.

David looked around. "There's a beaver who's blocked things off by the drain ditch," he said. "We can cross on the other side of the ditch 'cause the water's always shallow there. It's a long way around, but it's too deep here."

The boys walked along the lake bank to its southern-most tip. They came to a fortress of logs and sticks with a mud hut in the centre. The twins knew they were nearing the wide drainage ditch that channeled water from Pischke Lake into Lake Manitoba. They could see the spanse of water become narrow and shallower as rocks broke the surface in places.

The thought of walking through the cold water did not appeal to either boy.

"Why don't we just go to the road?" Dennis asked.

David looked in that direction and listened. He could hear a vehicle somewhere in the distance and there was a chance that Domko had gone back for the car and was looking for them along the road.

"We can't," David said. "He's wild 'bout us goin' to the neighbours. He's scared 'bout the police comin' and takin' him back to Selkirk. Hear that car? I bet it's him lookin' for us again."

Dennis' eyes widened. He remembered that they had twice run down the road and Domko had caught them easily. They were trying to run away, which made matters worse, and had received a horrible beating when they got home.

"Yeah. It won't be so bad in the water," Dennis said. "We can cross this ditch an' be on the other side in no time."

The boys looked at the glassy water. It was early May and although it had been a warm spring, the water temperature was undoubtedly just above the freezing point. Neither boy wanted to step into the frigid ditch.

Suddenly, they heard a noise behind them. The twins froze at the water's edge as they heard a faint rustling in the bushes directly behind them. Thinking it was Domko with the gun, David grabbed Dennis' arm and pulled him to the ground. The rustling abated as David slowly turned and strained to see into the dark bush. A moment later, the still, cool air was penetrated by the sound of footsteps in the underbrush, coming directly towards them.

Without further hesitation, they stepped into the cold water. The boys waded silently up to their thighs and the water rippled lightly as they tried not to splash. Dennis glanced nervously over his shoulder but saw nothing along the shore.

"Do you think it was him?" he asked.

"I dunno but I didn't wanna stand there an' find out," David said.

"Me neither. I'm freezin' my legs off - are we almost there?"

"We got to keep walkin', David coaxed, "it'll get shallow soon."

The boys waded as the water continued to get deeper. Deep ruts in the ditch made the bottom slippery and difficult to walk on. As they neared the other shore, they discovered the ruts became even deeper and soon they were up to their waists in water.

"C'mon we'll walk further south," David groaned, altering his direction slightly as Dennis followed closely behind.

Dry ground was less than 100 yards away when the boys' legs began to cramp.

"What should we do?" David gasped as he massaged his legs. "We gotta get outta the water before we freeze!"

Dennis agreed. "Just keep goin'. We can see the shore."

"Yeah, but it's getting deeper!" David cried.

But it's too far to go back!" Dennis yelled. "We'll just hurry."

David took a deep breath as he continued to wade. One more deep rut underfoot plunged the boys in up to their chests. Both boys groaned and cried out from the pains that shot sharply through their extremities.

"Keep going!" Dennis yelled, encouraging his brother and himself. "We're almost there!"

Gradually, the water began to recede and within a few minutes, they were standing on dry land. They shivered uncontrollably as they stood in the cold night. It was dark now and the only light they had come from the brightness of the moon. The wind was beginning to blow.

"You got any matches?" Dennis asked through chattering teeth.

"No."

"I didn't think so."

"Ole Squeezer keeps 'em in his bedroom now so I can't find 'em," David said. "We're not far from Koch's an' since there's no snow to walk through, it won't take long to get there."

The boys hurried through the field then into a bluff of trees. They followed the same light they'd seen the time they came through the reeds. They kept their minds busy by pointing out trees, rocks and other landmarks that looked vaguely familiar. Soon they found themselves on the same road they'd travelled the last time they crossed the lake, but this time the Kochs house was nowhere to be seen.

"Where'd the farm go?" Dennis asked.

"I dunno," David said looking around. "Which direction do you think we should go?"

Dennis pointed north. "We probably came out there last time. Maybe we're all turned around?"

The boys trudged along the road, expecting to arrive at Koch's house after rounding each unfamiliar bluff of trees.

The wind picked up slightly and a light rain began to fall. The boys were already wet and, the pelting of the cold rain just added to their misery. Soon they saw a light in the distance and hurried towards it. As they got closer, they realized this wasn't the Koch house.

"Should we ask to stay here?" Dennis asked.

"We better," David said. "We're all wet and we'll freeze if we don't."

The twins rapped on the door. A man answered and David recognized him immediately. This was the same man who had caught Dennis feeding Domko's cows in the man's grainfield. A huge fight had ensued between the man and Domko. As usual, Dennis had been blamed by Domko.

"C-can we c-come in," David asked meekly as the pair stood expectantly at the door.

The man looked at them suspiciously.

"You boys go back to where you came from," he said. "I don't want to get involved."

The door shut a moment later and the twins were left standing on the stoop in the pouring rain.

"Come on, Denny," David said angrily. "Let's get outta here."

They walked down the driveway and along the road when they noticed an abandoned building a short distance away. They saw no lights farther north on the road and decided they should spend the night in the old shed.

"We gotta dry off," Dennis said, walking ahead. "This is a good spot."

He opened the door and David followed him inside. There was nothing in the shed except a few rusted iron rails and an old red jerry can. The shed was reasonably dry, so the twins found themselves a place in a corner to gather their thoughts. Pressing their bodies together they listened to the patter of rain on the roof, which by now was falling in big drops. They could also hear the skittering of mice along the edges of the inside wall.

"Tomorrow we'll go to Schedlers an' find Eunice," David said. "She'll know what we should do. In the mornin', it'll be easier to find our way around instead of in the dark."

They boys resigned themselves to spending a long, cold, miserable night in the shed.

The next morning they emerged stiff and hungry. They headed in the general direction of Grahamdale and walked through the sloppy wet fields. They found themselves on a road and asked a motorist for directions. Soon they were standing in front of Schedler's house. The boys knocked on the door and were happy to see Eunice answer. She was surprised and pleased to see them, but slightly embarrassed by their dishevelled appearances. The boys explained what had happened and told her that they didn't want to go home again.

After discussing the boys' plight with Mr. Schedler, Eunice washed and dried her brothers' clothes. They boys were fed lunch while Mr. Schedler made a few telephone calls.

"Don't tell mom where we are," David whispered to Eunice. "We don't wanna go home no more."

Eunice nodded in understanding. She had a wonderful life with the Schedlers and shuddered at the thought of having to go back to the farm. She didn't want that for herself or for her brothers either.

Later that afternoon, Mr. Schedler found them a place to go where they could work for their room and board. The twins went to live with Fred and Mary Buztynski whose farm was very close to the Koch's. Had the boys continued along the road instead of sleeping in the shed the night before, they would have come to the Buztynski's home.

The Buztynski's needed two farm hands and agreed to keep the boys for a few months. Fred and his wife Mary were nice people who fed and treated them well. There was a lot of work for the boys to do, but they were strong, capable and willing workers when they weren't being beaten.

The twins began work the next day. They shoveled manure and picked stones from the fields. Near the end of the month, they seeded a field in oats. Occasionally they went to visit the Kochs who lived nearby.

"Do you think mom knows where we are?" Dennis asked one Sunday afternoon when they walked from the Kochs back to the Buztynski's house.

David thought for a moment. "No, or she woulda come to get us. She an' Domko probably think we died somewhere an' are too scared to phone the police in case they get blamed."

Dennis laughed. "I don't care just as long as they don't come."

They twins worked for the Buztynskis for nearly two months. Caroline and their brother Walter came to visit one Sunday afternoon. It was an awkward reunion as their mother tried to persuade them to go back to the farm. The twins were adamant about staying where they were and eventually their mother and Walter left. The boys fell back into a routine, but knew that the Buztynskis wouldn't be needing them much longer.

One day while the twins repaired fences by the road, a car slowly pulled up beside them. A man got out of the car and walked towards the boys. He introduced himself as Herman Bray from Grahamdale. He had heard that Buztynskis wouldn't be needing the twins anymore and wondered if one of them would like to work on his farm. The boys nodded favourably at first, but then it struck them. The man only wanted one of them.

Herman looked both boys over and then offered the job to Dennis. He was quick to say that he'd find a place for David too. The twins agreed and Herman came back the following day. The boys thanked the Buztynskis and soon were soon on their way, each to new homes.

The twins were not happy about being separated. Except for the time Dennis had run to the Brown and Sherbert homes, the boys had never been apart for more than a day. They knew that not everyone needed two farm hands, especially when they were growing boys who ate a lot. They knew they had to earn their keep.

David was upset and also jealous that Herman had chosen Dennis over him. They sat quietly in the back seat of Herman's car as he drove towards Highway No. 6. The boys parted company when David was dropped off at a farm on the highway at the Grahamdale curve. His new boss was a man named Mr. Whipper. After a minimal introduction, David was put to work immediately. He became discouraged when he was sent to shovel manure out of the barn. The barn hadn't been cleaned in so long that the manure was almost high enough for the cows to walk into the loft and live there instead of on the ground floor.

"It would be easier to pick up the barn an' move it," David muttered to himself as he began shoveling.

* * * * *

Dennis settled in nicely at the Bray home. Herman's wife Crystal was a lovely woman who treated Dennis like a son. She was an excellent cook and kept a clean, beautiful home. Herman was a little 'rough around the edges' but was a kind man who was always good to Dennis.

It was here that Dennis saw Nick Skleparik once again. Nick worked part time for the Brays and was a kind enough to teach Dennis the social skills he'd never learned at home.

Nick was a Witness, who, in Dennis' mind, was the epitome of human kindness. Nick had been thrown off the farm by Domko years before, much to the dismay of Dennis. The twin wished that all the Witnesses who came to visit were as principled as Nick. Dennis began studying the bible and watched intensely as Nick slowly converted Herman to the truth according to the Jehovah's Witnesses.

* * * * *

David stayed at the Whipper farm for only a few weeks. He was overwhelmed by the workload and despondent about not being allowed to see Dennis who was only three miles away. This prompted him to accept his mother's next offer to go home. He arrived back on the farm and immediately began haying. Rosie was happy to see him since she and her mother had been doing all the chores.

Domko was as belligerent as ever, but dared not ridicule David for fear he might run away again. It had been difficult getting the work done without the twins. Although Domko never admitted it, he was beginning to realize how valuable they were to the farming operation.

One afternoon in September, David was called to the kitchen and Domko gave him a watch. It was payment for the work he'd done in the hayfield. Domko was very pleased with himself for thinking of the present David accepted gratefully, even though he suspected the gift might be stolen. He put the watch on his wrist and was very pleased with how it looked. He'd never had such a nice present before and treasured it. He carefully took it off at night and put it on a small shelf, then strapped it back on in the morning.

David began grade eight near the end of September, but was only able to attend nine days in October because there was so much work on the farm. As time wore on he began to miss Dennis terribly but he kept busy and accompanied Rosie to school when he could.

David got dressed one morning in early December and reached for his watch but found it was missing. He looked all over the house but could not find it. Domko soon noticed the watch was missing and began asking him about it.

"Vere's be but a some vatch?" he asked suspiciously. "You's be trowink it in the bush?"

David protested that he didn't lose the watch. He said it had been misplaced and would find it soon. Domko berated him about the missing watch all winter while David looked everywhere for it. The stepfather knew that David wouldn't want to flee into the cold night by himself so when he tired of beating Rosie, he began attacking David again.

One afternoon in early spring, David was sitting at the kitchen table. He glanced into his mother's purse which sat open on the chair beside him. He noticed his watch inside and took it out, discovering it had been completely destroyed. He stuffed it in his pocket, then confronted his mother about it when she was alone.

"Ma, I found my watch in your purse," he whispered. "Why didn't you tell me you found it?"

Caroline flushed.

"You must have left it in your pocket," she whispered in reply. "I put it through the ringer on the washing machine by mistake."

"What? How come you didn't tell me?," he demanded. "How could you let him taunt me about it all winter?"

Caroline's eyes widened, then she began to cry softly. "I was too scared to tell him. I hoped that he would forget and I kept the watch hopin' that I could get you a new one that looked just like it. He never lets me go to town alone, though."

David sighed. He was angry at his mother for what she had done, but understood how it felt to be afraid of Domko.

"He's getting worse and I'm afraid of him," she said.

"Then why don't you call the police to take him back to Selkirk?" he asked, in a soft voice.

Caroline said nothing. "If he found out it was me, he'd kill me."

"Then get someone else to do it," David said. "Why do you let him get away with this?"

Caroline turned away, refusing to say anything more.

During the next few weeks, Domko continued to berate David about the missing watch while the boy and his mother sat in silence.

* * * * *

On an early April afternoon, David was shoveling manure beside the barn where the horses were kept over the winter. He was thinking about Dennis and wondering how life was treating his twin in his new home. David hummed softly to himself as he shoveled heavy chunks of half-frozen manure on the wagon. He chuckled as he thought of the huge manure pile in Mr. Whipper's barn. He wondered who the next unsuspecting farm hand might be.

Standing with his back to the house, he had an uneasy feeling suddenly pass over him. A tiny voice inside his head told him to turn around. He smelled the foul stench he recognized as Domko's body odour and turned quickly. At that second, a pitchfork came like a bullet through the air, its prongs sticking into the barn just inches from David's stomach. David looked in horror at the fork which protruded from the wall, the prongs deep in the weathered wood. Domko was less than three yards away and he lunged at the boy.

Instinctively, David dropped the shovel and darted around the edge of the barn. His boots slipped on wet manure as he ran towards the bush. He heard the footsteps behind him abate and realized he'd outrun Domko. He continued down the path at top speed until he could hear Domko swearing back in the distance.

He must have found the watch, David thought.*Or maybe it's something else. Who knows? Maybe he saw me eating lunch, or maybe I smiled when I thought of Whipper's manure pile and he saw that. All I know is, I can't go back now 'cause he'll kill me fore sure.*

David went to the lake and walked along the shore for a while. He turned and meandered back into the bush until he came to an old campfire site that he and Dennis had shared many times the winter before. He gathered wood, made a fire with matches he'd managed to steal from Domko's bedroom and sat down. It was then he realized how much he missed Dennis. While he hoped that his brother had a good life at the Bray house, he wished that he had been chosen as well.

What's wrong with me? he thought, feeling sorry for himself. *I'm a good worker too. Boy, is that Dennis ever lucky! When am I gonna get outta here anyway? I wanna go to Winnipeg and do some drawing, but I don't know who to ask for help.*

David snared and cooked a rabbit for supper then sat for hours after his meal, mulling over his life. No matter how hard he tried to escape, he couldn't get away from the farm.

The next time I go, I'm gone for good, he promised as he fell asleep.

The next afternoon David was daydreaming when he heard someone coming along the bush trail. Thinking it was Domko, he crouched down behind his small wood pile. He flared his nostrils, hoping to smell whatever might be coming. The rustling continued, then somebody called his name. David recognized the voice as Norman's.

"Hey Norman!" he called as he stood up. "I'm over here."

Norman waved, then left the trail and pushed his way through the bush.

"I finally found you," he said. "I've been lookin' for you all mornin'."

"What are you doin' here?" David asked.

"Ma phoned me an' asked if I'd come lookin' for you," Norman said. "I guess the ole bastard came in yesterday an' told her that he'd stabbed you with a pitchfork."

David shook his head. "Yeah, Squeezer missed me by that much," he said pressing his thumb and index finger a half inch apart. "If I hadn't turned around, he'd a killed me for sure."

Norman snorted in disgust. "What's wrong with him anyway? Who keeps lettin' him outta Selkirk?"

David shrugged.

"He sure is nuts. He thinks I'm gonna take the farm away from his kids, but he needs me to work. It don't make no sense."

"Why did he try to stab you?"

"I don't know," David said innocently. "I was just shovelin' when he did it."

"Does he still beat the hell outta you kids?" Norman asked.

"Yeah. Poor Rosie, he's gotten her good a few times. I was listenin' to him beatin' her the other night an' she finally just gave up screamin'."

"Bastard!" Norman said as he kicked his black boot into the ground. Then he reached into his breast pocket. "Guess what I got?"

"What?"

Norman smiled as he brought out a small, silver handgun. He stroked it carefully then grinned at David. "You can use it on him if you want." he offered.

David's eyes widened. "No, I can't. Me an' Denny already tried that once an' I'm too scared to do it again."

Norman laughed as he gave his brother a shove.

"C'mon, let's go back to the farm," he said. "I'm stayin' there tonight an tomorrow we're goin' to Moosehorn. You can come live with me."

David's mouth dropped open. He could hardly believe his good luck! To live with Norman would be a dream come true. He was fun, exciting and he had a motorcycle and a car. To live in Moosehorn would be much better than being a farm hand. David kicked out the fire then they both started walking towards the trail.

"I'm sleepin' with this tonight," Norman said lifting the gun over his shoulder and then shoving it in the waistband of his jeans. "If the ole bugger comes upstairs tonight, I'm gonna blow his head off."

Chapter 34

Moving to Moosehorn

THAT NIGHT NORMAN SLEPT with the gun in his jeans just as he'd promised. David sat awake for a long time, wondering if Domko would come upstairs or not. He had mixed feelings about Norman's threat. David believed that Norman would shoot Domko if provoked. He worried that if Norman killed Domko, it would spoil his plans to move to Moosehorn.

The next morning, Norman seemed slightly disappointed that he hadn't been given an excuse to shoot Domko. Their stepfather sat at the table and watched the pair finish their breakfast then go outside. Once away from Domko's watchful gaze, the boys began making plans.

"Do you got any money?" Norman whispered.

"No, I'm just workin' for room an' board," he said.

Then David remembered the bond he'd won in the art contest. "But I got a $50 bond at the bank from winnin' that contest."

"Do you think you can get it?"

"Yeah. They said I can have it when I finish school."

"Well, if you're movin' to Moosehorn with me," Norman said slyly. "Then I guess you've finished school."

"I guess so. We can go to the bank later."

"Hey," Norman asked as they crouched around the corner of the house. " Do you got your driver's license yet?"

"My driving license? No. Domko wouldn't let me."

"Christ, man you're missin' out!" Norman said whistling. "We gotta get you a driver's license! You'll never get a job without one."

"What do I gotta do?"

"You'll need your birth certificate to prove you're sixteen. Do you got that?"

"I don't but I can look through ma's papers an' see if I can find it," David suggested.

"O.k., you go do that an' I'll go help 'em in the barn," he said punching David in the arm. "We'll leave after lunch."

David nodded. The boys waited outside until Domko came out and motioned for them to go to the barn.

"What if he sees me go in the house?" David asked fearfully.

"Don't worry," Norman said confidently. "He ain't never gonna beat you again, 'specially not when I'm here."

David's heart swelled with pride. He went into the house to his mother's room. He assumed she kept all her important papers in the cardboard box that sat on top of her bureau.

David took the box down, sat on the bed and pulled back the flaps. There was a huge stack of papers inside, and for a moment finding the birth certificate seemed like a daunting task. He lifted out a handful of documents and letters.He felt guilty looking through his mother's personal things but reasoned she'd never give him the birth certificate if he asked. Once she knew he was leaving the farm, she'd likely become very uncooperative.

He began flipping through the papers. He discovered Mark and Raymond's birth certificates, plus and a clipped stack of official looking papers from the blind school. David was careful to put everything in the same order he'd found it, piling letters and pictures of the Kolodka family on top. There were invoices and the deed to their land. The further down he dug the older and more interesting the documents became.

Near the bottom of the box he found a folded paper and when he opened it, discovered a picture of his father. He recognized him immediately. That long nose, wide grin and laughing eyes - how he'd longed to see that face many times over the last 13 years! He stared at the picture then read the marriage certificate it had been wrapped in. David stared at the picture for a long time, suddenly feeling apprehensive about the changes coming in his life.

Was he ready? Could he live in Moosehorn and get a good job? What about Dennis?

David worried about his mother and wondered if he was doing the right thing by leaving the farm. He wondered what his father would have wanted him to do. He asked out loud if he should stay and take care of his mother and Rosie. He listened for the voice to answer his question, but heard nothing.

Would his father think he was a coward for running away?

Reluctantly, he set the picture and certificate aside. He reached into the box and brought out a handful of papers. In this bundle he found the birth certificates of Dennis and himself. He read them carefully to be sure he had the correct documents, then tucked them in one of his pant pockets.

Still unsure about what to do next, he put the other papers back inside the box then careful tucked his father's picture near the bottom.

He hoisted the box overhead and placed it back on the bureau. He stood back and surveyed it, to see if it looked as if it had been disturbed. It was then he saw a brown envelope that was sticking out a bit from an exposed rafter in the ceiling. He stood on the edge of the bed and pulled the envelope down. It was addressed to him and had been opened.

David read in disbelief a letter which said an application sent on his behalf had been accepted by a Winnipeg school. All he had to do was fill out the enclosed enrollment form and the bursary to pay the associated costs would be forwarded to the school. The Brooke Bond company was mentioned as well as the Manitoba Department of Education.The letter ended by saying that he was a very talented young man and that the school administration looked forward to having him as a pupil in their drafting-commercial art program for the 1963-64 school year.

The letter was dated April of 1963. He glanced at the calendar on the wall - April 20, 1964.

David had known many disappointments in his young life, but until this day had never experienced a hurt of such magnitude. His chest pounded heavily and his mind whirled as he realized the opportunity he'd missed. A chance to go to art school for free! It was almost more than he could stand to realize that his dream of becoming a professional artist had been dashed by his own mother.

How could she do this to me? he thought as he tossed the envelope on the bed and stormed out of the bedroom. He ran upstairs and packed a few clothes in a bag. He fell on the bed and cried, yelling in frustration as tears streamed down his cheeks.

I'm never gonna draw anything, ever again, he thought as he pounded the bed with his fists.

David stayed upstairs until heard everyone come inside from the barn. Norman dashed up the stairs.

"What's the matter with you?" Norman asked as he picked up David's bag of clothes.

"Nothin," David said rubbing his eyes with the cuff of his shirt.

"Did you get it?" Norman asked.

"Yeah," he sniffled. "Let's get outta here. Where's Flatfoot? I gotta talk to mom before we go."

"You're not gonna tell her are you?"

"I'm gonna tell her alright," David said. "But not what you think."

Norman shrugged. "He's feedin' his stupid birds."

David got up from the bed and stormed past Norman without looking at him.

His brother followed behind then whispered, "I'll be waitin' in the car. We gotta go 'cause I gotta get back to work. I already missed half a day."

David nodded as he went into the kitchen. The sight of his mother serving Kathy's lunch made him even angrier.

She sent Kathy to the blind school, he thought. *It's good enough for her but not for me. Mine wasn't even gonna cost no money.*

"Ma, I gotta talk to you," he said quietly.

Caroline turned to look at him. His eyes were bloodshot from crying.

"What's wrong with you?" she asked.

"What's wrong with me?" he said indignantly, slapping himself on the chest. "What's wrong with you? Ma, I found the envelope about the art school in your room. How come you never told me about it?"

Caroline flushed then turned away as she poured the fresh milk into the separator.

"What were you doing in my papers? she asked.

"Your papers? Ma, that letter was 'sposed to be for me," he said.

"I'm your mother, so I can read it if I want," she said indignantly. "Art school? What would you want to go there for?"

"What for? *What for?* So I can get a good job, that's why." he said.

"Good job? What kinda job can you get from learnin' art? Nothin, that's what. All they do is take your money an' then you end up with no job when it's finished."

"Money? It was free! I read the letter an' it said that 'cause we got no money some rich people were gonna pay for me to go. If you don't think goin' to school is good, then why'd you send Kathy?"

"That's different," she said. "Kathy's blind"

"An' she's Squeezer's kid, right? Dad's kids never got nothin! That was my chance Ma, and you wrecked it for me."

Caroline poured herself a cup of tea. "Domko would never let you go anyway," she said.

"Not let me? If I'd have known, he wouldn't have been able to stop me! I woulda went, Ma, I'm tellin' you that right now."

"And then when it didn't work out, what would you have done?" she yelled. "Come back home?"

"Back, here? To shovel shit for the rest of my life?" he yelled back in anger. " It was my best dream an' now I'm never gonna get the chance. You wrecked it, just like you wrecked everything else in our lives."

Caroline's shoulders slumped and she turned her back on him. Then she began to sob as she rubbed her hand across her abdomen. Her eleventh child was due in a few months.

David watched her for a moment then walked toward the door, a lump rising in his throat.

"Bye, Ma," he said as he closed it behind him.

* * * * *

Herman Bray had experienced summer financial difficulties and told Dennis he'd have to go home because there was no money to pay him what he was owed. Dennis had been very frightened by this prospect. He told Herman he could keep the $150 in back pay and Dennis would work for free as long as he was allowed to stay. Herman was agreeable and the deal was made.

A relative of Caroline's came one day to visit Dennis at Brays and took him aside. This farmer told him that he'd been swindled. He said that if Dennis went to work for him, he'd pay him $2 a day - double what Herman had said he'd pay before he ran out of money.

Dennis thought about this for a few days and decided he would accept the man's offer. The Brays had been very upset to see him leave.

Dennis arrived at the man's farm and soon found that there was double the amount of work he'd been doing. To add insult to injury, one of Domko's old horses, Darby, was there too! Dennis worked for three days then realized he'd made a mistake. He packed his clothes and climbed out of a bedroom window in the middle of the night. The Brays were happy to have him back.

"You have to be careful who you trust," Crystal had warned. "People will take advantage of nice boys like yourself."

Ashamed that he had not paid Dennis for working that summer, and for precipitating his leaving, Herman bought Dennis a motorcycle and began paying him an allowance. Dennis also noticed that Herman referred to him as 'Mine Dennis' when he spoke of him. This, the allowance and the motorcycle put Dennis on top of the world!

Dennis decided to visit his mother one Friday afternoon in early summer. He phoned first to be sure that Domko was not home. He told Crystal he'd be away for the afternoon then jumped on his motorbike and drove to the farm. He arrived to find his mother and Rosie working harder than ever.

Neither Caroline nor Rosie should have been working that hard. Caroline was pregnant and Rosie was suffering so badly from malnutrition that she had festering sores on her legs. Dennis felt sorry for his mother and sister, but a keen sense of self-preservation kept him from offering to come back.

He sat in the kitchen with his mother, making small talk and drinking tea. Raymond was in school while Kathy jogged on the spot in the front room. Mark played with toys on the floor.

Dennis looked at his half-brother jealously. Domko had never allowed him and David to have toys.

"Ma, I was wonderin' if I could have Dad's old gun," he asked.

"What for?" she asked as she refilled his tea cup.

"I'd just like to have it that's all," he said. "Satan's got his own guns an' I don't got nothin to remember dad by."

Caroline thought for a moment then agreed. "But don't tell Domko I gave it to you."

Dennis said he wouldn't. They visited a while longer then Caroline handed him the gun as he was leaving.

Dennis waved good bye to his mother, climbed on his motorcycle and drove on the back roads to Grahamdale. He arrived 'home' and went inside to tell Crystal he was back.

"I'm goin' out to the garage for a while," he said.

"Alright, I'll call you when it's supper time," she called from the kitchen.

Dennis hurried back out to his motorcycle and picked up the gun he had placed carefully on the ground. He walked confidently to Herman's garage and set the rifle on the work bench. A flood of memories returned as he looked at the old, somewhat rusted .22 calibre rifle.

Dennis remembered how his father would carry the rifle over his shoulder when he went hunting. He and David had learned to hunt with that same gun and it was the one Norman had used to kill Marjorie's dog, Sandy.

It was the the gun that jammed the day he had tried to shoot Domko, sealing the fate of the twins for the next eight years. It was the gun that Domko had pointed at them so many times in anger. He'd laugh at how ironic it would be to shoot the twins with 'Beel's' gun.

This was also the weapon that Dennis held on the lowest day in his life. Now his mother was handing it to him and it was up to him how it would be used in future.

He found a hacksaw and changed the blade, before placing the gun in a vise and sawing the rusty barrel. The blade squeaked back and forth as Dennis put all his strength into it. Tears of frustration streamed down his cheeks.

Never again will this gun be used to scare anybody, he thought. *Dad wouldn't have wanted his gun to be used against his own kids.*

David had been right - things were better over the beaver dam and he'd kept his promise by taking Dennis there. In a way, his mother had been right too. For himself, justice was right around the corner. He now lived with wonderful people who sincerely loved him. He'd waited and suffered and now his life was just beginning. Dennis was glad he hadn't given up and had chosen the right path. He'd learned how to survive and it had made him a stronger person.

The blade continued to squeak through the steel. Dennis sawed faster as the blade suddenly cut through and the piece dropped to the ground.

I'll never shoot anything again, he vowed as he measured another six inches and began to cut again. An hour later when he had finished and the barrel was in many pieces, he disassembled the stock and held the smooth bolt in his hand. He examined it closely then dropped it in his pocket. He picked up the rest of the gun and tossed it in Herman's scrap pile in a corner of the garage.

Dennis cried once more then opened the garage door. When he stepped out, it felt as if a twelve-year weight had been lifted from his young shoulders. He felt as if he'd already lived a thousand lives. He walked confidently to the house, knowing he was no longer the frightened little boy whom Domko loathed.

Dennis felt like a man.

* * * * *

Later that summer David went to visit Dennis and the twins had a cheerful reunion.

David had been managing on his own, but found himself consumed by loneliness. He missed his twin and hoped to lure Dennis to the bright lights further south.

"Do you ever come to Moosehorn?" David asked.

"Yeah," Dennis began. "I stopped at Norman's trailer once but you weren't there."

"Well, I'm in Winnipeg workin' now an' only come out on weekends."

"Where are you workin'?" Dennis asked.

"I got this great job with Ramsey-Bird Construction," David said, his eyes dancing. "You should see me Denny, I'm drivin' these big road construction machines, all different kinds, an' it's great work."

Dennis was impressed. "How much money do you make?"

"A hundred and fifty bucks every two weeks," he said proudly.

Dennis' mouth gaped wide, then he slowly repeated the figure.

"That's right and guess what the best part is? I asked the boss if he needs anybody else, an' you know what he said? He said, 'If you're brother works half as good as you do, then he can start on Monday.' Hear that Dennis? You can come work for Ramsey-Bird too."

"I can?"

"Sure, I can take you back with me today," David whispered, hoping the Brays hadn't overheard because he didn't want to be the one to tell them. "We can stay in Moosehorn tonight then go to Winnipeg tomorrow."

Dennis was speechless. He knew that this time his departure would be for good. He didn't think he'd have to leave the Brays so soon.

"I gotta talk to Herman an' Crystal first," he said quietly. "They're gonna be sad I'm going."

"Sure, I get it," David said. "Oh yeah, do you got your license yet?"

"Driver's license?"

"Yeah."

"No, not yet."

"Christ, man you're missin' out!" David said sounding just like Norman. "We gotta get you a license. I've got your birth certificate in my wallet - I took it when I got mine."

Dennis nodded cheerfully and asked David to wait outside while he told the Brays. His friend Nick was also there which gave him the opportunity to say good-bye to those close to him.

Crystal and Herman were upset about Dennis' decision. They were sorry to see him go since he'd become like a son to them over the past two years. He was also hard working and reliable.

Dennis packed his bag and climbed into the car beside David. As the vehicle slowly backed out the driveway, Dennis waved good bye to the Brays who stood together at the living room window.

Looking back, Dennis could see Crystal crying at the window.

Chapter 35

February 8, 1966

TWO YEARS LATER WHILE visiting friends in Moosehorn, David and Dennis heard rumours that things were deteriorating at the farm.

The boys weren't surprised by this news, and even chuckled. They had been saying for years that Domko didn't do a stitch of work and that he'd never manage without them. They were concerned about their mother and Rosie, though. Deciding they should visit, David phoned to see if they would be home and received an affirmative answer.

The twins climbed into David's cream coloured pick up truck for the trip.

"Happy Birthday to us," he said cheerfully. "We made it Denny, we're eighteen today."

"Yeah," Dennis said as he looked solemnly out the window. "Remember how we never thought we'd make it out of the bush?"

David shook his head in disbelief. "There were lots of times we almost didn't."

The twins drove to the edge of town and pulled onto the snow-packed highway. Just north of Moosehorn, they turned on the Township Line. The sun was just setting on what had been a beautiful day, sending streams of pink and gold across the sky.

"I couldn't go back to those days again," David said thoughtfully, enjoying the beautiful sky ahead. "I think it would kill me."

"Me too," Dennis said. "We've got it so good, I sometimes have to think hard to be sure it's real. We lived through hell, and I know it was hell 'cause the Devil was standin' there the whole time."

David laughed. "You've got that right."

"Sometimes bein' a kid seems so far away," Dennis said dreamily. "And sometimes it feels like yesterday. Remember our birthdays? Remember the time Squeezer got in the car accident, on the road right here - and how you smashed your teeth?"

David laughed. "Yeah, an' remember how stupid he was driving right into that guy like that?" David made an ugly face then gripped the steering wheel. "Aaarrrh!" he growled as he drove towards the ditch.

Dennis laughed as he grabbed the dashboard and pretended to be their mother. "Slow dow, slow down!" he screamed in his best woman's voice.

Then they laughed.

"And remember our best birthday ever?" David asked. "At Kochs an' you got to cut the cake first?"

"Yeah, and you took the biggest piece I've ever seen!"

"Yeah, but Denny, remember?" It was chocolate cake. Remember what I'd do for chocolate cake," he joked.

"And the socks!" Dennis exclaimed. "Five years ago today, we got the nicest presents we ever got. What happened to them anyway?"

"I never wore mine," David said. "I didn't wanna take them nice tags off. I hid the socks upstairs and I think he took him an' wore 'em for Walter's wedding. How 'bout you?"

"They were too nice to wear. I just saved 'em an' then they disappeared."

The boys sighed as they continued down the road. Dennis looked instinctively to his right when they came to the small bluff of trees that shielded Jim's house from the east. David slowed down and looked as well.

"How's Jim doin'?" Dennis asked.

"Good, I think."

"Anybody ever hear from Ruby?"

"Yeah, she's got a new husband named Harry Ratz," David said. "I heard she's happy an' I sure hope so. I'll never forget the time she kissed me."

"Kissed you?" Dennis exclaimed. "She never kissed me!"

"Yes she did, but you were asleep. She kissed me right here," David said gently touching his cheek.

"Jim was bravest guy I ever saw," Dennis said. "And he tells it like it is."

"That's for sure. Everyone else just kisses the ole bastard's ass or they stay the hell away from him," David said. "Except for Gus - he fought with him more than anybody. Poor Gus, do you remember?"

"Yeah, after Satan kicked him that time I never wanted to go to Harwarts again."

"Me neither."

David slowed and the truck slipped slightly as he turned towards towards the farm.

"Too bad Ma wasn't more like Emma," David said as he slowly accelerated. "She loved her kids an' never woulda put up with Satan's crap."

"That's for sure," Dennis said.

The boys drove slowly past the abandoned barn then Harwart's house, which now sat empty since Gus and Emma moved to Moosehorn in the fall of 1964. A warm feeling washed over Dennis as he looked at the old log house.

"I never told nobody but I used to wish that Emma an' Gus were my parents," he said, voice cracking.

David looked at him and smiled softly. "I know."

They drove in silence for a moment, then Dennis shivered as he looked toward the thick bush.

"Turn it up high," David said laughing. "We got lots of heat now!"

They looked towards the fields and trees. The bush had an ominous look that made both boys quake a little inside. They had no fond memories of their childhood and only a feeling of foreboding for the place they once called home. Instinctively, they knew what the other was thinking.

"I couldn't sleep in the bush again," Dennis said sadly. "Davey, how did we survive?"

"I don't know," he said, forcing a smile. "I think it was some of that tough German blood that the ole bastard hated so much."

The church sat as it always had, calm and unwavering in the cold wind.

"Do you ever talk to other people about what happened to us?" Dennis asked as he stared at the imposing structure.

"Sometimes I do, but mostly I just try to forget," David said as he slowly drove into the church's driveway. Looking to his left, he could see his mother's house through the bare trees. A flood of bad memories returned and he had to look away.

He wondered how long it would be before he could look into that bush without a horrible memory. His eyes were still drawn every time to the place where he'd seen the collie dogs hanging. The stick that had been placed horizontally between the two trees was still there. Looking away, he put the truck in reverse and backed out of the church driveway so that they would face the south. The sun had completely set now and he wondered how long it would take before his mother would be able to sneak out of the house.

"Was the church good or bad?" Dennis asked.

"That church?" David said pointing with his thumb over his shoulder.

Dennis nodded.

"It was a good place," he said. "I figure the church and the Harwarts are what saved us."

They sat remembering for a moment, then Dennis broke the silence.

"How do you think Rosie is?"

A pang of guilt stabbed David in the gut and he winced. He'd heard that Rosie had suffered more than any of them

"She's not good," he said. "We gotta get her out of there. I heard that her legs were so bad that she couldn't keep the bugs out of the sores. Lucky Doc Steenson gave her some medicine and cleared it up. Otherwise, they would have had to cut her legs off."

Dennis shuddered. He remembered how they'd come to visit soon after moving to Winnipeg. Domko was inconsolable that the boys were not coming back and had threatened to shoot them all. Dennis was thankful that he'd escaped and felt bad for his sister.

"How come the social workers don't take her away?" Dennis asked.

David shrugged. "Same reason they never came to get us, I guess. They're probably scared of old Satan."

"Yeah, everyone except Mrs. Patterson," Dennis laughed. "Boy, I wouldn't want to fight her!"

David laughed as he remembered how frustrated Domko had been with the confident woman.

"Maybe Rosie can come live with us?" Dennis suggested. "We'll have to sneak her out so he doesn't know."

David glanced in his rear view mirror and saw his mother approaching the back of the vehicle.

"Mom's comin'," he said.

Dennis looked out the back window. "Oh no, she's bringin' poker!"

David laughed. "Then he'll go tell the ole Bastard that we were here."

Opening his door he stepped out.

"How are you doin' mom?" he asked in a quiet voice.

"About the same," she said weakly. "I don't know what I'm gonna to do."

Where is she now? Carlorka is always going places without me. She shouldn't be going anywhere since there is still cooking and cleaning that needs to be done.

He was the head of the house and it was his responsibility to make sure things ran smoothly on the farm.

How can I do that when there is nobody there to work?

Now, Jenny is crying. He calls Carlorka but she doesn't answer. The baby, who's 18 months old, begins to cry louder. He likes to rest each evening after a hard day of work, but now has to get up to find his wife. He calls her name again, but she still doesn't answer.

He goes to the kitchen and looks out the window. It's dark so he sees nothing. He glances at his watch. *Where could she be?*

Maybe she's found another man. She was always looking for a new husband, and that was a fact. That's why she doesn't care when I'm sent to the hospital. She likely wraps herself around another man when I am gone. The thought of it made him angry as he pulled on his boots. *Carlorka never gives me enough love and attention. She always sides with the children instead of me. There is only one way to control that woman and it is through her religion. As long as I keep the members of the church on my side, she had to do as I say.*

That's why she is trying to kill me. Leaving is not permitted - so she is trying to work me to death instead. Just like she killed Bill.

She bought some rat poison the other day so he had been checking his food ever since.

She wants the farm for her kids. Those boys are going to come back and kill me, like so many people have said they would. He wasn't afraid of Steven, Walter or the girls, but those twins and Norman! They are always conspiring against me. They are waiting for their chance to kill me and take the farm. That's why they talk in that language - right from the very first day I arrived. It was a secret way of talking that everyone, even Harwarts and Deightons, understood, everyone except me.

So instead of turning his back, he just watched them all the time and beat them whenever he could.

He knew he was brutal towards the children. People said that beating children was wrong but but his father had beaten him and he turned into a good man. How else did you discipline children? And that's all he wanted the Pischkes to be - hardworking and obedient.

Nothing had worked! They were good for nothing little German bastards who hate me because I am Polish. They'll be nothing but punks some day, living off the government.

He thought of the labour camps he'd been in - where he'd learned to survive. He watched how the guards beat the strongest of the Polish soldiers and starved the rest. It became a habit, a way of survival. They taunted and exposed the weak and vulnerable then destroyed them one by one. This was a method that worked, it had broken many men's spirits. And it was the only way he knew to keep the twins under control.

The baby is still crying, this time frantically. He pulls on his coat and steps into the cool air. He carries his gun loaded all the time now.

Somebody followed me the other day in Moosehorn. Probably one of the twins.

He walked silently along the driveway then looked towards the church. He could see a vehicle parked there. Moving closer he squinted then recognized the truck.

David's truck and Dennis is there too.

He took a few more steps and could see Carlorka sitting between them. Then he notices Raymond on the seat beside his mother.

They are talking about me. Likely planning how they are going to kill me.They are telling Raymie lies about me, and then will send him spying. I've taught the boy well. How will I know who Raymie sides with?

He began running toward the truck.

I'll shoot them all, before they kill me.

Suddenly, David stiffened. His twin also sensed the feeling of danger nearby, a feeling they knew all too well. They shot a quick glance at each other then swinging around in the crowded cab, both teenagers caught sight of a dark figure running awkwardly towards the truck.

It was Domko and he was shaking a fist in the air while clutching a rifle in the other. All those familiar childhood feelings came flooding back. It was as if the boys had been propelled back to the days of being helpless nine year old children.

"It's that crazy bastard!" David yelled as he yanked the truck into gear, slamming the gas pedal to the floor. The tires spun trying to grip the slick, snow-packed road. Staring intently into the rear-view mirror, David could see Domko stop in the centre of the road and raise his rifle to eye level.

"He's gonna shoot!" he yelled, "everybody down!"

Instinctively Dennis' arms came up over his head as he slid low on the seat. Caroline pulled Raymond down and covered him with her body.

Got to get out of here, David thought to himself, clenching his jaw tight. His heart raced as adrenalin surged into his bloodstream. *We don't deserve to die like this, not after what we've been through. If only I can get out of range . . .*

Moments seemed like hours as the truck slipped sideways down the centre of the road, the back wheels sliding to the left.

Domko could barely see into the crowded cab. He took aim at Dennis' head or was it Raymond? Hesitating, he lowered the gun slightly and squinted.

Suddenly, the back wheel caught on a bare piece of the road, straightening the vehicle and propelling it forward. David pushed the gas pedal down hard and soon the truck was speeding toward the Township Line. He glanced in the mirror and could see that Domko was still standing on the road, but was now just a speck in the distance.

"We made it!" David gasped, as he struggled to catch his breath. He hadn't felt fear like that in nearly two years.

Dennis and Caroline still shaking from the ordeal, complimented his driving as they sighed in relief.

"David, can you take me to the police?" Caroline said. "We gotta send him back to Selkirk, but this time for good. I'm not putting up with this no more."

The twins looked at her. It appeared she meant what she was saying.

"I'm going to leave him and get a legal separation," their mother continued. "We just can't live like this no more."

The boys didn't ask any further questions as they drove to Ashern. Each silently wished that their mother had done this much sooner, but that was not her way. It took her a long time to make up her mind, but once she did, she never changed it.

It was the first time the twins had been at the Ashern RCMP office since they were youngsters. They rang the bell then stepped inside.

The officer who came to the front seemed much friendlier than the ones they remembered.

"Can I help you?" he asked.

They stood quietly for a moment, then David looked at his mother.

She nodded.

"Y-yes, you can," David began. "We want to report that our stepfather just tried to shoot us. We were talking with our m-mother out by the farm, and he snuck up behind the truck and pointed his rifle at us. If I hadn't noticed him, we'd all be dead right now."

The officer looked stunned.

"Who's your stepfather?" he asked.

"Bob Domko," David said without hesitation. It was then he realized how odd those words sounded coming from his mouth. Never once in his life had he consciously uttered the man's name, never in anger and certainly not in fondness. This man had been nothing to him but his tormenter - and he'd always addressed him in that fashion.

"Domko should have been locked up a long time ago, it's a miracle he hasn't killed somebody," the officer said. "He never should have been released from Selkirk."

The twins looked at each other in amazement. Where was this man when they'd sought refuge as children?

"H-he tried to kill us many times and more than once he almost did," Dennis said firmly. "We were beaten and starved for twelve years and nobody did anything about it. We want you to do something about it now."

The officer called in another constable and soon they were on their way to the farm. Caroline and Raymond sat in the back seat as the cruiser sped along the highway. The twins followed behind in the truck.

"Remember how we would ride like that?" David said, pointing at his mother's silhouette.

". . . and he'd beat the hell out of us when we got home," Dennis added. "But this time, they're taking him away."

"Do you think he's gone for good?" David asked.

"I don't know, but if he comes back we'll just keep callin' the police," Dennis said without hesitation. "Is Mom is gonna kick him out for good this time?"

David thought for a moment then nodded: "I think she means what she said. You know Mom when she makes up her mind."

Dennis leaned his head back against the window and sighed.

"Do you think that dad knows we made it?" he asked.

David looked at his twin and felt a warm strength flood over him.

"I know he does."

Then, as they had so many times in the bush, the twins shared their thoughts without speaking. They knew instinctively that never again would there be a reason so urgent, that they'd run screaming into the cold, windy night. They knew that whatever loomed ahead could be no worse than what lay behind. That no threat could equal and no struggle be more difficult than what they had already endured.

And at that moment, David and Dennis knew, they'd never run again.

Epilogue

The RCMP arrived at the farm shortly after the twins and their mother went to the police station. They took Domko to Ashern that night and during questioning, Domko admitted that he had planned to kill Caroline and the twins. He said he did not shoot because he was afraid that he'd hit his son Raymond.

Domko was held in the Ashern jail then taken to the Selkirk Mental Health Centre where he was admitted as a patient.

Caroline, Rosie and Domko's four children stayed on the farm. Domko was discharged June 6, 1966. Caroline kept her word and left the farm and obtained a legal separation from Domko.

Unable to do the farm work alone, he re-admitted himself to the Selkirk Mental Health Centre on July 6, 1966. Caroline returned to the farm and managed it until the fall of that year. She then sold all of the livestock. The land was leased to Hugo Russell, and is now owned by Arden and Barb Weigelt.

David Pischke: David continued work for Ramsey Bird Construction of Winnipeg as a heavy equipment operator during the summer months. He spent the winter working in sawmills in British Columbia, Canada. In 1970, he married Bonnie Shiells of Steep Rock and together they had two sons, Dale and Ian.

David and Lynne

In 1968 David became employed at Winnipeg Fuel & Supply in Spear Hill, Manitoba. The company now operates under the name Continental Lime, in Steep Rock and Dave is still employed there as a rock crusher. Dave and Bonnie divorced in 1984.

In 1985 David married Lynne Jensen of Ashern. They lived in Moosehorn until 1995, then moved their home to a lot in the town of Steep Rock.

David has three step-children, Bill, David and Sherry Jensen. David's wife Lynne says: "My children are extremely fond of David. He certainly hasn't inherited any of Domko's stepfather traits. If anything, he is the exact opposite. My children think the world of him."

On being bushed: David described his first years away from the farm as difficult. Moving to Winnipeg was a huge step for him and he was very frightened living in the city. He rented a small house with no plumbing in Birds Hill, on the outskirts of the city. He had only a few friends and things improved when Dennis moved to the city also.

David was so shy that he could barely order food in a restaurant or buy gas. His stuttering proved embarrassing but it has improved tremendously over the years.

At eighteen years old, David was still very naive about life and members of the opposite sex. He still believed that storks brought babies and he says, "It made sense at the time because the Ashern hospital has a flat roof, which is good for landing."

David often tells the story of his first date and how he naively jumped out of his car and ran to hide in the bushes from his amorous date. He waited there until the girl eventually walked home, then he got back in his car and drove off. Needless to say, he never saw her again.

David says that there were other people who helped them when they left the farm, including the Elizabeth Matheson family. David says that these were very poor, 'bushed' people who lived in Moosehorn. He remembers Mrs. Matheson allowing him and Norman to hook their trailer up to their hydro and also gave them food.

"That just goes to show that some of the kindest people aren't necessarily the richest." he said.

On his mother: David fluctuates between resenting his mother and feeling sorry for her. He never understood why she would leave them alone with Domko, yet feels badly that she received a number of beatings while trying to defend them. He admits that he did not understand his mother very well. She was a very private person who, in later years, would just cry and become upset whenever the past was discussed.

David visited his mother occasionally and outwardly was always very kind to her.

On Domko: "He meant absolutely nothing to me," David said. He only saw Domko on a few occasions after he was admitted as a permanent resident at the Selkirk hospital. He never understood him and can not forgive him for the way he treated them as children. He never remembers Domko being civil to them. He did attend Domko's funeral.

"But only to be sure that the s.o.b. was really dead," he said.

On Remembering: David says he has tried to shut out the abuse and seldom discussed his childhood over the years. For a number of years he was able to put it in the past, but gradually as time wore on memories began to creep back. He remembers telling friends some of the stories in "Where Children Run", but didn't begin discussing the abuse openly until

1994. His wife Lynne had no idea what he'd lived through until then.

Residual affects from the abuse: David is a self-proclaimed workaholic. He suffered from nightmares for many years, images of Domko stalking him and not being able to run away. He is a very tidy man who keeps himself and his surroundings very clean. He worries about not having enough food to eat and helps his wife can hundreds of sealers of vegetables and fruit each year. He is deathly afraid of the sight of blood and will not submit to having a blood test. He has a phobia about needles and 'puncturing' of skin.

David admits he has a bad temper and sometimes finds himself frustrated and unable to express his feelings and anger. He yells, but never lashes out phyically. David did not physically discipline his own children.

On religion: David has had no interest in the Jehovah's Witness religion as an adult. "I've seen the ugly side of that outfit and I don't want nothing to do with them," he said. He says some of the senior members of the congregation at the time ignored their situation and by 'turning a blind eye' made matters worse. He resents the fact that there was no enjoyment in their lives and that his mother's religious beliefs further deprived them of special occasions such as birthdays and Christmas.

"It gave people no opportunity to get to know us us. We were different than the rest, shunned by people in our religion and people outside. It was embarrassing." he said.

David belongs to no religious denomination, but does believe in an afterlife. He is confident that he will see his father again. He also is not afraid of dying.

"I've been to hell already," he says. "Nothing can be worse than that."

On writing this book: "It was like letting the monster out," David said. "It helped get a lot of things out in the open." David says that he and his brother have been plagued by rumours that carried over from their childhoods. He hopes that people will understand after reading this book how cruel and unfair abuse is to children and how devastating the after effects can be. He wants people to help children in these situations, not shun them because they are poor, dirty or misbehaving.

David says writing the book has helped him come to terms with his past. He says that it is nice to be believed and it is comforting to know that so many people supported the idea.

Dennis Pischke: Dennis continued work for Ramsey Bird Construction of Winnipeg as a heavy equipment operator during the summer months. He, along with David spent the winter working in sawmills in British Columbia, Canada.

In 1970, he married Robynne Shiells of Fort Whyte, Manitoba and together they had twin daughters Deanna and Dawn and a son, Ryan.

In 1968 he left Ramsey-Bird and became employed at Winnipeg Fuel & Supply in Spear Hill, Manitoba The company now operates under the name Continental Lime, in Steep Rock. Dennis is still employed there.

Dennis and Robynne live just outside the town of Steep Rock. Dennis credits Jack McInnis and George Rentz from Ramsey-Bird for giving him and David a job as well as John Brown who hired the both of them at the limestone plant.

Residual affects from the abuse: Dennis is a workaholic who is obsessed with cleanliness. While he will take a needle in the arm, he also becomes ill at the sight of blood. He suffered from nightmares for years - images of an ugly face suddenly appearing and not being able to get away. Dennis also suffers from back problems and has arthritis that he attributes to the beatings and being outside in the cold.

Dennis and Robynne

Dennis vowed that Domko would never harm his wife and children and kept them away from him. He never physically disciplined his children. His wife Robynne enjoys describing how Dennis would spank: "Clapping his own hands together behind their rear ends."

On Remembering: Dennis blocked out many of the incidents that happened to him when he was a child. He tried to forget, but found that living in the same area, associating with the same people brought back many of the memories.

"There are people who won't let us forget," Dennis said. Dennis says there are people who he calls 'cronies', former friends of Domko and members of the Ashern Jehovah's Witness congregation who have accused him of being a thief. "Once a thief, always a thief, they say," Dennis says. "This was said in front of a group of people and once the situation was resolved, and it was discovered I was not the thief, there was no apology."

Dennis also says that a senior member from their congregation made durogatory comments about his sister, based on the past. When Dennis asked for an apology, he was again refused.

"They are the ones who have opened the old wounds," Dennis says. "I want to forget but some of them continue to judge my siblings and myself unfairly."

Dennis says that since churches are made up of families of people, the 'church' has a moral responsibility to help its members in need. He says there were some in the church who helped, but only if they were never considered 'involved'. The remainder turned a blind eye. In some cases, the people made the situation worse by befriending Domko and turning against their mother. They tell us what 'good men' Domko made of us and that makes me so angry." Dennis says that he and David are the men they are today, not because of Domko but inspite of him.

"We were struggling everyday to survive and they were worried if my mother kept a clean house," he said. "Now that shows you the priorites of that particular church." Dennis went on to say that he recently believed that another family from within the same church was experiencing problems similar to what he and his siblings endured. He brought it to the attention of the elders of the church in 1979, and was told flat out to 'mind his own business.'

"And that is my point," he said. "If it isn't the church's business, then whose is it? And what is the purpose of organized religion - then? Just for show? To gather around and 'pretend' to be wonderful Christians while others are suffering?

On Religion: Dennis belonged to the Jehovah's Witness religion through his teens and adult years. In the early 1980's he began to question some of the beliefs and now considers some members of the religion hypocritical and stopped associating with them in the fall of 1994. He does not know if he has been disfellowshipped as of yet, but suspects his public comments could be the grounds for such action.

"It is a farce," he says. "I want nothing to do with them anymore."

On Writing this book: Dennis says that writing this book has helped him come to terms with his past. It has helped to unlock some of the pent up frustration that he has felt over the years, particularly with members of the church who he watched through a child's eyes virtually ignore his family.

"Now I can make friends with people and not feel like my past is hanging over my head all the time," he said. "I'm more relaxed."

The Twins : David and Dennis Pischke are two of the most animated and interesting storytellers you could ever meet. They are twins, no doubt, and we suspect they are identical although David would not submit to a blood test to verify the fact.

David and Dennis still use some of the 'secret' words in conversation, especially when telling stories from their past. They have an acute sense of one another - as you will notice in their biographies, the pattern has remained throughout their adult lives of being together. While working on this book, we noticed that more often than not, Dennis is either sitting or standing on David's right hand side and that the boys move in unison. When they tell stories, they alter back and forth as they did when children and still have some sympathy pains for eachother.

Like all siblings, they sometimes disagree and for a year, the twins were estranged from one another. They agree that sometimes they lock horns and halo, but cannot agree who has the horns and who wears the halo.

Boleslaw Domko: After re-admitting himself to the Selkirk Mental Health Centre on July 6, 1966, he was diagnosed as a Paranoid Schizophrenic with violent tendencies. Medical records from the institution show he stayed in the hospital until September 27, 1967 when he was released under the supervision of a farmer in Petersfield as a farmhand. Domko was brought back to Selkirk on October 3, 1967. The files show that on his release he arrived in Moosehorn and began harassing Caroline once again. She called the police and he was re-admitted to the hospital.

On May 14, 1968 he was released into a work situation once again, this time to the Gmitzyk family in Faulkner. He was returned to the hospital by his employers because he was unable to work, was depressed and had suicidal thoughts. In August Domko begged to be sent back to Caroline and while she previously refused, she decided to give him one last chance. He arrived in Moosehorn August 29, 1968 but the police were again called and he was returned to Selkirk September 7, 1968. He had one other short stint as a farmhand in East Selkirk in early December of that year but was again returned to the hospital.

Domko and Caroline in the early 1960's

Schizophrenia is a mental disorder that has the following symptoms: a split personality, escape from reality into a dream world, no interest in personal cleanliness and emotional indifference. The victims' behaviour is determined by their imagined thoughts, not by their real surroundings, and their answers to questions often sound silly and meaningless. Their speech may be garbled and unintelligible and their lack of concern with a serious situation, such as a death in the family, is astonishing. The onset of schizophrenia is most common in adolescence or early adult life and the course is regressive, with increasing mental deterioriation throughout life. There are three types: hebephrenic (simple mental regression), catatonic, with alternating phases of stupor and excitement. The third is paranoid with hallucinations and delusions of persecution, sometimes leading to violence.

This could explain some of Domko's irrational behaviour and lack of feeling towards the children. He also shows why some people liked the man. It is entirely possible that Caroline fell in love with one part of his personality, while he persecuted the children with the other.

Some people who knew him said that sometimes he said he couldn't control himself and appeared remorseful about beating the children. Nobody knows what his motivation for the confession was and the children never remember him being remorseful for his actions, except for injuring Kathy. As well, interviews recorded at Selkirk show none of this - he blames the children and complains about them constantly in his psychiatric evaluations.

Although people suffering from schizophrenia are not often violent, a search by the psychiatrist into Domko's childhood revealed that he was severely abused as a child by his father and that one of Domko's brothers also suffers from a mental illness, having received treatment in Britain.

Medical records show that his biological children visited him only once or twice each during his stay in Selkirk, and that nobody from Caroline's church nor his friends from Moosehorn and Grahamdale paid him a visit. Stephen Pischke did visit on occasion and Caroline visited him occasionally after she returned from British Columbia. The twins took their mother there, but refused to be kind towards Domko.

Domko's military record obtained from the Ministry of Defence in England shows that he was a single, Roman Catholic who worked as a butcher before enlisting.

He was deported from Poland to the former USSR in 1940. On the basis of the Sikorski-Maisky pact of July 30, 1941 he was released for the purpose of joining the Polish Armed Forces which were being organized in 1941-42 on the former Soviet territories. He enlisted in the Polish Army on February 1, 1942 and was posted to the 7th Heavy Artillery Regiment. Together with the Polish Army units crossed the Soviet-Iranian frontier, was evacuated to Iran, thereby came under British command with effect from August 15, 1942. On the re-organization of the Polish Army in the Middle East he was posted to the 8th Heavy Anti-Aircraft Artillery Regiment. He served in the Middle East (Iran, Iraq, Palestine) until 1944 then was sent to Italy.

His theatre of operations included Italy, February 1944-May 1945 action on the rivers Sangro and Rapido February 1944-April 1944; battle for Monte Cassino/Gustav-Hitler line of enemy defences April 1944-May 1944; battle for Ancona and Goths line of enemy defences June 1944-September 1944; rearguard of the 8th British Army September 1944-October 1944; Northern Apennines October 1944-January 1945; action on the river Senio January 1945-April 1945; battle for Bologna/Lombardy Plain April 1945-May 1945.

Private Domko was honourably discharged in December 1947 from the Polish Resettlement Corps. His conduct while in the army was classified as good. He received the following medals: Polish: Cross of Monte Cassino No. 36473, Army Medal. British: 1939-45 Star, Italy Star, Defence Medal, The War Medal 1939-45.

Nowhere does it show that Domko was injured in the war as he claimed.

In 1976 while a permanent resident at the Selkirk Mental Health Centre Villa, Domko suffered a stroke which left him impaired on his right hand side. He had another series of strokes that left him almost totally impaired before his death November 19, 1983. Although not a baptised Jehovah's Witness, he was laid to rest through the Kingdom Hall in Selkirk, Manitoba. His ashes were buried, rather uncerimoniously by Caroline and Eunice, under a fencepost at the farm.

Caroline Domko: Caroline lived in Moosehorn until the early 1970's, then she moved to British Columbia. She moved back to Moosehorn in the early 1980's, bought a house in Ashern and lived there with Kathy.

After returning to Manitoba from British Columbia, Caroline paid occasional visits to Domko in Selkirk. She remained a devout Jehovah's Witness until her death in March of 1987.

The Farm: An inspection of the rafters in the attic of the old house in 1995 revealed tin cans, cutlery, books, school work and notes. The bush where the premature infant had been buried was been bulldozed. Inspection of the area turned up eating utensils, broken cups and hundreds of nails from the makeshift houses the twins had built together.

Strange sightings and happenings on that particular parcel of land have led people in the area to believe that it is indeed cursed or haunted. While researching this book a number of people relayed other unsettling stories about the farm.

The farm yard. Taken in 1996.

The Lutheran Church:

The Lutheran Church where the boys stayed many nights still sits in the same location south of the farm. The church hasn't been used for services for a number of years.

Top: The church where the twins slept many nights.

Left: The inside of the church. The Bible that they tore pages from still sits on the podium

Walter Pischke: Walter worked for a number of years as a pressman in Winnipeg. He and his wife Laurie raised three children, Kimberly, Rhonda and Eugene. Walter and Laurie now raise cattle and are commercial fishing in Amaranth, Manitoba.

Steven Pischke: Steven spent his younger years in the rodeo circuit in Western Canada. He now lives in British Columbia and is not in contact with his siblings.

Norman Pischke: Norman worked as a truck driver for a number of years. He married Sharon Russell and they had two sons, Lee and Trevor. Norman obtained his pilot's license and soon afterwards bought his own plane. He operated a crop spraying business called NormAir out of Estevan, Saskatchewan. Norman died on a mountainside after the 172 Cessna

Norman Pischke in the early 1970's.

he was piloting crashed on it's way to Boise, Idaho May 5, 1979. Norman was 35 years old.

Gus and Emma Harwart: Retired to Moosehorn in the fall of 1964. Gus died October 21, 1981. Emma died April 25, 1984. Both are buried in the St. John's Cemetery.

Gus and Emma

Marjorie Harwart: Marjorie obtained her Grade twelve education then moved to Winnipeg, where she still resides. Marjorie still spends time in the Moosehorn area and is in contact with Eunice, David and Dennis.

Ruby Deighton: After leaving the farm, Ruby married Harry Ratz. Ruby died peacefully in her sleep of an apparent heart attack on October 31, 1991, at the age of 73 years. She was living in Radium Hot Springs, B.C.,

Jim Deighton: Eventually sold the farm to an American outfit who now use the house and land for hunting purposes. Jim stayed at the house until the early 1980's when he moved into the senior citizen's home in Moosehorn. In his mid-80's, Jim's health has been good over the years. His step-sons, Charles and especially Harold Boutilier have kept in close contact with Jim.

Eunice Pischke: Eunice has spent most of her life trying to forget the horrors of her childhood. In 1965 she married Mel Bullerwell, who was stationed at the Canadian Armed Forces base in Gypsumville. Eunice and Mel live north of Moosehorn. Together they raised three children, Marlo, Melissa and a foster daughter Dreena.

Eunice kept the yellow dress in storage until just a few years ago.

Rose Pischke: Rosie left the farm soon after Domko was arrested in 1966 and lived with Norman and his wife Sharon. Then she lived with David and Dennis, moved to Winnipeg where she met and married Al Gardner. Rosie and Al have three children, Theresa, Tiffany and Vanessa. They live near Steep Rock, Manitoba.

Kathy Domko: Kathy spent another year in Brantford's school for the blind, then lived with her mother until Caroline's death. After her mother's death, Kathy was taken to see a specialist in Winnipeg to see if there was anything that could be done about her eyesight. X-rays showed that her optic nerve was severed at some point in her young life, likely from a severe blow to the head. Kathy lives a quiet, contented life with Rose and her family near Moosehorn, Manitoba.

Raymond Domko: Raymond stayed with his mother until he began working with Norman in Estevan, Saskatchewan. In 1975, at the age of 18 years, Raymond was involved in a car accident between Moosehorn and Ashern. He remained a quadraplegic until his death in 1987 at the age of 30 years.

Mark Domko: Mark is married and lives in Winnipeg. He is not in contact with either David or Dennis.

Jenny Domko: Jenny is married and lives in British Columbia. She is not in contact with either David or Dennis.

Dennis and David with Marjorie Harwart and her sisters Violet and Evelyn. Taken in 1995.

Dennis with his boat which still sits in the bush beside the Church.

The hole on the floor of the house where the children were kept.

Dennis and David celebrating their 48th Birthdays on February 8, 1996.

Author's Note

The instinct to isolate and attack the weak and vulnerable in society is a trait that human beings, in spite of the evolutionary process, still exhibit.

To most people the Pischke children were nothing but dirty little beasts, misunderstood and shunned. Miraculously, these children survived their horrific childhoods and we are privileged that they have shared it with us. Unfortunately there are still people in the community where they were raised, who hold the twins' lack of a proper upbringing against them.

People do not want to believe that human beings exist who inflict horrible abuse upon others. Bob Domko is the perfect example of a man who could be friendly in public while tormenting his family behind the scenes.

I spoke with a few people who wanted to defend this man - people who say the twins are lying. I believe this comes from a natural tendency for people to want to shield themselves from awful truths. If they shift the blame to the victim then they can fool themselves into believing that they will never be a victim themselves.

Unfortunately, some people even receive a perverse pleasure in watching others suffer.

Researching this project was challenging. There were only a few files and records that hadn't been destroyed by various government agencies. I was able to obtain records from the Lakeshore School Division, Environment Canada, Selkirk Mental Health Centre, LGD of Grahamdale. By cross-referencing this information with the children's recollections and those of their former neighbours and friends, we were able to make this book as historically correct as possible after forty years.

While doing research for this book, a very interesting pattern developed. The people who turned a blind eye to Dennis and David's mistreatment when they were young, were the same people who when interviewed in 1995 and 1996 feigned ignorance or said they "didn't want to get involved".

David and Dennis have broken the cycle of abuse. They are productive, hardworking, upstanding citizens. No doubt there will be individuals who will be anxious to discredit their story based on biases established when the twins were children. To those people who claim to know the Pischke family so well and now offer criticism, I ask: where were you forty years ago when these children needed your help?

Talk is cheap. Actions like those of Gus and Emma Harwart, Jim and Ruby Deighton, Leon & Anna Koch, Margaret Burnett and Martha (Jeske) Patterson - show character and courage. I now understand the obstacles those people faced while trying to help these children in the 1950's and early 60's.

While the laws have changed people are still reluctant to step forward for fear of embarassment and retribution. Society does not reward 'interference' in other's lives even when the victims are defenseless chidren.

In that respect, things haven't changed much in forty years.

The Pischke children have been to hell and back and this book tells their story. The incidents of abuse, starvation, emotional torture, thievery, deception and fear are all true. If you doubt this, ask David or Dennis to tell you a story.

They will - and their tears don't lie.

- Karen Emilson

About the Author

Karen Snively was born and raised in Stoney Creek, Ontario. In 1982 she married Mark Emilson and moved to Winnipeg, Manitoba. In 1985, after their son's birth, Karen and Mark moved to the Emilson family farm near Vogar, along Lake Manitoba in the Interlake Region. They run a cow-calf operation.

Karen has written short stories and poetry and has kept a journal since she was a young girl. She began her writing career as a reporter with the Interlake Spectator in 1993.

The story about the Pischke twins, written by her, appeared in the Spectator in 1995. It won an award in the Manitoba Community Newspapers Association annual competition in the feature article category.

This is her first book.

Bibliography

Published Sources

Gzowski, Peter. The Sacrament. Toronto: McClelland and Stewart Limited, 1980.

The Moosehorn-Gypsumville History Book Committee. Northwest Interlake Heritage Museum History Book, Moosehorn: The Committee, 1991.

World Book Inc. The World Book Encyclopedia , 1991. Vol. 15, pg. 615

Lakeshore Women's Resource Centre, 1996 Newsletter, 1996.

Fishbein's Illustrated. Medical and Health Encyclopedia, H.S. Stuttman, Inc. 1985. Vol. 4, pg. 1288

Archival Sources

Lakeshore School Division

Bayton School registers, Sept. 1961 to June 1964.

Ashern School registers, Sept. 1953 to June 1956.

Manitoba Public Archives

Bayton School registers, Sept. 1950 to June 1961.

Local Government District of Grahamdale

Land Tax Registers, 1949 to 1965

Selkirk Mental Health Centre

Register Data Sheets for patient Boleslaw Domko, Feb. 6, 1961, May 19, 1962, Feb. 23, 1966, July 5, 1966, Oct. 3, 1967, June 28, 1968, Sept. 7, 1968, Dec. 9, 1968

Ministry of Defence - Bourne Ave. Hayes, Middlesex - Britan

Military Record - Private Boleslaw Domko